21,22

THE GREENHAVEN ENCYCLOPEDIA OF

ANCIENT MESOPOTAMIA

Other Books in the Greenhaven Encyclopedia Series

ANCIENT MESOPOTAMIA

by Don Nardo
Robert B. Kebric, *Consulting Editor*

Christine Nasso, *Publisher*
Elizabeth Des Chenes, *Managing Editor*

GREENHAVEN PRESS
A part of Gale, Cengage Learning

GALE
CENGAGE Learning

Detroit • New York • San Francisco • New Haven, Conn • Waterville, Maine • London

LIBRARY OF CONGRESS CATALOGING-IN-PUBLICATION DATA

Nardo, Don 1947–
    Ancient Mesopotamia / by Don Nardo.
        p. cm. -- (Greenhaven encyclopedia of)
    Includes bibliographical references and index.
    ISBN-13: 978-0-7377-3441-6 (hard cover : alk. paper)
    ISBN-10: 0-7377-3441-8 (hard cover : alk. paper)
    1. Iraq--History--To 634--Encyclopedias, Juvenile. 2. Iraq--Civilization--To 634--Encyclopedias, Juvenile.
I. Title. II. Series.
    DS70.62.N37 2006
    35--dc22

                                                                2006007298

Printed in the United States of America
3 4 5 6 7 13 12 11 10 09

Contents

Contents

C

D

E

Contents

The Greenhaven Encyclopedia of Ancient Mesopotamia

Contents

Contents

Preface

Today, Iraq and many other countries in the Middle East are struggling to achieve or maintain prosperity and political significance in a world largely dominated by major foreign powers. Throughout most of the modern era, those powers have been Western—European nations and their phenomenally successful offshoot, the United States. In contrast, throughout most of the modern era much of the Middle East has been mired in poverty, politically and militarily weak, and technologically backward.

Early in the twentieth century, the industrialized Western powers—primarily Britain, France, and the United States—set out to establish political and economic influence in the undeveloped Middle East, in part to gain control of the valuable stores of oil that lay beneath it. In the process, the outside powers created new, artificially constructed countries, often forcing rival local peoples, tribes, and religious groups to live together in shaky alliances. The roots of the sectarian violence and political chaos in Iraq in recent years lie in this period of intervention, for Iraq was originally one of those artificial nations pieced together by Western politicians.

The irony of this situation is that the outside powers that have sought to influence Middle Eastern governments and economies actually owe this region a huge cultural debt. Indeed, the plains and hills of Iraq and its surrounding territories were once the home of the world's first major civilizations. The Near East, the term scholars use to describe the region before the modern era, witnessed the birth of agriculture, the creation of the first cities and writing systems, the first law codes, the rise of the earliest complex religious institutions, and the world's first empires and standing armies.

At the heart of the ancient Near East lay Mesopotamia, the so-called land between the rivers, in reference to the Tigris and Euphrates. These waterways still wind their way across Iraq's mostly flat plains and empty into the azure waters of the Persian Gulf. Between and around these rivers the Sumerians erected the first cities and irrigation canals, the Akkadians molded the first empire, the Assyrians built the first road system and numerous royal palaces of incredible splendor, and the Babylonians charted the night sky and constructed the towering ziggurat that later inspired legends of the biblical Tower of Babel.

These and other important achievements are significant far beyond the immediate boundaries and cultures of the region. The fruits of civilization that had their first spurt of growth in Mesopotamia and neighboring areas steadily filtered outward across the ancient world. In the words of the late, great scholar of ancient Mesopotamia, Samuel N. Kramer, Mesopotamian culture had far-reaching affects on [human] economic, intellectual, and cultural progress. Ideas, techniques, and inventions originated by the Sumerians and nurtured by later Mesopotamian peoples . . . were diffused east and west to leave their mark on practically all the cultures of antiquity [ancient times] and even on those of our own day. . . . [Mesopotamian] kingship—the notion that a ruler's right to rule was bestowed by the gods . . . passed into the very fiber of Western society ... Mesopotamian law shed its light over much of the civilized world. Greece and Rome were influenced by it through their contacts with the Near East, and Islam acquired a formal legal code only after it had conquered the region that is now Iraq.

Today, most people, especially in Western countries, are unaware of these and other profound contributions ancient Mesopotamia made to world culture. This is partly because, as Kramer points out, "Mesopotamia's key role in the saga of civilization has become known only in recent times." The development of the science of archaeology in the 1800s and 1900s made it possible to uncover and begin to examine the remains of the great ancient Mesopotamian cities, many of which had long lain hidden under mounds of sand and debris. Perhaps in time, a majority of people living outside of the Near East will realize and appreciate how many of the oldest of their own cultural roots lie in those distant, cryptic mounds.

The *Greenhaven Encyclopedia of Ancient Mesopotamia* gives students and other readers a comprehensive, accurate, and easy-to-use overview of the ancient foundations of the region at the center of today's headlines. Entries encompass political and military figures and events; geography; religious and social life and customs; science, medicine, transportation, and invention; and cultural achievements in literature and architecture. An unusual feature is the inclusion of entries on the important archaeologists whose discoveries have revealed Mesopotamian civilization to the modern world and the important records and evidence that are crucial to historians' work and our understanding. A useful chronology presents a concise historical perspective, and an extensive bibliography, including valuable Web sites, points readers to general and specialized sources for further research.

Achaemenid dynasty

The family line of rulers to which the Persian Empire's founder, Cyrus II (born ca. 599 B.C.), and his royal successors belonged. They traced their lineage back to a nobleman named Achaemenes, also called Hakhamanish. They believed that in the fairly recent past Achaemenes had brought together the scattered hill tribes of Fars, the Persian homeland situated north of the Persian Gulf, into a small nation. A later Achaemenid king, Darius I, brags:

> I am Darius, the great king, king of kings, the king of Persia . . . grandson of Arsames, the Achaemenid. . . . We are called Achaemenids. From antiquity, we have been noble; from antiquity has our dynasty been royal. King Darius says: Eight of my dynasty were kings before me; I am the ninth. (*Behistun Inscription* 1–4)

The last of the Achaemenids was Darius III, whom the Macedonian Greek conqueror Alexander the Great defeated and deposed in 331 B.C. Modern scholars sometimes refer to the Persian Empire of that era as the Achaemenid Empire to distinguish it from the Parthian and Sassanian empires, which the Greeks, Romans, and other Europeans also characterized as Persian.

SEE ALSO: Cyrus II; Darius I; Darius III; Fars; Persian Empire

Adad-apla-iddina (reigned ca. 1082–1070 B.C.)

A king of the Second Dynasty of Isin, a group of Babylonian rulers who dominated southern Mesopotamia after the Elamites eradicated the Kassite dynasty in Babylon in 1155 B.C. Assyrian sources claim that Adad-apla-iddina was placed in charge of Babylon and its surrounding region by the Assyrian monarch Ashur-bel-kala (reigned ca. 1074–1057 B.C.). This may or may not be true, but evidence does suggest that Adad-apla-iddina married Ashur-bel-kala's daughter. Inscriptions commissioned by Adad-apla-iddina claim that he engaged in peaceful building projects. However, other local Babylonian records mention some sort of civil unrest and a military threat by the Assyrians.

SEE ALSO: Assyrian Empire; Babylon; Isin

Adad-nirari I (reigned ca. 1307–1275 B.C.)

A king of Assyria who has the distinction of being the first monarch of that nation for whom detailed annals of his exploits have survived. Some of his decrees, letters to other kings, and other writings have also survived. Among these is a curse placed on one of his stelae, or commemorative marker stones bearing inscriptions, to discourage would-be defacers:

> Whoever blots out my name and writes his own name in its place, or breaks my memorial stele, or consigns it to destruction, or throws it into the

A relief sculpture shows King Darius holding audience in his palace in the Persian capital of Persepolis. © GIANNI DAGLI ORTI/CORBIS

river, or covers it with earth, or burns it in the fire ... or if anyone because of these curses sends a hostile foe or an evil enemy ... and has him seize it ... may Assur, the mighty god ... look upon him in great anger, and curse him with an evil curse. His name, his seed, his kith and kin, may they [the gods] destroy from the land.

Adad-nirari left behind many such stelae during military campaigns that extended Assyrian borders in all directions from the Assyrian heartland. He was particularly successful in the west, where he defeated the king of Mitanni, a kingdom centered in eastern Syria, and reached the Syrian town of Carchemish, only 90 miles (145km) from the Mediterranean coast. In the southeast Adad-nirari defeated the Kassite ruler of Babylon and collected tribute, or payments acknowledging submission, from the peoples of that region. Such tribute, along with Adad-nirari's other successes, brought him great wealth, which he used in part to build walls around several Assyrian cities and some canals.

SEE ALSO: Assyrian Empire; Kassites; Mitanni

Adad-nirari II
(reigned ca. 911–891 B.C.)

An Assyrian king who effectively built on the efforts of his father, King Ashur-dan II, to restore the power and prestige of the Assyrian nation, which had recently undergone serious decline. According to an ancient account, Adad-nirari defeated Shamash-mudammiq, king of Babylon. Later Adad-nirari concluded a treaty with the new Babylonian king, which resulted in three generations of peace between the two peoples. On the eastern front, Adad-nirari drove the Aramaeans out of the Tigris valley and recaptured some of the cities that Assyria had formerly controlled on the plains west of the Tigris. In an inscription commemorating these deeds, he boasts:

The defeat of the desert folk, the Ara-

maeans, was accomplished. . . . I am he who returned the cities Hit, Idu, and Zakku, strongholds of Assyria, to the territory of this land. . . . The old city of Apku, which the kings who went before me had built, had fallen [in]to decay and was turned to a mound of ruins. That city I rebuilt. . . . I made it beautiful, I made it splendid, I made it greater than it had been before.

Significantly, Adad-nirari and his immediate successors initiated a consistent, relentless imperial policy best described as "greater than before"; that is, each ruler attempted to surpass his predecessor's efforts to acquire power and prestige and thereby glorify the god Ashur. These efforts mainly included foreign military campaigns and domestic building programs. Adad-nirari was succeeded by his son, Tukulti-Ninurta II.

SEE ALSO: Ashur-dan II; Assyrian Empire; Tukulti-Ninurta II

Adad-nirari III
(reigned ca. 810–783 B.C.)

An Assyrian king who tried to restore good relations with Babylonia after his father, King Shamshi-Adad V, had devastated that land. Adad-nirari's early military campaigns were conducted by his generals, perhaps because he ascended the throne as a child. He first led his own expedition circa 805 B.C., marching into Syria and demanding tribute from local leaders. On Assyria's eastern front, Adad-nirari allowed the thousands of Babylonians whom his father had deported from their homeland to return there, and gave back the religious statues that Shamshi-Adad's troops had removed from Babylonian shrines.

SEE ALSO: Assyrian Empire; Babylonia;

Shamshi-Adad V

Adapa

A Mesopotamian folk hero whose exploits were similar to those of the legendary Babylonian king Gilgamesh. Like the latter, Adapa, who hailed from the city of Eridu, likely originated in Sumerian folklore, and his story then passed along to the Babylonians and other later Mesopotamian peoples. Adapa was long respected as one of Mesopotamia's legendary wise men, the Seven Sages, and was also known for his ability to exorcise, or get rid of, demons. Like Gilgamesh, Adapa sought immortality but found this an elusive goal because it was a treasure with which the gods were reluctant to part. For Adapa's story, see *Adapa*.

SEE ALSO: *Epic of Gilgamesh*; Gilgamesh

Adapa

A Mesopotamian literary work that recounts the exploits of Adapa, originally a Sumerian folk hero. Fragments of the tale have been found in the ruins of the library of the Assyrian king Ashurbanipal, and a fuller version was unearthed in Egypt on a tablet inscribed in Akkadian.

Adapa's story begins in the city of Eridu, southeast of Uruk, where he serves as a priest in the local temple of Ea, god of freshwater. One of Adapa's jobs is to keep the shrine stocked with fresh food to use in sacrifices. So one day he takes his boat out into the Persian Gulf in hopes of catching some fish. But he has barely gotten started when a storm blows up and the boat capsizes, tossing him into the water and causing him to utter a curse against the god of the south wind. The curse proves effective because it causes one of the deity's wings to break.

The great sky god, Anu, soon finds out what has happened and angrily orders Ea to bring Adapa to Anu's throne room in the sky. Adapa realizes that he might suffer some kind of punishment. Yet he also recognizes that this is his big chance to become a hero to humanity by bringing back from the gods' abode the secret of immortality. The problem, Adapa tells Ea, is that, at the moment, Anu is upset and in no mood to give him any gifts. But Ea offers to help Adapa get on Anu's good side. Ea tells Adapa to heap flattery on Dumuzi and Gizzida, the minor gods who guard the gate of Anu's heavenly palace. After receiving this praise, they will gladly put in a good word with their superior, Anu, on Adapa's behalf.

Just as Ea foretold, Dumuzi and Gizzida persuade Anu to forgive Adapa for cursing the god of the south wind. In fact, Anu seems ready to reward Adapa for his years of service to the temple of Ea. However, the man makes a serious mistake during his audience with the great god. Ea told Adapa not to accept any food or drink during the audience because these would cause him to die. Sure enough, Anu offers Adapa some refreshments, and the man remembers Ea's warning and refuses to accept them. Later, however, after he has returned to Eridu, Adapa finds out that Anu has tricked him. The refreshments the god had offered had actually been the food and drink of life, the secret of immortality itself. For the ancient Mesopotamians, the story revealed two morals: First, the gods work in mysterious ways; and second, humans are not destined to know the secrets of eternal life.

SEE ALSO: Adapa; Ea; *Epic of Gilgamesh*

Adda-Guppi
(flourished ca. 649 B.C.–ca. 547 B.C.)

The mother of the Neo-Babylonian monarch Nabonidus (reigned ca. 555–539 B.C.). A stele erected by Nabonidus bears inscriptions that claim that Adda-Guppi was unusually influential in the royal court. This may have been partly because of her extraordinary longevity. She apparently lived to be 102 years old, which means that she knew, socialized with, and perhaps offered advice to several of Nabonidus's predecessors, including Nebuchadnezzar II (reigned ca. 605–562 B.C.), Amel-Marduk (ca. 561–560 B.C.), and Neriglissar (ca. 559–557 B.C.). According to her son, Adda-Guppi was an avid worshipper of the moon god, Sin (or Nanna), and a supporter of that deity's cult.

SEE ALSO: Nabonidus; Nanna; Neo-Babylonian Empire

adoption

Adoption was a fairly common practice in ancient Mesopotamia, as revealed by the survival of a number of adoption contracts and other related documents, mostly dating from the second and first millennia B.C. A common reason for adopting a child was to make sure the parents had someone to take care of them in their old age, assuming they lived long enough. In fact, the law required an adopted son or daughter to financially support the elderly parents and to pay for their funeral expenses. It was also common for parents without a son to adopt a boy so that he could inherit their estate and/or belongings and then carry on the family name. Another motive for adoption was humanitarian; some parents rescued and took in abandoned children who, helpless against predators, were said to be left "to the dog."

In addition, an older child whose parents had died, leaving him or her an orphan, could pay a married couple money in exchange for a legal adoption. The money was intended to reimburse the parents for the child's upkeep. Evidence suggests that on occasion some masters freed and adopted their slaves, presumably those who had come to be seen as cherished members of the family. It was also permissible in parts of Mesopotamia for an unmarried woman to adopt a daughter.

Once an adoption contract had been signed and witnessed, it was strongly binding; the authorities frowned on any party reneging on his or her duty to uphold the agreement. This is readily apparent from a surviving adoption contract from Mari, a prosperous Mesopotamian trading city located on the upper Euphrates River. The agreement, dating from the eighteenth century B.C., protects the adoptee, a boy name Yahatti-Il, from being abandoned by his adoptive parents, who stand to lose their house if they breach the contract. Also remarkable is the fact that Yahatti-Il becomes the sole heir, no matter how many children his parents have later:

> Yahatti-Il is [from this day forward to be the legal] son of Hillalum and of Alittum. He shall enjoy their good times and suffer their bad times. If Hillalum, his (adoptive) father, and Alittum, his (adoptive) mother, say to Yahatti-Il, their son, "You are not our son," they shall forfeit [their] house and property. If Yahatti-Il says to Hillalum, his father, and Alittum, his mother, "You are not my father, [or] you are not my mother," they shall shave him and sell him for silver. Even if Hillalum and Alittum have many sons, Yahatti-Il is the heir [to their estate], and he shall take two shares from the estate of Hillalum, his father. His younger brothers shall divide the

(remaining estate) in equal parts. A claimant who raises a claim against him infringes on the taboo of [the Sun god] Shamash, Iter-Mer (a god of Mari), [and] Shamshi-Adad [an Assyrian king who had conquered Mari and placed his son on its throne]; and he shall pay 31 minas of silver (as reparation) in a capital case. Eighteen witnesses [have overseen the creation of this contract]. (Translated by Karen R. Nemet-Nejat in *Daily Life in Ancient Mesopotamia*)

SEE ALSO: children; laws and justice; women

afterlife

Unlike Christians, Muslims, and members of some ancient Greek and Roman mystery religions, most ancient Mesopotamians did not envision an afterlife in which the good are rewarded and the wicked are punished. Nonetheless, the concept of immortality was clearly fascinating and appealing to the Sumerians, the Babylonians, and other peoples who inhabited Mesopotamia. This is revealed in the ancient literature of the region, notably in the *Epic of Gilgamesh* and the story *Adapa*. The title characters of these works expend considerable time and energy searching for the secrets of eternal life. However, these works also show that the gods consistently deny humans the gift of immortality. In Gilgamesh's tale, the boatman Siduri warns the hero:

No man walks on the deadly night sea as Shamash [god of the Sun] does. Shamash is the only one who can. When [a] mortal takes a step, quick he sinks, and just as quick comes death. ... O Mighty King, remember now that only gods stay in eternal watch. Humans come, then go; that is the way fate decreed on the Tablets of

Destiny. So someday you will depart, but till that distant day sing, and dance, eat your fill of warm cooked food and cool jugs of beer. Cherish the children your love gave life. Bathe away life's dirt in warm drawn waters. Pass the time in joy with your chosen wife. On the Tablets of Destiny it is decreed for you to enjoy short pleasures for your short days. (*Epic of Gilgamesh* 10.2–3)

Nevertheless, some ancient Mesopotamian texts mention a place where human souls might go following death. And evidence suggests that many people believed in its existence. Called variously the Land of the Dead, Great Earth, or the Land of No Return, it was ruled by the goddess Ereshkigal and the god Nergal, who lived in a palace made of the semiprecious stone lapis lazuli. Outside of that palace, the Land of No Return seems to have resembled the Plain of Asphodel in the Greco-Roman Underworld—a dismal, gray, uninviting place where souls simply existed, experiencing neither suffering nor joy, neither reward nor punishment. One surviving text describes it as "the house whose entrants are bereft of [lack] light, where dust is their sustenance and clay their food. They see no light but dwell in darkness." It was thought that ghosts of the dead could return to Earth on certain occasions, especially during a celebration known as "the return of the dead," held in the month of Abu (July/August). Any ghosts who harassed the living during these visits were punished by the Sun god, Shamash, who presided over a court in the Land of No Return. After the spirits were honored in the festival, they had to return to their dreary abode in the nether world.

Considering how uninviting the afterlife seemed to be, it is not surprising that most Mesopotamians were taught that they should make the best of their earthly lives since there was little if anything to look forward to after death. Thus, leading a decent, honest, constructive life was a common goal, not because of the rewards it might bring later, but because it was the will of the gods, who supposedly knew what was best for humanity.

SEE ALSO: *Epic of Gilgamesh;* religion

Ahura-Mazda

The supreme god of the ancient Persian religion. Ahura-Mazda was often called "the Lord of Wisdom," as the word *ahura* meant "lord" and *mazda* meant "wisdom." It is possible that he was first conceived as an early Indo-European sky god, as was the Greek Zeus. However, thanks to the religious teachings of the fourteenth-century B.C. Iranian religious prophet Zoroaster (or Zarathustra), founder of the Zoroastrian faith, Ahura-Mazda emerged as the one true god, more or less equivalent to the deity worshipped by the monotheistic Jews of the same period. Just as the Jews, and later the Christians, saw their god as the ultimate creator of all things, the Persians believed that Ahura-Mazda had fashioned the universe. This idea is expressed in surviving inscriptions, including one commissioned by King Xerxes I: "A great god is Ahura-Mazda, who created this Earth, who created yonder sky, who created man, who created happiness for man, who made Xerxes king, one king of many, one lord of many." The Persians also saw Ahura-Mazda as the chief source of truth, virtue, and light and thought that he would bring prosperity, peace, and happiness to those who faithfully worshipped him. Such ideas are repeated often in the *Avesta,* the collection of prayers and hymns constituting the Persian/Zoroastrian bible.

One of the texts known as the Yasnas (meaning "Reverence"), reads:

> I announce (and) carry out (this Yasna) for the creator Ahura Mazda, the radiant and glorious, the greatest and the best, the most Beautiful . . . the most firm, the wisest, and the one of all whose body is the most perfect, who attains His ends the most infallibly . . . to him who disposes our minds aright, who sends His joy-creating grace afar; who made us, and has fashioned us, and who has nourished and protected us, who is the most bounteous Spirit! (*Avesta, Older Yasnas* 1.1)

Ancient Persian artists almost always portrayed Ahura-Mazda as a bearded man sitting inside a winged vehicle that moved through the sky. He held a ring that symbolized his authority over human rulers and wielded lightning bolts representing his ability to enforce that authority, similar to the way Zeus enforced his own will using lightning bolts. According to Persian beliefs, the god also used his formidable weapons against his archfoe, the evil spirit Ahriman, somewhat equivalent to the Christian devil.

SEE ALSO: *Avesta;* Zoroaster; Zoroastrianism

Akitu

The Akkadian name for Mesopotamia's largest agricultural holiday and religious festival. (The original Sumerian name was *Akiti.*) Many communities celebrated Akitu directly after the spring barley harvest, barley being the region's principal grain. Because the spring equinox was viewed as the start of a new year, Akitu was often also a New Year's celebration. The holiday lasted for twelve days, beginning on March 20 or 21, in the month of Nisan. Based on surviving evidence from Babylon, the first six days or so featured private ceremonies conducted by a local high priest. The last six days involved lavish public rites dedicated to Marduk, chief god of the Babylonian pantheon. Also honored was Marduk's son, Nabu. The king accompanied the sacred image of Marduk as priests or worshippers carried it from that god's temple. The procession marched into Nabu's temple to a spot called the Shrine of Destinies, where supposedly the god revealed whether the king would enjoy success in the year to come. That destiny was announced with great pomp in public. And there were several elaborate feasts. When the sacred procession returned the image of Marduk to the main temple, the king may have made love to a specially chosen young woman in a reenactment of a mythical coupling of the goddess Inanna and the divine shepherd Dumuzi. However, this aspect of the festival is still uncertain and is debated by scholars. Versions of the festival held in other parts of Mesopotamia probably singled out different gods and had other local variations.

SEE ALSO: farming; Inanna; Marduk; religion

Akkad

In general regional terms, the northern portion of Babylonia, as opposed to the southern portion, called Sumer. In a more specific way, the term *Akkad* (or *Agade*) is used to designate the local homeland and home city of the great Akkadian conqueror Sargon of Akkad, or Sargon the Great, born circa 2370 B.C., who created the first great Mesopotamian empire. To the frustration of archaeologists, the location of the city of Akkad has not yet been determined. Some scholars propose that it might lie somewhere near modern Bagh-

dad, the capital of Iraq. The city fell, along with the empire, in about 2200 B.C.

SEE ALSO: Akkadian Empire; Mesopotamia, history of; Sargon of Akkad

Akkadian Empire

The first large-scale empire that rose in Mesopotamia, centered on the city of Akkad, situated perhaps east or northeast of Babylon. Modern scholars usually use the term *Akkadian* to describe the inhabitants of northern Babylonia—or, more generally, northern Mesopotamia—before Assyria rose to power in that region in the second millennium B.C. The Akkadians were culturally similar to their neighbors, the Sumerians. The main difference was language, as the Akkadians spoke a Semitic tongue quite different from Sumerian.

Local Akkadian rulers became active in the mid-third millennium B.C., the most successful of their number being Sargon, later called "the Great." It appears that he started out as a government official under the king of Kish, lying a few miles east of Babylon, then at some point founded a new city, Akkad, nearby. After capturing Kish, Sargon launched major campaigns that succeeded in defeating all of the Sumerian city-states lying southeast of Babylon and took him to the shores of the Persian Gulf. Either Sargon or one of his Akkadian successors, perhaps Rimush, Manishtusu, Naram-Sin, or Shar-kali-sharri, then overran Elam in southern Iran and made the then-minor Elamite city of Susa the regional capital. (Susa would later become an important Persian city.) On Akkad's western flank, members of the Sargonid dynasty conquered the powerful city-states of Mari on the upper Euphrates and Ebla in Syria, not far from the Mediterranean coast, and may have momen-

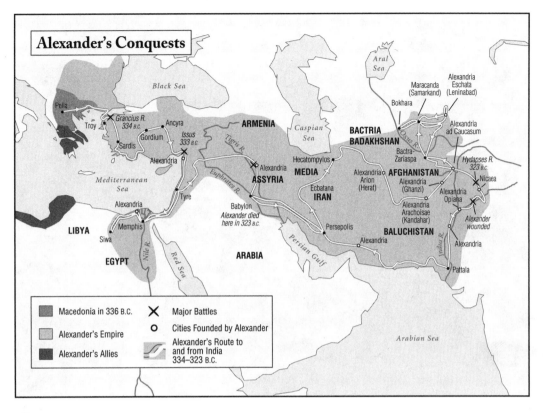

Alexander's Conquests

Black Sea

Aral Sea

Pella

Troy
Grancius R.
334 B.C.
Ancyra
Gordium
Sardis
Alexandria

ARMENIA

Caspian Sea

Maracanda (Samarkand)
Bokhara
Alexandria Eschata (Leninabad)

BACTRIA
BADAKHSHAN
Bactra-Zariaspa

Alexandria ad Caucasum

Issus
333 B.C.

Tigris R.

Euphrates R.

Alexandria

ASSYRIA

Hecatompylos

MEDIA

Ecbatana

IRAN

Alexandria Arion (Herat)

AFGHANISTAN
Alexandria (Ghazni)

Hydaspes R.
323 B.C.
Nicaea

Alexandria Opiana

Alexander wounded

Mediterranean Sea

Tyre

Babylon
Alexander died here in 323 B.C.

Persepolis

Alexandria Arachoisae (Kandahar)

BALUCHISTAN

Indus R.

Alexandria

Alexandria

LIBYA
Memphis
Siwa

Nile R.

Red Sea

Persian Gulf

Alexandria

Pattala

EGYPT

ARABIA

Arabian Sea

Macedonia in 336 B.C.   ✕ Major Battles

Alexander's Empire   ○ Cities Founded by Alexander

Alexander's Allies   Alexander's Route to and from India 334–323 B.C.

GALE

tarily reached the eastern reaches of Asia Minor.

For its time, this empire created by the Akkadian dynasty was seen as extensive, although it was smaller than the Assyrian and Persian empires that would later rise in the same region. Sargon was able to create and initially maintain this realm through the use of his army, the first-known permanent professional military force. As shown in the famous Stele of the Vultures, the army employed a formidable battlefield formation similar to the phalanx later developed by the Greeks. Sargon and his successors held the empire together partly by using this army to intimidate subject towns. In cases where local rulers were willing to swear allegiance to Akkad, these rulers were allowed to retain their positions; however, sometimes the Akka-

dian kings placed their own men in charge of subject cities. In these ways, Sargon and his successors were able to achieve at least some central control over their realm.

The Akkadian Empire was relatively short-lived, however. Rebellions by the Sumerian cities and wars with neighboring peoples weakened it. Then, around 2200 B.C., or perhaps shortly thereafter, a group of hill tribes collectively called the Guti attacked Akkad and the realm collapsed.

SEE ALSO: Akkad; Guti; Stele of the Vultures; Sumerians; weapons and warfare, land

Alexander III ("the Great") (356 B.C.–323 B.C.)

A Macedonian Greek king who, in the extraordinarily brief period of a decade,

This "Alexander Mosaic" depicts Alexander charging at his foe, the Persian king Darius III.

conquered all of Mesopotamia, along with Anatolia (or Asia Minor), Egypt, and what is now Afghanistan. Though Alexander's empire was equally brief in duration, it was the largest single centralized realm that ever existed in the Near East. Alexander was the son of Macedonia's King Philip II and Olympias, one of Philip's seven wives. The boy was an excellent student and early developed a driving ambition to achieve great deeds and everlasting fame. Like the legendary Greek warrior Achilles (the central character of Homer's epic poem the *Iliad*), with whom he often identified himself, Alexander consciously chose a brief life of fame and glory over a long one of obscurity. "Those who endure hardship and danger are the ones who achieve glory," Alexander said, according to his ancient biographer Arrian, "and the most gratifying thing is to live with courage and to die leaving behind eternal renown." (*Anabasis Alexandri* 5.26)

Alexander certainly fulfilled this singular, lofty goal. In 338 B.C., at the age of eighteen, he commanded the Macedonian cavalry in the Battle of Chaeronea, in which Philip defeated the major city-states of southern Greece. Soon afterward Philip was assassinated, and the twenty-year-old Alexander was king of Macedonia and captain-general of Greece. After ruthlessly putting down rebellions by those Greeks who had underestimated him because of his youth, he turned his attention to the invasion of the Persian Empire, which Philip had been planning for some time. In 334 B.C. Alexander led an army of some thirty-two thousand infantry and five thousand cavalry across the Hellespont (now the Dardenelles strait) and into Anatolia. He quickly won a major victory at the Granicus River, defeating an army led by some of the local Persian governors. Then he marched southward and at Issus in Syria defeated a larger army commanded by the Persian king, Darius III, although Darius escaped capture. Next, Alexander marched through Palestine and into Egypt, which he liberated from Persian control. In the Nile delta he founded the city of Alexandria, named after himself, which rapidly developed into one of the major commercial and cultural centers of the ancient world.

The hills and plains of Mesopotamia now beckoned Alexander. Early in 331 B.C. his forces penetrated the Persian heartland (now Iraq and Iran) and at Gaugamela, located 270 miles (435km) north of Babylon, he crushed another large army commanded by Darius. The Persian king escaped once more, but soon some of his own nobles, led by a provincial governor named Bessus, betrayed him and tried to trade him to Alexander in exchange for leniency for themselves. They murdered Darius, after which Alexander captured them.

The way Alexander dealt with Bessus is an excellent illustration of the young conqueror's often ruthless methods. It also shows how Alexander avidly, and in many cases quite strategically, adopted customs of the countries he conquered. For example, cutting off the nose and ears or tearing someone limb from limb were not normal means of punishment and execution in Greece, but they were in ancient Mesopotamia and Iran, including Assyria and Persia. So Alexander inflicted one or both of these gruesome penalties on Bessus. Two different accounts of Bessus's fate have survived. One, an account which Arrian purports was taken from a book written by one of Alexander's leading followers, Ptolemy, claims:

> Alexander [said] that he [Bessus] must be stripped of his clothes and led in a dog-collar and made to stand on the right [side] of the road, along which he [Alexander] and his army would pass. The order was obeyed, and when Alexander saw him [Bessus] there, he stopped his chariot and asked him why he had treated Darius, the king, kinsman and benefactor, so shamefully, first seizing him, then hurrying him off in chains, and finally murdering him. Bessus answered that . . . the object was to win Alexander's favor. . . . At this, Alexander ordered him to be [whipped]. . . . [Later] Alexander had Bessus brought before a full meeting of his officers and accused him of treachery to Darius. He then gave orders that his nose and the tips of his ears should be cut off. (*Anabasis Alexandri* 3.30, 4.8)

In contrast, Alexander's other major ancient biographer, the first-century A.D. Greek writer Plutarch, claims that Bessus was executed in the following manner:

> [Alexander] had the tops of two straight trees bent down so that they met, and part of Bessus's body was tied to each. Then, when each tree was let go and sprang back to its upright position, the part of the body attached to it was torn off by the recoil. (*Life of Alexander* 43)

During the months during which Alexander chased and dealt with Bessus and the other conspirators who had killed Darius, the Macedonian king occupied the three Persian capitals—Babylon, Susa, and Persepolis—none of which offered any resistance. Then Alexander completed his conquest of Persia, a process that took him to the western borders of India. There, in 326 B.C., he defeated a local king, Porus, on the banks of the Hydapses River. Though Alexander desired to press on and conquer the rest of India, his exhausted and homesick troops refused to go any farther. Reluctantly, therefore, Alexander ordered the army's return to Babylon, a difficult journey in which many soldiers died. Reaching Susa, he married Darius's eldest daughter, perhaps in hopes of initiating a lasting merger of Greek and Persian/Mesopotamian culture. Then he moved on to Babylon and began planning an invasion of Arabia. However, Alexander, then only thirty-three, suddenly died in Babylon on June 10, 323 B.C., perhaps of alcohol poisoning. Arrian later summed up this remarkable man this way:

> He had great personal beauty, invincible power of endurance, and a keen intellect. . . . He had an uncanny instinct for the right course in a difficult and complex situation. . . . Noble indeed was his power of inspiring his men, of filling them with confidence, and . . . sweeping away their fear by the spectacle of his own fearlessness. . . . Never in all the world was there another like him, and therefore I cannot but feel that some power more than human was concerned in his birth. (*Anabasis Alexandri* 7.28–29)

Alexander's vast empire did not last long, mainly because his principal generals and governors, the so-called Successors, engaged in a long and bloody power struggle for possession of it. A handful of victorious Successors, including Seleucus and Ptolemy, divided the realm into smaller units, including the Seleucid Empire, which encompassed most of Mesopotamia.

SEE ALSO: Battle of Gaugamela; Darius III; Greeks; Persian Empire

Ammi-saduqa
(reigned 1646–1626 B.C.)

The tenth king of the Babylonian dynasty that had earlier produced Hammurabi, the lawgiver (reigned 1792–1750 B.C.). Historically speaking, Ammi-saduqa's principal achievement was to have his royal astronomers make complex observations of the risings and settings of the planet Venus. The purpose was to use the heavenly positions of Venus and the stars to make predictions of future events. However, long after the demise of ancient Mesopotamia, modern scholars discovered the cuneiform tablets bearing this data and saw that it could be used to date the reigns of Babylonian rulers going back to Hammurabi. Unfortunately, though, interpretations of Venus's ancient cycle differ, allowing for three possible sets of dates that vary by as much as 120 years. Three differing modern chronologies exist for Babylonia, therefore, the High, Middle, and Low. This encyclopedia adopts the most widely used of these time lines, the Middle.

SEE ALSO: astrology and astronomy; Babylonia; Hammurabi

Amorites

Originally a pastoral, Semitic-speaking hill people who began settling in the region of northern Babylonia in the last years of the third millennium B.C. The city-dwelling Mesopotamians initially viewed the Amorites as odd and almost laughably primitive. The Amorites did not grow grains but rather raised sheep and goats; they had no cities, preferring a nomadic existence; they lived in tents rather than in houses; they wore animal skins rather than woven fabrics; and they ate most of their food raw. Whatever their social and cultural shortcomings, however, the Amorites vigorously moved onto Babylonian farmlands, which they used to graze their animals. Such Amorite intrusions are believed to be one of the causes of the downfall of the empire known as the Third Dynasty of Ur circa 2004 B.C. Thereafter, Amorites occupied various cities in the region. These cities included Larsa and eventually Babylon, where, in about 1894 B.C., an Amorite named Sumu-abum established the Babylonian dynasty that later produced the lawgiver Hammurabi.

SEE ALSO: Babylonia; Hammurabi; Third Dynasty of Ur

amulets

Objects thought to have magical properties that could either bring luck or protect a person from evil. In ancient Mesopotamia amulets were often attached to cords and were worn as pendants, although sometimes people placed them in strategic spots and left them to work their intended magic. Amulets were made of terra-cotta (baked clay), bone, metal, the semiprecious stone lapis lazuli, and other materials. They came in a wide variety of shapes, among the most popular being small figurines of animals, animal heads, and gods.

SEE ALSO: jewelry; magic; religion

Amurru

The chief god of the Amorites, a Semitic-speaking people who became absorbed into the Mesopotamian cultural mainstream in the early second millennium B.C. At first Amurru (or Martu), like the Amorites themselves, was viewed as a primitive being who lived in a tent and ate his food raw. The god's rustic image was reflected in his nickname, "the Man of the Desert." As Amorite tribes settled in Mesopotamian cities, Amurru was assimilated and "civilized" by the invention of myths in which he married a Sumerian goddess, the granddaughter of the moon god, Nanna.

SEE ALSO: Amorites; Nanna

Amytis (flourished late seventh century B.C.)

A Median princess who became the queen of Babylonia's King Nebuchadnezzar II circa 605 B.C. The marriage was designed to seal the alliance between the Babylonians and the Medes following their joint destruction of the Assyrian Empire. It was for Amytis that Nebuchadnezzar built the famous Hanging Gardens of Babylon, listed among the Seven Wonders of the Ancient World.

SEE ALSO: Hanging Gardens of Babylon; Media; Nebuchadnezzar II

An

A Sumerian, and later general Mesopotamian, god whose name meant "Heaven" or "Heavenly Deity" and who held moral authority over all other gods. An (or Anu) provided the universe with order, ruled the sky, and oversaw the administration of justice, including deciding the fate of other deities. Various myths list different wives for An, among them the earth goddess, Ki; the mother goddess, Nammu; and the sex goddess, Inanna (or Ishtar). The names of gods in lists found on tablets dating from the late fourth and third millennia B.C. often use An's name as a prefix, perhaps paying homage to his superior position in the divine pantheon. An's son, Enlil, ruler of Earth, eventually took over some of An's functions, such as bestowing kingship on human rulers.

SEE ALSO: Enlil; Inanna; Nammu

Anabasis

A major work by the fourth-century B.C. Greek writer and adventurer Xenophon (ZEN-uh-phon) detailing the exploits of a Greek army stranded on the Mesopotamian plains in the middle of the Persian Empire. In 401 B.C. Xenophon was one of ten thousand Greek troops who signed on to fight for a Persian prince named Cyrus the Younger. Cyrus's goal was to dethrone his older brother, Artaxerxes II, and to this end the prince raised a mixed army of Persians, other Mesopotamians, and Greek mercenaries. As described in the *Anabasis* (or *March Up-Country*), Cyrus led these forces from Sardis, in western Anatolia, overland to Cunaxa, about 50 miles (80km) from Babylon. There, Artaxerxes was waiting with a larger army and a huge battle took place. Xenophon recalls the advance and charge of the Greek infantry, which terrified the Persians:

> The two lines were hardly six or seven hundred yards [549 or 640m] apart when [we] began to chant the battle hymn and moved against the enemy. . . . Then altogether [we] broke into a ringing cheer [battle cry], "Eleleu, eleleu!" and all charged at the double. . . . Before one shot reached them, the barbarians turned and fled. At once [we] pursued with might and main. . . . Not one Greek was hurt in this battle, except one on the left wing, said to have been shot by an arrow. (*Anabasis* 1.7)

Though Xenophon and his comrades had acquitted themselves well in the battle, the main part of Cyrus's army was defeated and Cyrus himself was killed. The Greeks now found themselves marooned in the center of enemy territory and surrounded by hostile forces. Artaxerxes' officers invited the Greek commander to peace talks but then treacherously murdered him and his officers. The outraged Greek soldiers quickly elected new leaders, including Xenophon. They decided there was no other choice but to try fighting their way out of Persia. In an incredible overland trek of more than 1,000 miles (1,609km), they weathered daunting hardships, including fending off assaults by Persian troops and fierce hill tribesmen and trudging through deep mountain snows. "A north wind blew in [our] faces," Xenophon writes, "parching everything . . . and freezing the men. . . . The snow was a fathom [6 feet (1.8m)] deep, so that many animals . . . were lost, and [about thirty] soldiers, too. . . . [We] kept the fire burning all night." (*Anabasis* 2.5)

Eventually, the "Ten Thousand," as they became known to Greeks everywhere, reached the shores of the Black Sea, where several Greek cities were located. A number of men sailed or hiked from there to their home cities. Xenophon's *Anabasis* proved important because many Greeks in the following generation saw it as a sort of manual on how to defeat "inferior" Mesopotamian troops in their own homeland; it was, therefore, one of the factors leading to the invasion and destruction of the Persian Empire by Alexander the Great.

SEE ALSO: Artaxerxes; Battle of Cunaxa; Cyrus the Younger; Xenophon

Anatolia

The large peninsula presently occupied by the nation of Turkey. Throughout much of antiquity, Anatolia (or Asia Minor) was viewed as part of the Near East, what many Greeks and Romans called Asia. And because it lay on the northwestern periphery of the Mesopotamian plains, the region was often sought after or occupied by empires centered in those plains. As early as the third millennium B.C., important trade routes linking Mesopotamia to southeastern Europe by way of the Hellespont and the Aegean Sea ran east to west through Anatolia. The first Mesopotamian conqueror to reach the area was Sargon of Akkad, who in the 2300s B.C. may have campaigned in the Taurus Mountains in southeastern Anatolia. About five centuries later the Hittites, an Indo-European people, established a powerful kingdom, Hatti, centered on the Halys River in Anatolia's eastern sector. For several centuries the Hittites played a major role in Near Eastern history, as they attacked Syria, sacked Babylon in 1595 B.C., and fought the Egyptians in Palestine. Long after the Hittites' demise, in the seventh century B.C. the Assyrians occupied the Taurus Mountains and may have penetrated farther into Anatolia if their empire had not suddenly collapsed. This goal was achieved in the following century, however, by the Persians, led by their founder, Cyrus II. He conquered the kingdom of Lydia, then occupying the western portion of Anatolia; and took charge of the Greek cities lying along the Aegean seaboard. For the first time in history, this brought a Mesopotamian power into direct contact with the Greek city-states. For two centuries most of Anatolia remained under Persian rule, until the Macedonian king Alexander III, later called "the Great," took over the region in the late 330s B.C. Following Alexander's death in 323 B.C., Anatolia became a battleground for his leading generals, the so-called Successors. And by about 280 B.C. one of these men, Seleucus, had control of large portions of the peninsula. Only a century later, however, the Seleucids were driven from the area, which increasingly came under Roman rule.

SEE ALSO: Hittites; Persian Empire; Romans

annals

Royal inscriptions, most often carved in stone, describing the military exploits, building programs, and other works of kings. The most numerous and striking versions were those of the Assyrian monarchs, beginning in the early thirteenth century B.C.

SEE ALSO: historical accounts

Annunaki

In Sumerian, Babylonian, and some other Mesopotamian mythologies, a group of minor gods and goddesses often mentioned in literature and religious inscriptions. Their number varied in the telling, from as few as seven to as many as six hundred. In some ways the Annunaki resembled, as well as interacted with, another assemblage of minor gods, the Igigi. In Sumerian lore the Annunaki performed various labors and errands for more important gods and in some ways resembled the angels of Christian lore. In fact, the Hebrew writers of the Old Testament, who lived in the Near East and were familiar with the Annunaki, incorporated a version of them into the book of Genesis, in which they are angels called Jedi or Nephilim. The Assyrians viewed the Annunaki as members of a very early race of gods who taught humans to farm and then became judges of the dead in the Underworld.

SEE ALSO: Bible; Igigi; religion

Anshar and Kishar

Two very ancient divine beings mentioned in the Babylonian *Epic of Creation*. Anshar, who personified the sky or heaven, and Kishar, who personified Earth, were the offspring of the primordial forces Apsu, deity of freshwater, and Tiamat, goddess of saltwater. In turn, Anshar and Kishar gave rise to the god An, or Anu, who oversaw universal order and justice.

SEE ALSO: An; *Epic of Creation*

Antigonus Monophthalmos (ca. 382 B.C.–301 B.C.)

One of the so-called Successors of Alexander the Great and for a while a powerful Macedonian Greek warlord who illegally controlled and looted Mesopotamia. Not much is known about Antigonus's life before he was in his sixties, except that he lost an eye in battle as a young man. This was the origin of his nickname Monophthalmos, meaning "the One-Eyed." Antigonus accompanied Alexander in the latter's invasion of the Persian Empire in the late 330s B.C. During these campaigns, Alexander appointed him governor of Phrygia, the region encompassing much of central Anatolia, but Antigonus soon proved that he was not satisfied with a mere governorship. Following Alexander's death in 323 B.C., Antigonus joined with several of Alexander's other former generals and governors in a struggle to gain control of all or parts of the vast empire Alexander had carved out.

During these seemingly relentless wars, Antigonus claimed he had a right to the title "supreme commander in Asia," which would in effect give him control of much of Alexander's realm. However, another of the Successors, Eumenes, made the same claim, and the two were staunch rivals until Eumenes was killed in 316 B.C. After this, Antigonus arrogantly began acting as if he was master of most of the Near East, including Mesopotamia. Another Successor, Seleucus, had been made governor of Babylonia soon after Alexander's death in an agreement approved by most of the Successors. But he now felt himself overshadowed by Antigonus, who suddenly arrived on the scene and began plundering the region at will. Antigonus looted the former Persian capitals of Persepolis and Susa, taking an estimated twenty-five thousand talents' worth of booty. (At the time, a person with assets worth just a single talent was seen as very well-to-do.) Eventually Seleucus had no choice but to flee to Egypt, where he was sheltered by another Successor, Ptolemy (TAW-luh-mee). Antigonus then marched across upper Mesopotamia toward Syria, stealing another ten thousand talents' worth of loot along the way. He also occupied Sidon, Byblos, and other Phoenician cities. There he put shipbuilders to work to create a fleet with which to make war on the other Successors.

But many of these rivals of Antigonus were as ambitious and ruthless as he was. And on more than one occasion they formed coalitions against him and his equally power-hungry son, Demetrius Poliorcetes, who later became famous for his massive siege of the island of Rhodes. Antigonus's day of reckoning came when one of these coalitions defeated and killed him at Ipsus in Phrygia in 301 B.C. Incredibly, he went down fighting, though he was now eighty. Among the victors that day was the resilient Seleucus, who had already reestablished himself in Mesopotamia. There, the Seleucid Empire, which was destined to hold sway in that region for more than a century, was in its birth pangs.

SEE ALSO: Alexander III ("the Great"); Seleucid Empire; Seleucus I

Antiochus

The name of several rulers of the Greek Seleucid Empire, which controlled Mesopotamia for about a century following the wars of the Successors of Alexander the Great. Antiochus I Soter (reigned 281–260 B.C.) was the son of the kingdom's founder, Seleucus, who had been one of Alexander's generals. The first Antiochus restored a number of temples in Babylon. On these his artisans carved inscriptions, including the last ones in Mesopotamia to be composed in the old cuneiform symbols. The following example, carved in the temple of Nabu, god of the written word, perpetuates the haughty, grandiose style of earlier non-Greek Mesopotamian rulers:

> Antiochus, the great king ... king of the world, king of Babylon ... the first son of Seleucus, the king ... of Babylon, am I. ... In the month of Addaru, on the twentieth day, year 43 [i.e., the forty-third year since Seleucus established his empire], the ... true temple, the house of Nabu, which is in [the town of] Borsippa, I did lay. O Nabu ... regard [me] joyfully and, at your lofty command which is unchanging, may the overthrow of the countries of my enemies ... just kingship, [and] a happy reign ... be [your] gift for the kingship of Antiochus ... forever.

Antiochus II Theos (260–246 B.C.) inher-

ited a war with Ptolemaic Egypt; and to help facilitate peace, he married Berenice, daughter of Ptolemy II. However, in the process Antiochus dismissed his first wife, Laodice, who achieved her revenge by poisoning him.

Perhaps the most famous of the Seleucid rulers after Seleucus himself, Antiochus III "the Great" (222–187 B.C.), did his best to keep his disintegrating realm intact. He put down some rebellions in Mesopotamia. But he lost a major battle at Raphia in southern Palestine to Ptolemy IV in 217. Soon Antiochus rebounded and defeated the Parthians, who had been chipping away at the Seleucid Empire's eastern portions. He also managed to restore some lost territories in Anatolia. However, he then came up against the Romans, who had recently brought the powerful Greek Macedonian kingdom to its knees. In 190 B.C., at Magnesia in western Anatolia, the Romans delivered Antiochus a shattering defeat, and he ended up losing much of the territory he had recently gained.

Antiochus's later namesakes were weak kings who were unable to halt the onrush of the Parthians in the east and the Romans in the west. Antiochus IV Epiphanes (175–164 B.C.) lost Jerusalem in Palestine to Jewish rebels and, like his father, Antiochus III, was defeated in battle by the Romans. Antiochus VII Sidetes (138–129 B.C.) managed briefly to recover Babylon, but soon afterward he died fighting the Parthians. During the reign of the last ruler of the Seleucid dynasty, Antiochus XIII Asiaticus (69–65 B.C.), the Romans captured Antioch, the capital of the last remnant of the Seleucid Empire.

SEE ALSO: Parthian Empire; Romans; Seleucid Empire

aqueducts

Water channels that carry freshwater from lakes or streams to distant towns. The Arabic word for aqueduct was *qanat;* the Persian word was *kariz.* In ancient Mesopotamia, the Assyrians and the Persians built aqueducts, mainly underground.

SEE ALSO: water supplies

Arabs

Before the Muslim era, most ancient Arabs inhabited dry wastelands lacking arable fields and pastures, and their populations, organized into competing tribes, were small and often nomadic. For these reasons, they did not create any strong, well-organized kingdoms and generally remained outside the political and cultural mainstream of the empires of Mesopotamia and the eastern Mediterranean.

The first historical references to Arabs, called Aribi in the Akkadian tongue, appear in the book of Genesis in the Hebrew Old Testament and in Assyrian annals of the early first millennium B.C. Assyria's King Shalmaneser III mentioned Arabs as one of the peoples he defeated circa 853 B.C. Later Assyrian bas-reliefs show battles in which Arab warriors ride camels. Some evidence suggests that Persia's King Darius I conquered parts of Arabia in the late sixth century B.C. and collected tribute from local sheikhs.

Following the fall of Persia nearly two centuries later, the Arabs remained autonomous until A.D. 106, when the Romans annexed the northwestern portion of Arabia and made it a province of their empire. The Romans called this region, roughly corresponding to modern Jordan, Arabia Petraea. It was one of the three general divisions of Arabia recognized throughout antiquity. The other two were, in Roman terminology, Arabia Deserta, the remote, nearly waterless interior of the country; and Arabia Felix, the southern coastal region now occupied by Yemen and Oman. For many centuries the ports of Arabia Felix were vital links in a trade route that received goods from the Far East and funneled them via camel caravans northward into Mesopotamia and Palestine.

SEE ALSO: Muslim period; Shalmaneser III; trade

Aramaeans

A group of tribal peoples who emerged in the middle of the second millennium B.C. from the Syrian deserts and established small kingdoms in Syria and along the Mediterranean coast, one of them centered in the town of Guzana. Some Aramaeans also migrated into northern and western Mesopotamia and settled wherever they could, which brought them into contact with the Assyrians, who then controlled that region. The Assyrians at first called them Ahlamu. As time went on, Aramaean tribesmen raided Assyrian and Babylonian farms and settlements and long remained a nuisance. The main contribution of the Aramaeans to Mesopotamian culture—indeed a major one—was their language, Aramaic, which eventually spread throughout Mesopotamia and other parts of the Near East.

SEE ALSO: Aramaic; Guzana; languages

Aramaic

The language of the Aramaeans, a Syrian people who migrated into Mesopotamia in the late second millennium B.C. A Semitic tongue related to Hebrew, Aramaic utilized a simple alphabet based on that of the Phoenicians, a maritime people inhabiting coastal Palestine. The simplicity of written Aramaic appealed to literate Mesopotamians who were used to dealing with the more complex and cumbersome cuneiform writing system. Over time Aramaic spread through the Near East and replaced Akkadian as Mesopotamia's lingua franca, or universal language.

SEE ALSO: Aramaeans; cuneiform; languages

Arbil

One of the leading cities of ancient Assyria. Situated between the Upper and Lower Zab rivers in the Assyrian heartland, Arbil (or Arbela) was noted for its sacred temple of Ishtar, goddess of sexual desire. Of Ishtar's many shrines across the wide Assyrian Empire, this one was second only to that in Ashur, Assyria's first royal capital. Later, following Assyria's demise, the town became momentarily famous because of the great battle fought there in 331 B.C. between Alexander the Great and Persia's King Darius III at nearby Gaugamela. Early modern scholars called it the Battle of Arbela. Because the modern city of Erbil completely overlays ancient Arbil, the latter has so far undergone very little excavation.

SEE ALSO: Ashur; Battle of Gaugamela; Ishtar; Zab rivers

Ardashir I
(reigned A.D. 226–241)

The founder and first ruler of the Sassanian Empire, a Neo-Persian realm that supplanted the Parthian Empire. Like Cyrus II, founder of the Achaemenid Persian Empire, Ardashir was born in the old Persian heartland of Fars, north of the Persian Gulf, then a small vassal kingdom within the greater Parthian realm. In 208 Ardashir deposed his brother, Sapur, then the ruler of the kingdom. The new leader of Fars proceeded to expand his power by obtaining the loyalty of the rulers of the surrounding regions. Hoping to stop him, the Parthian king, Artabanus IV, assembled an army and attacked, but Ardashir defeated and killed him in 224. Two years later Ardashir was crowned king of what he viewed as a reborn Persian Empire. He began to create a strong centralized government and oversaw a resurgence of Zoroastrian worship, which had declined under the Parthians. Ardashir also twice invaded western Mesopotamia, then part of the Roman province of that name. In the first campaign he defeated a Roman army but suffered heavy losses and temporarily withdrew. He returned in 237 and captured a number of towns in the area, including Hatra, located southwest of Nineveh. At his death in 241, Ardashir left a firm national and imperial foundation for his son and successor, Shapur I, to build on.

SEE ALSO: Artabanus IV; Parthian Empire; Romans

Armenia

The mountainous region lying directly north of Mesopotamia. Armenia was repeatedly attacked and/or conquered by rulers of various Mesopotamian empires as well as by other peoples. In the early first millennium B.C., and for many centuries to come, the region was called Urartu, and its inhabitants clashed with the armies of several Assyrian kings. In about 600 B.C. the Armenians, an Indo-European tribal people, entered and took over the area. Almost immediately, they came under the

An investiture of Ardarshir I by the god Ahura-Mazda. © ROGER WOOD/CORBIS

sway of the Median king Cyaxares II, whose own realm soon fell to Persia's King Cyrus II.

About a century and a half later, the Greek mercenary soldier and writer Xenophon passed through Armenia during the retreat of the Greek army known as the Ten Thousand. He later described some typical Armenian houses and their contents, including primitive versions of straws to sip beer:

The houses were underground structures with an aperture like the mouth of a well by which to enter, but they were broad and spacious below. The entrance for the beasts of burden was dug out, but the human occupants descended by a ladder. In these dwellings were to be found goats and sheep and cattle, and cocks and hens. . . . There were stores within of wheat and barley and vegetables, and wine made from barley [beer] in great big bowls; the grains of barley malt lay floating in the beverage up to the lip of the vessel, and reeds lay in them, some longer, some shorter, without joints; when you were thirsty you must take one of these into your mouth, and suck. (*Anabasis* 4.24–26)

Not long after Xenophon wrote these words, Armenia became part of Alexander the Great's empire. Then the region was ruled by the Seleucids, the dynasty established by Alexander's general Seleucus, until the Romans defeated the Seleucids and backed a series of independent Armenian rulers. Much later, in the fourth century A.D., Armenia was divided into two sections, the western one controlled by Rome and the eastern part by the Sassanian Empire.

SEE ALSO: Assyrian Empire; Mesopotamia, history of; Cyaxares II

Artabanus IV (reigned ca. A.D. 216–224)

The last ruler of the Arsacid dynasty and the Parthian Empire. After the death of his father, King Vologases V, in about 208, Artabanus fought with the new king, his brother Vologases VI, and eventually won. Not long afterward the Roman emperor Caracalla invaded Parthia, but Artabanus assembled an army and forced him to retreat. However, Artabanus was less fortunate when he marched his forces against Ardashir, king of Parthia's vassal state of Fars, who was leading a major rebellion. Ardashir was victorious, and Artabanus died in battle, extinguishing the Arsacid line of rulers. Several of the coins Artabanus issued have survived, most of which show him wearing a forked beard and a crown with ear flaps; the reverses usually display an archer seated on a throne.

SEE ALSO: Ardashir I; Parthian Empire; Sassanian Empire

Artaxerxes

The name of four rulers of the Persian Achaemenid dynasty, which controlled most or all of Mesopotamia from about 550 to 330 B.C. (*Artaxerxes* is a Greek corruption of the Persian name *Artakhshathra*.) The first Artaxerxes (ar-ta-ZERK-seez), who reigned from 464 to 424 B.C., was the son of King Xerxes I, who had invaded but failed to conquer Greece in 480 B.C. The new king had to deal with many rebellions in the empire's provinces, including Egypt, and his capable general Megabyzus defeated a large force of Athenian troops who were aiding the Egyptian rebels. Artaxerxes is well spoken of in the biblical books of Ezra and Nehemiah for his benevolence to the Jews who lived under his rule. The first of these books includes the text of a letter given by Artaxerxes to the Jewish priest Ezra, which reads in part:

> You are to be sent by the king [Artaxerxes] . . . to convey the silver and gold which the king . . . [has] freely offered to the God of Israel, whose dwelling is in Jerusalem. . . . With this money . . . you shall buy bulls, rams, and lambs . . . and you shall offer them [in sacrifice] upon the altar of the house of your God. . . . Whatever seems good to you and your brethren to do with the rest of the silver and gold, you may do so. (Ezra 7.14–18)

The second Artaxerxes ruled Persia from 404 to 358 B.C. The son of King Darius II, he was highly influenced by his wife and mother, and many of his decisions seem to have been based on the advice of two strong Persian governors, Tissaphernes and Pharnabazus. Artaxerxes II is best known for putting down a major rebellion led by his brother, Cyrus the

Younger, in 401 B.C. Artaxerxes defeated and killed Cyrus at Cunaxa in central Mesopotamia, then murdered the leaders of the Greek mercenaries Cyrus had hired, among them the writer Xenophon, who later recalled the expedition in his *Anabasis*.

Artaxerxes III (reigned 358–338 B.C.), whose original name was Ochus, was the son of Artaxerxes II. The new king reconquered Egypt, which had rebelled again. But he was unable to stop his own assassination, as he and many other members of his family were slain, perhaps by a powerful adviser, Bagoas, or else by the king's own son, Arses, with Bagoas's support. Arses then took the title Artaxerxes IV and ruled from 338 to 336 B.C. That reign witnessed frequent rebellions, and the king was finally killed by Bagoas and was replaced by Darius III.

SEE ALSO: *Anabasis*; Battle of Cunaxa; Persian Empire; Xerxes

Aruru

A Sumerian, and later general Mesopotamian, mother goddess, who, it was said, helped create human beings from clay. The kindly and gentle Aruru (or Ninmah) appears most prominently in the traditional *Epic of Gilgamesh*, in which she fashions the wild man Enkidu to check the arrogance and power of Gilgamesh. "I created humans," she proudly states in the narrative.

> "I shall create again the image of Gilgamesh. This creation now shall be as quick in heart and as strong in arm. This creation will speak word to word, blow to blow, so Uruk's children will live in peace." With this thought she did bend and scoop and spit and fling, with flick of wrist, mud that fell deep into the woods below.

> Thus did Enkidu come about. Thus did Enkidu, wild man, hairy man, forest man, come about. (*Epic of Gilgamesh* 1.2)

SEE ALSO: *Epic of Gilgamesh*

Aryans

A general, imprecise term designating groups of nomadic Indo-European peoples who, in the second millennium B.C., migrated in waves from somewhere in what is now southern Russia. Evidence suggests that some Aryans entered northern India circa 1500 B.C. And other Aryan waves may have pushed into Afghanistan (originally called Aryana, meaning "Land of the Aryans") and the Iranian plateau. The latter may have given rise to the early Persians; in one of his inscriptions, the Persian king Darius I claimed that the Achaemenid ruling family was of Aryan stock. Some scholars suggest that a later wave of Aryans became known as the Hurrians, who established the kingdom of Mitanni in western Mesopotamia. Almost nothing is known about the Aryans, except that they were pastoral (herded livestock) and used bronze weapons and horse-drawn chariots.

SEE ALSO: Hurrians; Mitanni; Persians

Asag

In Sumerian mythology, a terrifying demon who supposedly caused all manner of human suffering. (The Babylonians and the Assyrians called him Asakku.) Among the foul deeds attributed to him were making people ill, drying up wells, provoking fights, and squirting poison at people and animals. Asag was pictured in art as having three arms, three legs, repulsive skin, and many eyes located all over his body. One well-known Mesopotamian myth tells how the heroic god Ninurta defeated Asag.

See Also: Ninurta

Ashur (capital)

Long the capital and one of the chief cities of the Assyrian Empire as well as the root word for the terms *Assyria* and *Assyrian*. Located on the west bank of the Tigris River, about 60 miles (97km) south of the modern Iraqi city of Mosul, Ashur (or Assur) seems to have been settled circa 2500 B.C. by immigrants from Syria. The early Assyrian king Shamshi-Adad I (reigned ca. 1809–1766 B.C.) and his successors made the city a ceremonial center and their imperial capital. It retained that status until 883 B.C., when Kalhu (modern Nimrud) became the Assyrian capital; still, Ashur remained important as the burial site of the Assyrian monarchs. The city met its end in 614 B.C., when the Babylonians and the Medes sacked it during their conquest of Assyria.

The principal modern excavations of Ashur were conducted by the German Oriental Society, under the direction of Walter Andrae, between 1903 and 1911. Andrae and later researchers determined that the city was originally surrounded by a high circuit wall about 2.5 miles (4km) long. Ashur eventually boasted at least thirty-four temples honoring a range of Mesopotamian gods, three palace complexes, and three ziggurats, or pyramid-like structures. Today, tragically, the ruins of Ashur lie unprotected, and archaeologists list the site as seriously endangered.

See Also: Assyrian Empire; palaces; ziggurat

Ashur (god)

The chief god of the Assyrian pantheon of deities. Ashur (or Asshur) started out as the local god of the town of Ashur and its surrounding region. But after the Assyrians made that town their capital and expanded outward, creating an empire, the god Ashur grew in importance until he was the state war god and the supreme divinity, more or less equivalent to the Babylonian Marduk. People swore oaths to Ashur, whom artists usually depicted as a bearded, well-dressed man wearing a horned cap and sometimes riding a giant snake. In time the Assyrian kings came to associate themselves directly with Ashur, each claiming to be his earthly representative and deserving of the same loyalty.

See Also: Ashur, 1; Assyrian Empire; religion

Ashurbanipal (reigned ca. 668–627 B.C.)

The last powerful and important king of Assyria. Ashurbanipal succeeded his father, Esarhaddon, on the Assyrian throne. After Esarhaddon died while campaigning in Egypt, the new king proceeded to consolidate Assyria's hold on the region of Syria-Palestine, then invaded Egypt. The Egyptian pharaoh, Taharqa, fled and eventually died in exile. After most of the Assyrian forces had left Egypt, Taharqa's son, Tanuatamun, launched a rebellion, and Ashurbanipal responded by invading Egypt again. Although Ashurbanipal sacked the major Egyptian city of Thebes, a few years later (ca. 655 B.C.) he once more lost control of Egypt when the forces of the pharaoh Psamtik expelled the Assyrians from the country.

It appears that Ashurbanipal failed to invade Egypt still again because he suddenly found himself embroiled in a major war with Elam, a strong kingdom situated southeast of the Mesopotamian plains. He drove the Elamites back into their own country. But then Ashurbanipal's own brother, Shamash-shuma-ukin, who had administered the city of Babylon for seventeen years, challenged him for the Assyrian throne. At first the king attempted to deal with the problem diplomatically. He issued a public appeal to the Babylonian people, admonishing them not to follow his rebellious brother. But this approach came to nothing. A full-scale war soon broke out, in which some Babylonian towns backed Shamash-shuma-ukin and others sided with Ashurbanipal. After three years of bloodshed, the rebellion collapsed; in despair, Shamash-shuma-ukin, set fire to his own palace and died in the blaze.

Shortly after the civil war ended, Ashurbanipal was forced to deal with more unrest in Elam. This time the king showed the Elamites no mercy. His armies swept into Elam and went on a rampage of destruction, virtually erasing that kingdom from the map. Ashurbanipal's scribes recorded the campaign in his annals, which read in part:

> The sanctuaries of Elam I destroyed totally. Its gods and goddesses I scattered to the winds. . . . The tombs of their earlier and later kings, who did not fear Ashur . . . and who had plagued the kings, my fathers, I destroyed. . . . I exposed them to the sun. Their bones I carried off to Assyria. . . . I devastated the provinces of Elam. Salt . . . I scattered over them.

Ashurbanipal apparently did not have much time to gloat over his victory. It appears that a series of disasters—rebellions, invasions by foreign tribes, and civil strife—occurred more or less simultaneously. Details are lacking, however, because late in 639 B.C. the king's scribes stopped producing annals. As a result, the last twelve years of Ashurbanipal's reign are extremely obscure. Perhaps he abdicated the throne; or maybe he died in battle. What is more certain is that at the time of his passing the Assyrian realm was caught in a rapid and fatal decline.

SEE ALSO: Assyrian Empire; Elam; Esarhaddon

Ashur-dan II
(reigned 934–912 B.C.)

An Assyrian king best known for his attempts to restore vigor, purpose, and prestige to the declining Assyrian Empire after it reached its lowest ebb in the decades following the assassination of King Tiglathpileser I in 1077 B.C. West of the Assyrian heartland, Ashur-dan fought the Aramaeans and took back land they had earlier usurped from Assyria. He also pushed eastward and reestablished Assyrian access to trade routes running through the Iranian plateau and beyond. However, his main efforts were in the domestic sphere. There, he began rebuilding the land's damaged economy by settling farmers on uncultivated lands, built up the nation's military forces, and restored crumbling temples and palaces. His energetic efforts gave his immediate successors, beginning with his son, Adad-nirari I, a solid base on which to forge a new Assyrian nation.

SEE ALSO: Adad-nirari I; Assyrian Empire; Tiglathpileser I

Ashurnasirpal II
(ca. 883 B.C.–859 B.C.)

The first great king of the so-called Neo-Assyrian Empire that emerged in the early first millennium B.C. Ashurnasirpal first consolidated the territorial gains made by

A statue representing King Ashurnasirpal II. © WERNER FORMAN/CORBIS

his father, Tukulti-Ninurta II. Then, circa 877, the new Assyrian monarch moved westward in hopes of reaching the Mediterranean coast. An excerpt from his annals confirms that he achieved this goal:

> At that time I marched along the side of Mount Lebanon, and to the Great Sea. . . . In the Great Sea I washed my weapons, and I made offerings unto the gods. The tribute of the kings of the seacoast, of the people of Tyre, Sidon, Byblos . . . silver, gold, lead, copper, vessels of copper, garments made of brightly colored wool . . . maplewood, boxwood, and ivory . . . I received as tribute from them, and they embraced my feet.

On the way back to Assyria, Ashurnasirpal and his soldiers sacked and plundered many towns, firmly establishing the now familiar Assyrian reputation for terror and cruelty. "Three thousand captives I burned with fire," he boasts in his annals. "Their corpses I formed into pillars [piles]." Other typical atrocities included cutting off noses, ears, fingers, and impaling people on sharp stakes. Surprisingly, however, this clearly sadistic ruler was also a great builder. At Kalhu (modern Nimrud) he erected temples, military barracks, and dozens of other structures; and it was said that he inaugurated these works with a feast that fed almost seventy thousand people for ten days.

SEE ALSO: Assyrian Empire; Nimrud

Ashur-uballit I (ca. 1365 B.C.–1330 B.C.)

The first king to preside over the Assyrian realm as it emerged as the leading power of Mesopotamia following the collapse of Mitanni. The kingdom of Mitanni had managed to keep the Assyrians in check on their eastern flank. But after civil strife and an invasion of the Hittites combined to destroy Mitanni, Ashur-uballit was free to pursue territorial expansion. He was strong enough to depose the Babylonian king and place his own man on Babylon's throne.

SEE ALSO: Assyrian Empire; Hittites; Mitanni

Ashur-uballit II (late seventh century B.C.)

The last monarch of the Assyrian Empire. Following the destruction of Nineveh and other Assyrian cities by the Medes and the Babylonians in about 612 to 611 B.C., Sinshar-ishkun, the last surviving son of King Ashurbanipal, was killed. Afterward a military officer took charge of the pitiful remnants of the Assyrian royal court and army. Perhaps for propaganda value, he took the throne name Ashur-uballit, an earlier Assyrian king known for his ferocity. In 610 B.C. he made a last stand at Harran on the upper reaches of the Euphrates; but the Medes and the Babylonians took the city, and the short-lived Assyrian king was heard of no more.

SEE ALSO: Assyrian Empire; Medes; Nineveh

Assyria

A region of ancient Mesopotamia that became the heartland of a series of Assyrian empires. Assyria was located in the region now occupied by northern Iraq, near the Tigris River. It stretched northward toward the foothills of the mountains of Armenia and eastward over the Jezirah plateau and Upper and Lower Zab rivers, tributaries of the Tigris. In ancient times most of the land in this region was a good deal more fertile than it is today. Consequently, in the late Stone Age (ca. 6000–3000 B.C.) Assyria was densely inhabited by farmers and herders. However, in the third millennium B.C., while urban centers were rising across Sumeria in the southwest, Assyria remained mostly rural. The area was absorbed into the Akkadian Empire in the 2300s B.C. But Assyria rose from near obscurity in the nineteenth century B.C. under an Amorite leader named Shamshi-Adad I, who established the first Assyrian Empire. After the collapse of the last Assyrian realm in the late 600s B.C., the region of Assyria faded back into obscurity and came under the control of a succession of outside powers, among them the Medes, Persians, Seleucid Greeks, Parthians, Sassanians, and Arabs.

SEE ALSO: Assyrian Empire; Babylonia; Medes

Assyrian Empire

One of the largest and most powerful of the many imperial realms that rose in and around the Mesopotamian plains in ancient times. Actually, Assyrian territory and influence expanded and diminished more than once over the course of more than a thousand years, so one can, in a sense, speak of multiple Assyrian empires. They were centered on Assyria, the region dominated by two major tributaries of the Tigris River, the Upper and Lower Zab. The leading cities in the area were Ashur, whose patron god, also called Ashur, became the chief Assyrian deity; Kalhu (Nimrud), Mosul, Arbil, and Ninua (later Nineveh).

Early Assyria The history of the Assyrian Empire can be conveniently divided into three phases. The first phase, in which the Assyrians began to develop a national identity, began in the two centuries after Sumer and Akkad declined at the end of the third millennium B.C. A series of energetic Assyrian rulers erected temples and other public buildings and marched small armies into neighboring regions. These forays are probably better termed *raiding parties* than *full-scale conquests*. But they gained the Assyrians control of considerable amounts of new territory, even if only temporarily. The most successful of these early kings was Shamshi-Adad I (reigned ca. 1813–1781 B.C.). He captured the small kingdom of Mari, located about 140 miles (225km) southwest of Ashur, and marched all the way to what is now Lebanon, on the Mediterranean coast.

Not long after Shamshi-Adad died, Assyria experienced its first reversal of fortune. In about 1759 B.C. Hammurabi, king of Babylon, launched his own campaign of expansion. He, too, captured

A modern architect's sketch reconstructs the original appearance of the façade of the main palace of King Sennacherib. © BETTMANN/CORBIS

Mari, completely destroying it in the process, then overran Ashur and the other Assyrian cities. The Assyrians, who were always open to foreign cultural ideas, now became conflicted about their relationship with Babylonia. Cultural ideas had traditionally flowed into Assyria from Sumer, located in southeastern Mesopotamia; and now that the Babylonians had absorbed the Sumerian lands, some Assyrians felt comfortable giving allegiance to the Babylonian monarchs. In contrast, other Assyrians were strongly anti-Babylonian and kept alive native traditions and feelings of patriotism and nationalism. In the meantime, for roughly three centuries the Assyrians remained vassals or subjects of larger, more powerful states, not only Babylonia but also Mitanni, lying west of Assyria. Other imperialistic states also began to intrude into the general region in this period. The Hittites marched south-ward from Anatolia and occupied Syria, and in the southwest the Egyptians took control of Palestine.

Assyria's Second Phase of Expansion It was a sudden power imbalance among these competing major powers that allowed the Assyrians to launch the second phase of their own imperial expansion. In the fourteenth century B.C. a combination of increasing pressure by the Hittites in the north and civil war among Mitanni's own rulers brought Mitanni to the brink of collapse. And Assyrian leaders took advantage of the situation. Beginning with Ashur-uballit I (ca. 1365–1330 B.C.), a series of strong Assyrian kings seized large sections of former Mitannian territory and set their sights on further conquests.

From this time on, the foreign and military policy of Assyria's rulers operated on three major fronts. The first consisted of the broad arc of foothills stretching eastward from the borders of Anatolia through Armenia to the Zagros Mountains. The Assyrians conducted frequent small-scale raids into these northern hills, taking human captives, horses, and other booty. They also built fortresses and roads with which to defend this frontier against periodic incursions by various aggressive peoples. Assyria's second major front was the ever-changing border with Babylonia in the southeast. Numerous confrontations between the two powers culminated in the capture of Babylon by the vigorous Assyrian monarch Tukulti-Ninurta I (ca. 1244–1208 B.C.) sometime early in his reign. Assyria's third major military front was the western corridor to Syria and the Mediterranean Sea. Here, the Assyrian monarchs launched relentless offensives, gaining, losing, and then regaining territory in cycles. King Adad-nirari I (ca. 1305–1274 B.C.) reached Carchemish in northern Syria, as did his immediate successor, Shalmaneser I (ca. 1274–1245). These and later Assyrian conquests posed an almost constant threat to the stability of the many small kingdoms in the region, including the early Jewish states of Israel and Judah.

The complicated balance of power in Mesopotamia and the greater Near East underwent another sudden shock circa 1200 B.C., when the leading towns of Anatolia, Syria, and other parts of the eastern Mediterranean sphere were sacked and burned, most never to be rebuilt. The exact causes of this widespread catastrophe are still uncertain. Much of the destruction seems to have been caused by groups of invaders who are today collectively called the Sea Peoples, who originated in southeastern Europe. The Assyrian cities escaped destruction; however, the confusion and dislocations caused by the disaster led to the sudden rise in power and influence of several formerly insignificant local peoples. Among these were the Aramaeans, tribal inhabitants of the Syrian deserts, who now presented a partial barrier to Assyrian expansion. Still, the Assyrian kings continued their relentless military expeditions, occasionally enjoying success. The most outstanding gains in this period were those of Tiglathpileser I (ca. 1115–1077 B.C.), who expanded the realm on all three of its major fronts. After he was assassinated, his immediate successors turned out to be far less capable men. In the course of only a few decades the realm shrank, shedding its conquered territories one by one until all that remained was the traditional Assyrian heartland centered around Ashur and Nineveh. This period is sometimes referred to as Assyria's dark age.

The Rise of the Neo-Assyrian Realm However dark these lean years may have been for the Assyrians, their leaders kept alive the dream of reviving the glories of their ancestors. And this national pride was the seed from which the third and greatest phase of Assyrian expansion would grow. Beginning with Ashur-dan II (ca. 934–912 B.C.) and Adad-nirari II (ca. 911–891 B.C.), a series of strong kings transformed Assyria into the largest, most feared empire the world had yet seen. Each of the military campaigns of these rulers was partly self-defense, partly piracy, and partly a religious crusade undertaken in the name of the supreme god, Ashur. Because of the religious dimension, Assyrian leaders deemed it justifiable to employ any means, no matter how harsh or brutal, to achieve their goals. And this is the basis for the Assyrians' famous reputation for cruelty. Exemplifying the aggressive, pitiless attitude of many of these rulers is this statement by Adad-nirari II:

Powerful in battle, who overthrows cities, who burns the mountains of the lands, am I, strong hero, who consumes his enemies, who burns up the wicked and the evil, am I. . . . Like the onset of a storm, I press on. Like an evil downpour, I rage. . . . Like a net, I entangle. . . . At the mention of my mighty name, the princes of the four regions (of the world) trembled.

As these vigorous kings brought more and more towns and territory into the empire, it became increasingly more difficult to collect tribute from and suppress rebellions in distant areas. For expediency, therefore, the royal government made many of these areas official provinces, each ruled by an Assyrian governor appointed by the king in Ashur. Thus, a true empire with complex administrative machinery gradually grew. The economic aspects of this administration were self-centered and severe. Precious metals, foodstuffs, livestock, and other valuable commodities regularly flowed into the empire's heartland from outlying areas. But very little, if anything, flowed out to compensate the subject peoples for their losses. This naturally inspired these peoples to hate the Assyrian monarchs even more.

The Sargonid Dynasty The first truly great rulers among these monarchs were Ashurnasirpal II (ca. 883–859 B.C.) and his son, Shalmaneser III (ca. 858–824 B.C.). The latter devoted fully thirty-one of his reign's nearly thirty-five years to expensive, violent military campaigns launched on all three of the nation's traditional fronts. But even these efforts paled in comparison to those of his successors. Tiglathpileser III (ca. 744–727 B.C.) further increased the powers of the central authority over the provinces and subject peoples. This helped pave the way for the conquests of Sargon II (ca. 721–705 B.C.) and his immediate

successors—Sennacherib, Esarhaddon, and Ashurbanipal—collectively referred to as the Sargonids. The best documented of all the Assyrian rulers—indeed of all the Mesopotamian rulers—they expanded the realm until it encompassed the entire courses of the Tigris and Euphrates rivers, parts of the Zagros Mountains in the east, Armenia (Urartu) in the north, eastern Anatolia in the northwest, and Babylonia in the southeast.

Because this great empire was composed of diverse lands and peoples, each with their own customs and ambitions, it was difficult to control. And rebellions occurred frequently. Indeed, Sargon's reign was wracked by insurrections, yet he and his son, Sennacherib (ca. 704–681 B.C.), managed to keep the realm in one piece. Sennacherib also found time for domestic and cultural projects, including enlarging and beautifying the city of Nineveh and erecting the magnificent Palace Without Rival there. Esarhaddon (ca. 680–669 B.C.), also a noteworthy builder, refurbished Babylon. But he was no less a ruthless conqueror than his immediate predecessors, as his bold invasion of Egypt demonstrated. In reference to the Egyptian pharaoh, Esarhaddon states:

Without cessation I slew multitudes of his men and him I smote five times with the point of my javelin. . . . Memphis, his royal city, in half a day, with mines, tunnels, assaults, I besieged, I captured . . . I burned with fire. His queen, his harem, his . . . sons and daughters, his property and his goods, his horses, his cattle, his sheep, in countless numbers, I carried off to Assyria.

Esarhaddon's son, Ashurbanipal (ca. 668–627), also invaded Egypt, and in 639 B.C. he destroyed the kingdom of Elam, lying along Mesopotamia's southeastern fringe.

However, Ashurbanipal's reign was also marred by rebellions and civil strife. As time went on, Assyria's vassals and subject peoples grew more daring and either resisted the central authority or severed ties with it. As the crisis worsened, the Babylonians, led by a Chaldean named Nabopolassar, invaded the Assyrian heartland. Soon the Medes, commanded by Cyaxares II, joined forces with the Babylonians and the two armies swept across central Mesopotamia, burning and pillaging one Assyrian stronghold after another. Assyria's heartland was devastated, and within the space of only a few years all that remained of the once-mighty Assyrian Empire was the memory of the cruelty of its rulers.

SEE ALSO: Ashur; Cyaxares II; Mari; Mitanni; Nimrud; Nineveh; and the names of individual Assyrian rulers

Assyriology

The archaeological and historical study of ancient Mesopotamia. The reference to Assyria in this term reflects the fact that most of the earliest scholars in the field spent their careers unearthing Assyrian ruins. However, Assyriology came to incorporate the remnants of the Sumerian and Babylonian civilizations as well as those of other ancient cities, kingdoms, and peoples of the region. Much of what is known about these long-dead cultures comes from surviving writings on clay tablets, stone markers, bas-reliefs, and so forth. Thus, Assyriologists have the daunting task of becoming proficient in several ancient languages, including Hebrew, Aramaic, and Akkadian, which had several dialects. They must also learn to read the hundreds of cuneiform characters used in Mesopotamian writings for thousands of years. In addition, many scholars in the field are trained in archaeological field methods and comparative anthropology so that they can recognize and interpret various Mesopotamian artifacts unearthed over the years. Among the early pioneers of Assyriology were Paul Emile Botta, Georg F. Grotefend, Robert Koldewey, Samuel N. Kramer, Austen Henry Layard, Seton Lloyd, William K. Loftus, Karsten Niebuhr, Hormuzd Rassam, Henry C. Rawlinson, Claudius James Rich, George Smith, and Charles Leonard Woolley. For details on the discoveries these scholars made, see their individual names.

SEE ALSO: cuneiform; languages; writing materials

astrology and astronomy

Today, astronomy is the serious study of the universe and how it works, and astrology is considered a false science that claims that the movements of celestial objects directly affect life on Earth. The ancient Mesopotamians did not make such distinctions between the two disciplines, however. Their observations of the heavens were made mainly to discern how the movements of the stars and planets affected earthly events. Because these bodies were seen as divine or divinely inspired objects, Mesopotamian astronomy also had a strong religious dimension.

All of the Mesopotamian peoples observed the heavens, but the Babylonians, Assyrians, and Persians were particularly meticulous and often ingenious in their methods. Their "astronomers" were specially trained scribes. These men used hollow tubes as viewfinders and water clocks to time the risings and settings of stars and planets, Venus's disappearance behind the Sun and subsequent reappearance, and other celestial movements. The data thus collected was frequently recorded on clay tablets and kept in archives. The earliest surviving examples date from circa 1700 B.C., and many were discovered in the great library of the Assyrian king Ashurbanipal at Nineveh. Of particular importance today are the so-called Venus tablets, compiled by the astronomers of the Babylonian king Ammi-saduqa (reigned 1646–1626 B.C.). The observations recorded on the tablets were originally used to determine omens that might affect that monarch, but modern scholars use them to help date Mesopotamian events.

Surviving records of the Mesopotamian astronomers indicate that they paid close attention to unusual heavenly phenomena, such as lunar and solar eclipses and halos around the Sun. This is not surprising since the rarer and more dramatic celestial events were viewed as most likely to represent divine omens. Eventually these observers were able to predict eclipses with considerable accuracy. But observations of the regular, mundane movements of the Sun, the Moon, and the planets were also seen as important. Repeated observations of the Moon's movements, for instance, led to the introduction of a fairly accurate lunar calendar by the seventh century B.C. The year was thus divided into twelve lunar months, each of which corresponded to one of twelve constellations in the sky. These star groups, which were associated with various gods and mythical characters, made up the zodiac, which was firmly established by the early Persian period (ca. 400s B.C.) but probably existed earlier. About a century or two later, in the Seleucid period, horoscopes based on the signs of the zodiac were introduced.

Regular observations of the movements of celestial objects also allowed Mesopotamian astronomers to develop useful methods of and units for reckoning time, including hours and minutes. The Babylonians divided an hour into sixty minutes and counted twelve "double hours" in each day. (Greek astronomers later divided these into twenty-four single hours, creating the system familiar today.) Likewise, the Babylonian astronomer Kidenas (or Kidinnu) calculated the length of the solar year with an error of only about four minutes.

In general, the Mesopotamian astronomers were just as bright and diligent as their Greek counterparts, who established the true science of astronomy between the sixth and third centuries B.C. The main difference was that the Greeks saw the heavenly bodies as lifeless objects following natural laws rather than as being divinely inspired; also, the Greeks incorporated their celestial observations into scientific theories in an effort to explain how the universe works.

SEE ALSO: Ammi-saduqa; Greeks; mathematics

Astyages
(reigned ca. 585–550 B.C.)

The last king of the Medes, who were defeated and absorbed by the Persians led by Cyrus II. According to the Greek historian Herodotus, the main ancient source for Astyages, the latter was the son of Media's King Cyaxares II. As a boy Cyrus, the son of a Median vassal king, had known Astyages. When the younger man launched a rebellion against the Medes, Astyages prepared to put down the uprising. He "armed the Medes to a man," Herodotus says. But once the war was under way, a mutiny occurred in the Median ranks, apparently led by a general named Harpagus. "When Astyages learned of the disgraceful collapse of the Median army, he swore that ... Cyrus should not get away with it so easily." However Astyages' "men were killed and he himself was taken alive." (*Histories* 1.130) It is revealing of Cyrus's merciful nature that he did not execute or punish Astyages. Instead, the defeated Median monarch was allowed to live out the rest of his days as one of Cyrus's royal courtiers.

SEE ALSO: Cyrus II; Medes; Persian Empire

Atrahasis

A mythical Mesopotamian hero who survived a great flood sent by the gods. In the original Sumerian version of his story, he is called Ziusudra. In the Hebrew Old Testament, which later incorporated the tale, he is called Noah. For the details of the story, **see** *Atrahasis*.

SEE ALSO: *Epic of Gilgamesh;* flood legends

Atrahasis

An epic poem originally dating from Mesopotamia's Sumerian period (the second millennium B.C.) and perpetuated by the Babylonians and other peoples who later dwelled in the region. The most complete written copy, made by a Babylonian scribe, dates from circa 1700 to 1650 B.C. A fragment, representing about a fifth of the work, was discovered in 1876; more came to light in 1965, and about 80 percent of the original has now been recovered. One of the most important of the Mesopotamian creation stories, the tale of Atrahasis also provides biblical scholars with a link between the ancient Mesopotamian and Hebrew cultures, as the story of Noah and the flood from the book of Genesis is clearly based on the *Atrahasis*.

According to legend, Atrahasis was the pious king of the Sumerian city of Shuruppak, lying northwest of the Persian Gulf. He was forced to deal with a series of epic, dramatic events when the powerful storm god, Enlil, decided to destroy the human race because he felt that people had become too noisy and annoying. As his instrument of destruction, Enlil chose a great flood. However, Ea, god of wisdom and freshwater, felt bad for the humans. Behind Enlil's back, Ea went to Atrahasis and warned him of the coming deluge. The god told the man to dismantle his house, use the materials to build a big boat, and try to save as many plant and animal species as possible by loading them onto the ark. "I loaded her with everything there was," Atrahasis later recalled. "I loaded her with all the seeds of living things, all of them. I put on board the boat all my kith and kin. I put on board the cattle from open country and all kinds of craftsmen." Then the floods came and covered the land far and wide, drowning all those humans and animals that were not in Atrahasis's boat. Finally, on the seventh day, the storm subsided and Atrahasis looked out at the ruined world. "Silence reigned, for all of humanity had returned to clay," he says.

> The flood-plain was as flat as a roof. I opened a porthole and light fell on my cheeks. .... Tears ran down my cheeks. .... The boat had come to rest on [the top of] Mount Nimush. .... When the seventh day arrived, I put out and released a dove. The dove went; it came back, for no perching place was visible to it, and it turned around. [Later] I put out and released a raven. The raven went and saw the waters receding. And it ate ... and did not turn round. Then I put all [on board the ark] out to the four winds [i.e., in all directions] and I made a sacrifice [to the gods].

Two winged sphinxes topped by a winged disk, which is an emblem of the god Ahura-Mazda. ERICH LESSING/ART RESOURCE, NY

After the catastrophe, some gods were glad that humanity had survived, but Enlil was upset that Ea had interfered in his plans to destroy the human race. Fortunately for Atrahasis and his family, the tactful Ea convinced Enlil that saving humanity was a good thing. Enlil decided to commemorate the event by giving Atrahasis and his wife—but no other humans—the gift of immortality.

SEE ALSO: Enlil; flood legends; literature

Avesta

The collective name of the holy writings of Zoroastrianism, the religion of ancient Persia. The numerous sacred texts making up the *Avesta* were composed over the course of many centuries in different languages. Unlike the books of the Judeo-Christian Bible, the texts of the *Avesta* consist mainly of prayers and hymns and contain little in the way of narrative storytelling. The first written versions of the *Avesta* seem to have appeared in the

Parthian period (ca. 228 B.C.–A.D. 224). Others may have been compiled in the fourth or third centuries B.C., during the Persian period. And some of the texts undoubtedly date from much earlier, a few of them from the second millennium B.C., when Zoroaster was thought to have lived.

Of these parts, the oldest are the *Older Yasnas*, which include the *Gathas*. Most of these are prayers or statements of devotion directed to the supreme god of the faith—Ahura-Mazda—and thought by the ancients to have been written by Zoroaster himself. One or more of these prayers were recited by worshippers on a daily basis. Many are similar in style and tone to this one:

> I shall recognize you as strong and holy, Ahura-Mazda, when you will help me . . . through the heat of your truth-strong fire, to the wicked man and the just, and when the might of Good Purpose shall come to me. Then as holy I have recognized you, Ahura-Mazda, when I saw you as first at the birth of life, when you appointed rewards for acts and words, bad for the bad, a good recompense for the good [just rewards that will be handed out] at the final turning point [last judgment]. (*Avesta, Older Yasnas* 43.4–5)

Another section of the *Avesta* consists of the *Yashts*, hymns directed to lesser-divine spirits. Later additions were the *Younger Yasnas*, describing various religious rituals, including sacrifices of water and fire; and the *Vendidad*, a series of prose texts about mythical people and events. In the Sassanian period (ca. A.D. 224–651), the *Khorda Avesta*, a collection of short prayers for use by everyday worshippers, was introduced. The Sassanians, who were devout Zoroastrians, also edited the older texts and added some supportive material, including a biography of Zoroaster, thereby creating the largest compilation of all—the *Great Avesta*. About a quarter of that work survives.

SEE ALSO: Ahura-Mazda; Persian Empire; Zoroaster; Zoroastrianism

Baba

An ancient Sumerian goddess of fertility and motherhood who began as the wife of Ningirsu, the patron deity of the city-state of Lagash. Baba (also Bawa or Bau) was frequently called the Lady of Abundance in reference to her ability to make the earth fertile. She was also known as the Mistress of the Animals. In later Mesopotamian ages she came to be associated with healing and magic spells.

SEE ALSO: Lagash; Ningirsu

Babylon

The most famous city of ancient Mesopotamia and possibly the entire Near East, and the capital or main stronghold of a number of succeeding political states and empires. The term *Babylon* is the Greek version of *Babili* or *Bab-ilim*, meaning "Gate of the Gods." The city was located on the Euphrates River about 60 miles (96km) south of modern Baghdad, Iraq. Indeed, the river originally flowed right through Babylon, dividing it into two sections, the "old city" and "new city." In late antiquity, however, the river shifted, leaving the city dry and contributing to its decline. Babylon's founding date is lost in the mists of time, but evidence indicates it existed at least as early as the mid-third millennium B.C. The early empires of Sargon of Akkad and the Third Dynasty of Ur seized and occupied it. But it was the Babylonian ruler Hammurabi (reigned 1792–1750 B.C.) who expanded the city into a sprawling metropolis and heavily fortified it.

Fortification of Babylon continued under later rulers, and eventually an outer defensive wall more than 12 miles (20km) long surrounded it. This barrier was some 85 feet (25m) thick and featured guard towers at intervals of 65 feet (20m). The Greek historian Herodotus, who visited Babylon in the mid-fifth century B.C., recalls, "On the top of the wall they constructed, along each edge, a row of one-room buildings facing inwards with enough space between for a four-horse chariot to pass." (*Histories* 1.181)

Inside the fortified walls were thousands of buildings, ranging from ordinary houses and shops to enormous temples and palaces. At least by Herodotus's day, they were aligned along a well-organized grid. "There are a great many houses of three and four stories," he writes. "The main streets and the side streets which lead to the river are all dead straight." (*Histories* 1.181) The larger structures in the city included the great temple of the god Marduk and, situated slightly north of it, an immense ziggurat standing some 300 feet (90m) high, perhaps the Tower of Babel mentioned in the Bible. This tower, which supposedly took seventeen years to erect, was called the Etemenanki, or "House of Heaven's and Earth's Foundation." Babylon was also home to the famous Hanging Gardens, constructed by King Nebuchadnezzar II (reigned 605–562 B.C.), who, it was said, also built the Etemananki. A theater and a large open-air marketplace were added later by the early Seleucid rulers.

As a much-coveted center of power, wealth, and culture, ancient Babylon endured a tumultuous existence. Soon after it had achieved greatness under Hammurabi and his immediate successors, the Hittites swept into Mesopotamia and sacked the city circa 1595 B.C. The Kassites then moved in, rebuilt Babylon, and ruled it until circa 1174 B.C., when the Elamites invaded and wrecked it. Slowly, the city recovered once more, and eventually, under Nebuchadnezzar, it achieved greatness once more. Subsequently, the Persians made it one of their three capitals, along with Susa and Persepolis, and it was in Babylon that Alexander the Great died in 323 B.C., after making it the capital of his own empire. Under the Seleucids, however, a new city, Seleucia-on-the-Tigris, steadily drew commerce and residents away from Babylon, which went into decline. That decline continued under Parthian rule, and by the first century A.D. the site of Babylon was largely deserted. Principal modern excavations there were conducted between 1899 and 1914 by the German Oriental Society under the direction of the great Robert Koldewey. At that time, the city's famous Ishtar Gate was removed to a museum in Berlin.

SEE ALSO: Babylonia; Elam; Hammurabi; Hanging Gardens of Babylon; Kassites; Nebuchadnezzar II; Tower of Babel

Babylonaica

A history of Mesopotamia composed in the third century B.C. by Berossus, a Babylonian scholar who lived during the early years of Seleucid rule in the area. The work is unfortunately lost, but a few fragments survive in the form of quotations in the writings of later Greek and Roman historians. Apparently it consisted of three volumes. The first covered the region's geography and the origins of civilization; the second chronicled the Assyrian and Babylonian kings and their exploits down to the eighth century B.C.; and the third dealt with the fall of Assyria, the period of Persian domination, and Alexander's conquest of Persia. The loss of the *Babylonaica* left Herodotus's *Histories* as the principal surviving ancient account (outside of the annals and chronicles of various Mesopotamian kings) of the region's history.

SEE ALSO: Herodotus; historical accounts

Babylonia

The name *Babylonia* was and still is used in a variety of contexts. In the geographical sense, it is a general term for southeastern Mesopotamia, as opposed to the term *Assyria*, denoting northwestern Mesopotamia. In a political context, Babylonia usually consisted of the national unit—country, land, province, or whatever—that included the city of Babylon and the surrounding territories that its rulers controlled. The Kassites, whose dynasty ruled the area from the sixteenth to the twelfth centuries B.C., called Babylonia Karduniash.

Babylonia is also sometimes used to describe one or more of the larger Mesopotamian empires carved out by Babylonian rulers. When Hammurabi ascended Babylon's throne circa 1792 B.C., Babylonia encompassed an area barely 100 miles (161km) in extent; however, at the height of his conquests imperial Babylonia stretched from the Persian Gulf in the southeast to the foothills of the Zagros range in the northwest, an area hundreds of times larger. Later, following the fall of the Assyrian Empire in about 612 B.C., the short-lived but splendid Neo-Babylonian Empire, created by Nebuchadnezzar II, encompassed all of Mesopotamia plus Syria and Palestine.

SEE ALSO: Babylon; Hammurabi; Kassites; Neo-Babylonian Empire

Babylonian Chronicles

The general, collective name for a series of historical writings compiled by Babylonian scribes over the course of several centuries. Apparently commissioned by Babylonian rulers, they describe people and events from a local, biased Babylonian perspective. Modern scholars, therefore, are careful not to take everything in these works at face value. They are, nonetheless, extremely valuable when combined with other sources, such as the Assyrian royal annals. The oldest of the Babylonian Chronicles dates from the Kassite dynasty in the late second millennium B.C. The rest, making up the bulk of the work, cover the period beginning with the reign of the Babylonian king Nabonassar (747–734 B.C.) and ending with the start of the Parthian period in the late second century B.C. These later chronicles bear names such as the *Fall of Nineveh Chronicle*, *Artaxerxes III Chronicle*, and *Alexander the Great Chronicle*. This excerpt from the *Fall of Nineveh Chronicle* describes incidents in 612 and 611 B.C., when the Babylonians and the Medes were attacking Assyria:

> The king of Babylonia mustered his army and marched to [?]. . . . The king of the Medes [Cyaxares] marched towards the king of Babylonia. . . . They met one another. The king of Babylonia [and] Cyaxares . . . marched along the bank of the Tigris [and] encamped against Nineveh. From the month Simanu [June] until the month

> Abu [August] . . . they subjected the city to a heavy siege. . . . They inflicted a major defeat upon a great people. . . . They carried off the vast booty of the city and the temple and turned the city into a ruin heap.

SEE ALSO: Assyrian Empire; historical accounts; Nineveh

Balawat

An Assyrian town situated about 9 miles (16km) northeast of the larger city of Kalhu, or modern-day Nimrud. While digging at Balawat (or Imgur-Enlil) in 1877, archaeologist Hormuzd Rassam unearthed some bronze decorations from the doors of a palace of the kings Ashurnasirpal II and Shalmaneser III. Some scholars theorize that a small palace in this town was used as a country residence by these and other Assyrian kings.

SEE ALSO: Assyrian Empire; Nimrud; Rassam, Hormuzd

Bardiya
(flourished late sixth century B.C.)

The name of the younger son of the Persian king Cyrus II, who was successfully, though briefly, impersonated by a royal pretender in 522 B.C. After Cyrus's death, his elder son, Cambyses, murdered the real Bardiya (whom the Greeks called Smerdis) to eliminate any potential rivals. Later, when Cambyses was away campaigning in Egypt, he received news that a priest named Gaumata (the "false-Smerdis" to the Greeks), who bore a close resemblance to Bardiya, had seized the throne. Because the murder of the real Bardiya was a secret, most Persians had no reason to suspect that Gaumata was a phony. As later recorded by another Persian king, Darius I:

This stone bas-relief shows the soldiers of the Assyrian king Ashurnasirpal laying siege to an enemy city. ERICH LESSING/ART RESOURCE, NY

After Cambyses went to Egypt . . . there was great deceit in the land. . . . There arose a Magian [Median priest], by name Gaumata. . . . He deceived the people, saying, "I am Bardiya, son of Cyrus, brother of Cambyses." Then all the people became estranged from Cambyses and went over to him [Gaumata]. . . . He seized the kingdom. (*Behistun Inscription* 10–11)

Shortly after hearing about the deception, Cambyses died. Gaumata held power in the capital for several months before a small group of leading Persian nobles finally slew him and placed one of their own number—Darius—on the throne. Because Darius belonged to a branch of the Achaemenid family, he did have a legitimate claim.

SEE ALSO: Cambyses; Darius I; Persian Empire

bas-reliefs

Carved images raised slightly from a flat background. They are also often termed simply *reliefs*. The technique was used widely in the ancient Near East, the most outstanding examples being the large panels of reliefs that decorated the palaces and temples of the Assyrian and Egyptian kings.

SEE ALSO: Layard, Austen Henry; palaces; sculpture

bathing

Although it is unknown how often people bathed in ancient Mesopotamia, archaeological evidence provides a fairly clear picture of how and where they bathed. The vast majority of people could not afford separate rooms for bathing in their homes, so they washed in the nearest river or canal. People also used buckets to carry water from these sources back to their homes, and those whose houses had small courtyards sometimes installed terra-cotta cisterns, or shallow basins that collected rainwater. The water from buckets and cisterns was used not only for cooking and drinking but also for what today would be called a sponge bath.

Actual bathrooms in Mesopotamia were a luxury of royalty and the well-to-do. Palaces, including that of the Neo-Babylonian king Nebuchadnezzar II, had bathrooms, the floors and lower walls of which were made of baked bricks waterproofed with a coating of bitumen, a tar-like substance. The bather sat or stood in the middle of the room while servants poured buckets of water over him or her—a crude sort of shower. No modern-style bathtubs have yet been found. "Soap" consisted of plant ashes or animal fats. The dirty water drained into clay or stone conduits in the floor that led outside, sometimes to primitive sewers. There is also evidence that it was customary for people to wash their hands before entering the royal throne room for an audience or other gathering.

SEE ALSO: grooming; houses; water supplies

Battle of Cunaxa (401 B.C.)

A major military engagement fought between Persia's King Artaxerxes II and his younger brother, Cyrus the Younger, who sought to usurp the throne. Cyrus marched an army composed of handpicked Persian cavalrymen, some assorted troops from Persian subject nations, and ten thousand or more Greek mercenaries to Cunaxa, situated about 50 miles (80km) north of Babylon. Soon Artaxerxes' much larger army approached. The Greek writer Xenophon, who stood among the Greek ranks, recalls the moment:

> When afternoon came, dust appeared like a white cloud, and sometime afterwards a sort of blackness spreading far over the plain. But when they came nearer, quickly there were flashes of bronze and spears and the lines [of soldiers] were visible. Cavalry in white corselets [chest protectors] were on the enemy's left wing. . . . Next came wicker-shield men, next men-at-arms with wooden shields . . . then more cavalry, [and] bowmen, too. . . . In front of all were chariots. . . . They had the scythes [sharp blades] sticking out sideways from the axles . . . to cut through any [enemies] they met. (*Anabasis* 1.7)

As the battle commenced, the Greeks, commanded by Clearchos, surged forward and attacked. (See *Anabasis* for Xenophon's description of the charge.) They chased a large contingent of Persians off the field, but in the meantime Artaxerxes' remaining troops began outflanking (moving around the sides and back of) Cyrus's lines. In a desperate move, Cyrus himself charged with some six hundred cavalry at the six thousand horsemen guarding his royal brother. Artaxerxes was knocked to the ground and was whisked away to safety, but Cyrus was struck in the eye and slain. The Greeks returned from their chase to find Artaxerxes the victor. Xenophon later described how he and his comrades spent more than a year fighting their way out of Persia.

SEE ALSO: *Anabasis*; Artaxerxes; Greeks; Xenophon

Battle of Gaugamela (331 B.C.)

A huge battle fought between the forces of the twenty-five-year-old Macedonian king Alexander III, later called "the Great," and Persia's King Darius III. Alexander had already defeated Darius at Issus in northern Syria in 333 B.C. After capturing Palestine and Egypt, Alexander marched his army, consisting of some seven thousand cavalry and forty thousand infantry, northeastward into the Mesopotamian plains. Darius was waiting near the village of Gaugamela, about 70 miles (113km) from Arbil (or Arbela). The size of his army is uncertain, but it was likely at least three or four times larger than Alexander's. The Greeks arrived to find that the Persians had cleared the plain of obstacles to make it easier for chariots and horsemen to maneuver. The Persians were already formed into lines; they remained in them throughout the night for fear the Greeks might attack under the cover of darkness. Alexander wisely refrained from such a risky maneuver and got a good night's sleep.

The next day, perhaps October 1, Alexander opened the battle by leading the cavalry on his right wing sideways to the right, as if trying to outflank the enemy. Darius and his generals responded by sending troops from their center to deal with the battle forming on their far left (corresponding to Alexander's right). Just as Alexander had anticipated, this eventually caused a large gap to form in the Persian center. And into that opening charged the main force of the Macedonian cavalry, led by Alexander himself. According to his principal ancient biographer, Arrian, the young king

> drove in his wedge [i.e., a wedge-shaped formation] and raising the battle cry pressed forward at the double straight for the point where Darius stood. A close struggle ensued. . . . Alexander himself . . . vigorously pressed the assault, fighting hand to hand. . . . Darius, who now saw nothing but terrors all around him, was the first to turn tail and ride for safety. (*Anabasis Alexandri* 3.14)

Many of Darius's troops followed him in flight. Meanwhile, other Persian units made it through the Greek lines and attacked the Greek baggage train. These soldiers were driven back by a reserve unit of Macedonian infantry, and soon the entire Persian army was in full retreat. Alexander chased Darius to Arbil but there found only the king's abandoned chariot and bow. To call Alexander's victory decisive would be an understatement. He lost only a few hundred men, whereas Persian losses numbered forty thousand or more. In a single stroke, Alexander and his men had brought the mighty Persian Empire to its knees and ensured that it could never recover.

SEE ALSO: Alexander III ("the Great"); Darius III; Greeks

Battle of Kadesh (ca. 1274 B.C.)

Perhaps the largest battle fought in the Near East in the second millennium B.C. and the earliest battle in world history for which a specific play-by-play account can be reconstructed. The confrontation took place in Syria and did not involve Mesopotamian armies. However, the major players—the Hittite Empire (centered in Anatolia) and Egypt—were part of a delicate balance of power that included and affected the fortunes of the leading Mesopotamian realms, including Mitanni, Assyria, and Kassite-controlled Babylonia. The Hittites long had a loose alliance with the Kassites, whom the Hittites had helped place in power in Babylon, for example. And pressure brought to bear by both the Egyptians and the Hittites on Mitanni's western flank served to limit the aggressions of that large and powerful kingdom. By about 1300 B.C. or so, however, the balance of power in the Near East was upset when the Hittites and the Assyrians destroyed Mitanni. This allowed the Assyrians to expand westward and the Hittites to move southward into Syria and Palestine and capture the cities of Aleppo, Ugarit, Carchemish, and Kadesh (or Qadesh). The Egyptians, who had long controlled or influenced Syria-Palestine, viewed the Hittites' presence in that region as unacceptable, thereby setting the scene for the great battle between the two peoples.

In the summer of 1275 B.C., Egypt's new pharaoh, Ramesses II, marched through Palestine and captured much of southern Syria. No Hittite army tried to stop him, so he returned to Egypt in triumph. The following year the Hittite king, Muwatallis, retaliated by leading a force of some thirty-seven thousand infantry and twenty-five hundred chariots—a very large army for that time—into Syria and taking a stand near Kadesh. Ramesses marched northward with about eighteen thousand foot soldiers and perhaps two thousand chariots. Following custom, the Egyptian forces were divided into four large field units, each named after gods—Amun, Ra, Ptah, and Seth. These units were separated from one another by several miles as they approached Kadesh. At first Ramesses was tricked into thinking the Hittite army was camped many miles to the north. But then some of his men captured two Hittite spies who, under torture, revealed that Muwatallis and his forces were hiding on the far side of Kadesh, preparing to ambush the Egyptians.

Hearing this unwelcome news, Ramesses scrambled to prepare, but it was too late. A few miles to the south of the city, near the Orontes River, his Ra unit was suddenly struck by a massed charge of Hittite chariots, which did tremendous damage and sent the survivors into flight. These refugees made it to Ramesses' camp, which began to fall into confusion. The pharaoh realized he had to act quickly to avert total disaster. According to an official Egyptian account of the event:

> Taking up weapons and donning his armor, he was like [the formidable god] Seth in the moment of his power. He mounted his [chariot, pulled by his prized horses named] "Victory in Thebes" [and "Mut is Content"], and started out quickly. . . . His majesty was mighty, his heart stout, [and] one could not stand before him.

Ramesses and a small force of his soldiers assaulted the enemy chariots from the side or rear. For several hours the two armies clashed in sight of the city, perhaps until darkness forced them to retire. Evidence suggests that the battle was largely indecisive. After agreeing to a temporary peace, the opposing kings returned to their countries and each claimed victory. Nearly a generation of uneasy standoff ensued until about circa 1259 B.C., when Ramesses signed a treaty with a new Hittite king, Hattusilis III. As a result of the battle and the treaty, the Egyptians and the Hittites remained in control of Syria-Palestine. And Assyria and other Mesopotamian realms were temporarily discouraged from expanding westward into the area.

SEE ALSO: Egypt; Hittites; Palestine; Syria

Battle of Pelusium (525 B.C.)

A battle fought between the Egyptians and the Persians near Pelusium, a town strategically situated southwest of the Palestinian town of Gaza and east of the Nile delta. (In ancient times, a branch of the Nile emptied into the Mediterranean Sea not far from Pelusium; that branch later dried up.) The Persians were led by their king, Cambyses, son of Cyrus II, who sought to invade Egypt and make it part of the growing Persian Empire. The Egyptian commander was the reigning pharaoh, Psammetichus III. Most of the details of the battle itself are unknown. Ctesias, a fourth-century Greek historian who worked at the Persian court and wrote a history of Persia, which is now lost except for a few fragments, claimed that seven thousand Persians and fifty thousand Egyptians were killed. These numbers may well be exaggerated, but there is no doubt that Cambyses was the victor and went on to capture most of the rest of Egypt. This was confirmed by Herodotus in his own book, which survives. Herodotus writes that he visited Pelusium a few decades later, and "at the place where the battle was fought . . . the bones still lay there, those of the Persian dead separate from those of the Egyptian, just as they were originally divided." (*Histories* 3.13)

SEE ALSO: Cambyses; Egypt; Persian Empire

Behistun Rock

A huge boulder on which the Persian king Darius I (reigned 522–586 B.C.) carved some of the major records of his reign—the so-called *Behistun Inscription*. The rock was located near the village of Bagastana, on the road connecting Babylon with the old Median capital of Ecbatana. Darius's artisans carved the inscriptions, along with

A drawing based on the great carving on the Behistun Rock. © NORTH WIND/NORTH WIND PICTURE ARCHIVES. ALL RIGHTS RESERVED.

some human figures, on the face of a cliff at a height of some 328 feet (100m). The figures form a large tableau in which Darius exerts his superiority over nine defeated enemies, who are tied together by ropes around their necks. A tenth opponent lies beneath his feet. The text accompanying the figures is presented in three languages using cuneiform symbols—Old Persian, Babylonian, and Elamite, which the Achaemenid Persians used for administrative purposes. The words, largely deciphered by scholar Henry C. Rawlinson, tell how Darius was chosen by the great god Ahura-Mazda to overthrow the royal pretender Gaumata (who was impersonating Bardiya, son of King Cyrus II), and how, after assuming the throne, Darius defeated various rebels and enemies and captured their cities and lands. Part of the section describing his capture of Babylon reads:

> I marched against that [Babylonian ruler] Nidintu-Bêl, who called himself Nebuchadnezzar. The army of Nidintu-Bêl held the Tigris [River] and there it took its stand, and on account of the [high] waters [the river] was unfordable. Thereupon I supported my army on [inflated] skins,

The Greenhaven Encyclopedia of Ancient Mesopotamia

[while for] others I . . . brought horses. Ahuramazda brought me help; by the grace of Ahuramazda we crossed the Tigris. Then did I utterly overthrow that host [army] of Nidintu-Bêl. . . . Then did Nidintu-Bêl flee with a few horsemen into Babylon. Thereupon I marched to Babylon. By the grace of Ahuramazda I took Babylon, and captured Nidintu-Bêl. Then I slew that Nidintu-Bêl in Babylon. (*Behistun Inscription* 18–20)

SEE ALSO: cuneiform; Darius I; Rawlinson, Henry C.

Belet-ekallim

A Babylonian goddess who was best known as a patron deity of the city of Mari, located on the Euphrates near the border between western Mesopotamia and Syria. Called the Lady of the Great House, she was thought to protect the local ruler and his family.

SEE ALSO: Mari

Bell, Gertrude L. (1868–1926)

A noted English diplomat and scholar whose championing of archaeologists and founding of a major museum in Iraq greatly advanced modern studies of ancient Mesopotamia. Bell early made a name for herself by becoming the first woman to graduate with honors from Oxford University. She then traveled extensively throughout Europe and earned a reputation as an expert mountain climber, tackling some of the tallest peaks in the Alps.

Eventually Bell made her way to Iraq, where she fell in love with the local Persian and Arab cultures. She taught herself Arabic and became so knowledgeable about Arab customs that local Arabs

respectfully dubbed her "Daughter of the Desert," and "the Uncrowned Queen of Iraq." In 1920 she was appointed as an assistant to the British high commissioner in Iraq, which at the time was under British rule. Bell helped to install as king of Iraq the renowned Arab chieftain Faisal, who was a close friend of England's T.E. Lawrence, or "Lawrence of Arabia." During these years, in her official government capacity, Bell strongly encouraged ongoing archaeological digs across Iraq. She also established Baghdad's prestigious Archaeological Museum and served as Iraq's director of antiquities. Westerners and local Iraqis alike were saddened when she died of an overdose of sleeping pills in 1926. As a final service to Mesopotamian archaeology, Bell left behind some seven thousand photographs she had taken of the region. Many showed local archaeological sites in fair detail. These remain crucial to scholars because in many cases they are the only surviving visual records of sites that have since that time been altered or built over.

SEE ALSO: Assyriology

Bible

Several books of the Bible, specifically the Hebrew Old Testament, contain valuable references to Mesopotamian empires, rulers, events, and customs. This is not surprising since Palestine, where the Hebrews lived, adjoined Mesopotamia and was frequently conquered or culturally and commercially influenced by Mesopotamian peoples, especially the Babylonians and the Assyrians. Also, the books of the Old Testament were written, or their initial oral traditions were formed, during the period when the Assyrian and the Babylonian empires were at their heights. The Old Testament not only records figures and events of this period but also incorporates traditional Mesopotamian myths and traditions, such as the flood legend of Atrahasis, which became the biblical Noah's flood.

The Creation, Garden of Eden, and Flood: Cross-Cultural References The first section of the Old Testament, the book of Genesis, is especially rich in cross-cultural references with Mesopotamian civilization. The writers of Genesis were clearly influenced by the main Babylonian creation epic, the *Enuma Elish*. Both works describe the chaos and nothingness that existed before the intervention of a deity:

> The earth was without form and void, and darkness was on the face of the deep. (Genesis 1.2)

> When on high the heaven had not been named, firm ground below had not been called by name . . . no reed hut had sprung forth, no marshland had appeared, [and] none of the gods had been brought into being. (*Enuma Elish* 1–7)

In each work the heavens, Earth, and humanity are then created. The major difference, of course, is that the Hebrew version names a single god as the creator, whereas the Mesopotamian work invokes multiple gods.

Later in Genesis, the Garden of Eden appears. *Eden* was a Sumerian word meaning "fertile plain." Genesis claims that Eden was situated in the "east" and that a river in Eden split into branches called Hiddekel and Pherath. These were the Hebrew names for the Tigris and Euphrates rivers; thus, from the Hebrew point of view, Eden was located somewhere in the heart of Mesopotamia. Ancient Sumerian texts also mentioned an Eden-like paradise, called Dilmun. And the biblical episode in which

God creates Eve from one of Adam's ribs seems to have been inspired by a Sumerian myth set in Dilmun. In that myth, the goddess Ninhursag tries to help the god Enki, whose rib is injured, by creating the goddess Nin-ti, "the lady of the rib."

Perhaps the closest and most famous parallel between Genesis and the Mesopotamian legends is the flood story. The hero, known to the Mesopotamians variously as Ziusudra, Utnapishtim, and Atrahasis, is the equivalent of Noah. All are given instructions by a god on how to build a large boat to survive a coming deluge. And later, all release birds in an effort to determine if the floodwaters have abated. Recent evidence suggests that all of the hauntingly similar flood legends of the Near East, including the biblical one, may have been based on a real natural catastrophe in the Black Sea region some seven thousand years ago. Genesis also mentions the Tower of Babel. Most modern scholars think this is a reference to the great ziggurat erected in Babylon by King Nebuchadnezzar II and that the term *Babel* derived from *Babylon*.

The biblical book of Exodus also shows Mesopotamian influences. Particularly striking is the way the story of the Hebrew prophet Moses's birth and upbringing parallel those attributed to the great early Mesopotamian conqueror Sargon of Akkad. Sargon is supposedly born in secret to a priestess who places him in a basket made of reeds and sets the basket adrift in a river. A man finds the basket and raises the boy, who later rises to become king. Similarly, in Exodus, "the woman conceived and bore a son. . . . And when she could hide him no longer, she took for him a basket made of bulrushes [reeds] . . . and she put the child in it and placed it among the reeds at the river's bank."

(Exodus 2.2–3) In the biblical version, Moses, like Sargon, is rescued and grows up among royalty, in this case the family of Egypt's pharaoh.

Political and Military References Other books of the Old Testament record, with varying degrees of detail and accuracy, actual military and political events of first-millennium B.C. Mesopotamia. They therefore constitute important supplementary historical sources for these happenings. Among them were the Assyrian capture of the northern kingdom of Israel in the 720s B.C., the Assyrian king Sennacherib's siege of Jerusalem two decades later, and the sack of Jerusalem and exile of its resident Jews by Babylonia's King Nebuchadnezzar II circa 597 B.C. The biblical prophets who recorded these events usually gave them a moral dimension, suggesting that the Jews' misfortunes were a form of divine retribution. For example:

> Then the king of Assyria invaded all the land [of Israel] and came to Samaria and for three years he besieged it. . . . The king of Assyria captured Samaria and he carried the Israelites away to Assyria. . . . And this was so because the people of Israel had sinned against the Lord. (2 Kings 17.5–7)

One of the most vivid historical biblical passages is the prophet Nahum's description of the destruction of the Assyrian city of Nineveh by the Babylonians and the Medes in 612 B.C.:

> The shatterer [the hand of God?] has come up against you. . . . The chariots flash like flame when mustered in array; the chargers prance. The chariots rage in the streets, they rush to and fro through the squares; they gleam like torches, they dart like lightning. . . . The river gates are opened, the palace is in dismay. . . . Nineveh is like

> a pool whose waters run away. "Halt! Halt!" they cry; but none turns back. Plunder the silver, plunder the gold! . . . Desolate! Desolation and ruin! (Nahum 2.1–10)

SEE ALSO: flood legends; historical accounts; Israel; Judah; literature; Nahum; Tower of Babel

Borsippa

An important Babylonian city located about 7 miles (11km) southwest of Babylon. Dating from at least as early as the late third millennium B.C., Borsippa (today called Birs Nimrud) was most famous as the home of the god Nabu, son of the chief Babylonian god, Marduk. Nabu's main temple, called the Ezida ("Enduring House") was in the city and a large ziggurat was erected nearby. Because the ruins of the ziggurat still rise to a height of 150 feet (45m) and lie so close to Babylon, many early modern travelers incorrectly assumed that Borsippa was Babylon and that this ancient pyramidal structure was what remained of the Tower of Babel. In reality, in the city's heyday worshippers carried the cult image, or sacred statue, of Nabu from its temple and bore it along a special processional road to Babylon, where it "communed" with a statue of Marduk. Various early Assyriologists, including Austen Henry Layard, Hormuzd Rassam, and Henry C. Rawlinson, conducted excavations at Borsippa in the nineteenth century. The latest archaeological dig at the site was an Austrian expedition in the 1980s.

SEE ALSO: Babylon; Nabu; Tower of Babel

Botta, Paul Emile (1802–1870)

A French diplomat and archaeologist who is sometimes called the world's first As-

A bridge of boats erected for Xerxes' Persian army to cross the Hellespont into Greek territory in 480 B.C. © NORTH WIND/NORTH WIND PICTURE ARCHIVES

syriologist because he was the first person to excavate an Assyrian palace. While working in an official capacity for the French government in Iraq, Botta was drawn to some of the spectacular ruins in the area. In 1842 he began digging at the site of ancient Nineveh, although he did not know the city's true identity at first. The following year he abandoned that dig and began excavating at the site of Dur-Sharukkin (or Khorsabad), incorrectly thinking that it was Nineveh. It did not take him long to bring to light a palace of the Assyrian monarch Sargon II. In the years that followed, Botta shipped numerous statues from the palace back to Paris, where many are still on display in the Louvre Museum. Botta's work proved an inspiration to other young Europeans fascinated by ancient Mesopotamia, including the great Austen Henry Layard.

SEE ALSO: Dur-Sharukkin; Layard, Austen Henry; Nineveh

bridges

Not many large-scale, permanent bridges were built in ancient Mesopotamia, partly because supplies of stone and timber were fairly scarce on the Mesopotamian plains. Also, the Tigris and Euphrates rivers tended to shift their courses from time to time, rendering permanent bridges obsolete. As a rule, people forded rivers by using rafts and small boats as ferries. Or sometimes pontoon bridges, temporary structures made by laying boards across rows of boats, were constructed. These were especially useful for moving armies across waterways, as in the case of the bridge of boats erected by Persia's King Xerxes I to get his men across the Hellespont on the way to invade Greece in 480 B.C.

Nevertheless, a few major, permanent bridges were built in ancient Mesopotamia. One, erected by King Nabopolassar circa 600 B.C. across the Euphrates in Babylon, is the oldest-known large-scale, permanent bridge in the world. The Greek historian Herodotus, who saw this bridge when he visited Babylon in the fifth century B.C., describes its construction:

> [The builder] ordered long stone blocks to be cut, and when they were ready . . . diverted the river into [a pre-dug] basin. And while the . . . original bed of the stream was drying up, [the builder erected] an embankment on each side of the water's edge . . . then built a bridge over the river with the blocks of stone which had been prepared, using iron and lead [clamps] to bind the blocks together. Between the piers [vertical supports] of the bridge, squared lengths of timber [were] laid down for the inhabitants to cross by. . . . Finally, when the . . . bridge [was] finished, the river was brought back into its original bed. (*Histories* 1.186)

The remains of this impressive structure have been excavated and reveal that it was 380 feet (115m) long and rested on seven massive stone piers. The engineering was sound enough that the bridge was still in use at least six hundred years later, when another Greek historian, Diodorus Siculus, saw it.

Another noteworthy Mesopotamian bridge was one built by the Assyrian king Sennacherib to carry the water channel of an aqueduct across a stream. Located at Jerwan, north of Nineveh, the bridge was some 90 feet (27m) long and 30 feet (9m) high and rested on five stone arches made of stone blocks measuring 20 inches (51cm) on a side. The king's inaugural inscription can still be read, proclaiming, in part, "I caused a canal to be dug to the meadows of Nineveh. I spanned a bridge of white stone blocks. These waters I caused to pass over it."

SEE ALSO: building materials and methods; water supplies

building materials and methods

The choice of materials for constructing houses, temples, and other structures in ancient Mesopotamia was dictated largely by the natural geology and topography of the area. The Mesopotamian plains were composed mostly of alluvial materials— silts and clays laid down by rivers and streams over the course of many millennia. There were few trees or outcrops of stone from which to get suitable building materials, except on Mesopotamia's northern rim, in the foothills of the Zagros range and other mountain chains. Thus, the most common building materials by far in the region were clay and marsh reeds.

Raw Materials The clay was used to make bricks. Some bricks were composed of clay only, but others contained a mix of clay and various binding materials, such as straw or sand, to add strength. The biblical book of Exodus (5.10–14) features a famous reference to the use of bricks containing straw. Typically the moist clay mixture was pressed into wooden or pottery molds, then deposited in rows on the ground to dry in the sun. The best time of the year for making sun-dried bricks was during the heat of summer. In fact, the first month of summer came to be known as "the month of bricks." Bricks were also sometimes fired in kilns, which made them harder and longer lasting. However, partly because of the scarcity of wood to fuel the kilns, fired bricks were more expensive, so they were used mainly for prestigious structures such as palaces. The earliest bricks used in Mesopotamia before circa 3500 B.C. were long and thin. By the late fourth millennium B.C., however, a standard brick with a length twice its width had evolved. Later the Akkadians developed a square brick measuring about 14 inches (35cm) on a side. Another popular variation that developed was a brick with one end that was convex (outwardly curved), which produced a variegated (motley), three-dimensional exterior surface.

When building with brick, workers usually employed some kind of mortar. One common kind was a plaster made by mixing moist mud with powdered lime. Bitumen, a tarlike, petroleum-based substance, was also used for mortar and had the added benefit of being more or less waterproof. Abundant in what is now Iraq, the bitumen came from sticky deposits that formed at ground level in certain areas. Still, no matter what kind of mortar was used, sun-dried clay bricks disintegrated rapidly, necessitating frequent repairs. Often houses and other structures became so dilapidated that people simply leveled them and built over them. These new structures also decayed, and slowly but steadily cities came to rest on mounds of debris from past ages. When the cities were eventually abandoned, the still-disintegrating mounds became known as "tells."

Whenever possible, roofs and doorways in the newer structures were made of wood or stone. The cheapest, softest wood came from the date palm, which was native to Mesopotamia. Or if the builders could afford it, they imported hardwoods from cedars and other trees that were plentiful in Syria and Palestine. Small timbers were used to frame doors or windows. Sometimes the upright supports, or posts, of the frame were wood, but the horizontal piece at the top, called a lintel, was a slab of stone. This was one of the few uses for stone in building, the others being bridges and canals. Because they had some access to stone from the mountains north of their homeland, the Assyrians sometimes used stone for the foundations and lower courses of the walls of some structures.

Methods Most bricks and stone blocks were simply stacked, one on top another, in Mesopotamian structures. However, the arch was occasionally used, though not nearly to the extent the Romans later used it. Mesopotamian builders used both corbelled and true arches. As explained by L. Sprague de Camp in his classic book about ancient builders:

> Corbelling is laying courses or layers of stone or brick so that each course overhangs the one below. When walls are corbelled out from two sides until they meet, a corbelled arch or vault results. Although a structure of this kind is [not as strong] as a true arch, it is easy to

make. (*The Ancient Engineers*, p. 26)

Whether or not arches were employed in them, large-scale structures often featured commemorative inscriptions by the builders. Carved onto stone or metal tablets, these sometimes consisted simply of the builder's name and perhaps the date. Others consisted of short or long messages. It was common to urge future kings and builders to treat the structure with respect, and sometimes the builder placed a written curse on any and all who might not do so. The inscribed tablets were placed in a box and buried beneath the foundation or were inserted into spaces between the wall bricks.

Though brick structures were erected in many parts of Mesopotamia, in the marshy regions, by contrast, excessive water and moisture made building with clay bricks impractical. So most people who lived in the swampy lowlands near some of the rivers—especially in the region lying northwest of the Persian Gulf—used marsh reeds for their houses. The chief method of erecting such structures was to tie clusters of tall reeds into thick, sturdy bundles and then dig holes and sink the ends of the bundles into the ground. The bundles, which stood upright like columns, were bent over and their tops were attached to the tops of other bundles, forming rounded arches. Crosspieces, also made of bundled reeds, connected and braced the arches, after which thick reed mats were tied to the top and sides, forming the structure's roof and walls. The light, narrow boats these marsh dwellers used to catch fish and water foul were also made of reeds.

See Also: bridges; houses; palaces; temples; ziggurat

burial customs

In ancient Mesopotamia people often referred to death as "going to one's fate," "taking refuge on one's mountain," or "going to the road of one's forefathers." Whatever one called it, it was seen as a journey, and it was customary to prepare the deceased for that journey. If it was clear that a person was dying, he or she was laid in a special funerary bed, and a chair was placed beside the bed. It was thought that the deceased's soul would rest and receive its first offerings in that chair. These initial offerings—usually bread and beer—were meant to sustain the soul during its long journey to the Land of No Return.

In preparation for the funeral, mourners washed the body, rubbed it with oil, dressed it in clean clothes, and sewed the mouth shut. A few personal items—such as toiletries and jewelry—were placed beside the body. There was a wake, in which relatives and friends came to view the body and mourn. For average people these were likely brief, small-scale gatherings, whereas the death of a ruler could inspire a long period of national mourning. Perhaps to enhance or maintain their social status, those families who could afford it sometimes hired professional mourners to supplement the real ones. During the funeral procession people sang dirges (sad songs) and uttered words of lament, perhaps not unlike the funeral speeches common today. The famous Mesopotamian epic about the hero Gilgamesh preserves an example in the episode in which Gilgamesh openly mourns for his recently deceased friend Enkidu:

> It is for my friend Enkidu that I weep. He brought joy to the feast. He was a shield before me in the confusion of battle. . . . Great evil has taken Enkidu my friend. . . . Enkidu your eyes no longer move. Why is that? . . . Enkidu I cannot feel the beat of your heart. Why is that? Great evil has taken Enkidu my friend. . . . May every wild beast mourn for Enkidu. . . . May the mountain, the hill, the valley, the very fertile earth mourn for Enkidu. . . . May the water in the sea, in the lake, in the rivers, in the dew mourn for Enkidu. . . . May the farmers [who work in their] fields mourn for Enkidu. . . . May you Elders hear my words, I weep and I mourn for Enkidu. Enkidu was my friend. (*Epic of Gilgamesh* 8.1–2)

Also during the funeral procession, as well as after it, mourners went unbathed and ungroomed, and some tore their clothes in a display of grief, a custom still observed in some modern cultures.

Meanwhile, the body rested within a terra-cotta coffin, although the poorest people had to resort to wrapping the corpse in reed mats. Ordinary folk buried the coffin in the ground, preferably near the family house, so the deceased could symbolically be near his or her loved ones. Those who could afford a family crypt, made of clay bricks and frequently dug directly beneath the family home, stacked the coffin in the crypt. However, archaeologists have found some communal cemeteries, too.

In addition, modern excavators have discovered a number of royal Mesopotamian tombs, which were larger and much more elaborate than those of common people. In the 1920s the great Assyriologist Charles Leonard Woolley uncovered the royal burial site at Ur in southeastern Sumeria, in which he found sixteen graves of kings and queens. The royals were buried with their servants, who probably drank overdoses of sleeping potion so that they could follow their masters and mistresses into the afterlife. In one tomb, Woolley found the remains of thirty-eight serving women. Most of these tombs had been plundered in ancient times; but two were more or less intact and showed that many grave goods were buried with the bodies, including jewelry, grooming items, weapons, cups and utensils, parlor games, musical instruments, and more. Whether the deceased person was rich or poor, relatives continued to make periodic offerings in his or her honor in the years that followed. These included water, bread, broth, beer, oil, wine, honey, or other commodities, left in containers in the tomb or at the burial spot.

SEE ALSO: afterlife; religion; Woolley, Charles Leonard

Burnaburiash II (reigned ca. 1375–1347 B.C.)

One of the more prominent Kassite kings of Babylonia. Burnaburiash maintained good relations with Assyria by marrying the daughter of the Assyrian king Ashuruballit I. Burnaburiash also sought good relations and commercial ties with Egypt, as revealed in three of the famous *Amarna Letters*, a surviving set of correspondence between the pharaoh Akhenaten (reigned 1352–1336 B.C.) and other Near Eastern rulers. These letters reveal Burnaburiash to be somewhat pompous and quite demanding, as when he chides the Egyptian ruler for not sending enough gold as an official gift. In the letter excerpted here, Burnaburiash complains about his agents and merchants being robbed and killed in Egyptian-controlled Canaan in Palestine:

> To Akhenaten, King of Egypt, my brother, to say: Thus speaks Burnaburiash King of Babylon, your brother. I am well. To your country, your house, your women, your sons, your ministers, your horses, your chariots, many greetings. . . . And now, my merchants who traveled with Ahutabu delayed in Canaan for business. After Ahutabu set out on his way to my brother and in the town of Hanatun . . . [men working for the local ruler] beat my merchants and stole their money. . . . Canaan is your country and its kings are your slaves. . . . [I ask you to] bind them and return the money they robbed. And the men who murdered my slaves, kill them and avenge their blood. Because if you do not kill these men, they will again murder my caravans and even my ambassadors, and the ambassadors between us will cease. (*Amarna Letters* EA 8)

See also Babylon; Kassites. And for an excerpt from another of the *Amarna Letters*, see *Tushratta*

Byblos

An important Phoenician city, called Gebal by the Phoenicians and Byblos by the Greeks, located on the Mediterranean coast in what is now Lebanon. In the second millennium B.C. merchants from Byblos traded far and wide, reaching many Mediterranean ports, Egypt, and most major Mesopotamian cities. Skilled painters and other artisans from Byblos and other Phoenician cities also helped to decorate palaces for various Mesopotamian kings. In the first millennium B.C. Byblos was repeatedly conquered by Mesopotamian peoples, including the Assyrians, the Babylonians, and the Persians. Today the city is most famous for developing the alphabet later borrowed by the Greeks, the ancestor of today's Western alphabets.

Systematic excavation of Byblos took place in the 1920s.

SEE ALSO: Phoenicians

Cambyses
(reigned 530–522 B.C.)

The son of Cyrus II and the second king of the Achaemenid Persian Empire. The first important assignment Cyrus gave Cambyses (cam-BEE-seez) was to rule Babylon after Cyrus had captured it. Not long afterward Cambyses received the task of beginning preparations for an invasion of Egypt, and when Cyrus died Cambyses ascended the throne and decided to follow through with the grand expedition. The new king arranged for Persia's first fleet of warships, foreseeing that the vessels would be needed to supply his land army while it was crossing the arid region lying between Palestine and the Nile River. In 526 B.C., shortly before leaving for Egypt, Cambyses disposed of his younger brother, Bardiya, who had been Cyrus's favorite, to ensure that Bardiya would not attempt to usurp the throne while the king was away.

Early in 525 B.C. Cambyses reached northern Egypt, defeated the inexperienced young pharaoh Psammetichus III at Pelusium on the seacoast east of the Nile delta, and marched southward into the heart of the country. After taking control of Egypt, the Persian king stayed there for three years. His activities during this period are unclear. Rumors abounded that he committed cruel and sacrilegious acts, including burning the mummy of the former pharaoh, Psammetichus's father, Amasis, and looting several Egyptian temples.

Whatever Cambyses did in Egypt, he struck out for home early in 522 B.C. On the way, news arrived that a priest named Gaumata was impersonating the dead Bardiya and had seized the throne. Before Cambyses could rectify the situation, however, he died under mysterious circumstances. Some accounts say he committed suicide after hearing about Gaumata's rebellion; others claimed Cambyses developed an infection after an accidental knife wound. The latter explanation is by far the more likely.

SEE ALSO: Bardiya; Battle of Pelusium; Egypt

Canaanites

In ancient times, a general name given to the peoples who dwelled in the region of Palestine and spoke Semitic languages. The term *Canaan* sometimes denoted Phoenicia, home of the famous trading people, and some passages of the Hebrew Old

Persians hurling cats at Pelusium's defenders during Cambyses II's conquest of Egypt early in 525 B.C. © NORTH WIND/NORTH WIND PICTURE ARCHIVES

Testament use the term *Canaanite* as a synonym for *merchant*. An eighteenth-century B.C. Mesopotamian document found in the ruins of Mari, located on the Euphrates near the Syrian desert, mentions Canaan, which at the time may have consisted of a loose alliance of local Palestinian city-states. A century later the Hyksos, a people who invaded Egypt and took over the northern part of that country, seem to have come from Canaan, although they may not have originated there. After the Hyksos invasion, Amorites, who are mentioned in the Old Testament (Joshua 9.10, 10.5; Numbers 21.13), settled in the area of Canaan. After the Egyptians expelled the Hittites and began building an empire in the 1500s and 1400s B.C., Egypt controlled Canaan. The Egyptians hotly contested the area with the Hittites in the great Battle of Kadesh in Syria in 1274 B.C. In the centuries that followed that conflict, the early Hebrews became prominent in Palestine. The writers of the Old Testament sometimes used the term *Canaanite* to refer to one of a group of peoples they displaced, as in this passage:

> When the Lord your god brings you into the land you are entering to take possession of it, and clears away many nations before you, the Hittites, the Girgashites, the Amorites, [and] the Canaanites . . . then you must utterly destroy them. (Deuteronomy 7.1)

Whoever the Canaanites were at this historical juncture, as the first millennium B.C. progressed they, the Hebrews, and other Palestinian peoples fell under the control of a series of Mesopotamian peoples, including the Assyrians, the Babylonians, and the Persians.

SEE ALSO: Amorites; Israel; Palestine; Phoenicians

canals

At least by the third millennium B.C., the peoples of Mesopotamia were building irrigation canals to regulate the flow of water across the plains and thereby aid agricultural activities.

SEE ALSO: water supplies

Carchemish

An ancient Near Eastern city strategically located—on the upper Euphrates in northern Syria—on one of the main trade routes linking Mesopotamia to the Mediterranean world. Archaeological evidence indicates that the site of Carchemish was inhabited at least as early as circa 3000 B.C. Over time its involvement in trade made it prosperous, and it became an alluring prize for the large empires that rose around it in the second millennium B.C. Mitanni, Hatti (land of the Hittites), and Assyria all captured Carchemish. Under Hittite domination, which lasted more than two centuries, the city's patron goddess was Kubaba, who may have been an early version of Cybele, an Anatolian deity widely worshipped in the Mediterranean world in the late first millennium B.C. Assyria's King Sargon II seized Carchemish in about 717 B.C., but only a century later Assyria collapsed. In 605 B.C. the city was the site of a large battle fought between the Babylonian king Nebuchadnezzar II and the Egyptian pharaoh Necho, in which the Babylonians were victorious.

In modern times, the ruined site of Carchemish was first surveyed in 1876 by Assyriologist George Smith. After his death a team from the British Museum explored the site between 1911 and 1914. Among the diggers were the great archaeologist Charles Leonard Woolley and T.E. Lawrence, who later became famous as

"Lawrence of Arabia." They uncovered temples, a fortress, and many sculpted reliefs and statues.

SEE ALSO: Hittites; Mitanni; Smith, George; trade

Caspian Sea

An inland sea whose southern portion lies east of Armenia and north of Iran and that came under the control of several ancient Mesopotamian peoples. The Caspian Sea is the world's largest inland waterway, measuring some 143,000 square miles (371,000 sq. km). It bore numerous names in ancient times, among them the Hyrcanian Ocean, after Hyrcania (also called Gorgan), the region lying along its southwestern shore. The Persians called it the Mazandaran Sea. The name *Caspian* may derive from the Arabic name for it—the Qasvin Sea.

Archaeological evidence shows that humans lived along the edge of the sea seventy-five thousand years ago. But Hyrcania and other areas lying along its southern coasts remained on the periphery of the major civilizations until the Medes established their kingdom in the area in the mid-first millennium B.C. Soon afterward Cyrus II brought the southern Caspian into the Persian Empire. After the latter's fall, the Seleucid Greeks briefly held the area. In the 200s B.C., however, the Parthians arose there and went on to create a major Mesopotamian empire that lasted until the Sassanians overcame Parthia in A.D. 224.

SEE ALSO: Medes; Parthian Empire; Seleucid Empire

Çatal Hüyük

An important early agricultural town in southeastern Anatolia, located in an area that was once part of the northern reaches of the Fertile Crescent. It was in the Fertile Crescent, an arc-shaped region lying along the western and northern borders of ancient Mesopotamia, that agriculture first began. Eventually, people from the Fertile Crescent migrated to Mesopotamia, so many scholars contend that the first agriculturalists can, in a sense, be thought of as "Proto-Mesopotamians." Farming and herding animals such as sheep and goats provided more food for people who were used to sustaining themselves through hunting and gathering. Thus, after they settled down to work the land, the inhabitants of the Fertile Crescent felt secure enough to stay in one place permanently. Villages began to appear, and over time a few grew into towns of a thousand people or more. The larger villages and towns, which possessed more crops, animals, and other valuable items than the smaller ones, must have become tempting targets for bandits and local enemies. This is proven by the fact that, by the late ninth and early eighth millennia B.C., some of these settlements began to protect themselves with defensive walls of brick or stone.

Çatal Hüyük (chat-al-hoo-YUK) was one of the first and also the largest of these fortified towns. In fact, it covered an area of about 32 acres (13ha), making it the largest Neolithic, or New Stone Age, site in the Near East. (Experts define Neolithic cultures as those that practiced agriculture but still used stone, rather than metal, tools and weapons.) It appears that Çatal Hüyük was established as early as 8000 B.C. But its period of greatest prosperity was in the seventh and sixth millennia B.C. By that era the inhabitants had built a sturdy complex of houses that were connected to one another for the sake of mutual security. As noted archaeologist Trevor Watkins puts it, the town's

> square, flat-roofed houses were built side by side like a pile of children's building blocks, pushed together. Access to each house was by means of a door at roof-level, from which a steep ladder led down into the living area. Circulation [movement] around the settlement was across the flat roofs. The edge of such a settlement would have presented a solid, blank wall to any intruder or attacker. Once the ladders . . . were drawn up, the settlement would have been impregnable. ("The Beginnings of Warfare," in John Hackett, *Warfare in the Ancient World*, p. 16)

Although Çatal Hüyük's defenses were designed mainly to keep out local bands of marauders, they foreshadowed the large-scale international warfare that characterized the area later. In the second millennium B.C., the region in which the town was located became part of the Hittite Empire, which fought with Assyria, Babylonia, and other Mesopotamian empires for dominance in the Near East.

Considerably less is known about the social and political organization at Çatal Hüyük and other early Near Eastern agricultural sites than about their building methods. But some evidence does indicate that religion played an important role in the life of such communities. At Çatal Hüyük, for example, the remains of small mud-brick shrines dating from about 6150 B.C. have been found. These shrines featured primitive altars used for worshipping bulls as well as an early form of a mother goddess. Her name is unknown. But it may be significant that the earliest major cultures to inhabit the Mesopotamian plains, including the Ubaidians and the Sumerians, worshipped a number of powerful female deities; this lends support

to those scholars who argue that some of the people who lived in the Fertile Crescent in Neolithic times were the direct ancestors of the first Mesopotamians.

The remains of Çatal Hüyük were first discovered in the 1950s, and major excavations of the site took place between 1961 and 1965 under the direction of English archaeologist James Mellaart. Since 1993 an ongoing series of digs there have been carried out by an international team led by Ian Hodder of the University of Cambridge. These teams uncovered evidence that the residents of Çatal Hüyük grew peas, lentils, and grains. They also raised sheep, goats, cattle, pigs, and chickens. Dogs and cats, presumably already domesticated, also roamed the town in its heyday.

SEE ALSO: farming; Fertile Crescent; Mesopotamia, history of; Ubaidian culture

Cedars of Lebanon

The general name used both in ancient and modern times to describe a huge cedar forest that covered large areas of what is now Lebanon in Palestine. The Phoenicians, especially the inhabitants of Byblos, grew wealthy partly through lucrative trade of cedar timber. Peoples who dwelled in Palestine regularly used Lebanese cedar for large-scale building projects, the most famous being the Hebrew king Solomon's temple in Jerusalem:

> He built the House of the Forest of Lebanon. Its length was a hundred cubits [about 150 feet (45m)] and its breadth fifty cubits, and it was built upon three rows of cedar pillars, with cedar beams upon the pillars. And it was covered with cedar above the chambers that were upon the forty-five pillars, fifteen in each row. (1 Kings 7.2–3)

In addition to local use of the Cedars of

Ancient workers harvest cedars from the forests of Lebanon. © BETTMANN/CORBIS

Lebanon, Mesopotamian rulers regularly imported them for their palaces and temples because the Mesopotamian plains lacked hardwood forests. Workers transported the logs overland to the upper Euphrates and floated them downstream to building sites in Assyria and Babylonia. These cedars were so widely used and were seen as so important to constructing cities that they became a sort of metaphor for civilization itself. In the biblical book of Ezekiel, God tells that prophet that the Lebanese cedar "was beautiful in its greatness" and that "the cedars in the garden of God could not rival it." But these trees were destined to be destroyed. "Foreigners, the most terrible of the nations [perhaps a reference to Assyria], will cut it down . . . and in all the valleys [of Lebanon] its branches will fall." (Ezekiel 31.7–8, 12) This prophecy was fulfilled, for the vast majority of Lebanon's cedars were gone by the end of antiquity. Today about three hundred trees from the original forest remain, some of them believed to be up to fifteen hundred years old.

SEE ALSO: Byblos; Palestine; Phoenicians

Chaldean dynasty

A family of rulers and a regime that controlled Babylonia and its empire, usually called the Neo-Babylonian Empire, from 626 to 539 B.C. The term *Chaldean* originally referred to a group of tribal, Semitic-speaking peoples who entered southern Mesopotamia sometime between 1000 and 900 B.C. and from whom the members of the Chaldean dynasty descended. Also, *Chaldea* was a general name used to denote Babylonia from the mid-first millennium B.C. onward. The Chaldean dynasty was established by King Nabopolassar (reigned 626–605 B.C.), who, with the aid of the Medes, destroyed the rival Assyrian Empire in about 612 B.C. He was succeeded by Nebuchadnezzar II (604–562 B.C.), Amel-Marduk (561–560 B.C.), Neriglissar (559–557 B.C.), Labashi-Marduk (556 B.C.), and Nabonidus (555–539 B.C.). Nabonidus was forced to submit himself and his empire to the control of the first Persian king, Cyrus II. For details about the leading rulers of the dynasty and their realm, **see** Nabonidus; Nabopolassar; Nebuchadnezzar II; and Neo-Babylonian Empire.

SEE ALSO: Babylon; Cyrus II; Medes

chariots

Chariots were used widely in ancient Mesopotamia for transportation, hunting, and warfare. War chariots were depicted in the Stele of the Vultures and other sculptures during the third millennium B.C. The earliest versions are better termed *battlewag-ons*, as they were clumsy, solid-wheeled carts pulled by four donkeys or onagers (wild Asiatic asses). Because they were heavy and not very maneuverable, they must not have been very effective on the battlefield; it is likely, therefore, that they were used primarily as "prestige vehicles" to carry the king and his officers to and from the battlefield or as pursuit vehicles to chase down fleeing enemies.

This situation changed radically as two major innovations swept Mesopotamia and other parts of the Near East in the second millennium B.C. First, horses, which had been rare in the area before, began to be bred on a wider scale and were har-nessed to chariots, especially by the Kas-sites in Babylonia. Horses were consider-ably stronger and faster than donkeys and onagers. Second, Mesopotamian artisans perfected woodworking techniques that al-lowed the construction of spoked wheels and the manufacture of lightweight chariot bodies. The combination of lighter, more maneuverable chariots and stronger ani-mals pulling them revolutionized warfare in the Near East. Massed charges of chari-ots could now be used to smash through or chase away groups of infantry (foot soldiers). Particularly maneuverable and effective were the chariots developed by the Assyrians in the thirteenth and twelfth centuries B.C. and improved in the centu-ries that followed. According to military historian D.J. Wiseman:

Changes in technology enabled iron-smiths to design a light vehicle with a wooden frame set on a metal under-carriage with the wheel axis moved back from the center to the rear. The result was a highly maneuverable vehicle which required less traction effort. ... The chariot's driver was held steady against the front screen

while the rigid shaft, originally ellipti-cal but later straight, made control of the two yoked horses easier. The car became increasingly rectangular in shape to accommodate more armor and crew. (*Warfare in the Ancient World*, p. 43)

In fact, after the ninth century B.C. the standard chariot crew of a driver and an archer was supplemented by a third man, a shield bearer to protect the other two from enemy missiles. (The Hittites had used three-man crews in the late second millennium B.C.) The chariot archer also came to be protected by body armor. Sculptures and paintings from Egypt, Palestine, and other parts of the ancient Near East show armored outfits made of copper or bronze scales sewn or glued to leather or linen jerkins, along with metal helmets to protect the head.

Later, in the mid-first millennium B.C., the Persian king Cyrus II further improved on Assyrian chariot designs. In his account of Cyrus's life, the fourth-century B.C. Greek historian Xenophon states:

He had chariots of war constructed with strong wheels, so that they might not easily be broken, and with long axles; for anything broad is less likely to be overturned. The box for the driver he constructed out of strong timbers in the form of a turret; and this rose in height to the driver's elbows, so that they could manage the horses by reaching over the top of the box; and besides, he covered the driv-ers with mail [armor], all except their eyes. On both sides of the wheels, moreover, he attached to the axles steel scythes [blades] ... with the intention of hurling the chariots into the midst of the enemy. (*Cyropaedia* 6.1.29–30)

Despite these improvements in chariot

design, by the advent of the Persian Empire these war vehicles were used less frequently in battle than they had been in the past. First, cavalry increasingly came to replace chariotry. Also, whenever possible enemies of armies with chariot corps avoided fighting on flat plains where chariots could be used with maximum efficiency. In addition, the Persians came up against the Greeks, whose infantrymen were very well armored and trained to repel chariot charges. When King Darius III used scythed chariots against Alexander the Great in the 330s B.C., the Macedonian pikemen simply stepped aside and allowed the Persian vehicles to pass through the gaps that had formed in their line; the Greeks then surrounded the vehicles and showered their crews with javelins, putting them permanently out of action.

SEE ALSO: hunting and fishing; Stele of the Vultures; transportation and travel; weapons and warfare, land

childbirth

Children were customarily born in the home in ancient Mesopotamia. Female relatives and a midwife, when possible, aided in the delivery. Birthing stools are mentioned in the Old Testament, which was written in Palestine in the first millennium B.C., so it is likely that these were used in nearby Mesopotamia as well. Otherwise, the expectant mother adopted a squatting position in the latter stages of labor. Evidence suggests that amulets and other charms were regularly used to ward off potential evil and increase the chances of a successful birth. For example, a pregnant woman sometimes wore an amulet depicting the demon Pazuzu, which had a canine face and a scaly body, to hinder the female demon Lamashtu, who was thought to cause miscarriages and crib death or to kidnap babies from wet nurses. Also, wearing a charm necklace made of twenty-one stones was thought to make delivery easier. During labor the woman might chew a piece of tree bark while a female attendant rubbed her abdomen with oil, and if the delivery was difficult, another woman recited an appropriate incantation.

The incidences of infant mortality and of mothers dying during childbirth in ancient Mesopotamia are unknown. But they must have been similar to those in ancient Greece. There, 10 percent or more of women delivering babies died, as compared to only .01 percent in the United States today; likewise, perhaps 20 to 30 percent of babies died either in childbirth or by the age of one, compared to less than 1 percent in the United States today. In Mesopotamia babies seen as deformed (missing limbs, conjoined twins, hermaphrodites) were customarily rejected as cursed and thrown into the river. As in nearly all ancient cultures, even if they were physically sound, unwanted baby girls were exposed, or left outside to die, as male offspring tended to be more prized than female ones.

SEE ALSO: amulets; magic; women

children

Soon after a child was born, he or she received a name. In those homes that could afford it, the infant was nursed for two or more years by a wet nurse. In the case of a poor family in which the mother could not produce milk, the baby usually died. At home, the infant was placed in a basket lined with linen; outside the house, the mother or wet nurse carried it in a linen sling.

Very little is known about child-rearing

practices and societal views of children in ancient Mesopotamia. That children played with toys, like their counterparts in most other cultures, is evident from a number of toys that have survived. These include terra-cotta rattles for babies; small slingshots and bows and miniature chariots, wagons, and ships for young boys; dolls and miniature furniture for young girls; and balls, hoops, and jump ropes for both boys and girls. In rural areas of Egypt and other parts of the ancient world, children helped with agricultural work. And this was undoubtedly the case in Mesopotamia, too, though the average age at which this began is uncertain.

More is specifically known about adopting children in Mesopotamia. The main reason for adoption was to ensure that parents had someone to look after them in their old age. In fact, in many places an adopted son was required by law to bury and mourn his adoptive parents. The simplest form of adoption was to rescue an infant who had been abandoned. But older children could be adopted by paying a fee to reimburse the costs of raising the child up to that point and by signing a contract with someone who was willing to give up a child. A surviving adoption contract shows that the adoptive parents were expected to provide the child with an inheritance, no matter how many children they already had. Slaves could be freed and then adopted. And it was permissible for an unmarried woman to adopt a daughter and thereby become a single mother.

SEE ALSO: childbirth; education; women

Choga Mami

An important prehistoric Mesopotamian village located about 70 miles (113km) northeast of modern Baghdad. The site, which covers about 15 acres (6ha), may date to the sixth millennium B.C., making it a part of what scholars call the Hassunah culture. These early Mesopotamians, among the first who migrated onto the alluvial plains from the Fertile Crescent, are termed *pre-urban*, or "before cities," and typically inhabited small villages of about five hundred to one thousand people. Nevertheless, Choga Mami had a defensive wall and a stone tower that guarded one of the entrances. Broken pottery has been found in the ruins, along with figurines of women, though it is unclear whether they represent real people or goddesses. The houses were made of sun-baked bricks and had several small rooms. Choga Mami also contains the earliest-known example of an irrigation canal in Mesopotamia. It was excavated primarily by archaeologist Joan Oates of the University of Cambridge.

SEE ALSO: cities and city planning; Fertile Crescent; Ubaidian culture

Cimmerians

A nomadic Indo-European people who originally inhabited the region north of the Black Sea. According to the Greek historian Herodotus, sometime in the eighth century B.C. they were displaced by the Scythians, to whom they may have been related. The Cimmerians then migrated into Urartu (Armenia), where they settled in an area the Assyrians called Gamir. (The Assyrians called the Cimmerians the Gimirri, and the Old Testament refers to them as the Gomer.) It appears that the Cimmerians would have tried to conquer Mesopotamia next; however, the Assyrian king Sargon II defeated them in 705 B.C. (He died in the battle.) The Cimmerians then invaded Anatolia, taking over the region later known as Phrygia. After an unsuccessful attempt at conquering the

Sumerian ruins at Uruk. © Nik Wheeler/Corbis

kingdom of Lydia in western Anatolia, they more or less disappeared from the historical record.

SEE ALSO: Anatolia; Armenia; Sargon II

cities and city planning

The world's first examples of what people today view as cities—urban centers with considerable populations and numerous houses and public buildings—appeared in Sumer, the region lying northwest of the Persian Gulf, shortly before 3000 B.C. But, of course, before there were cities there had to be towns and villages; and this was certainly the case in Mesopotamia. The first settled, permanent villages on the Mesopotamian plains appeared sometime in the seventh millennium B.C. This was the result of the rapid spread of agriculture in the region, since the regular maintenance of fields and crops required that farmers remain in one place year after year. By the early 5000s B.C., villages like Hassunah, near the modern Iraqi city of Mosul, had populations of five hundred or more. Somewhat later, Tell-es-Sawwan, on the Tigris near Samarra, and Choga Mami, north of Baghdad, had up to one thousand or more inhabitants each. Local populations grew as high as five thousand in the Ubaidian period (ca. 5000–4000 B.C.), perhaps qualifying the villages as towns. At least by this era, each city associated itself with a patron deity, who, it was thought, protected the inhabitants and brought the town prosperity. Thus, the sun god, Shamash, was the patron of Sippar, northwest of Babylon; and Enki, god of the primeval waters, oversaw the town of Eridu, then only a few miles west of the shores of the Persian Gulf.

Eridu, which flourished during the

Ubaidian period, steadily grew larger than its neighbors and is often called the first true city. Certainly the Sumerians themselves, who appeared in Mesopotamia in the mid-fourth millennium B.C., viewed it as such. They claimed that it was the site of the original mound of creation, the first land that rose from the sea at the beginning of time. They also saw Eridu as the home of the first Mesopotamian king. Some modern scholars agree that Eridu was the first true city, although others think that Uruk, not far northwest of Eridu, is also a candidate for that distinction. Perhaps both views are correct. The older Eridu may have been used mainly as a ceremonial center, and Uruk may have featured the first actual urban center with large numbers of houses.

Other prominent Sumerian cities included Ur, a few miles north of Eridu; Lagash, some 50 miles (80km) to the northwest; and, farther to the northwest, Larsa and Nippur. By 2700 B.C. each of these may have covered several square miles and had thirty thousand or more inhabitants. They were not dependent units within a larger Sumerian nation but rather independent city-states, each in a sense a tiny national unit in its own right. Each consisted of a densely populated central town with houses, shops, and temples, surrounded by dependent villages and farmland supported by irrigation ditches.

At first none of these early cities followed any logical or systematic plan. All were very old and had grown organically, adding streets, houses, and public buildings haphazardly, as human needs dictated. Streets tended to be narrow and winding. Over time religious precincts, where the temples were, became separate entities with walls to protect the shrines; likewise, the entire city was surrounded by a larger

defensive wall to keep attackers at bay. Only later, in the Assyrian, Babylonian, Persian, and Greek eras, when rich kings decided to refurbish an old city or build a new one from scratch, did cities have formal plans. Thus, the grid of straight avenues that Herodotus saw in Babylon in the fifth century B.C. was the result of a renovation of part of that city in the recent Neo-Babylonian period. By Herodotus's day, Babylon was the largest city in the world, covering more than 300 square miles (780 sq. km). Before its destruction by the Babylonians and the Medes, the Assyrian city of Nineveh was almost as large, at an estimated 290 square miles (750 sq. km). The populations of these cities are unknown but must have been in the hundreds of thousands.

SEE ALSO: Babylon; Choga Mami; Lagash; Nineveh; Ur; Uruk

clothing

The first good indications of clothing in ancient Mesopotamia come from about 3300 B.C., when early sculpture and writing appeared. At that time and in the next several centuries, the Sumerians were the dominant people of the region. At first Sumerian men and women wore sheepskins or goatskins. The men were generally bare above the waist and wore their skins ankle-length and belted; the women covered themselves above the waist and draped their outfits more like a toga, with one shoulder covered and the other bare. When textiles came into wide use in the third millennium B.C., they steadily replaced animal skins, although for a while the style of dress remained roughly the same. Some leather was still used, but the chief fabric became sheep's wool; linen, made from plant fibers, was reserved for formal dress or for priests and nobles. Shoes, hats, and some other accessories were made of felt, consisting of crushed sheep's or goat's hair. Cotton was not used until the Assyrians imported it from Egypt circa 700 B.C. And silk, which came from China, was unknown until the early first millennium A.D.

A major change of fashion swept Mesopotamia in the Akkadian period, beginning circa 2300 B.C. Many men adopted robes that draped over one shoulder, and women covered both shoulders and adopted a V-neck style. Women also wore short-sleeved dresses. In the first half of the second millennium B.C., fashions retained the same basic look, except that the hems of men's garments became much more elaborate. Another change of dress occurred beginning in about 1400 B.C., when Assyrian men and women began wearing wide robes belted at the waist, with tassels hanging down between the legs. Men also wore decorated kilts. In the first half of the first millennium B.C., many Mesopotamian men adopted short-sleeved, belted tunics that stretched from the neck to the knees. Upper-class men added an elegant linen cloak dyed blue, red, or purple. The nature of footwear in these periods is somewhat uncertain. It appears that many people went barefoot much of the time, although some Assyrian men—mostly hunters and warriors—wore sandals or high boots, and some women wore sandals or slippers.

The simple tunics and kilts adopted in the early first millennium B.C. seem to have long remained the standard dress of common folk, who always made up the bulk of Mesopotamia's population. Sometimes people accessorized these garments, for instance, adding outer cloaks and/or jewelry items or sporting fancy walking sticks. The Greek historian Herodotus, who visited Babylon in the fifth century B.C., observes:

> The dress of the Babylonians consists of a linen tunic reaching to the feet, with a woolen one over it, and a short white cloak on top. They have their own fashion in shoes, which resemble ... slippers. ... They grow their hair long, wear turbans, and ... everyone owns a ... walking stick specially made for him, with a device carved on top of it—an apple or rose or lily or eagle or something of that sort. (*Histories* 1.195)

Not everyone in Mesopotamia dressed this way in Herodotus's day, however. At the time, the region was part of the Persian Empire, and he also described the outfits worn by soldiers and many courtiers, which featured the usual tunic but added trousers and a felt cap. The Persians had borrowed this style, Herodotus said, from the Medes, whom they had conquered and absorbed in the preceding century. This fashion borrowing was corroborated by the Greek adventurer and writer Xenophon, whose biography of the Persian king Cyrus II tells how upper-class Persian men also adopted Median shoe lifts and makeup to enhance their appearance:

> He [Cyrus the Great] chose to wear the Median dress himself and persuaded his associates also to adopt it; for he thought that if anyone had any personal defect, that dress would help to conceal it, and that it made the wearer look very tall and very handsome. For they have shoes of such a form that without being detected the wearer can easily put something into the soles so as to make him look taller than he is. He encouraged also the fashion of penciling the eyes, that they might seem more lustrous than they are, and of using cosmetics to make the complexion look better than nature made it. (*Cyropaedia* 8.1.40)

Later, following Persia's downfall at the hands of the Greeks, the Seleucid rulers introduced Greek fashions of the day. Evidence suggests, however, that the only locals who readily adopted these foreign styles were members of the upper classes who were trying to get ahead in a society controlled by Greeks. The common people of Mesopotamia continued to wear the traditional clothes of their regions, usually some mixture of tunics, kilts, and/or trousers.

SEE ALSO: grooming; jewelry; Medes

Code of Hammurabi

The most famous of the law codes created in ancient Mesopotamia. The Babylonian king Hammurabi (reigned ca. 1792–1750 B.C.) issued it toward the end of his reign, marking the first time that a ruler of the region had attempted to implement a set of laws affecting all people at all times with an air of impartiality. It is unknown to what degree the Babylonian justice system actually enforced or interpreted these laws, but they were held in high regard by later Mesopotamians and were often used as models for later law codes. For more information about and excerpts from Hammurabi's code,

SEE ALSO: crime and punishment; Hammurabi; laws and justice; magic; marriage and divorce

cosmetics

Beginning with the Sumerians in the third millennium B.C., and perhaps earlier, ancient Mesopotamian women, along with some men, used makeup products to enhance their appearance.

SEE ALSO: grooming

An embossed terra-cotta relief from Uruk depicting the activity of a carpenter during the 3rd–2nd millennium B.C. ERICH LESSING/ ART RESOURCE, NY

crafts and craftspeople

Some basic and essential crafts, such as pottery, leatherwork, brick making, and basket making, developed very early in Mesopotamia, in the late Stone Age (or Neolithic Age, ca. 10,000–6,000 B.C.). Crude forms of a few crafts—leatherworking, for example—likely existed a good deal earlier. With the development of cities by the Sumerians in the fourth and third millennia B.C. and their continued growth under the Akkadians, the Babylonians, and the Assyrians, a wide range of crafts developed. Some achieved high levels of refinement by the second millennium B.C. The major craftspeople in the large Mesopotamian cities included potters; stonemasons; sculptors; architects; brick makers; carpenters and house builders; painters; metalworkers, including specialists in bronze, silver, and gold; bakers and brewers; glassmakers; leatherworkers; weavers and basket makers; jewelers; seal makers, sometimes called seal cutters; wagon makers; shipwrights; blacksmiths; and fullers, who cleaned and dyed fabrics.

Most of these workers belonged to the lower classes or occasionally to the middle class. They made things individually, by hand, and did not make very much profit from any single item; thus, rich artists or craftspeople with their own companies and mass-market products did not exist in ancient Mesopotamia or anywhere else in the ancient world. The vast majority of craftspeople employed the apprentice system, in which a father passed his knowledge and skills on to his sons or other male relatives. Apprenticeships were typically long—up to eight years for a house builder and up to four for a seal maker. Many craftspeople plied their trades in their homes. However, workshops employing several or even dozens of people (the ancient version of factories) existed in the larger Mesopotamian cities. Evidence has been found of a jewelry workshop at Ur; a larger workshop in that city featured workers with assorted skills— among them metalworkers, sculptors, blacksmiths, carpenters, and basket makers.

Some workers were organized into guilds, although these were not unions that staged strikes to achieve political goals like many modern versions. An ancient Mesopotamian craft guild was more of a brotherhood of like-minded or like-skilled people. Each had an administrator who answered to the authority of the local royal palace. Individual artists and workers within the guild could achieve some measure of popularity, fame, and independence. But the guilds themselves could not become independent of government control because in most cases only the govern-

ment had the financial and other means of obtaining the necessary raw materials.

Although ancient guilds differed from modern ones, the modern phenomenon of craft specialization, including within a single worksite, was very much in evidence in ancient Mesopotamia. For example, when a temple or other public building was under construction, architects, brick makers, sculptors, painters, carpenters, and others took part, all working only within their areas of specialty. Carpenters specialized in building the doors, door frames, and roof, for example.

Carpentry was typically a male profession. By contrast, weavers were mostly women. They used looms, at first a horizontal version set up on the floor or ground. Later they employed a vertical loom, essentially the same as the kind used in Egypt, Greece, and other parts of the ancient world. Fullers not only cleaned the fabrics made by weavers, but they also dyed them using a variety of colors derived from animal, plant, and mineral products. The most coveted textile dye was a purple one derived from a mollusk, supplies of which came mainly from Phoenicia on the eastern Mediterranean coast. (Purple was seen as a "royal" hue in ancient times.)

The fabrics made and dyed by weavers and fullers are examples of craft products used by people at all levels of society. Similarly, basket makers, whose work was related in some ways to that of weavers (since one group wove thread, the other reeds or hemp), created numerous products used by people of all walks of life. In addition to baskets, these included boxes of all sizes, small boats used by fishermen in marshy regions, reed mats for floors and beds, chairs and other furniture items, inexpensive coffins, and doghouses. The products of leatherworkers were no less diverse and practical. These craftspeople not only cleaned and tanned animal skins using tree bark, fats, oils, and other products, but they also fashioned sandals, boots, straps for armor and helmets, quivers for arrows, horse bridles, and chariot linings. In contrast, some craftspeople specialized in a single product. A good example was the seal maker, who created the rounded clay stamps people used to make their individual marks on clay tablets and other documents. For more details on several of the leading Mesopotamian crafts and their products,

SEE ALSO: clothing; cylinder seals; furniture; glass; houses; jewelry; metalworking; mosaics; painting; pottery; sculpture; writing

crime and punishment

Human nature in ancient times was as human nature is today, and the inhabitants of ancient Mesopotamia committed many of the same crimes common in modern societies, including theft, bearing false witness, cheating the customer in a business deal, assault, rape, and murder. And then as now, a person found guilty of one of these crimes suffered some kind of punishment. In general, none of the societies that thrived in Mesopotamia used imprisonment as a penalty, as is commonly the case in modern societies. The theory was that imprisoning someone did not benefit either the victim or society. Compensating the victim, making the criminal do forced labor, or killing or mutilating the criminal as an example to others seemed more beneficial to society as a whole.

For instance, in Sumerian society, the first major culture that developed in Mesopotamia, many penalties forced the guilty party to compensate the victim of the crime. For example, one law stated, "If a man acts in violation of the rights of another and deflowers the virgin slave woman of a man, he shall weigh and deliver [to the victim] 5 shekels of silver." However, harsher punishments, including the death penalty, were inflicted for crimes such as rape or murder.

By the early second millennium B.C., Babylonian law codes, exemplified by that of Hammurabi dating from ca. 1760–1750 B.C., concentrated much more on physical punishments, perhaps based on the theory that these would more effectively deter potential criminals. The famous statement about crime and punishment from Leviticus in the Old Testament was a later product of the uncompromising view of justice that developed in Babylonian culture:

> When a man causes a disfigurement in his neighbor, as he has done, it shall be done to him; fracture for fracture, eye for eye, tooth for tooth, as he has disfigured a man he shall be disfigured. He who kills . . . a man shall be put to death. (Leviticus 24.19–21)

(Nevertheless, Hammurabi's code did include some provisions for victims' compensation. For example, law number twenty-three said that if a man was robbed and the thief was not apprehended, local officials had to reimburse the victim for his or her losses.) Indeed, penalties under the Babylonian system were in general quite harsh compared to those in modern democracies. For instance, the death penalty was imposed for theft or falsely accusing someone of murder, crimes that today are punished by fines or brief imprisonment. A Babylonian man and woman found guilty of committing adultery were tied together and thrown into the river to drown. And under some decrees issued by one of Hammurabi's immediate successors, Ammi-saduqa (reigned 1646–1626 B.C.), other relatively minor offenses were also punished by death:

> The wholesale and retail merchants [who use] a false seal [to try to cheat their customers] will be put to death. The representative of the king . . . who has forced . . . the family of a worker [to] harvest or perform work for his own profit, will be put to death.

Penalties under the Assyrian justice system were equally harsh and often more gruesome. A female thief could have her ears or nose cut off, for instance. A male adulterer was castrated and had his face sliced to shreds; the woman with whom he had committed the crime had her nose cut off. A man who touched another man's wife had a finger cut off; if he kissed her, his lower lip was sliced off. The degree to which these punishments actually deterred crime, if they did at all, remains unknown.

SEE ALSO: Ammi-saduqa; Hammurabi; laws and justice

Ctesias
(flourished late fifth and early fourth centuries B.C.)

A Greek physician and historian who wrote extensively about the Achaemenid Persians when they controlled Mesopotamia and most of the rest of the Near East. Ctesias (TEE-see-us, or TEE-shee-us) was born in the Greek city of Cnidus in southern Anatolia. Cnidus was known for its medical schools, and as a young man Ctesias avidly studied medicine. At some unknown date he was captured by the Persians and, because of his medical expertise, was asked to become a doctor in the Persian royal court in Persepolis; in fact, he eventually became the personal physician of King Artaxerxes II (reigned 404–358 B.C.).

The exact period in which Ctesias served the Persians is uncertain and is often disputed by modern scholars. The best guess is between about 414 and 397 B.C. All agree that he was present when Artaxerxes' brother, Cyrus the Younger, attempted to usurp the throne in 401 B.C. and the royal siblings fought each other in the great Battle of Cunaxa, not far from Babylon. Cyrus had brought with him some ten thousand Greek mercenaries, and though he was defeated and slain, they survived the battle. It is possible, because of his command of the Greek language, that Ctesias was present during the negotiations between the Persian generals and the Greek leaders following the battle. Ctesias also tended to Artaxerxes' wounds both during and after the battle.

What is more certain is that Ctesias eventually returned to his native Cnidus. There he set to work writing several long books describing the histories and customs of some of the Near Eastern peoples he had encountered. Regrettably, these works are now lost, but they were used and frequently quoted from by other ancient writers, including the first-century A.D. Greek biographer Plutarch. In particular, Ctesias's *History of the Persians* provides valuable information about Persian-controlled Mesopotamia and Iran. Ctesias's importance as a historian in the years following his passing, as well as his attention to detail as a writer, can be seen in the following quote from *History of the Persians*, which Plutarch integrated in paraphrased form into his own biography of Artaxerxes. The passage describes Cyrus's death at the height of the struggle at Cunaxa:

> Cyrus rode up against the king . . . neither exchanging a word with the other. . . . The king cast his spear at his brother, but missed him, though he both hit and killed Satiphernes, a

nobleman and Cyrus's faithful friend. Then Cyrus directed his spear against the king, and through his armor pierced his breast, five centimeters deep, so that the king fell from his horse. Those who attended him were put to flight and disorder. The king and others, among whom was Ctesias, made his way to a little hill not far off. . . . [Meanwhile] Cyrus was carried off a great way by the wildness of his horse. . . . He passed through his enemies, crying out, "Clear the way, villains, clear the way!" They did as they were ordered, throwing themselves down at his feet. But his tiara [royal cap] dropped off his head, and a young Persian named Mithridates struck a dart into one of his temples near his eye. . . . So much blood gushed out of the wound that Cyrus, swooning and senseless, fell off his horse. . . . [Later] the vein under [his] knee was cut open, [and] Cyrus fell, struck his wounded temple against a stone, and died. (Quoted in Plutarch, *Life of Artaxerxes* 11, part of Plutarch's *Parallel Lives*)

SEE ALSO: *Anabasis*; Artaxerxes; Battle of Cunaxa; historical accounts

Ctesiphon

An important Mesopotamian city lying about 22 miles (35km) south of modern Baghdad, Iraq. Ctesiphon was constructed by the Parthians after they took central Mesopotamia from the Seleucids in the second century B.C. The city became the Parthian capital, the central storehouse of the national treasures, and the place where the Parthian kings were crowned. The Romans captured Ctesiphon twice, once under the emperor Trajan in A.D. 114 and again under the emperor Marcus Aurelius a few decades later. However, the Romans were unable to hold onto either the city or Parthia for very long. Ctesiphon was

Tablet with cuneiform characters tallying sheep and goats. © GIANNI DAGLI ORTI/CORBIS

captured still again when the Sassanian Persians conquered the Parthian Empire in 224. The Sassanian rulers restored the city, making it more splendid than ever before, and for a while it was one of the world's leading cultural centers. Then the Byzantines, or eastern Romans, captured it in 627, and shortly afterward a Muslim army sacked it. Thereafter, Ctesiphon was steadily abandoned and dismantled and its stones were used for construction in Baghdad and other new cities erected nearby.

SEE ALSO: Parthian Empire; Romans; Seleucid Empire

cuneiform

An early form of writing developed by the Sumerians perhaps between 3500 and 3000 B.C. The earliest examples were discovered in the ruins of the city of Uruk. Whether or not it originated there, after its introduction cuneiform writing rapidly spread to other parts of the Near East and eventually beyond. Modern scholars named it *cuneiform* after the Latin word *cuneus*, meaning "wedge-shaped or nail-shaped." This is because in its most mature form the system consisted mainly of small wedge-shaped marks arranged in various combinations. The marks were made by pressing pointed sticks or styluses, often made of reeds, into soft clay tablets, which, when dry and hard, became cumbersome but permanent records.

The first cuneiform signs were based on pictographs, or picture signs, each representing an animal or an object. The pictogram for a fish, for example, began to be rendered in wedge-shaped marks instead of curved, drawn lines. In time, those wedge marks became more abstract, and sometimes they were rotated ninety degrees, so that they no longer bore any visual relation to a fish. Nonetheless, that sign still signified a fish, whereas some cuneiform marks came to be phonetic, each standing for a spoken sound or syllable. As if mixing pictures and sound signs was not complex enough, there seem to have originally been more than a thousand separate signs. By the mid-third millennium B.C. this number had been reduced to around six hundred. But this was still a great many, making reading and writing cuneiform very time-consuming and difficult and ensuring that only a handful of dedicated scholars, called scribes, achieved literacy.

Another complication was that cuneiform signs, originally intended to express the Sumerian language, were steadily adapted to other Mesopotamian and Near Eastern languages. These included, among others, Akkadian, Elamite, Hittite, Hurrian, Babylonian, Assyrian, and Old Persian, each with its own variations and peculiarities, although some elements of the original Sumerian marks and meanings remained in all of them. In the

thirteenth century B.C. the Syrian kingdom of Ugarit instituted a considerably simplified version of cuneiform with thirty to thirty-two characters that represented alphabetic sounds. This subsequently influenced the script alphabet introduced by the Phoenicians, versions of which are still in use today. In the first millennium B.C. the Persians adopted their own simplified version of cuneiform to express the Old Persian tongue.

The modern study and decipherment of cuneiform began in the 1770s, when Danish scholar Karsten Niebuhr visited the old Persian capital of Persepolis in southern Iran and observed three different forms of cuneiform script in the ruins. He correctly concluded that the one with fewer than forty signs must be alphabetic in nature. Not long afterward, German scholar Georg F. Grotefend began studying the script, and by 1802 he had deciphered roughly a third of the signs, which turned out to represent Old Persian. In the 1830s and the 1840s, English linguist Henry C. Rawlinson completed the decipherment of the Old Persian cuneiform, then tackled the two other scripts from Persepolis. He was greatly aided by his study of another set of three different cuneiform inscriptions on the Behistun Rock, carved by the artisans of Persia's King Darius I. Another scholar, Irish Assyriologist Edward Hincks, also became involved. By 1851 Rawlinson and Hincks were able to read some two hundred signs of the second cuneiform script. It turned out to be Babylonian, a dialect of Akkadian. With the help of German scholar Julius Oppert and British scholar William Talbot, Rawlinson and Hincks showed that Assyrian was another form of Akkadian. The third script from the Behistun Rock was Elamite, a language very different from others in Mesopotamia, and it was not until the mid-twentieth century that Elamite cuneiform was satisfactorily understood. Meanwhile, the decipherment of Akkadian cuneiform greatly aided other scholars in understanding other kinds of cuneiform, including Sumerian.

SEE ALSO: Behistun Rock; languages; Niebuhr, Karsten; writing

Cyaxares II
(reigned 625–585 B.C.)

The first and greatest king of the Median Empire, which immediately preceded the rise of the Persian Empire in what is now Iran. Cyaxares achieved success, partly because he instituted sweeping military reforms, including dividing his spearmen, archers, and cavalry into distinct units and standardizing weapons and uniforms. Many of Cyaxares' soldiers were native Medes, but he also collected troops from minor Iranian peoples that were vassals to the Medes, including the Persians, who lived in the region of Fars.

Having prepared his army, in about 614 B.C. Cyaxares launched an attack on Assyria, which had declined in strength in recent years. He was wise enough to form an alliance with Babylonia's King Nabopolassar, who hated the Assyrians as much as he did. The combined Median-Babylonian forces captured one Assyrian town after another, a campaign that culminated in the destruction of Nineveh in 612.

After disposing of Assyria, Cyaxares pursued other foreign conquests, subjugating the Cadusii, who lived along the southern border of the Caspian Sea; and the Armenians, centered in Urartu, directly north of Assyria. Then he moved westward into Anatolia and struck at the kingdom of Lydia. The Lydian king, Alyattes, fought

back with every soldier he had. But it was a natural rather than a human force that brought the conflict to a sudden and unexpected halt. On May 28, 585 B.C., at the height of a great battle between the opposing forces, a total eclipse of the Sun occurred. "Day was suddenly turned into night," the Greek historian Herodotus records.

> This change from daylight to darkness had been foretold by [the Greek scientist] Thales of Miletus, who fixed the date for it in the year in which it did, in fact, take place. Both Lydians and Medes broke off the engagement when they saw this darkening of the day. (*Histories* 1.74)

Viewing the sudden onset of darkness at noon to be an evil omen, Cyaxares hastily led his soldiers out of Lydia and died soon afterward.

SEE ALSO: Medes; Median Empire; Nabopolassar

cylinder seals

Short pieces of stone, and sometimes other materials, that were engraved with pictures or words that formed recessed impressions in their surfaces. When pressed into moist clay, these cylinder seals produced raised images. These images denoted the official identity, ownership, or authority of an individual or institution, in the manner of a modern signature or stamp. Before cylinder seals came into use, curved stone stamps were produced in Syria as early as the 7000s B.C. The cylindrical versions, which appeared in Sumeria in the mid-fourth millennium B.C., had the advantages of covering more area and allowing for more detail and information when rolled into wet clay. In the centuries that followed, hundreds of thousands of these objects were produced all over Mesopotamia. Images made by such seals have been found not only on tablets bearing palace inventories and decrees but also on legal documents, marriage contracts, doors, jars, and elsewhere.

Cylinder seals were created by seal makers, or seal cutters, who used copper, bronze, or flint chisels and gravers (pointed tools), cutting blades, and small hand-driven drills. Although most seals were made of stone, some utilized copper, bronze, gold, ivory, bone, or shell. Varieties of stone included limestone, crystal, lapis lazuli, talc, and agate. The scenes carved into the seals depicted activities such as weaving, baking, feasting, dancing, combat, and mythical incidents involving gods and human heroes. They often had artistic value and aesthetic appeal since many of the seal makers were accomplished artists. In fact, it took a considerable amount of technical virtuosity to carve shapes and etch details within sunken impressions—the reverse of normal sculpture work. The fact that the seals' surfaces were curved rather than flat made the production of correctly proportioned scenes and figures all the more difficult and amazing.

Cylinder seals also possess a certain amount of archaeological value. First, some of the scenes and inscriptions on them provide information about Mesopotamian mythology and everyday life. Second, some surviving seals bear names of rulers or dates or follow styles distinct to a specific place and time, allowing scholars to roughly date the sites where they are found.

SEE ALSO: crafts and craftspeople; sculpture; writing materials

Cyrus II
(reigned 559–530 B.C.)

The first and arguably greatest king of the Persian Empire. Born in the Persian homeland of Fars, located north of the Persian Gulf, Cyrus traced his ancestry back to Achaemenes, a legendary character who had supposedly brought together the original Persian hill tribes. When Cyrus became ruler of Fars at the age of about forty-one, the Persians and other subject peoples of the Medes were discontented with the reigning Median king, Astyages. Cyrus correctly reasoned that many of these peoples would offer Astyages little support if he were attacked. Thus, after careful preparations, Cyrus launched a rebellion against the Medes in 553 B.C. Three years later the Persians took the Median capital of Ecbatana and captured Astyages.

Cyrus had bigger plans than merely taking over the territories then under Median control, however. In 546 B.C. he marched his army northwestward into Anatolia and invaded the kingdom of Lydia, which the Median king Cyaxares II had failed to capture a generation before. After Lydia had been brought into the Persian fold, Cyrus returned to Fars and began construction on some palaces and other large-scale structures at his capital of Pasargadae. Then he turned eastward and conquered the peoples who lived in northern Iran and in Bactria (now part of Afghanistan). These eastern conquests nearly doubled the size of the Persian Empire. Finally, Cyrus felt confident enough to attack the Babylonians, who then controlled most of Mesopotamia. Late in 539 B.C. the Persians reached Babylon itself, which capitulated without a fight. Cyrus's first official proclamation after seizing the greatest city in the world stated, in part, "I am Cyrus, king of the universe, Great King, mighty king, king of Babylon, king of Sumer and Akkad, king of the world quarters."

Babylonia's imperial possessions, including most of Palestine, now belonged to Cyrus. But his own imperial ambitions were still not satisfied. He desired to add the land of Egypt to his realm, and he charged his son, Cambyses, with raising and training a huge new army for that purpose. But Cyrus did not live to see the conquest of Egypt. In about 530 B.C. he died of a wound suffered in battle while campaigning in the east near the Aral Sea. His body was carried back to Pasargadae and placed in a simple but beautiful stone tomb, which today survives almost completely intact, and Cambyses succeeded him on Persia's throne.

However, the memory of Cyrus and his deeds persisted. Though he had conquered by the sword, he had created a reputation as an unusually wise and fair ruler who inspired people to follow him. More than a century later, the Greek adventurer and writer Xenophon wrote a long account of Cyrus's early years, saying of him in the introduction:

> He ruled over [a great many] nations, even though they did not speak the same language as he, nor one nation the same as another; for all that, he was able to cover so vast a region with the fear which he inspired, that he struck all men with terror and no one tried to withstand him; and he was able to awaken in all so lively a desire to please him, that they always wished to be guided by his will. Moreover, the tribes that he brought into subjection to himself were so many that it is a difficult matter even to travel to them all, in whatever direction one

begins one's journey from the palace, whether toward the east or the west, toward the north or the south. Believing this man to be deserving of all admiration, we have therefore investigated who he was in his origin, what natural endowments he possessed, and what sort of education he had enjoyed, that he so greatly excelled in governing men. (*Cyropaedia* 1.1.5–6)

SEE ALSO: Astyages; Cyaxares II; Persian Empire

Cyrus the Younger
(ca. 424 B.C.–401 B.C.)

A Persian prince, the younger brother of King Artaxerxes II, who tried but failed to depose Artaxerxes, bringing about one of the greatest battles ever fought in Mesopotamia. The second son of King Darius II, Cyrus was so energetic, capable, and well liked as a youth that he was made a satrap, or governor, of two provinces in Anatolia while still a teenager. A former Persian governor, Tissaphernes, evidently did not like Cyrus, however. After Artaxerxes became king, Tissaphernes told him that Cyrus was planning to overthrow him. It is unclear whether this was true, but the king believed it was and would have killed Cyrus had their mother not intervened and demanded the boy be pardoned.

Perhaps because he no longer trusted his brother, Cyrus now began planning a real rebellion. As told by the Greek writer Xenophon, who worked as a mercenary soldier in Cyrus's army:

> The native troops he had [charge of as governor] he carefully trained to take the field, and made them loyal to himself. Greek mercenaries he assembled in as great a force as possible, secretly, in order to keep the king quite unprepared. (*Anabasis* 1.1)

A painting depicting the head and hand of Cyrus being paraded through the field after the Battle of Cunaxa, north of Babylon. TIME LIFE PICTURES/MANSELL/TIME LIFE PICTURES/GETTY IMAGES

Artaxerxes eventually found out what Cyrus was up to, however. When the latter marched his army to Cunaxa, not far from Babylon, his older brother was waiting with a larger army. Cyrus was defeated and killed, and his Greek mercenaries, Xeno- phon among them, had to fight their way out of Persia.

See Also: *Anabasis*; Battle of Cunaxa; Xe- nophon

Dagan

An important storm god worshipped by the Semitic peoples who inhabited Syria and western Mesopotamia in the late third millennium B.C. Dagan was the principal deity at Ebla in Syria, and he was one of the chief gods at Terqua and Mari, both on the upper Euphrates. Sargon of Akkad and his successors introduced the god to the region of Sumer, and the Sumerian city of Nippur became Dagan's main cult center. Over time the worship of Dagan merged with that of the major Mesopotamian weather god, Ishkur (or Adad). Dagan was also worshipped as a protector of grain, one of the staples of the Mesopotamian diet.

SEE ALSO: Ebla; Mari; Terqua

Damgalnuna

In Sumerian and Mesopotamian mythology, the wife of Enki, god of freshwaters and wisdom. Later Babylonian texts call her the mother of Marduk, the chief Babylonian god. Damgalnuna (or Damkina) was often identified with the mother-goddess Ninhursag, and their names are used interchangeably in the Sumerian epic poem *Enki and Ninhursag*, in which Enki impregnates his wife, giving rise to a daughter whom he also impregnates.

SEE ALSO: Enki; *Enki and Ninhursag*; Marduk

Darius I
(reigned 522–486 B.C.)

One of the greatest monarchs of the Achaemenid Persian Empire and the first Persian king to attack mainland Greece. Darius belonged to a different branch of the Achaemenid line than Cyrus II and Cambyses, the first two rulers of the Persian Empire. An imposter usurped the throne while Cambyses was away campaigning in Egypt. Not long after Cambyses died while on his way home, a group of nobles, Darius among them, slew the usurper and Darius became king. The new ruler's first order of business was to keep the empire, now wracked by rebellions, from falling apart. In an impressive display of military skill and sheer determination, Darius crushed all of the insurrections in less than a year. He then divided the realm into twenty satrapies (provinces) and began work on some long roads to better facilitate the movements of his couriers and armies as well as trade goods.

Partly to keep his large standing army busy, and also to further expand the empire, Darius launched a series of military campaigns. In the east he seized large tracts of northwestern India, and in the west he initiated the conquest of Europe by crossing into Scythia, the region lying east of the Black Sea. The Scythian campaign was more difficult than expected, however, because the locals adopted a scorched-earth policy and kept always ahead and out of reach of Darius's forces. Seeing these tactics as cowardly, he sent a messenger to Idanthyrsus, the chief of the Scythians, saying in part:

Why on earth, my good sir, do you

keep running away? . . . If you think yourself strong enough to oppose me, stand up and fight, instead of wandering all over the world. . . . Or if you admit that you are too weak . . . you should send earth and water [signifying submission] to your master. (Quoted in Herodotus, *Histories* 4.126)

Idanthyrsus answered:

Persian, I have never yet run from any man in fear; and I am not doing so now from you. . . . As for your being my master, I acknowledge no masters but God from whom I sprang. . . . I will send you no gifts of earth and water . . . and your claim to be my master is easily answered—be damned to you! (Quoted in Herodotus, *Histories* 4.127–130)

Darius was eventually forced to abandon Scythia, but he did take control of Thrace, the area located directly north of the Aegean Sea.

Also, between 499 and 494 B.C. Darius put down a rebellion of the Greek cities on Anatolia's western coast, which Cyrus II had acquired by conquering Lydia. This brought Darius into a confrontation with the mainland Greeks because the city of Athens had sent ships, supplies, and troops to aid the revolt of the Anatolian Greeks. Herodotus records how Darius was enraged over this interference in his affairs and

asked who the Athenians were, and then, on being told, called for his bow. He took it, set an arrow on the string, shot it up into the air and cried: "Grant, O God, that I may punish the Athenians." Then he commanded one of his servants to repeat to him the words, "Master, remember the Athenians," three times, whenever he sat down to dinner. (*Histories* 5.106)

Darius sent an army to punish the Athenians in 490 B.C. But his troops were decisively defeated at Marathon, northeast of Athens, and he died four years later before he could achieve his revenge for this embarrassment.

At the time of Darius's passing, the Persian Empire had reached its greatest extent, stretching from Thrace in the west to India in the east and incorporating all of Mesopotamia and many dozens of peoples speaking numerous different languages. He bragged about the number and diversity of his subjects in a building inscription carved at one of his capitals, Persepolis:

King Darius [says]: This country Persia which [the god] Ahura-Mazda gave to me is a good country, full of good horses, full of good men. By the favor of Ahura-Mazda and of me, King Darius, this country fears no other country. . . . By the favor of Ahura-Mazda, these are the countries which I got into my possession . . . which felt fear of me and bore me tribute: Elam, Media, Babylonia, Arabia, Assyria, Egypt, Armenia, Cappadocia (in Anatolia), Lydia, the Greeks who are . . . by the sea [i.e., in western Anatolia], and countries [in the east], Sagartia, Parthia . . . Aria, Bactria, Sogdia, Chorasmia . . . [and in India] Hindus, Gandara, Sakae, [and] Maka.

SEE ALSO: Ahura-Mazda; Cambyses; Greeks; Persepolis

Darius III
(reigned 336–330 B.C.)

The last king of the Achaemenid Persian Empire. Darius III was the throne name of an obscure Achaemenid man named Codomannus. In the wake of the murder of King Artaxerxes IV, he was selected for the kingship by the assassin, the treacherous royal adviser Bagoas. After becoming king, Darius saw that Bagoas intended to dispose of him as well and had the king-maker executed. Despite this violent act, Darius appears to have been a mild-mannered and generous person who only wanted the best for his country and empire. Yet this was not destined to happen, partly because by this time the Persian Empire was weak and corrupt.

Also, during Darius's reign his realm became the target of the Greeks, led by the young Macedonian king Alexander III, later called "the Great." Alexander invaded Anatolia in 334 B.C., and the following year he faced off with Darius at Issus in northern Syria. Darius was defeated and fled the field, but Alexander was unable to catch up to him. The Greeks did manage to capture the Persian king's wife, children, and mother, all of whom were treated with great respect. The two monarchs exchanged letters, the essence of which was preserved by the Greek historian Arrian. Darius told Alexander:

> [I] took the field in defense of [my] country and of [my] ancestral throne. . . . Now Darius the King asks Alexander the King to restore from captivity his wife, his mother, and his children, and is willing to make friends with him and be his ally. For this cause [I] urge Alexander to send to [me] . . . representatives of his own in order that proper guarantees may be exchanged.

Alexander answered:

> Your ancestors invaded . . . Greece and caused havoc in our country, though we had done nothing to provoke them. As supreme commander of all Greece I invaded Asia because I wished to punish Persia for this act. . . . By God's help I am master of your country. . . . Come to me, therefore, as you would come to the lord of the continent of Asia. . . . And in the future let any communication you wish to make with me be addressed to the King of all Asia. Do not write to me as an equal . . . or I shall take steps to deal with you as a criminal. (Anabasis Alexandri 2.14–15)

Darius rejected Alexander's arrogant talk and raised another army. The two forces met in October 331 B.C. at Gaugamela in central Mesopotamia, and once more Darius suffered defeat and fled for his life. Again Alexander was unable to catch his foe. But then Bessus, the satrap (governor) of Persia's Bactrian province, and some other high Persian officials took Darius prisoner and tried to exchange him for favorable terms with Alexander. The latter hunted them down; when the conspirators learned that he was approaching, they stabbed Darius with their spears and ran. Less than an hour later, one of Alexander's men found the dying Persian king in a covered wagon, accompanied only by a faithful dog. After the man had given Darius some water, the king said:

> This is the final stroke of misfortune, that I should accept a service from you, and not be able to return it, but Alexander will reward you for your kindness, and the gods will repay him for his courtesy towards my mother and my wife and my children. And so through you, I give him my hand. (Quoted in Plutarch, Life of Alexander 43)

With these words, Darius died. Alexander soon arrived and used his own cloak to cover the body, and not long afterward the conqueror of Persia caught up to Bessus and had him torn limb from limb.

SEE ALSO: Alexander III ("the Great"); Battle of Gaugamela; Persian Empire

Anzu, a mythological divine bird, fights two bisons in order to gain power and control.
ERICH LESSING/ART RESOURCE, NY

Defeat of Anzu, The

An ancient Sumerian myth and epic poem, which is also sometimes called *The Defeat of Zu*. It explores the evils of treason and tyranny in both human and divine dealings. Hoping to become ruler of the universe, Anzu, a divine bird, steals the Tablet of Destiny, a magical object on which, supposedly, the futures and fates of all beings were recorded. "I shall take the gods' Tablet of Destiny for myself," Anzu says, "and control the orders for all the gods, and shall possess the throne and be master of the [divine religious] rites!" The chief god, Enlil, who originally controlled the tablet, is outraged at the theft. Enlil sends the war god, Ninurta, after Anzu. But Ninurta's first attack on the great bird is unsuccessful because Anzu uses the innate powers of the tablet to render the war god's weapons useless. Ninurta then changes his tactics. He sends a powerful wind against Anzu, and the bird's wings are torn off. Ninurta then attacks Anzu again, and this time he successfully kills the creature, in the process spreading destruction far and wide:

> He slew the mountains, inundated their proud pastures, inundated the broad Earth in his fury, inundated the midst of the mountains, [and] slew wicked Anzu, and [the] warrior [god] Ninurta regained the Tablets of Destiny for his own hand.

SEE ALSO: Enlil; literature; Ninurta

Deioces (flourished early seventh century B.C.?)

An early and perhaps legendary Median ruler who was said to be the grandfather of King Cyaxares II. According to the Greek historian Herodotus, Deioces and his son Phraortes were the first leaders to unify the Median tribes, who had long lived in scattered villages. "The Medes had established themselves in small settlements," Herodotus writes,

> and Deioces, who was already a man of mark in his own village, now entered wholeheartedly into the task of distinguishing himself for just dealing. In this he had a purpose; for throughout the country at that time there was no sort of organized government whatever. . . . Bent upon getting all power into his own hands, he performed this office with perfect integrity. (*Histories* 1.96)

Herodotus adds that Deioces went on to build a palace and to erect the Median capital of Ecbatana. However, most modern scholars are unsure that Deioces was an actual historical figure, as the stories about him recorded by Herodotus may have been based on memories of the exploits of several different early Median leaders.

See Also: Cyaxares II; Ecbatana; Phraortes

Descent of Inanna, The

An ancient Sumerian myth and epic poem dealing with Inanna (or Ishtar), goddess of love and sexual desire, and her lover/consort, the shepherd Dumuzi. Several versions of the story, which is sometimes called *The Descent of Ishtar*, were written on clay tablets during ancient Mesopotamia's long history. The original Sumerian version, however, dating from the third millennium B.C. and consisting of 410 lines, is the most detailed. Like the famous Greek myth of Demeter and Persephone, which has many similarities, *The Descent of Inanna* demonstrates how even the status of divinity and feelings of love between gods cannot contradict the ultimate power and fate of death.

In the story, Inanna decides to pay a visit to the Land of No Return (Underworld), where her sister, Ereshkigal, reigns. Ereshkigal agrees to admit the goddess of love to the nether realm. However, Inanna is forced to remove all her clothes before gaining an audience with her grim sister. Then, quite unexpectedly, Ereshkigal kills Inanna and hangs her body from a hook. When Inanna fails to return home, her servant, Ninshubur, enlists the aid of the god Enki, who fashions two special rescuers. These beings descend into the Underworld and trick Ereshkigal into giving them Inanna's remains. They then inject into her corpse the magical food and water of life, which revives her. Unfortunately for Inanna, however, a group of divine judges tells her that once a person or god enters the Land of No Return, he or she must stay there forever unless a substitute can be found. Guarded by demons, Inanna searches for a substitute. She finally chooses her consort Dumuzi, who is taken down into the depths. The lovers strike a deal in which each agrees to spend half of each year in the Underworld and half on Earth.

See Also: afterlife; Ereshkigal; Inanna

divination

Various human attempts to read and interpret the will of the gods and/or predict future events. In ancient Mesopotamia, specially trained priests or scribes, known as *baru*, closely studied the livers or lungs of sacred animals; the movements of the heavenly bodies; the behavior of animals, including the flight patterns of birds; the layout of cities; the movements of clouds and puffs of smoke; the occurrence of famines, disease epidemics, floods, and other disasters; and other naturally occurring phenomena or objects. The diviners regarded any deviations from the "normal" patterns of these phenomena as possible candidates for omens, divine signs of impending change, either good or bad. Through repeated observations, diviners came to believe that certain specific events or phenomena were sure signs of specific outcomes. For example, the seventh-century B.C. Assyrian king Esarhaddon asked his chief diviner to interpret the behavior of some ravens he had witnessed. The diviner's answer, which was preserved on a clay tablet, was as follows:

> As to Your Majesty's request addressed to me concerning the incident with the ravens, here are the relevant omens: If a raven brings something into a person's house, this man will obtain something that does not belong to him. If a falcon or a raven drops something he is carrying upon a person's house or in front of a man, this house will have much traffic—traffic means profit. If a bird carries

meat, another bird, or anything else, and drops it upon a person's house, this man will obtain a large inheritance.

Of particular note were two unusual or noteworthy events that occurred at approximately the same time. It was commonly believed that this did not happen by mere coincidence; rather, one event must have a causal relationship with the other. If a king died soon after a great disaster, for instance, the disaster was seen as an omen foreshadowing the monarch's death. Because of such beliefs, Mesopotamian rulers like Esarhaddon generally consulted their royal diviners before embarking on a trip or a military campaign to make sure the signs were favorable.

SEE ALSO: astrology and astronomy; doctors and medicine; oracles

doctors and medicine

Healers no doubt existed in Mesopotamia well before the advent of cities in the late fourth millennium B.C. However, it was not until writing was invented and the healers began writing down their cures that tangible evidence for medical practices in the region began to accumulate. The oldest-known medical text in the world was discovered in the Sumerian city of Nippur. It dates to the late third millennium B.C. and was recorded in cuneiform symbols on a clay tablet. A much larger store of medical information—consisting of roughly eight hundred tablets—was found in the palace library of the Assyrian king Ashurbanipal at Nineveh.

Common Medicines These tablets list some 370 substances purportedly possessing medicinal properties, about 250 of them derived from plants and the rest from minerals. The plant substances include tree bark and gum; roots; leaves; seeds; fruits, including pears, dates, and figs; spices such as thyme and myrrh; castor oil; and licorice. Among the minerals listed are potassium nitrate (saltpeter), sodium chloride (salt), and sulfur. Doctors kept many of these substances in containers, and when need arose they poured one or more of them into a liquid such as milk, wine, honey, or beer. The patient drank the liquid, ingesting the medicine in the process. To make an ointment for the skin, appropriate medicinal substances were added to animal fat or wax. Some healing substances were injected directly into the eyes, ears, rectum, vagina, or penis.

The exact amounts of the medicinal substances to be used for a particular cure were decided by the individual doctor. Two general kinds of physicians existed in Mesopotamia—the *asu*, who primarily relied on these substances to effect physical cures; and the *ashipu*, who employed spiritual cures. From time to time a doctor might feel the need to resort to both physical and spiritual methods. The symbol used by Sumerian doctors to identify themselves was a staff with snakes encircling it. This image was later adopted by ancient Greek physicians, who inspired its adoption by the modern medical profession. Mesopotamian doctors often plied their trade on the grounds of religious temples, so some temples were thought of as medical clinics as well as places of worship.

The surviving Mesopotamian medical texts reveal that these doctors diagnosed and treated a wide variety of conditions and diseases, with mixed success. Among them were typhus, smallpox, bubonic plague, gonorrhea, gout, tuberculosis, epilepsy, colic, diarrhea, and various intestinal problems. Some forms of mental illness were also recognized, though not properly understood. The germ theory of disease was unknown, of course, and was not discovered and proven until the nineteenth century; yet it appears that some doctors were aware that a disease could be passed from person to person and therefore that it was helpful to limit a sick person's contact with other people.

Because no one in ancient Mesopotamia knew about the existence of germs, it was assumed that most illness was caused by evil spirits or demons sent by the gods to punish humans. (This was the main factor that differentiated Mesopotamian doctors from Greek doctors. The latter came to reject the idea of divine causes of disease and advocated that sickness had natural causes.) Something like six thousand different demons were recognized, and it was a doctor's job to identify which specific demon was making his patient ill. It was thought that the demon or spirit afflicting the patient was punishing the person for some kind of sin; thus, it was seen as necessary to perform appropriate religious rituals to counteract the bad effects of the supernatural visitor. In some cases exorcism, or the act of driving a demon from a person's body, was called for.

Common Practices Some Mesopotamian doctors also performed surgery, although very little specific information about the actual operations has survived. More plentiful are references to surgeons in law codes, which set fees for surgical procedures and recorded the penalties doctors suffered if their surgeries failed. Fees were set on a scale based on the patient's ability to pay. A doctor treating a commoner was allowed to charge only half as much as he charged a noble, and the fee for treating a slave was somewhat less than half of that

for treating a commoner. As for penalties for malpractice, a surgeon who caused the death of a noble had his hand cut off.

Some mention of dentistry is also made in ancient Mesopotamian texts, though there do not appear to have been doctors who specialized in this area. People believed that tooth decay was caused by an insidious worm that had been spawned in a swamp when Earth was first created. The traditional story of how the gods allowed this worm to feed on people's teeth was as follows:

> Came the worm before Shamash [the sun god]. Before Ea [god of freshwater] came her tears: "What will you give me to eat and destroy?" "Ripe figs will I give you," Ea answered. [Then the worm asked,] "What good are ripe figs to me? Take me up and let me reside between the teeth and the gums [of humans], so that I may destroy the blood of the tooth and ruin their strength; the roots of the tooth I will eat." [The gods then granted the worm's request.]

To remove an infected tooth, the doctor grasped it with a medical instrument, perhaps a kind of forceps, cursed the worm three times in a row, then yanked. Afterward the patient was instructed to rinse several times a day with a mouthwash made of beer and sesame oil.

SEE ALSO: divination; exorcism

dowry

Money and/or valuables given to a groom by a bride's father for the young woman's maintenance during the marriage.

SEE ALSO: marriage and divorce

Dumuzi

The Sumerian god of shepherds and their flocks and the lover/consort of Inanna (or

Ishtar), goddess of love and sexual passion. In the myth and epic poem known as *The Descent of Inanna*, the goddess chooses Dumuzi (or Tammuz) as a substitute for her in the Underworld so that she can spend half of each year on Earth.

SEE ALSO: *Descent of Inanna, The*; Inanna

Dur-Katlimmu

An Assyrian city located about 140 miles (225km) southwest of Mosul, Iraq. Although archaeologists did some initial work at the site of Dur-Katlimmu (modern Shiekh Hamid) in 1879, principal excavations took place in the late twentieth century. The chief find consisted of a group of some five hundred clay tablets bearing cuneiform characters in the Assyrian dialect of Akkadian. The tablets date to about 600 B.C., shortly after the destruction of the Assyrian Empire by the Medes and the Babylonians, and show that Assyrians still spoke and wrote their language after the empire's fall.

SEE ALSO: Assyrian Empire; cuneiform

Dur-Kurigalzu

A small city constructed by and named for a Kassite king, Kurigalzu I, in the late fifteenth century B.C. Located about 18 miles (29km) west of Baghdad, Dur-Kurigalzu (modern Aqar Quf) served as the Kassite administrative/political capital, but Babylon remained the religious and ceremonial Kassite center. Dur-Kurigalzu was abandoned after the Kassite dynasty fell in the twelfth century B.C. The city originally featured a fortified defensive wall on its perimeter and a large ziggurat dedicated to the god Enlil. The remains of the ziggurat—mainly its mud-brick core—still reach a height of 187 feet (57m). Some painted murals from the royal palace

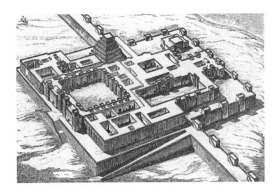

Known today as Khorsabad in Iraq, Dur-Sharrukin was the capital of the Assyrian Empire. It was erected from 713–708 B.C. AKG-IMAGES, LONDON.

survive as well, along with some statues. Dur-Kurigalzu was excavated between 1943 and 1945 by a team of Iraqi archaeologists.

SEE ALSO: Babylonia; Kassites; Kurigalzu

Dur-Sharukkin

Meaning "Fortress of Sargon," a new capital of the Assyrian Empire built in the last years of the eighth century B.C. by King Sargon II. The city was located about 7 miles (11km) northeast of the modern Iraqi city of Mosul. Dur-Sharukkin (modern Khorsabad) was surrounded by an imposing brick defensive wall some 46 feet (14m) thick and 39 feet (12m) high and covered about 1 square mile (2.6 sq. km). The corners of the square marked out by the walls pointed to the north, south, east, and west.

One of the city's outstanding structures was Sargon's palace, which he claimed was "without rival." His inauguration inscription, which has survived, reads, "For me, Sargon, who dwells in this palace, may he [the god Ashur] decree as my destiny, eternal life." The palace originally featured more than two hundred rooms grouped around three large courtyards, and the entrances were guarded by giant stone, winged bulls. The interior walls of the palace are still covered with magnificent relief sculptures depicting Sargon's military exploits. There are so many panels of reliefs that if they were laid end to end they would stretch for nearly a mile (1.6km)! The city also had a number of temples and shrines, the most important of which was dedicated to Nabu, god of literacy and wisdom.

The first modern excavations of Dur-Sharukkin were conducted by archaeologists Paul Emile Botta and Victor Place in the 1840s and the 1850s, during the golden age of Assyriology. A later expedition to the site mounted by the University of Chicago's Oriental Institute between 1929 and 1934 uncovered the so-called Khorsabad King List, a list of the names and lengths of the reigns of Assyria's rulers from about 2200 B.C. down to Sargon's day.

SEE ALSO: Botta, Paul Emile; Sargon II; sculpture

Ea

The Babylonian name of the Sumerian god Enki, who had charge of freshwater and was also a patron of craftsmen and artisans.

SEE ALSO: Enki

Ebla

An important independent city-state and commercial center in the Orontes Valley in northern Syria. Ebla (modern Tell Mardikh), which had close ties with nearby Mesopotamia, rose to prominence twice. The first time was in the late third millennium B.C., when it thrived by trading timber, textiles, and cattle, of which it was said to own more than two hundred thousand head. The local palace contained numerous workshops and employed nearly five thousand artisans and servants. The principal deity worshipped in the city was the Semitic storm god, Dagan. Ebla was sacked circa 2250 B.C., apparently by an Akkadian army, although the ruler who led that army is still disputed by scholars. Ebla's second period of prosperity was about 1800 to 1650 B.C., when Amorites controlled it. Little is known about the city in this era, which ended when the Hittites destroyed it for good.

Ebla was largely forgotten until 1964, when excavations began by Italy's University of Rome La Sapienza under the direction of Paolo Matthiae. The Italians uncovered an archaeological bonanza in the form of the city's archive, consisting of some twenty thousand clay tablets. These bear cuneiform symbols in Sumerian and Ebalite, a Semitic language related to Akkadian. Translations have revealed tribute lists, trade contracts, law cases, diplomatic letters, and more, providing important insights about the economic and cultural life of the inhabitants.

SEE ALSO: Dagan; Hittites; Syria; trade

Ecbatana

Originally the capital of the Median Empire and later a key city in the Persian, Seleucid, and Parthian empires. According to the Greek historian Herodotus, Ecbatana (modern Hamadan), located in the Zagros Mountains directly east of central Mesopotamia, was first erected by the early Median ruler Deioces in the seventh century B.C. "Deioces' first act was to command his subjects to build a palace worthy of a king," Herodotus claims.

> The Medes complied. They built a large and well-defended palace on a site he himself indicated. . . . Deioces [then] put pressure on the Medes to build a single great city to which, as the capital of the country, all other towns were to be held of secondary importance. Again they complied, and the city now known as Ecbatana was built, a place of great size and strength fortified by concentric walls, these so planned that each successive circle was higher than the one below it by the height of the battlements. . . . The circles are seven in number, and the

innermost contains the royal palace and treasury. . . . The battlements of the five outer rings are painted in different colors, the first white, the second black, the third crimson, the fourth blue, the fifth orange; the battlements of the two inner rings are plated with silver and gold respectively. (*Histories* 1.98–99)

Modern scholars suspect that Herodotus's description of Ecbatana, which he never saw in person, may be partly fanciful. The concentric battlements rising in height may be a garbled account of a ziggurat, a structure common to cities of the region in that era. Unfortunately, the truth may never be known. Modern Hamadan almost completely overlays ancient Ecbatana, so very little archaeological work has been done there, and the prospect of future digs remains uncertain. Herodotus's mention of silver and gold does square with other ancient accounts of Ecbatana, which say that its palace was splendidly decorated with these precious metals. What is more certain is that after the fall of Media, the Persian kings used Ecbatana as their summer residence, and the city served as a capital under the Seleucids and the Parthians.

SEE ALSO: Deioces; Median Empire; Persian Empire

education

The first-known formal schools were in ancient Mesopotamia. It is uncertain exactly when they first appeared, but lists of vocabulary words obviously intended for students were found in the ruins of the Sumerian city of Uruk and date from roughly 3000 B.C. More abundant evidence comes from the period of 2500 to 1500 B.C., including hundreds of cuneiform tablets that were used for classroom and homework exercises. These and/or sometimes the remains of actual schoolhouses have been found not only in Uruk but also in Nippur, Ur, Mari, and elsewhere in and around Mesopotamia. Such a school, called an *edubba*, or "tablet house" after the clay tablets used by the students, was at first located on the grounds of a temple, but later it was common to set up schools in private buildings. A private school excavated at Mari had two rooms, one containing mud-brick benches, each of which accommodated two to four students. Scholars believe that the walls, which are now largely missing, featured wide shelves on which to stack the students' exercise tablets. In addition to such tablets, the children may also have used wooden writing boards like those used by Egyptian children. These boards were covered with wax; a student used a pointed stick to inscribe letters in the wax and later smoothed out the wax to create a fresh surface.

All schools in Mesopotamia were privately run and paid for by students' parents, so only the well-to-do could afford to send their children to a formal school. Thus, the vast majority of people were illiterate. In the mid-twentieth century, a scholar from Luxembourg, Nikolaus Schneider, examined a large collection of economic and administrative tablets dating from circa 2000 B.C. and found that most of the scribes who created these documents also added the names and occupations of their fathers. The fathers were invariably governors, mayors, military officers, priests, high tax officials, temple administrators, scribes, and so forth. Schneider's study showed not only that education was a privilege of the well-to-do but also that most students were male. Only one woman was listed as a scribe in all the documents he examined. As was the case in other ancient societies, it was not seen as necessary to educate girls since nearly all major positions in government and business were held by men.

As for the actual running of a Mesopotamian school, the school day lasted from early morning to sundown. It appears that schools were open on twenty-four days of each month, the other days being devoted to religious holidays or vacation. The headmaster was called the *ummia* ("school father"), a scribe who commanded great respect in society because he had attained a high level of learning. One surviving tablet contains a passage in which a student tells his headmaster, "You have opened my eyes as though I were a puppy. You have formed humanity within me." The teachers who worked under the *ummia* were also scribes. They specialized in various intellectual disciplines, as modern high school and college instructors still do. There was a "scribe of counting," who taught arithmetic, for instance; and a "scribe of Sumerian," who taught students how to read and write that language. Later, after Akkadian came to be used widely across Mesopotamia, students were required to learn both Sumerian and Akkadian. Not all students became totally literate because early forms of cuneiform were tremendously complex and difficult to master; but it was probably expected that average students would become literate enough to write simple letters, read military dispatches, compute taxes, and read some standard prayers and poems, including the famous *Epic of Gilgamesh*. The best and most diligent students, however, went on to become scribes, including teachers, government administrators, astrologers, and priests. The main method of teaching was rote—constant repetition, both by writing and reciting the lessons. The teachers also showed the students how to fashion and bake the clay tablets used in the classroom.

The teachers and the *ummia* were both respected and feared because proper behavior in the schools was strictly enforced, when necessary by the use of corporal punishment. A surviving essay, titled "Schooldays," written in about 2000 B.C. by a teacher recalling his own youthful education, tells how the boy's mother gave him his lunch and sent him off to school. But unfortunately for him, he was late. "Afraid and with pounding heart," the boy stood before the headmaster and "made a respectful curtsy," after which the teacher beat him severely with a stick. "My headmaster read my tablet," the text goes on,

> and said: "There is something missing," [and then he] beat me. The fellow in charge of neatness said: "You loitered in the street and did not straighten up your clothes," [and he also] beat me. The fellow in charge of silence said: "Why did you talk without permission?" [and he also] beat me.

The beatings continued for some time. Finally, the boy convinced his father to pay the headmaster more money and to invite him over for dinner, after which the *ummia* stopped using physical means to discipline the boy.

SEE ALSO: cuneiform; literature; priests and priestesses; scribe; writing materials

Egypt

Although ancient Egypt was geographically separate from ancient Mesopotamia, the Egyptians long had cultural and trade connections with Mesopotamian peoples. Eventually, some of the more aggressive of

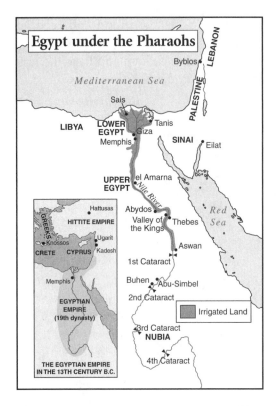

Egypt under the Pharaohs

Mediterranean Sea

Byblos

LEBANON

PALESTINE

Sais

LIBYA

LOWER EGYPT

Tanis

Giza

Memphis

SINAI

Eilat

UPPER EGYPT

el Amarna

Nile River

Hattusas

HITTITE EMPIRE

GREEKS

Knossos

CRETE

CYPRUS

Ugarit

Kadesh

Abydos

Valley of the Kings

Thebes

Red Sea

Aswan

1st Cataract

Memphis

Buhen

Abu-Simbel

2nd Cataract

EGYPTIAN EMPIRE (19th dynasty)

Irrigated Land

3rd Cataract

NUBIA

4th Cataract

THE EGYPTIAN EMPIRE IN THE 13TH CENTURY B.C.

BILDARCHIV PREUSSISCHER KULTURBESITZ/ART RESOURCE, NY

these peoples conquered Egypt and incorporated it into their empires. No direct contacts between the two peoples occurred in the third millennium B.C. But some modern scholars think that early Egyptian architects and artists may have been influenced by Mesopotamian models based on similarities between Egyptian buildings and structures depicted on Mesopotamian cylinder seals.

In the first half of the second millennium B.C., various ideas, including some important military ones, filtered into Egypt from Mesopotamia or from areas of Palestine controlled by Mesopotamian realms. These included the *khopesh* (a sickle-like sword), the composite bow, and horse-drawn chariots. In the seventeenth century B.C., Egypt was invaded by a people

called the Hyksos, who entered the country from southern Palestine. Some scholars think they were native to that region; others suspect that some of them may have been Hurrians, a people who had earlier settled in various parts of Mesopotamia and established the kingdom of Mitanni.

Beginning in about 1550 B.C., the start of what historians call Egypt's New Kingdom, the Egyptians began building an empire and expanded into Syria-Palestine. This brought them into more direct contact and often confrontation with the major Mesopotamian and other Near Eastern states of the era. These included Hatti, land of the Hittites; Mitanni; and Assyria. The chief bone of contention between Egypt and these other powers long remained control of Syria-Palestine. To counter the influence of the Hittites, the Egyptian pharaoh Amenhotep IV (or Akhenaten; reigned 1352–1336 B.C.) made a pact with the Mitannian king Tushratta. Amenhotep promised to send military aid if Mitanni was attacked by the Hittites, but he did not follow through with the aid when the Hittites invaded Mitanni and laid siege to its capital of Wassukanni. Not long after Amenhotep's reign, the Assyrians finished off Mitanni, leaving the Egyptians to contend with the Hittites on their own. Tensions escalated until the Egyptians under Ramesses II (reigned 1279–1213 B.C.) clashed with the Hittites at Kadesh in Syria in 1274 B.C. Ramesses later signed a treaty with Hatti, and relations between the two countries remained cordial until the Hittite realm collapsed circa 1200 B.C.

In the early centuries of the first millennium B.C., Egypt was weakened by civil strife and the division of the country into two parts ruled by separate and competing royal courts, one in the Nile delta region, the other in the area of Thebes. That left

Egypt more susceptible to invasion by big Mesopotamian powers. Egyptian rulers worried most about the rise of Assyria in this period. Sure enough, the Assyrian king Esarhaddon invaded Egypt twice—in 674 B.C. and again three years later. Esarhaddon's son, Ashurbanipal, also overran Egypt and laid waste to many of its towns and public buildings. Soon the Assyrian Empire was destroyed, but the Egyptians did not remain independent for long. In 525 B.C. another Mesopotamian ruler, Persia's King Cambyses, invaded Egypt. In the roughly two centuries that followed, the Egyptians rebelled against the Persians several times, but the latter eventually managed to regain control. It took the Macedonian Greek king Alexander III, later called "the Great," to oust the Persians from Egypt for good.

After Alexander's death, one of his generals, Ptolemy, seized control of Egypt and established the new Ptolemaic dynasty, which ruled until the country was annexed by Rome in 30 B.C. Even during the early years of the Ptolemaic period, Egypt still found itself in opposition to Mesopotamian rulers, in this case the Greek Seleucids, who had absorbed much of the old Persian Empire, including the plains of Mesopotamia.

SEE ALSO: Assyrian Empire; Battle of Kadesh; Cambyses; Greeks; Seleucid Empire

Ekallatum

A Mesopotamian city-state situated on the Tigris south of the city of Ashur. An early Assyrian king, Shamshi-Adad I (reigned ca. 1813–1781 B.C.) captured Ekallatum and installed one of his sons, Ishme-Dagan, as the city's ruler.

SEE ALSO: Assyrian Empire; Shamshi-Adad I

Elam

The area of southwestern Iran now called Khuzistan and long one of the leading kingdoms of the ancient Near East. In fact, Elam, centered in the hill country northwest of the Persian Gulf and adjoining the eastern Mesopotamian plains, was a thriving nation and a major player in Mesopotamian political history far longer than Sumeria, Assyria, or Babylonia. The site of Elam's principal city, Susa (originally Susiana), existed as a village by circa 4000 B.C. and may have been inhabited long before. Modern scholars divide the major portions of Elamite history into four periods: Proto-Elamite (ca. 3200–ca. 2700 B.C.), Old Elamite (ca. 2700–ca. 1600 B.C.), Middle Elamite (ca. 1500–ca. 1100 B.C.), and Neo-Elamite (ca. 1100–539 B.C.).

Not much is known about Elam in the Proto-Elamite period. The first major Elamite dynasty, centered in the city of Awan—the location of which is still unknown—arose at the start of the Old Elamite period. Some of the early Elamite rulers tried to extend their power into Sumeria, and surviving writings from the region mention wars between the Elamites and a number of Sumerian cities, notably Ur and Lagash. In about 2300 B.C. the Akkadians under King Sargon seized control of much of Elam and tried to impose the Akkadian language. Soon after Sargon's death, however, the Elamites regained their independence and reinstated their own language. Although it utilized cuneiform characters in its written form, it was completely different than Sumerian, Semitic, or any of the Indo-European languages used in Mesopotamia. Some scholars think Elamite may have been related to some of the languages spoken in southern India. In the 1700s B.C., during the last phase of the Old Elamite period, the Elamites fought Babylonia's King Hammurabi, who delivered them a decisive defeat.

The Elamites steadily recovered from the shock of their defeat, and beginning in 1500 B.C., marking the beginning of the Middle Elamite period, the Elamite kingdom enjoyed its greatest power, influence, and expansion. The rulers of the period belonged to three dynasties—the Kidinuid, the Igihalkid, and the Shutrukid—and generally took the title "king of Anshan and Susa." Elamite artisans became known far and wide for their skills in metalworking, weaving, and embroidery. Elamite traders roved across Mesopotamia to Palestine in the west and as far as India in the east. Some of the Shutrukid kings erected a new royal ceremonial center at Dur-Untash (now called Choga Zanbil), about 25 miles (40km) south of Susa. It featured a huge ziggurat, which is still well preserved and remains the largest human-made structure in Iran, along with palaces and shrines. Meanwhile, a sort of running feud developed between Elam and Kassite-controlled Babylonia. A number of wars and battles culminated with a major attack on Babylon in the early 1100s B.C. by the Elamite king Shutruk-Nahhunte I, in which the sacred statue of the god Marduk and the tablets of Hammurabi's law code were removed to Susa. The Elamites completely destroyed Kassite power in Babylon in about 1158 B.C. Very soon afterward, a new Babylonian king, Nebuchadnezzar I, raided Elam and took back the stolen items.

Very little is known about Elam in the next three centuries, making up more than half of the Neo-Elamite period, because of a lack of written records. Sometime in the 700s B.C., Elam became involved in the ongoing power struggles between Assyria

and Babylonia. When an Elamite ruler tried to help an Assyrian usurper steal the throne from King Ashurbanipal circa 645 B.C., that Assyrian monarch invaded Elam and devastated it, sacking Susa in the process. Although Assyrian power suddenly waned a few years later, the Medes, who had conquered Assyria, eliminated the last remaining remnants of Elamite independence. In 539 B.C. the Persians took control of the region of Elam. Susa was rebuilt under Persia's King Darius I and became one of the capitals of the Persian Empire. The Persians, whose homeland of Fars adjoined Elam, were highly influenced by Elamite culture and retained much of it, including the Elamite language, which the Persians used for administrative purposes.

SEE ALSO: Hammurabi; Sargon of Akkad; Shutruk-Nahhunte I; Susa

Enki

The Sumerian god of freshwaters and wisdom and one of the most important gods worshipped throughout Mesopotamia. Enki, called Ea by the Assyrians and the Babylonians, was sometimes referred to as the god of the deep or of deep waters, a reference to the Abzu, a freshwater ocean on which, according to Sumerian tradition, Earth floated; it was thought that Enki oversaw these underground waters. Myths also said that the Tigris and Euphrates rivers had flown out of Enki's body. For this reason, artists often depicted him with springs of water flowing from his shoulders or from a vase he held in his hands. The wisdom aspect of Enki's character derived from the belief that he possessed secret knowledge of magic and how the world worked, which also explains why he was the patron deity of craftsmen. Enki had shrines all across Mesopotamia, but his main one was in the Sumerian city of Eridu. His wife was the goddess Damgalnuna, associated with Ninhursag, and the divine couple figure prominently in the epic poem *Enki and Ninhursag*. Enki and Damgalnuna were said to be the parents of the deities Marduk, Enbililu, Asarluhi, and Nanse and the wise human Adapa.

SEE ALSO: Adapa; Damgalnuna; *Enki and Ninhursag*

Enki and Ninhursag

An ancient Mesopotamian myth and epic poem about the highly productive sexual relations between Enki, god of freshwaters and wisdom, and his wife, Damgalnuna, or Ninhursag, an earth goddess. Their union ultimately results in the creation of many other gods, as well as various plants. The setting is the primeval region of Dilmun, a paradise on which the biblical Garden of Eden may have been based. The primary theme of the work is fertility and the notion that it springs ultimately from the bodies and loins of selected divinities. Some aspects of the tale, including brazen incest among the gods, may seem strange and somewhat disconcerting to modern Western readers; to the ancient Mesopotamians, however, such ideas were perfectly acceptable within the context of divine creation.

As the story begins, Enki and Ninhursag fall in love, and she enjoys watching him create rivers to irrigate Dilmun and make it more lush and livable. The following passage captures the carefree, romantic mood of the lovers:

> Ninhursag rejoiced in Enki's mighty prowess and said to him: "Beloved, the powerful touch of your sweet waters, the essence of Mother Nammu that lies deep within you, transformed the land, my stony body. I feel the power of life throbbing within to be revealed throughout my very depths as I give joyously birth and sustenance to the marshes and reed-beds, that from now on will shelter fish, plant, beasts and all that breathes. Thus I call myself Nintur, the lady who gives birth, the Womb of the Damp Lands by the riverbanks." Enki replied: "Ninhursag, dearest Nintur, beloved, how can anyone quite compare to you? I cannot resist your wild, sweet ways, so lie with me one more time and fill my body, heart, soul and mind with endless delights! For me you will forever be my fierce Damgalnuna, my Great Spouse, passionate and very much loved!"

The product of Enki and Ninhursag's lovemaking is a daughter, Ninsar. Ninsar grows to maturity in just nine days. And while Ninhursag is away on a trip, Enki is taken with his daughter's beauty and impregnates her. She gives birth to a daughter named Ninkurra. Like her mother, Ninkurra grows up in a mere nine days; and as he did with Ninsar, Enki makes love to his new granddaughter. The result is Enki's great-granddaughter, Uttu. He has sex with her, too, but this time no child results. Instead, Ninhursag, who has found out what has happened in her absence, ensures that Enki's sperm produces eight varieties of plants. Enki eats the plants, which angers Ninhursag, and she leaves in a huff. But a clever fox convinces her to return. She makes love with Enki again, and the experience causes him pain in eight parts of his body. A new god is born for each of the eight pains, and Enki makes one of these deities the ruler of Dilmun.

SEE ALSO: Damgalnuna; Enki

Enkidu

In ancient Mesopotamian mythology and

A relief shows Enkidu and his friend Gilgamesh battling with Huwawa, a mythical monster. BILDARCHIV PREUSSUSCHER KULTURBESITZ/ART RESOURCE, NY

literature, one of the principal characters in the great *Epic of Gilgamesh*. Enkidu is a wild man roaming the woods near the city of Uruk. He was created by the goddess Aruru to counter the arrogance and abuse of power recently displayed by the young king of Uruk, Gilgamesh. Enkidu and Gilgamesh become friends. When Enkidu dies, Gilgamesh mourns him deeply and is inspired to search for the secret of immortality in order to save humanity from the scourge of death.

SEE ALSO: *Epic of Gilgamesh*

Enlil

In Mesopotamian mythology, the god who ruled Earth's domain, lorded over most of the other gods, and bestowed kingship on human beings. From Sumerian times on, Enlil (called Ellil by the Assyrians and the Babylonians), was one of the chief gods, along with An, who ruled the heavens, and

Enki, who controlled the freshwaters beneath Earth. Enlil began as a Sumerian weather god and retained this function when worshipped by later Mesopotamian peoples. Thus, he brought wind and rain and thereby ensured that agriculture was possible; at the same time, he could bring torrential rains and floods to punish people when he saw fit. Enlil married Ninlil, and they begat several divine beings, including the sun god, Utu (or Shamash); the moon god, Nanna (or Sin); and Inanna (or Ishtar), goddess of love and sexual passion.

Although Enlil was worshipped throughout Mesopotamia, his main shrine was in the city of Nippur in central Sumeria. To worshippers, he was the keeper of the Tablet of Destiny, on which the fate of the gods and humans was supposedly written. Thus, it was thought that he could "see all" and knew what would happen in the future. These powerful attributes, among others, are described in the following Sumerian hymn of praise to Enlil, composed in the mid-to-late third millennium B.C.:

> Enlil! his authority is far-reaching, his word is sublime and holy. His decisions are unalterable, he decides fates forever! His eyes scrutinize the entire world! When the honorable Enlil sits down in majesty on his sacred and sublime throne, when he exercises with perfection his power as Lord and King, spontaneously the other gods prostrate [lie flat on their faces] before him and obey his orders without protest! He is the great and powerful ruler who dominates Heaven and Earth, Who knows all and understands all!

Later, in Babylonia, the god Marduk came to wield many of the same powers Enlil had long wielded and to assume Enlil's general role of chief god.

SEE ALSO: *Defeat of Anzu, The*; Enki; Nippur; Utu

ephemerides

Important astronomical tables that noted the changing positions of the Sun, the Moon, and the planets Venus, Mars, Mercury, Saturn, and Jupiter in the sky. The chief *ephemerides* were those of the Babylonian astronomers Nabu-rimanni and Kidinnu, who flourished in the late first millennium B.C. The tables kept track of both daily and monthly positions of the roving heavenly bodies and helped observers predict how these bodies would move in the future.

SEE ALSO: astrology and astronomy

Epic of Creation

One of the major ancient Mesopotamian myths and epic poems, describing the primeval battle between cosmic order and chaos and celebrating the rise to power of Marduk, chief god of Babylonian civilization. The work was known as the *Enuma Elish* in ancient times, a title derived from its opening words, which translate as "when on high." The *Epic of Creation* was recited aloud in public each year on the fourth day of the Babylonian New Year's festival. It is based on an earlier Sumerian epic that tells basically the same story, only features Sumerian gods such as An, Enlil, and Nammu, while the Babylonian version stars the local Babylonian deities Anu, Marduk, and Tiamat. The Babylonian version, consisting of about a thousand lines on seven cuneiform tablets, dates from the twelfth century B.C. and was found in the library of the Assyrian king Ashurbanipal at Nineveh. The great Assyriologist George Smith published the first translation in 1876, and people immediately noted similarities between the *Enuma Elish* and the creation story in the Old Testament's book of Genesis. Indeed, although there are numerous differences between the two, the similarities are enough to prove that Genesis was at least partly based on the Babylonian myth. One of the main differences in the two works is that Genesis places a heavy emphasis on the creation of humans by God; whereas the *Enuma Elish* deals with human origins only in passing. This illustrates how the ancient Mesopotamians viewed humanity—as only an inferior species, completely dependent on and subject to the power and will of the gods.

The *Epic of Creation* begins with three gods—Apsu (a version of Enki), lord of subterranean waters; Mammu, Apsu's adviser; and Tiamat, goddess of saltwater.

Apsu and Tiamat mate and produce a deity named Anshar, who in turn gives rise to Anu, god of the sky. Many other gods are created, too, and they become so noisy that Apsu considers killing them all. But Ea, a son of Anu, objects to Apsu's murderous plan and overthrows Apsu. Ea then has a son—the glorious Marduk. Meanwhile, Tiamat wants to get revenge on Ea for his rebellion, so she creates several hideous monsters, led by Kingu, who is given control of the Tablet of Destiny, on which is written the fates of the gods and the humans.

Ea eventually finds out what Tiamat is up to and tells his grandfather Anshar about her army of frightening creatures:

> Sharp of tooth, unsparing of fang, with venom for blood she has filled their bodies. Roaring dragons she has clothed with terror, has crowned them with haloes, making them like gods, so that he who beholds them is overcome by terror. Their bodies rear up and none can withstand their attack. She has set up the Viper, the Dragon, and the Sphinx, the Great-Lion, the Mad-Dog, and the Scorpion-Man, mighty lion-demons, the Dragon-Fly, the Centaur—[all] bearing weapons that spare not, fearless in battle. (Enuma Elish 2.21–30)

Ea himself feels he lacks the strength to destroy these villains. So he calls on his son Marduk to fight Kingu and his evil minions. The gods still loyal to Ea then meet and give supreme authority to Marduk, making him king of the universe. After that Marduk dons his armor and goes out to face Tiamat, Kingu, and the monsters. The latter are terrified at the very sight of mighty Marduk and retreat, which greatly angers Tiamat. She charges forward and engages Marduk in single combat.

After slaying Tiamat, Marduk captures Kingu, takes from him the Tablet of Destiny, and finally slices Tiamat's lifeless body in half and uses the top half to create the sky. Marduk next places the stars in the sky, establishes the phases of the Moon, and sets the seasons in motion. After executing the evil Kingu, Marduk uses the creature's blood to fashion humanity. "I will take blood and fashion bone," Marduk says. "I will establish a savage. 'Man' shall be his name. Truly, savage-man I will create. He shall be charged with the service of the gods, that they might be at ease!" (Enuma Elish 6.5–9) After witnessing this ambitious bout of creation, the other gods applaud Marduk, sing his praises, and promise to be loyal to him.

SEE ALSO: Bible; Marduk; Smith, George

Epic of Gilgamesh

The most famous and influential of all the ancient Mesopotamian myths and epic poems, telling the story of the hero Gilgamesh, the tragic loss of his friend Enkidu, and Gilgamesh's quest to find the secret of eternal life. In the third millennium B.C. the Sumerians had several different minor epics about Gilgamesh and his exploits. Four of these—Gilgamesh and the Land of the Living; Gilgamesh and the Bull of Heaven; Gilgamesh, Enkidu, and the Netherworld; and The Death of Gilgamesh—were combined into one roughly three-thousand-line poem circa 2000 B.C. by an unknown Babylonian scribe. Only scattered fragments of this Babylonian version have survived. About 80 percent of a later Assyrian/Babylonian version was found in the ruins of King Ashurbanipal's library at Nineveh. Divided into twelve tablets, these have become the standard version used in modern translations.

A carved bust of Huwawa, in mythology the chief guardian of the cedar forest. ERICH LESSING/ART RESOURCE, NY

A Story Within a Story In the truest function of myth, the story explores certain fundamental truths about nature and humanity while capturing the imagination of and entertaining the reader/listener. Gilgamesh and Enkidu, heroes of epic proportions, represent humanity as a whole and illustrate major ideas or truths that lie at the core of the human experience. As in Greek tragedy, human worth and destiny are questioned, and the heroes must ultimately turn to the gods for answers. But will the gods reveal the deepest, darkest secrets of the universe to puny humans? In particular, will they allow humankind to share with them the gift of immortality? Gilgamesh's attempts to acquire that precious gift lead him to Utnapishtim, or Atrahasis, a wise man and hero who saved humanity by building a large boat that enabled him and a select few people to survive a great flood sent by the gods. In a story within the story, Utnapishtim tells the tale of the flood to Gilgamesh, who is sorely disappointed by what he finds at the end of his ambitious quest.

Adding extra depth and interest to the epic is the fact that the title character may have been a real Sumerian ruler. The Sumerian King List mentions a man named Gilgamesh who ruled Uruk, perhaps the oldest of the Sumerian cities, in about 2700 B.C. Nothing is known about his reign, but it stands to reason that his deeds were extraordinary enough to cause later generations to remember him as a heroic figure.

A Rival for an Arrogant King Gilgamesh is anything but a hero in the opening of the story, however. Though physically strong and a skilled, valiant warrior, he is an arrogant and somewhat disreputable person. One of his chief weaknesses is that no single woman can satisfy him; he shows his arrogance and disrespect for others by abducting young women off the streets or from the fields and forcing them to make love to him: "The people of Uruk did lament: 'Is this shepherd of Uruk's flocks protecting the women of other men by himself laying with them?'" (*Epic of Gilgamesh* 1.2)

Eventually, when the people of Uruk become completely fed up with Gilgamesh's bad behavior, the great mother goddess, Aruru, Uruk's patron deity, intervenes. The city's elders ask her to create a rival for Gilgamesh, someone who can match his great strength and fighting skill. Let that rival challenge Gilgamesh and teach him a lesson, they plead, so that their city might live in peace and security. Aruru agrees to do this for the people of her city. She exits her splendid temple, departs Uruk, and goes to the riverbank.

There, she takes some moist clay and fashions a primitive man, Enkidu, whose body is naked and covered by hair. At first Enkidu goes out into the fields with the cattle and chomps on grass and drinks from a watering hole with other wild beasts.

The arrival of a wild man in the countryside near Uruk does not go unnoticed, of course. Word soon reaches Gilgamesh. The curious king decides to bring Enkidu into the city and tries to civilize him. Gilgamesh sends a beautiful young woman out to lure the wild man into Uruk. In the months that follow, Enkidu lives in Gilgamesh's palace, where servants cut his hair, dress him in fine clothes, and teach him proper table manners. Fulfilling Gilgamesh's plan, the former wild man steadily becomes civilized. But as it turns out, Enkidu becomes even more civilized than the king. This is inevitable because Aruru has instilled in Enkidu a powerful sense of right and wrong and justice. One night Gilgamesh invites Enkidu to go for a walk through the city with him and some other companions. When the king is about to enter a house without being invited, Enkidu bars his way and says that Gilgamesh has no business barging into someone's private dwelling. Furious at being told what to do by one of his subjects, Gilgamesh jumps at Enkidu and a ferocious fight ensues:

> Each body on the other did meet with . . . heavy blows. Stray swings [of their fists] did the door break, did the door jamb break, and the walls did crack. On to the streets did the pair wrestle, wild heart to wild heart. Doors fell, corners [of walls] were broken off, stalls knocked down, and still on they fought. They fought to the city gates, which trembled with their blows. (*Epic of Gilgamesh* 2.3)

The fight ends in a draw, and Gilgamesh is astounded to find that his opponent can match him in strength, fighting skill, and courage. The two become instant, inseparable friends. And with Enkidu as a moral example, Gilgamesh suddenly sees how wrong his past behavior had been and becomes a model ruler, inspiring cheers and praises from his subjects.

A Heroic Mission The people of Uruk are not the only ones who notice the new friendship between Gilgamesh and Enkidu and the improvements in the king's behavior. Indeed, the gods heartily approve of Gilgamesh's transformation into a hero. Shamash, god of the Sun, suggests that the two friends embark on a heroic mission—to kill a monstrous giant named Huwawa (rendered Hawawa in some texts) who has been terrorizing the land of the Cedar Mountain, which lies far to the west of the Mesopotamian plains. Gilgamesh and Enkidu agree to do so and journey to the cedar forest that blankets the slopes of the Cedar Mountain. Somehow, Huwawa has heard that the heroes are coming and is prepared to fight them. There is a terrible battle in the forest; many trees come crashing to the ground, and the god Shamash unleashes a mighty wind on Huwawa.

> Hawawa fell to his knees . . . [and] cried out: "I, Hawawa, [will become] your servant. I will cut down the trees for you. Shamash has blown me down. . . . Gilgamesh you are king of Uruk. I, Hawawa can guard the wood for Uruk's gates." Enkidu with a mighty roar did say: "The demon lies. He must be killed." . . . Gilgamesh did take heart from Enkidu's words . . . [and] with his sword did slice into Hawawa's neck from the right. . . . So Enkidu with his ax did chop into Hawawa's neck from the left. And Hawawa's tongue spoke never more.

(Epic of Gilgamesh 5.4)

After killing the giant, Gilgamesh and Enkidu are congratulated and praised by the people who live in the region.

Gilgamesh's Grief The two human heroes soon face situations even more harrowing than the fight with Huwawa. Ishtar, goddess of love, tries to take Gilgamesh as a lover, and when he refuses she tries to punish him by causing a giant bull to attack the city of Uruk. Gilgamesh and Enkidu come to the rescue and slay the bull. However, this only makes Ishtar angrier. She proceeds to cast a lethal curse on Enkidu, which makes him fall ill and die. Completely devastated, Gilgamesh mourns and calls upon all things, living or nonliving, to mourn, too:

> Gilgamesh on [Enkidu] looked and fell to weeping like a child. May every wild beast mourn for Enkidu, both predator and prey. May the mountain, the hill, the valley, the very fertile earth mourn for Enkidu. May the trees, and the grass and moss on every rock mourn for Enkidu. May the water in the sea, in the lake, in the rivers, in the dew mourn for Enkidu. May old men, may young men who fought the Bull, may children and women of every kind mourn for Enkidu. (*Epic of Gilgamesh 8.2*)

Still grieving, Gilgamesh goes out into the desert and wanders for many weeks, all the while thinking about death and how it can take away a person forever when least expected. If the good and courageous Enkidu can die, Gilgamesh decides, then all people everywhere must someday face death. Yet there has to be some way to keep this terrible fate from coming to pass. Suddenly, Gilgamesh realizes what his greatest and most heroic mission must be—to hunt down the secret of immortality so that he might save humanity from the terrible fate of death. But where should he search for this highly coveted secret? There is a rumor that the gods have awarded eternal life to the former king of Shuruppak—Utnapishtim, whom some called Atrahasis, the "wise one." This old man dwells far to the west of Mesopotamia on an island in the great sea, now called the Mediterranean.

The Quest for Immortality Gilgamesh makes the long, difficult, and dangerous journey to Mt. Mashu, the home of the god Shamash. To get to the sea, which lies on the far side of the mountain, the man sees that he must pass through a tunnel that goes clear through the bowels of the mountain. However, the tunnel's entrance is guarded by an army of scary scorpion-men. These creatures tell Gilgamesh to go away, but he fearlessly strides right up to the leader of the scorpion-men and introduces himself. Gilgamesh explains the nature of his mission, which, if successful, will benefit the scorpion-men as much as it will humans. So the chief scorpion-man allows him to enter the tunnel. It is so dark inside that Gilgamesh has to feel his way through, running his hands along the slimy rock walls.

Reaching the far side of the mountain, Gilgamesh finds himself in a fragrant garden tended by Siduri, a goddess known for her wisdom. Siduri attempts to convince the man that he should turn around and go back to Uruk. The waters around the forbidden island are deadly, she tells him. But Gilgamesh refuses to listen to reason and persuades the goddess to take him to Utnapishtim's boatman. The boatman helps Gilgamesh into his vessel, and the two sail over the waves for more than a month.

Eventually they reached the fabled

island, and Gilgamesh enters Utnapishtim's mansion, which stands on a tall bluff overlooking the sea. Gilgamesh sees that Utnapishtim has a bald, wrinkled head and a long white beard. The old man is well aware of his visitor's identity and the reason for his journey. Utnapishtim wastes no time in telling Gilgamesh the story of how he became the only immortal human being. In the dim past, Utnapishtim recalls, he rose to the challenge when the human race was threatened by a flood sent by the gods. The god Ea had warned Utnapishtim about the coming deluge and told him to build a large boat. Put aboard it the seeds of all the living things on the face of the earth, Ea had ordered. Utnapishtim did as the god commanded, built the ark, and then loaded it:

> We loaded up the living things and then my gold, jewels, [and] every precious thing. We loaded up every household man, woman and child. We grasped sixty poles in our hands and pushed the boat towards the setting sun. We pushed then pulled the ungainly boat till solid in the river water did it lay. And in the sky the dark water heavy clouds did form as Ea had foretold. (*Epic of Gilgamesh* 11.2)

For six days and seven nights the wind howled, torrents of rain flooded down onto the land, and millions of people and animals drowned, Utnapishtim tells Gilgamesh. Finally, on the seventh day, the storm subsided and Utnapishtim looked out upon a devastated world. To reward him for saving the remnants of humanity, one of the gods gave him and his wife—but no other humans—the gift of immortality.

Because eternal life has been a special gift, Utnapishtim tells Gilgamesh, it is not possible for all people to acquire immortality. Yet Gilgamesh insists that the old man tell him where to find the "flower of youth," which will give eternal life to anyone who tastes it. The flower grows at the bottom of the sea, says Utnapishtim, at such a depth that no mortal person can hold his breath long enough to reach it. Gilgamesh's strength and courage is greater than that of most mortals, however, so he dives into the sea and brings up the magical flower.

After thanking Utnapishtim, Gilgamesh sets out for home, intent on bringing the gift of immortality to his people. Many months pass. When he is only a few miles from Uruk, he stops to rest beside a small lake. Unfortunately for humanity, Gilgamesh makes the mistake of putting the magical flower down for a moment; when he does, a snake snatches it and slithers away. No matter how hard he tries, Gilgamesh is never able to find the snake. The greatest human hero fails in his most difficult quest. Yet he learns an equally great truth, namely that only the gods are immortal, while human beings, no matter how powerful, good, or brave, must face death in the end.

SEE ALSO: *Atrahasis*; flood legends; literature

epic poetry

In ancient Mesopotamia, epic poetry consisted of literary works that were generally long, explored major myths or heroic legends, and dealt thematically with weighty issues such as the origins of the world and humanity, the relationship of humans with the gods, and the meaning of life. Modern scholars believe that such works were at first passed along orally, gaining length and detail until someone finally wrote them down. After that, they became part of the collective literature of the region and were copied and recopied over the centuries.

SEE ALSO: *Adapa; Atrahasis; Defeat of Anzu, The; Descent of Inanna, The; Enki and Ninhursag; Epic of Creation; Epic of Gilgamesh; Etana; Nergal and Ereshkigal; Ninurta and Agag;* and *Wrath of Erra, The*

epigraphy

The study of inscriptions—written words or messages cut or scratched into stone, metal, or other durable materials. Much of the information that scholars have collected about ancient Mesopotamia has come from inscriptions. The earliest Mesopotamian inscriptions were pictograms, simple drawings of objects, plants, or animals, which were inscribed on chips of clay as early as 9000 B.C., about eleven thousand years ago. At some undetermined date, people started to string the pictograms together on clay tablets in an effort to express ideas and messages. By about 3400 B.C. in Sumeria, the pictograms had begun to give way to wedge-shaped cuneiform characters. Cuneiform inscriptions on tablets and cylinder seals, as well as inscriptions in alphabetic scripts and carved bas-reliefs of people, animals, ships, and battles on tablets, seals, walls, rocks, and so on, continued to be used throughout Mesopotamia for the rest of antiquity. One of the most imposing and famous of all the Mesopotamian inscriptions are those carved by Persia's King Darius I on the Behistun Rock, east of Babylon. It features a huge carved scene showing the king and a group of captured enemies and a long message displayed in three different Mesopotamian languages. One of these languages was deciphered in the 1830s and the 1840s by pioneering Assyriologist Henry C. Rawlinson.

SEE ALSO: Behistun Rock; cuneiform; cylinder seals; Rawlinson, Henry C

Ereshkigal

In Mesopotamian mythology, the goddess who ruled the Land of No Return (the Underworld). Ereshkigal was the older sister of Inanna (or Ishtar), goddess of love and sexual passion, of whom Ereshkigal was very jealous because she was unable to find either love or sex. As told in the epic poem *The Descent of Inanna*, when Inanna tried to enter the Underworld, Ereshkigal slew her. Fortunately for Inanna, some other gods revived her. Sometime in the early second millennium B.C., the Old Babylonian period, a myth developed in which Ereshkigal agreed to share her authority over the Land of No Return with Nergal, a god associated with war and pestilence.

SEE ALSO: *Descent of Inanna, The;* Nergal; *Nergal and Ereshkigal*

Eridu

A very ancient Sumerian city located about 14 miles (22km) southwest of Ur and a few miles west of the ancient coastline of the Persian Gulf, which has since that time receded more than 100 miles (161km) to the southeast. The Sumerian scribes, who compiled lists of the kings of Sumeria, claimed Eridu (modern Abu Shahrein) was the oldest city in the world. Supposedly, the gods first granted kingship to a human being in Eridu; the first king, Alulim, ruled 28,800 years, and his successor, Alalgar, held the throne for 36,000 years. These impossibly long reigns aside, modern scholars are unsure whether Eridu was actually the first city in Mesopotamia. Some suggest that nearby Uruk was the first true city, with substantial urban housing, and that Eridu was mainly a ceremonial center. Eridu was sacred to Enki, god of freshwaters and wisdom.

Modern excavations of Eridu, particularly some brief digs in 1854 and more extensive ones by Iraqi archaeologists between 1946 and 1949, have revealed that Enki's shrine at Eridu was built and rebuilt many times over the centuries. In all, the diggers found at least eighteen levels of occupation, or build levels, the earliest dating back to circa 5500 to 5000 B.C. This primordial temple, the oldest known in the world, measured just 12 by 15 feet (3.6 by 4.5m); it was made of sun-dried clay bricks and featured a simple platformlike altar for performing sacrifices. Later, in about 2100 B.C., the excavators showed, a king of Ur erected a large ziggurat at Eridu. The remains of that structure still reach a height of 30 feet (9m). For reasons unknown, Eridu was largely abandoned sometime in the second millennium B.C.

SEE ALSO: Enki; king lists; Ur; ziggurat

Esarhaddon
(reigned ca. 680–669 B.C.)

One of the most accomplished of the kings of the Assyrian Empire and the first to successfully invade Egypt. Esarhaddon and his brothers assassinated their father, Sennacherib, in 681 B.C.; after a struggle among the royal usurpers, Esarhaddon, the youngest, seized the throne. The new king's first significant act was to rebuild the city of Babylon, including the temple area, which his father had demolished. This large-scale project continued throughout Esarhaddon's reign, and he bragged about the achievement in an inscription:

> I built [Babylon] anew, I enlarged [it], I raised [it] aloft, I made [it] magnificent. The images of the great gods I restored and had them replaced in

Assyrian soldiers lead a group of prisoners after King Esarhaddon' sack of the Phoenician city of Sidon. © BETTMANN/CORBIS

> their shrines to adorn them forever. ... The sons of Babylon ... their clientship I established anew.

Esarhaddon also concluded a treaty with the Medes, with whom the Assyrians had been at odds for some time. These excerpts from the treaty were discovered in the ruins of Kalhu (Nimrud):

> This is the treaty that Esarhaddon, king of the world, king of Assyria, son of Sennacherib ... concludes with Ramataia, prince of the city of Urakazabarna [in Media], with his sons, his grandsons, with all the people of [his] realm. ... In the presence of the [gods] Ashur, An, Enlil, Ea, [and] Sin. ... Assurbanipal, the [Assyrian] crown prince, son of your lord Esarhaddon ... will exercise the kingship and

sovereignty of Assyria over you [when I die]. You shall protect him in town and country. You shall fight and die for him. . . . You swear that you shall not be hostile to him. . . . You swear that you will not alter this treaty, that you will not consign it to the fire, or cast it into the water. . . . If you do so . . . let [the god] Sin . . . invest you with leprosy.

Not all of Esarhaddon's pursuits were as constructive as building projects and treaties, however. He showed that he was willing and able to employ the same aggressive foreign policy and harsh military methods as the Assyrian monarchs who had preceded him. When the Phoenician city of Sidon rebelled against his rule, for example, he crushed the revolt, beheaded the city's ruler, destroyed all the buildings, and deported the surviving inhabitants to Assyria. Esarhaddon also launched two invasions of Egypt, in 674 and 671 B.C. The Egyptians managed to keep the Assyrians more or less at bay in the first attack but they lacked the military resources to stop Esarhaddon's second and bigger offensive. He subdued the capital, Memphis, and most of the countryside, surrounding it in less than a month. Still, the proud and stubborn Egyptians continued to resist; only two years after the main Assyrian army left the country, they staged a large insurrection. Esarhaddon was on his way back to put down this revolt when he died unexpectedly. His son, Ashurbanipal, succeeded him on Assyria's throne.

SEE ALSO: Ashurbanipal; Egypt; Sennacherib

Eshnunna

An important Mesopotamian city situated on the Diyala River, a tributary of the Tigris, about 50 miles (80km) northeast of modern Baghdad. Eshnunna (modern Tell Asmar) was inhabited by Sumerians as early as the fourth millennium B.C. Its period of greatest prosperity and influence, however, was between about 2000 and 1800 B.C., when it was the capital of a small, independent kingdom called Warum. Eshnunna eventually fell to the armies of the Babylonian king Hammurabi in about 1763 B.C.

Many revealing archaeological discoveries have been made at the site of Eshnunna. The principal excavations took place in the 1930s, sponsored by Chicago's Oriental Institute and led by excavator Henri Frankfort. The diggers uncovered a temple that may have honored Abu, a vegetation god. Under the floor stones, Frankfort and archaeologist Seton Lloyd discovered a cache of gypsum and alabaster figurines depicting some gods and their human worshippers. The faces feature abnormally large, round eyes. The ruins of a palace were also found at Eshnunna. Buried beneath its floor the excavators found exquisite artifacts of silver and lapis lazuli, children's toys, and seal stones with engraved images of elephants and other motifs suggesting that Eshnunnian merchants traded with the people of faraway India.

SEE ALSO: Hammurabi; sculpture; Sumerians

Etana

A Mesopotamian myth and epic poem that follows the adventures of a human hero, Etana, who seeks to acquire from the gods the secret of having children. The story also features elements of animal fables similar to those of the legendary Greek writer Aesop. As the tale begins, the god Enlil selects Etana to be king of the city of Kish. But Etana is worried because he does not have a son who can become his royal successor when he dies. The king prays to the sun god, Shamash, and asks for a son. Shamash tells Etana to seek out an eagle who had lost its ability to fly when a snake, retaliating after the eagle devoured the snake's offspring, had bitten off its wings. The eagle and the snake had originally made a pact, promising not to eat each other's children, but the eagle had reneged on the deal, as told in the second of the four tablets bearing the story:

> He [the eagle] descended and ate up the serpent's children. In the evening of the same day, the serpent came [home]. . . . He [looked around and saw that] his children were [gone]. . . . The serpent [wept] before Shamash. . . . "My young are destroyed, while his [the eagle's] young are safe." When he had heard the serpent's lament, Shamash . . . said to him: "Set an ambush [for the eagle]. . . . When he comes . . . seize him by his wings, [and] cut off his wings. . . . Pluck him and cast him into a bottomless pit. Let him die there of hunger and thirst."

The snake had done as Shamash instructed.

Etana finds the eagle in the pit and carefully mends its broken wings. After a great deal of rehabilitation, the great bird is able to fly once more, and it carries Etana up into the sky, where the man hopes to find Inanna, goddess of sexual passion. Supposedly she possesses a magical plant that can make a person capable of having many children. The end of the story has been lost, but the Sumerian King List states that Etana did have an heir, so it seems likely that the epic originally concluded with Etana reaching heaven and obtaining the fertility plant.

SEE ALSO: Enlil; Inanna; Kish

Euphrates

Along with the Tigris, one of the two major rivers of Mesopotamia. Indeed, the term *Mesopotamia* means "the Land Between the Rivers."

SEE ALSO: Tigris and Euphrates; transportation and travel

exorcism

The process of driving a demon or evil spirit from a person's body. In ancient Mesopotamia it was widely believed that illness was caused by such demons and spirits. Doctors known as *ashpu* specialized in spiritual cures, including exorcisms. The exact manner in which exorcistic rituals were performed is uncertain, but evidence suggests that recitation of special magical spells was involved as well as cleansing rituals and special diets. The following seventh-century B.C. prescription, given to King Esarhaddon by one of his royal diviners, includes all of these methods:

> As to Your Majesty's writing to me concerning the ritual, they should perform the exorcistic ritual [to expel the sickness-causing demon] exactly as Your Majesty did several times already. As to . . . the formulas [spells] to be pronounced, the king should watch the formulas carefully. The king should not eat what has been cooked on fire; he should put on a loose robe of a nurse; the day after tomorrow he should go down to the river to wash himself. The king should perform these rituals . . . several times.

SEE ALSO: divination; doctors and medicine; religion

farming

Farming was the mainstay of the economies of the societies of the ancient world, including those of Mesopotamia and the regions that adjoined it. In fact, most modern scholars think that agriculture originated around 9000 B.C. in the Near East in the so-called Fertile Crescent, the hilly region arcing eastward from Syria across the northern rim of Mesopotamia to the Persian Gulf. The prevailing theory is that farming spread southward into the northern Mesopotamian plains during the next few millennia. By the seventh millennium (the 6000s) B.C., agriculture was well established on the alluvial plains of Sumeria, to the northwest of the Persian Gulf.

A Sumerian terracotta tablet, which describes in detail a harvest report. ERICH LESSING/ART RESOURCE, NY

Thereafter, and for the rest of antiquity, a majority of people in Mesopotamia participated in agriculture either directly as farmers and herders or indirectly as land surveyors and administrators, tax collectors, food merchants, slaves, and so forth. Most of the farmers lived in small huts, often clustered in small rural villages for mutual protection. Typically, the farmers walked or rode in wagons to the fields at dawn and returned to the villages at sunset. Some of the prehistoric farming villages eventually grew into cities surrounded by tall defensive walls. These became the nuclei of city-states, such as Uruk, Ur, and Nippur, each of which was surrounded by its own farmlands and small villages.

Chief Crops and Tools The chief crop raised by Mesopotamian farmers was barley, a salt-tolerant kind of wheat that grows well in Mesopotamia's somewhat salty soil. The barley kernels were used either in a thick porridge or were ground up into flour to make a flat bread that is still popular in most parts of the Near East. Barley grains were also used to make a tasty beer popular across Mesopotamia. Other common food crops included oil-rich sesame and linseed plants, lentils, peas, beans, garlic, cucumbers, lettuce, apples, figs, date palms, and grapes. To help shade ground crops such as beans and lettuce from the hot sun, Mesopotamian farmers developed a technique known as shade-tree gardening, in which these crops grew beneath the branches of palm and other fruit trees. Another important way to combat the heat and the evaporation it caused was to dig irrigation ditches, or canals, from nearby rivers. Such artificial waterways were employed particularly in southern Mesopotamia, where rainfall was less plentiful than it was in the northern plains.

The tools used by Mesopotamian farmers were made mainly of wood. These included a wooden plow drawn by oxen, metal-tipped axes mounted on wooden handles, and, for harvesting crops, wooden sickles with sharpened flint blades attached to them. At first a helper followed the plowman and tossed seeds into the furrows the plow had created. But sometime in the second millennium B.C. a plow with a vertical funnel attached was introduced. The farmer filled the funnel with seeds, which fell into the furrows as the oxen pulled the plow through the field, although the older method was still widely used. Such planting took place in the fall or early winter. Harvest time was generally in April or May. Through centuries of trial and error, farmers in different parts of the region learned to follow the yearly timetables for planting and harvesting that produced the most plentiful crop yields. Some of this valuable information was eventually written down. In the twentieth century, archaeologists pieced together a farmer's almanac from scattered fragments, one of which was found at Ur by noted Assyriologist Charles Leonard Woolley. The document dates to about 1700 B.C. Another famous scholar, Samuel N. Kramer, made the following translation:

> When you are about to take hold of your field (for cultivation), keep a sharp eye on the opening of the dikes, ditches, and mounds (so that) when you flood the field the water will not rise too high in it. When you have emptied it of water, watch the field's water-soaked ground that it stays virile [fertile] ground for you. Let shod oxen (that is, oxen whose hooves are protected in one way or another) trample it for you; (and) after having

its weeds ripped out (by them) (and) the field made level ground, dress it evenly with narrow axes weighing (no more than) two-thirds of a pound each. [Then] let the pickax wielder eradicate [the marks left by] the ox hooves for you (and) smooth them out. . . . When you are about to plow your field, keep your eye on the man who puts in the barley seed. Let him drop the grain uniformly two fingers deep (and) use up one shekel of barley for each *garush* [an area equal to about 27 square yards (22 sq. m)].

Even when the farmers followed the correct methods and schedules, their crops sometimes grew poorly or, on occasion, failed completely. Among the factors contributing to low crop yield were insect pests, including locusts; plant diseases; mice and other rodents; and, of course, drought. Pest control was limited to barrier methods: One way to keep rodents away from harvested crops was to store the crops in baked clay or stone silos.

Domesticated Animals Farmers also bred a number of domesticated animals. In addition to the oxen used for plowing, and eventually for eating, these included donkeys, cattle, sheep, goats, pigs, ducks, and geese. Perhaps the most numerous of these creatures were sheep, valuable as a food source as well as for their wool, which was used for making clothes. Flocks of sheep were typically tended by the farmer's children, although adult shepherds were not uncommon. Herds of sheep and goats were often moved from pasture to pasture, whereas cattle and pigs were usually kept in one area year-round. Cattle, sheep, and goats were also important for their milk and for their use as sacrificial animals. In addition to individual farmers and herders, large, wealthy organizations—notably temples and royal palaces—kept herds of animals.

SEE ALSO: Fertile Crescent; water supplies; Woolley, Charles Leonard

Fars

The modern and most commonly used name for Parsa (Persis to the Greeks), the ancient homeland of the Persians, located directly north of the Persian Gulf in southern Iran. Scholars are still uncertain about and divided on the issue of where the original Persian tribes came from and when they settled in Fars. It does seem fairly certain that a people known as the Parsua had established themselves in central Fars by the seventh century B.C. The early Persians were closely associated with the Medes, who inhabited the region of west-central Iran. It also appears that the early Persian inhabitants of Fars were culturally influenced by the Elamites, whose lands overlapped to some extent with the western part of Fars. In fact, Assyria's destruction of Elam in the 600s B.C. seems to have allowed the Persians to expand into western Fars and set the stage for the sudden and spectacular rise of the Persian Empire under Cyrus II in the following century.

SEE ALSO: Cyrus II; Medes; Persian Empire

Fertile Crescent

The earliest inhabited zone of the Near East—often referred to as the Cradle of Civilization—in which agriculture and the ancestors of the Mesopotamian peoples first developed. The term *Fertile Crescent* was coined in the early twentieth century by the noted University of Chicago scholar James Henry Breasted. The so-called crescent ran through the wide belt of

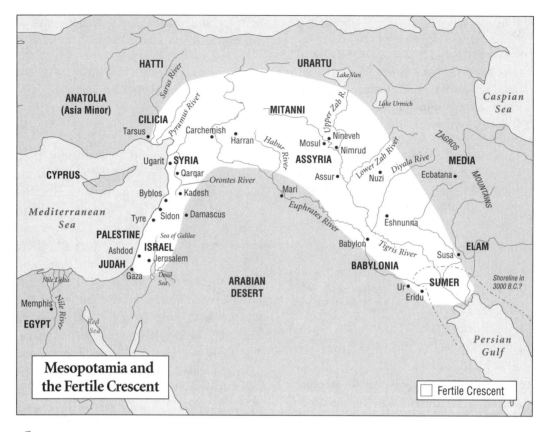

Mesopotamia and the Fertile Crescent

Fertile Crescent

GALE

foothills stretching from Palestine, northward through Syria, and across the northern rim of the Mesopotamian plains (modern Iraq) to the northeastern shores of the Persian Gulf. Exactly who the earliest inhabitants of this region were and where they came from remains uncertain. It seems clear, though, that they made the crucial transition from hunter-gatherer societies to agricultural ones, beginning perhaps in about 9000 B.C. or somewhat earlier. The crescent's low, hilly terrain provided the minimum of 12 inches (30cm) of rainfall a year needed to sustain rain-fed farming (as opposed to farming that requires supplemental irrigation). In the centuries that followed, the farmers of the region developed or domesticated the progenitors, or earliest forms, of the future staple crops of Mesopotamia, including barley, emmer wheat, flax, chick peas, and lentils. The inhabitants also raised domesticated animals, particularly cattle, sheep, and goats. Many of these people may have remained seminomadic at first, but by about 7000 B.C. permanent settlements were more common, among them villages with houses having stone foundations. Surviving examples include Jarmo (or Qalat Jarmo), situated not far north of the Sumerian plains, and Jericho (Tell-es-Sultan) in Palestine.

Over time successful agriculture and herding provided more food. This, in turn, stimulated population growth and increased the size and complexity of human settlements. By about 6000 to 5500 B.C. or so, the population of the upland regions of the Fertile Crescent had grown enough to stimulate expansion southward into the Tigris and Euphrates plains. Modern scholars call this pivotal era the Hassunah period; they refer to the early inhabitants of the northern alluvial plains, typified by the residents of the village of Choga Mami, the Hassunah culture. It is possible, though still unproven, that the great migration onto the plains was stimulated in part by the arrival in the crescent of refugees displaced by a huge natural disaster that struck northern Anatolia near the start of the Hassunah period.

SEE ALSO: Choga Mami; farming; flood legends

flood legends

Some scholars and other observers find it remarkable that the peoples of the ancient Near East had several legends of a great and disastrous flood, all featuring similar events and characters. A notable myth and epic poem, the *Atrahasis*, for example, tells how the god Enlil decided to rid the world of humans by flooding it. But Enki, god of freshwaters, warned a man named Atrahasis, whom the Sumerians called Ziusudra, and instructed him to build a large boat and thereby save a few people and animals. A very similar tale, in which the ark builder was called Utnapishtim, appears as a story within a story in the great Babylonian *Epic of Gilgamesh*. These tales are surely the bases of the story of Noah and the flood told in the biblical book of Genesis.

Archaeologists and other scholars who excavated in the Middle East in early modern times were divided about these legendary stories. Some assumed that they were mere fables, perhaps ancient allegories designed to teach moral lessons. Others felt confident that the flood legends

were based on a real disaster that had struck prehistoric Mesopotamia and had been remembered, in exaggerated form, in the later literature of the region. In this second group was the great British archaeologist Charles Leonard Woolley. While excavating at Ur in the 1920s, he discovered an 8-foot-thick (2m) layer of alluvial soil embedded between two layers of human habitation debris. The soil layer dated from the fourth millennium B.C., when cities were first starting to appear in Mesopotamia. Woolley concluded that a great flood had deposited the soil layer on top of one human settlement and that a new settlement had been built later atop the flood layer. Other excavators began looking for evidence of this same disaster at other Mesopotamian sites. Some did find flood-borne soil deposits similar to the one Woolley had uncovered at Ur. However, the evidence showed that most of these deposits had been laid down by an assortment of localized floods spanning almost two thousand years of Mesopotamian history. Thus, it appeared that there were many periodic local floods, rather than one huge, universal one, in the region in ancient times. Some scholars theorized that the "great" flood that had inspired the legends of Atrahasis and Noah might have been a major overflow of the Persian Gulf that had occurred eight to ten thousand years ago.

This is more or less the way the matter rested until 1998. In that year two Columbia University scientists, William Ryan and Walter Pitman, published their original and provocative thesis about the origins of the flood legends. They presented evidence showing that before the sixth millennium B.C. the Black Sea, located to the north of the Fertile Crescent, was a large freshwater lake. Today that sea is joined to the Aegean and Mediterranean seas via two straits, the Bosporus and the Dardanelles. In prehistoric times, however, the Bosporus was blocked by a massive earthen dam, and the lake's level was hundreds of feet lower than that of the seas beyond. In about 5600 B.C., Ryan and Pitman claimed, the dam burst and mighty torrents of water rushed into the Black Sea lake, flooding its shores for many miles inland. In all, up to 60,000 square miles (155,000 sq. km) may have been inundated in a matter of only a few weeks or months. "The soil and debris that had once damned the valley were quickly swept away," Ryan and Pitman later wrote,

> and the water, now several tens of feet deep, was a thundering flume twisting and churning with rubble. . . . Ten cubic miles of water poured through each day, two-hundred times what flows over Niagara Falls, enough to cover Manhattan Island each day to a depth of over half a mile. . . . It is hard to imagine the terror of those farmers, forced from their fields by an event they could not understand, a force of such incredible violence that it was as if the collected fury of all the gods was being hurled at them. (*Noah's Flood*, pp. 234–35)

Ryan and Pitman also pointed out that the date of this tremendous flood event roughly coincides with that of the initial migrations of peoples from the Fertile Crescent southward into Mesopotamia. Perhaps, they said, large numbers of refugees fleeing their lakeside villages and farms fled into the crescent, creating population pressures that induced some people to move onto the alluvial plains. The memories of the great flood would have been passed from generation to generation by word of mouth, until they were written down in the now-famous Mesopotamian and biblical texts. Though this scenario remains unproven and some scholars dispute it, many other researchers think there is enough circumstantial evidence to warrant continued research and discussion.

SEE ALSO: Bible; *Epic of Gilgamesh*; Fertile Crescent; Woolley, Charles Leonard

food and drink

The diversity of the diet of an ancient Mesopotamian depended in large part on his or her income and social class. In general, poorer folk, who made up the vast bulk of the population, consumed mainly food products made from cereals (grains), with a few vegetables and fruits to break the monotony. The poor only occasionally ate meat, which was expensive, with the exception of birds and other game, which people hunted in some areas. Well-to-do households—those of kings, courtiers, army officers, priests, and so on—could afford to eat meat on a regular basis. The wealthy could also afford full-time chefs and other kitchen staff to prepare varied, complex, highly appetizing mealtime fare.

Whether rich or poor, all Mesopotamians ate at least some bread and porridge, the chief products made from grains. The principal grain was barley, while emmer wheat and rye were available in smaller quantities. The simplest, cheapest kind of bread was flat and unleavened as well as coarse because it was made from crudely milled flour. Breads made from better-milled, finer flour were available but more expensive. Archaeologists found pieces of the latter variety of bread in the tomb of a queen of the Sumerian city of Ur. The more pricey breads sometimes had animal fat, milk, sesame oil, or fish oil added to the dough for extra consistency and taste or even mixed in fruit juices, fruit pieces, and/or cheese.

A fairly wide variety of vegetables and fruits were available, although some grew poorly or not at all in some areas, depending on the amount of rainfall. The most popular vegetables were onions and garlic, which people of all classes used in a wide variety of dishes. Also eaten when and where they were available were lentils, peas, cabbage, carrots, radishes, beets, and other vegetables. Common fruits included dates, from the date palm; apricots; apples; cherries; figs; plums; quinces; and nuts. The date palm also provided the most common food sweetener—date juice—as sugar was unknown and honey had to be imported (and was therefore expensive) because the Mesopotamians did not raise bees, as the Egyptians did.

For those who could afford to eat meat on a regular basis, mutton and pork were popular choices. Beef was more expensive and eaten less often because Mesopotamia had limited ranges of meadowland to support herds of cattle. Ducks, geese, game birds, gazelle, and deer were also consumed often in well-to-do households and on occasion in poorer ones. Because there was no refrigeration, raw meat did not keep long in Mesopotamia's hot climate and therefore had to be preserved; salting, drying in the sun, and smoking were the standard methods. Much more common in poorer homes—although wealthy people ate them too—were fish, of which more than fifty varieties were known in the region. Fish were also the source of a tasty sauce used to spice up many dishes. (Among the other common spices were mustard, coriander, cumin, marjoram, rosemary, and thyme.) Animals like sheep, goats, and cattle also provided dairy products, including milk, butter, and cheese.

As for drinks, by far the most popular in the region was beer, made mainly from barley. In fact, some scholars think that beer making may have predated bread making in Mesopotamia. There was even a goddess of beer brewing, Ninkasi, and an often-repeated proverb, with words to this effect: "He who does not know beer does not know what is good." More than seventy different kinds of beer were known, which varied considerably in strength, clarity, bitterness, sweetness, and so on. Wine was popular, too, but was much more expensive. Local grapes grew well only in the highlands, mostly in northern Assyria, prompting a common nickname for wine, "mountain beer"; so most wine had to be imported from Syria or Palestine and appeared mainly on the tables of the well-to-do.

Because of a fortunate archaeological find, a fair amount is known about ancient Mesopotamian cooking and recipes. The discovery consisted of part of a cookbook belonging to, and perhaps written by, the chief chef of the king of Mari, a city on the upper Euphrates. Dating to about 1700 B.C., the text contains thirty-five recipes and lists hundreds of individual ingredients. Among the dishes described are gazelle broth, lamb broth, and Assyrian stew. Each main dish was accompanied by several side dishes and garnishes, including fresh greens and vinegar, similar to a standard modern salad. The chef used sesame seed oil or linseed oil as a cooking medium. It also appears that kitchens in well-to-do households, like that of Mari's ruler, were staffed mainly by men, although women were likely the main cooks in poorer homes.

SEE ALSO: farming; hunting and fishing; trade

A carbonized representation of a wooden armrest that came from a chair decorated with shells. ERICH LESSING/ART RESOURCE, NY

furniture

Archaeological finds of the remains of ancient Mesopotamian furniture are relatively few, mainly because most furniture items were made of wood, reeds, and other highly perishable materials. Most of the evidence for such items comes from Assyrian artifacts of the first millennium B.C. It consists of some surviving pieces, many taken as booty from foreign cities sacked by Assyrian armies, along with depictions of furniture in art and written texts.

As is still true today, the kind and quality of one's furniture depended to a great degree on one's financial means. Poorer homes featured a minimal amount of furniture. Common items included stools and chairs made of palm wood, the cheapest, softest variety of wood in the region, and/or woven reeds. A poor home might feature one or two low wooden tables on which people had their meals or stacked personal belongings. Since no modern-style closets existed, other belongings were stored in reed baskets or in bins made of sun-dried clay, palm wood, or reeds. People of average means or less slept on reed mats or cheap mattresses, composed of cloth stuffed with palm fibers, on the floor.

In contrast, the well-to-do had beds not unlike modern ones—with wooden frames, mattresses stuffed with wool or goat's hair, linen sheets, and woolen blankets. The better households could also afford wooden chairs with leather upholstery, sometimes padded with felt. Excavators have found evidence of seventeen kinds of hardwood, most of which were imported from Syria, Palestine, and elsewhere. Many chairs were painted in bright colors. The most expensive chairs of all, used by royalty, were inlaid with copper, bronze, silver, or gold, some with bronze panels featuring carved figures of griffins and other mythical creatures as well as elaborately carved wooden or ivory finials decorating the arms. Some Assyrian art shows wealthy people lounging on sofas upholstered and decorated similarly to the chairs. Like the poor, the rich ate their meals on tables; however, the tables in better households were made of imported woods and were decorated with various metals. Linen tablecloths and napkins were used as well as cups, bowls, plates, and trays made of wood, pottery, or metals. Many well-to-do Mesopotamians stored their clothes and other belongings in handsomely carved wooden chests.

SEE ALSO: crafts and craftspeople; food and drink; houses

Gallas

In ancient Sumerian mythology, frightful demons who snatched people and dragged them down into the Underworld. The Gallas (or Galla) also did other tasks for the queen of that nether realm, Ereshkigal, and for the Annunaki, who in some ancient myths were judges of the dead who worked with Ereshkigal. In one celebrated instance, described in the epic poem *The Descent of Inanna*, the Gallas guarded the goddess Inanna after she had been allowed to return to the earth after visiting Ereshkigal's dark kingdom. The following passage from the poem provides a vivid picture of these creatures:

> As Inanna ascended from the underworld, The Gallas, the demons of the Underworld, clung to her side. The Gallas were demons who know no food, who know no drink, who eat no offerings, who drink no libations [liquid sacrificial offerings], who accept no gifts. They enjoy no lovemaking. They have no sweet children to kiss. They tear the wife from the husband's arms; they tear the child from the father's knees; they steal the bride from her marriage home. The demons clung to Inanna.

SEE ALSO: Annunaki; *Descent of Inanna, The*; Ereshkigal

Gandash
(flourished ca. 1730 B.C.)

According to one of the surviving Mesopotamian king lists, the first king of the Kassite dynasty established in eastern Mesopotamia sometime in the late eighteenth century B.C. A surviving first-millennium B.C. text contains what purports to be a copy of one of Gandash's inscriptions. In it he brags about conquering Babylon. Modern scholars think this was blatant propaganda since all available evidence shows that the Kassites did not seize power in Babylon until the early sixteenth century B.C. The prevailing view is that Gandash (or Gaddash) and his immediate royal successors occupied a region near Babylon, probably around the former Sumerian city of Sippar, and perhaps posed an ongoing threat to Babylon.

SEE ALSO: Babylon; Kassites; king lists

Gaza

In the second and first millennia B.C., an important Palestinian town located southwest of Jerusalem and northeast of the Egyptian town of Pelusium. Like Pelusium, Gaza was strategically situated in the coastal corridor connecting Egypt to lower Palestine. Thus, traders and armies passing from Mesopotamia and Palestine into Egypt, or vice versa, had to pass through or near Gaza. Archaeology shows that Gaza was inhabited as early as the fourth millennium B.C., but the first written mention of the town was in the war annals of the Egyptian pharaoh Thutmose III in about 1470 B.C. After Egyptian power in Palestine waned in the twelfth century B.C., those venerable biblical folk, the Hebrews and the Philistines, fought over Gaza, and the

Philistines held it for some time. In about 720 B.C. the Assyrian king Sargon II captured Gaza. One of his successors, Esarhaddon, also occupied the town on his way to conquer Egypt. In the late 600s B.C., after Assyria's fall, Babylonia's King Nebuchadnezzar II seized Gaza, and later the town's unfortunate inhabitants had to contend with still more foreign occupiers, notably the Persians and the Greeks. The Hebrews destroyed Gaza circa 96 B.C., but the Romans rebuilt it a few decades later.

SEE ALSO: Egypt; Esarhaddon; Palestine

Geshtinanna

A minor Sumerian goddess associated with vineyards and sheep. In mythology, she was also the sister of Dumuzi, male consort of the love goddess Inanna. After Dumuzi was consigned to spend half of each year in the Land of No Return (the Underworld), in rotation with Inanna, Geshtinanna was also forced to alternate with her brother and spend half of each year beneath the ground. It was said that while in the Underworld Geshtinanna married the god Ningishzida, grandson of Ereshkigal, ruler of the Underworld, and worked as a scribe.

SEE ALSO: Descent of Inanna, The; Ereshkigal; Inanna

Gilgamesh

In ancient Mesopotamian culture and literature, the greatest and most popular human hero, who went on a quest to find the secret of immortality and thereby save humanity from the fate of death.

SEE ALSO: Epic of Gilgamesh

Girsu

In the third millennium B.C., one of the more important Sumerian cities, located

A high relief depicts Gilgamesh, a legendary hero and king of Uruk, taming a lion. ERICH LESSING/ART RESOURCE, NY

on the plain stretching between the Tigris and Euphrates rivers in southern Mesopotamia. Initially, modern scholars thought that Girsu (modern Tello) and Lagash were one and the same. However, it soon became clear that Girsu was situated several miles south of Lagash. It is possible that at first Girsu may have served as an administrative center for Lagash, but later Girsu became mainly a religious center, with a major temple of Ningirsu ("Lord of Girsu"), a god associated with farming and the plow. Principal excavation of Girsu was undertaken by French archaeologists between 1877 and 1897. They found numerous important artifacts, including some forty thousand cuneiform tablets; the famous Stele of the Vultures, depicting a Sumerian battle formation; and a statue of Gudea, a noted king of Lagash.

SEE ALSO: Lagash; Ningirsu; Stele of the Vultures

glass

Mesopotamian artisans began making glass objects sometime in the third millennium B.C. This is evident from the discovery of small lumps of glass scraps or debris in the ruins of ancient artisans' workshops. Whatever glass products these workers made have long since disappeared, as the earliest surviving Mesopotamian glass artifacts date from the period of 1600 to 1500 B.C. In the centuries that followed, typical glass objects included bottles, especially perfume bottles; vases; jewelry, including pendants and amulets; small figurines; and the pupils of the eyes of stone statues to give these sculptures a more lifelike appearance. When much of the western Near East underwent devastation due to causes still not fully understood around 1200 B.C., many of the markets for Mesopotamian glass dried up; so glassmaking in the region declined. It revived in the eighth century B.C., however, and remained a major craft industry for many centuries to come. Glassmaking was also highly respected among the crafts and, for reasons that are unclear, required practitioners to employ religious rituals as well as skill and experience. Tablets found in the famous library of the Assyrian king Ashurbanipal describe such rituals as a regular part of the art of glassmaking. The glassmaker was obliged to sacrifice a sheep before heating the glass, for instance, and to make sure that he and all of his assistants were ritually clean.

There were three kinds of Mesopotamian glass—opaque, translucent, and clear, which began to be made circa 700 B.C. The chief ingredients were silicates, particularly quartzite sand; plant ashes; and lime. When combined and heated to high temperatures in a fire or kiln, these produced molten (liquid) glass, which could be cut and/or molded in various ways before it cooled and solidified. In fact, molding, in which the molten glass was poured into wooden molds, was one of the chief and simplest glassmaking techniques in Mesopotamia and in other parts of the Near East. Another common method, core forming, utilized preformed pottery objects, or cores. Using a metal handling rod, the glassmaker dipped a core into some molten glass, causing a layer of glass to stick to the core. Next, he allowed the glass to cool, a process known as annealing. Finally, he stuck pointed instruments through an opening in the glass and broke up and removed the core material, leaving behind the finished glass artifact. A third and more difficult method, cold cutting, involved making a mass of molten glass, then cutting off lumps of it. The artisan carefully molded each lump into the shape desired and allowed it to cool.

Most glass artifacts made in Mesopotamia remained fairly expensive until the first century B.C., when a glassmaker in Syria invented the technique of glassblowing. Glassblowing allowed artisans to make glass objects faster and more cheaply as well as of higher quality. Thus, by the end of that century even low-income Mesopotamians could afford to own several glass items.

SEE ALSO: crafts and craftspeople; jewelry

Gordon, Cyrus H.
(1908–2001)

A prominent American scholar of Near Eastern cultures and a renowned expert on ancient languages. Born in Philadelphia, Gordon early showed a talent for learning languages and became fluent in Hebrew, Greek, and Latin as a child. He then added Old Persian, Sanskrit, and others to his repertoire while earning degrees at the University of Pennsylvania. Wasting no time following his graduation, Gordon headed for Mesopotamia, and in the early 1930s he worked with the great archaeologist Charles Leonard Woolley, who was directing the pivotal excavations at the ancient Sumerian site of Ur. Not long afterward, Gordon assisted another giant of archaeology, Flinders Petrie, at a site in Palestine. During World War II Gordon enlisted and, because of his expertise in languages, served with distinction as a cryptologist for the U.S. military. The German Nazis sometimes coded their secret messages in Arabic and ancient Persian, and Gordon was instrumental in deciphering them. Also during the war, he was stationed for a while in Iraq, where he learned still more ancient languages and toured the leading archaeological sites. Following the war Gordon returned to the United States and taught at various universities, including Brandeis University and New York University. He also greatly advanced modern scholarship by turning out numerous books. These covered, among other subjects, the science of archaeology, Mesopotamian cuneiform writing, the Bible and its connections with ancient Near Eastern history, the Hebrew language, Hittite culture, and Sumerian culture. Especially important were Gordon's studies of and writings about Ugaritic, the lan-guage of the important ancient Syrian port of Ugarit.

SEE ALSO: Petrie, Flinders; Ugarit; Woolley, Charles Leonard

government

For the most part, government in the city-states, nations, and empires of ancient Mesopotamia was defined and shaped by the political power of selected individuals and groups. And much of that political power was based on landownership. Those who owned the most land—kings and priests, who ran large temple estates—were the richest, most influential, and most powerful and therefore had the most say in governing average people.

Kings existed in Mesopotamia from very early times, as revealed by the surviving king lists. However, it remains unknown when the first kings appeared and whether they were the first governmental officials. It may be revealing that one of the Sumerian epic poems, *Gilgamesh and Agga*, mentions a local government with three branches, so to speak: a chief executive, the king; a sort of senate, consisting of a group of elders who advised the king; and another legislative branch in the form of an assembly of warriors, who approved or disapproved of the king's policies. It is unknown if such separation of powers existed in any of the real Sumerian city-states. It may be only a literary fiction. In any case, as larger nations and empires emerged in Mesopotamia, absolute monarchies became the rule.

Still, it was impossible for one person

A wall relief depicts a Median officer with two Persian guards before King Darius the Great. © GIANNI DAGLI ORTI/CORBIS

to handle all the administrative, military, and religious duties of the government of a major state. So the king had to delegate much of his authority, even if he had the final say in affairs of state. High priests helped the king with his religious duties, advised him on certain matters, and ran the temple estates on which many Mesopotamians worked. The king also appointed generals and other military officers to run the army, although many Assyrian, Babylonian, and Persian monarchs led the army themselves on many of their campaigns.

When an empire had many provinces, as the Assyrian and Persian realms did, the king also chose governors, usually from his leading nobles, to run those provinces. The Assyrians were the first to institute a large-scale system of provinces with governors, royal inspectors who traveled around and checked up on the governors, garrisons of soldiers installed in each province to enforce the king's authority, and royal roads on which the king's inspectors and soldiers journeyed to and from the provinces. The Medes and the Persians adopted this same sort of administrative system for their own empires, calling the governors satraps. When the Macedonian king Alexander the Great conquered Persia, he also kept the system in place, although he reduced the powers of the satraps. The Seleucid monarchs who controlled Mesopotamia after Alexander used the satrap system, too. A satrap in the Seleucid Empire was called an *assirategus*. As in other Near Eastern monarchies ruled by Greeks in the late first millennium B.C., the Seleucids made no attempt to install democracy, the enlightened form of government pioneered on the Greek mainland in the fifth and fourth centuries B.C.

SEE ALSO: Alexander III ("the Great"); king lists; kingship; satrapy

Greeks

In the fourth millennium B.C., when the first large-scale cities appeared on the Mesopotamian plains, the inhabitants of mainland Greece still used crude stone and copper weapons and tools. Modern scholars think that knowledge of bronze—a tougher metal made by combining copper and tin—filtered into the Greek sphere from the higher civilizations of the Near East around 3000 B.C. But there was still no direct contact between Greece and Mesopotamia. In fact, Greek-speakers did not arrive in mainland Greece until circa 2100 to 2000 B.C., and they remained in a culturally primitive state for several more centuries. The non-Greek-speaking Minoans, who inhabited Crete and some of the Aegean Islands, developed a high civilization between 2000 and 1400 B.C.; and they evidently did have vigorous trade contacts with Mesopotamia, via middlemen in Anatolia and Syria-Palestine. The mainland Greeks, whom scholars call the Mycenaeans, conquered the Minoans circa 1400 B.C. and took over their trade routes. Then the Bronze Age civilizations of Greece, Anatolia, Syria, and other nearby regions underwent widespread destruction in the period of 1200 to 1100 B.C. and there were

no direct contacts between Greece and Mesopotamia in the dark age that followed.

Eventually sophisticated and prosperous city-states appeared across Greece, which rose from its state of cultural backwardness between 800 and 500 B.C. The rise of the classical Greeks coincided with major political changes in Mesopotamia. By the mid-530s B.C. the Assyrian Empire had been swept away, and the Babylonians and the Medes had been conquered by the Persians under King Cyrus II. Cyrus swiftly created the largest empire the world had yet seen. And his western expansion and conquest of Lydia in western Anatolia gave him control of the prosperous Greek cities that had recently grown up along Anatolia's Aegean coast. This marked the first direct political, economic, and cultural contact between Greeks and Mesopotamians. In the years that followed, there were numerous intermarriages between Anatolian Greeks and Persians, and as many as three hundred Greeks became permanent members of the Achaemenid Persian court in Persepolis, located north of the Persian Gulf. Cyrus's operatives recognized the talents of Greek sculptors and other artisans and brought many of them to Persepolis and Susa to work on Persian palaces and other public buildings. At the same time, extensive trade developed between the Anatolian Greeks and many Persian-controlled Mesopotamian cities.

Persian-Greek Hostility Persia's relationship with the Greeks was not destined to be a congenial one, however. Several factors contributed to tensions between the two. The Anatolian Greeks, for one thing, wanted to be independent, like the mainland Greeks, and chafed under Persian rule. Then, some of Cyrus's successors made the mistake of trying to expand their empire into Europe; this put them on a collision course with the freedom-loving mainland Greeks, who had recently developed a devastating new military system based on heavily armored infantry soldiers called hoplites. King Darius I conquered Thrace, the region lying directly north of the Aegean Sea, in the late 500s B.C. He also decisively crushed a rebellion of the Anatolian Greeks between 499 and 494 B.C. During the revolt, two mainland Greek cities, Athens and Eretria, sent ships and troops to help the Anatolian Greeks, which greatly angered Darius. In 490 B.C. he sent another army, which sacked Eretria but was soundly defeated by the Athenians on the plain of Marathon. The Persian monarch decided to raise a larger army and conquer all of Greece and use it as a base from which to invade the rest of Europe. But Darius died in 486 B.C., and the great invasion was launched by his son, Xerxes, in 480. Much to the surprise of the Persians and other Mesopotamians who fought in Xerxes' army, the considerably smaller Greek armies smashed the intruders in a series of epic battles, thereby saving Western civilization from an almost certain future of Eastern domination.

In the decades that followed, relations between Persia and Greece remained hostile. There was a brief period of more cordial relations after King Artaxerxes I made a treaty with the Greeks—the Peace of Callias—in 449 B.C. But the Persians never gave up on achieving whatever revenge they could against the Greeks, particularly the Athenians. During the disastrous Peloponnesian War (431–404 B.C.), in which Athens and Sparta battled for supremacy in Greece, the Persians ended up helping the Spartans build a fleet of warships. These proved instrumental in Athens's defeat.

Greek Conquest of Mesopotamia Soon after the end of the great war, large numbers of Greeks saw the plains of Mesopotamia for the first time. An army of Greek mercenaries fought for the Persian prince known as Cyrus the Younger, who wanted to dethrone his brother, King Artaxerxes II. In 401 B.C., at Cunaxa, not far from Babylon, Artaxerxes was victorious. The Greeks, who became known as the Ten Thousand, were forced to fight their way across Mesopotamia and through Armenia to the Black Sea. Their adventure and survival, which were recorded in graphic detail by the Greek writer Xenophon in his *Anabasis*, made it clear to the next generation of Greeks that Mesopotamia and the rest of the Persian Empire were vulnerable. Indeed, after Macedonia's King Philip II conquered the major Greek city-states in the 330s B.C., he began planning a major invasion of Persia. Philip was suddenly assassinated, however, and it was his son, Alexander III (later called "the Great"), who led an army into Anatolia in 334 B.C. Alexander defeated King Darius III at Issus in northern Syria and at Gaugamela near Arbil in Assyria, and he quickly brought the Persian Empire to its knees.

Alexander ushered in an era of almost two centuries in which Mesopotamia was ruled by Greeks. Alexander intended to Hellenize, or infuse Greek culture into, the region to whatever degree was practical. To this end, he made Greek the official language of administration and business and ordered ten thousand of his men to marry Persian and other Mesopotamian women. Greek-style temples, markets, gymnasia, theaters, and entire cities sprang up across Mesopotamia. Even after Alexander died unexpectedly at age thirty-three in 323 B.C., his plans for Hellenizing the Near East were taken up by some of the Successors, his generals who fought over control of his empire. One of these men, Seleucus, founded the Seleucid Empire, which encompassed all of Mesopotamia and parts of Anatolia and Syria-Palestine. Perhaps Mesopotamia would have been slowly transformed into a Greek cultural sphere, as Alexander had hoped, if the Seleucid monarchs had had more time. But their realm was short-lived. Caught between two aggressive peoples—the Romans in the west and the Parthians in the east—the Seleucids rapidly lost ground; as their empire shrank, Greek culture in Mesopotamia steadily declined and eventually all but disappeared.

SEE ALSO: Alexander III ("the Great"); *Anabasis*; battles of Cunaxa and Gaugamela; Persian Empire; Seleucid Empire

grooming

Representations of ancient Mesopotamian men and women in paintings, sculptures, statues, figurines, and cylinder seals show that they were very well groomed and spent a great deal of time making their hair and beards look stylish. However, the vast majority of people pictured in such art were members of the upper classes. They had money, leisure time, and servants. All of these probably allowed them to engage in elaborate, sometimes expensive grooming activities that may not have been practical for people in the lower, working classes. It can likely be safely assumed that average people did adopt the same hair and beard styles, as well as clothing styles, of the well-to-do. But poorer folk could not afford expensive fabrics and jewelry and probably did not

have the time to fuss with their hair and beards to the degree that wealthy people did.

As for hairstyles, artistic renderings show that in the third millennium B.C. Mesopotamian women grew their hair long. But they usually braided and plaited it on top of the head and held it in place with scarves or nets. Well-to-do women also frequently wore jewelry items in their hair, wedging them between the plaited locks. Excavations of graves in the royal cemetery at Ur dating to circa 2600 B.C. brought to light evidence of women with gold leaves, lapis lazuli beads, silver hairpins, and blue lapis lazuli flowers in their hair. Meanwhile, men were either bald or had long hair and long beards. The latter group carefully waved and groomed their hair and beards. These same styles carried over into the second millennium B.C., as Assyrian reliefs from that period show men with elaborately curled beards and mustaches. There is some evidence that men (again, probably mainly upper-class men) dyed their hair when it started to turn gray.

Unfortunately, the surviving evidence for the use of cosmetics in ancient Mesopotamia is scarce. But enough remnants of cosmetic and grooming items have been found to show that women, at least upper-class women, did use them on a regular basis. For example, archaeologists discovered some women's makeup kits in the cemetery at Ur. Included were seashells containing blue, green, yellow, red, and black eye makeup, which was made from antimony paste. A woman applied it with a wooden or ivory pin. Also found in the graves, as well as in the ruins of a few Mesopotamian houses, were wooden and ivory combs, metal tweezers, and hand mirrors made of highly polished copper, bronze, and silver.

Mesopotamian women, and possibly men, too, also used perfume. Perfumes were made by soaking fragrant-smelling plants in water for several days to extract their essence and then mixing that essence with sesame oil or other plant oils. Evidence shows that aromatic resins taken from imported cypress, cedar, and myrtle trees were used to make perfumes in Mari, located on the upper Euphrates.

SEE ALSO: bathing; clothing; women

Grotefend, Georg F. (1775–1853)

A noted German philologist (language expert) who made the initial, crucial breakthroughs in deciphering Mesopotamian cuneiform writing. Grotefend taught in German universities for several decades and wrote a number of books about early Italian languages, notably Latin, Umbrian, and Oscan. But his most celebrated achievement came when he tackled the then-mysterious wedge-shaped cuneiform characters from ancient Mesopotamia. Between 1800 and 1802 Grotefend studied the carvings on the Behistun Rock, lying in the plain east of Babylon. He determined first that the cuneiform writing on the cliff face was in three different languages, one of them Old Persian. He also showed that Old Persian cuneiform is alphabetic, with forty characters, and that it is read from left to right. These discoveries paved the way for later scholars, including Henry C. Rawlinson, to make full translations of the cuneiform inscriptions at Behistun and elsewhere.

SEE ALSO: Behistun Rock; cuneiform; languages

This statue of Gudea, king of Lagash, dates from 2120 B.C. ERICH LESSING/ART RESOURCE, NY

Gudea (reigned ca. 2141–2122 B.C.)

A noted ruler of the Sumerian city of Lagash. Gudea reigned during an unstable period in which a hill people known as the Guti were raiding large portions of Sumeria. Evidence suggests that he made some sort of alliance with the intruders and even helped them attack other Mesopotamian cities. Gudea also raided Elam, lying northeast of Lagash. His most lasting accomplishments, however, were in domestic affairs, especially the arts and architecture. Gudea erected more than a dozen temples, including a major one in the nearby ceremonial center of Girsu. To show his devotion to the gods, he placed statues of himself in many of the temples. Some of the surviving ones show him holding what look like architectural blueprints on his lap, perhaps to advertise that he was a great builder. Gudea also left behind numerous long inscriptions in well-phrased, classical Sumerian.

SEE ALSO: Girsu; Lagash; sculpture

Gula

The Babylonian goddess of healing and the patron deity of doctors, who was in essence the Babylonian version of an older Sumerian goddess, Ninisina. Gula's main temple was at Isin, a few miles southeast of Uruk. Her sacred animal was the dog, and worshippers placed pottery dogs on the altars of her shrines. Various male gods, including Ninurta, originally an agricultural deity and later a war god, were said to be Gula's husband. In mythology, both of her children, Damua and Ninazu, became healers, too.

SEE ALSO: doctors and medicine; Isin; Ninurta

Guti

A tribal, pastoral people who originally inhabited the northeastern reaches of the Zagros Mountains, a region called Gutium in ancient times. For an undetermined period, the Guti (or Gutians) existed on the periphery of Mesopotamian culture and the Sumerians dismissed them as uncouth mountain men and savages. In about 2230 B.C., however, the Guti began raiding the cities of northern Mesopotamia and eventually managed to capture Akkad and put an end to the Akkadian dynasty, which had earlier produced the successful conqueror Sargon. The invaders continued to attack nearby cities. Yet they seem never to have

formed a centralized Gutian nation; instead, they formed shifting, temporary alliances with various Sumerian city-states, including Lagash, while trying to adopt Mesopotamian culture and manners. Finally, in about 2120 B.C., a coalition of local rulers led by the strong king of the city of Uruk, Utuhegal, decisively defeated the Guti, putting an end to the period of disorder and decline they had created. The Guti were long remembered in the region, as they became archetypical villains in literature.

SEE ALSO: Gudea; Lagash; Utuhegal

Guzana

A small but influential city that existed on the fringes of northern Mesopotamia, situated near the modern border between Syria and Turkey. The site of Guzana (modern Tell Halaf) was first inhabited in the sixth millennium B.C. at about the time that people were moving southward from the Fertile Crescent onto the Mesopotamian plains. Modern scholars call the people of the town and those who were culturally similar to them in northwestern Mesopotamia the Halaf culture. They used a distinctive form of pottery, called Halaf-ware, that spread as far away as southern Iran. In the second millennium B.C. Guzana briefly became the capital of a small kingdom established by the Aramaeans, which was soon absorbed by the expanding Assyrian Empire. The site was first investigated by German engineer Max von Oppenheim between 1911 and 1913. Further excavations were conducted by a French team from 1927 to 1929. In addition to a good deal of Halaf-ware, the diggers found a small palace featuring sculpted scenes of war, hunting, and mythical creatures, including a scorpion-man, perhaps inspired by a character in the *Epic of Gilgamesh*.

SEE ALSO: Assyrian Empire; Fertile Crescent; Halaf culture

Halaf culture

The name given by modern scholars to the early inhabitants of the town of Guzana, in northeastern Syria, and other towns in nearby northern Mesopotamia. Halaf culture is dated variously from circa 6000 to 5000 B.C. to circa 5500 to 4500 B.C. Accordingly, the era is referred to as the Halaf period, and the distinctive pottery made by its artisans is often called Halaf-ware. These early ceramics, which seem to have originated in Guzana, featured geometric shapes and patterns handsomely painted in black, red, and white. They were made from a local type of clay that was distinct from other Mesopotamian clays. Examples of Halaf-ware have been found at nearby Carchemish and Tepe Gawra and in ancient ruins stretching across northern Mesopotamia and southern Iran, suggesting that fairly extensive trade routes had been established in the region by this period. Other distinctive aspects of Halaf culture were stamp seals and amulets bearing the same geometric designs as those on the pottery; pottery figurines of women, probably goddesses; and clusters of small, round, domed structures (dubbed *tholoi* by scholars) made from boulders, mud bricks, and straw. Some of the latter may have been houses, but others were likely places for religious worship. The people of the Halaf culture practiced "dry" farming, which depended on rainfall rather than irrigation, and raised cattle, sheep, and goats.

SEE ALSO: pottery; Tepe Gawra; Ubaidian culture

Hammurabi
(reigned ca. 1792–1750 B.C.)

An important early king of Babylon who created the first Babylonian empire and became even more famous for issuing an extensive law code. Hammurabi was the sixth king of an Amorite dynasty that had been established in Babylon in about 1850 B.C. At first he controlled only that city and a few others in the immediate area, including Kish, Sippar, and Borsippa. The early years of his reign were largely peaceful, as he concentrated on strengthening Babylon's administrative institutions, building local irrigation canals, and forging alliances with neighboring city-states, including Mari, Larsa, and Eshnunna.

It is unknown whether these agreements were part of a long-standing secret plan to put these states off guard or whether Hammurabi simply grew more aggressive and ambitious as he aged. In any case, in the late 1760s B.C. he suddenly initiated a policy of military and imperial expansion. One by one, he captured and absorbed neighboring Mesopotamian cities, first Larsa, which gave him control of most of southern Mesopotamia, then Eshnunna and Mari, which was largely leveled circa 1759 B.C. Not long afterward, Hammurabi attacked and seized Ashur, Nineveh, and the other Assyrian strongholds. These conquests made him the first ruler since Sargon of Akkad to rule over all of

Mesopotamia.

Hammurabi was not only an ardent imperialist and skilled military commander. He was also a highly capable administrator who took an interest in a wide range of domestic, economic, and other affairs. During his reign trade flourished throughout Mesopotamia, which made Babylon wealthy and allowed the king to erect many new religious shrines and canals. In addition, he ordered the old Sumerian creation myths to be recited at the New Year's festival of the Babylonian god Marduk and encouraged scholarly pursuits.

Most importantly, Hammurabi issued a major law code, based to some extent on earlier Sumerian and Akkadian models. The Code of Hammurabi became the most famous and influential set of laws before those created by the Greeks and Romans in the first millennium B.C. In addition to the laws themselves, the code contains a lengthy introduction and epilogue in which the king presents a rationale for issuing his laws. These sections of text are priceless relics in that they are among the few surviving statements that came directly from the lips of one of Mesopotamia's greatest rulers. In this excerpt from the epilogue, Hammurabi speaks not only to his subjects but also in a sense to the ages, declaring that his extreme wisdom, piety, and righteousness, bolstered by the sanction of the gods, have compelled him to create laws for the good of his people:

> A righteous law, and pious statute did he teach the land. Hammurabi, the protecting king am I. . . . The great gods have called me. I am the salvation-bearing shepherd, whose staff is straight, the good shadow that is spread over my city; on my breast I cherish the inhabitants of the land of Sumer and Akkad; in my shelter I have let them repose in peace; in my deep wisdom have I enclosed them. . . . The king who rules among the kings of the cities am I. My words are well considered; there is no wisdom like unto mine. By the command of Shamash, the great judge of heaven and earth, let righteousness go forth in the land. By the order of Marduk, my lord, let no destruction befall my monument. . . . Let my name be ever repeated; let the oppressed, who has a case at law, come and stand before this my image as king of righteousness; let him read the inscription, and understand my precious words. The inscription will explain his case to him; he will find out what is just, and his heart will be glad, so that he will say: "Hammurabi is a ruler, who is as a father to his subjects, who holds the words of Marduk in reverence, who has achieved conquest for Marduk over the north and south, who rejoices the heart of Marduk, his lord, who has bestowed benefits for ever and ever on his subjects, and has established order in the land."

Hammurabi also appointed judges, who reported directly to him, to administer these laws. He did not live to see widespread application of these laws, however, for he died shortly after introducing them.

SEE ALSO: Babylon; crime and punishment; laws and justice

Hanging Gardens of Babylon

An architectural wonder created in Babylon by the Neo-Babylonian king Nebuchadnezzar II in the early sixth century B.C. Ancient sources claim that Nebuchadnezzar's wife, Amytis, daughter of the Median king Umakishtar, missed the trees and hills of her homeland, Media, and her husband erected the gardens to make her happy. Supposedly they consisted of a

An illustration depicting the Hanging Gardens of Babylon during the early sixth century B.C. © Bettmann/Corbis

series of massive terraces, some hundreds of feet high. Workmen covered them with soil and planted trees and bushes, which were irrigated with water brought in from the Euphrates River. According to one of the more detailed ancient accounts of the gardens, that of the first-century B.C. Greek historian Diodorus Siculus, when the tiers of the structure were built,

> there had been constructed beneath them galleries which carried the entire weight of the planted garden and rose little by little one above the other. . . . the roofs of the galleries were covered over with beams of stone sixteen feet [5m] long. . . . The roof above these beams had first a layer of reeds laid in great quantities of bitumen [tar], over this two courses of baked brick bonded by cement, and as a third layer a covering of lead, to the end

that the moisture from the soil might not penetrate beneath. On all this again the earth had been piled to the depth sufficient for the roots of the largest trees; and the ground . . . was thickly planted with trees of every kind. . . . The galleries . . . contained many royal lodges of every description; and there was one gallery which contained openings leading from . . . machines [mechanically operated pumps] for supplying the gardens with water, the machines raising the water in great abundance from the river. (*Library of History* 2.10)

Not surprisingly, modern excavators have long sought to find the remains of the Hanging Gardens of Babylon, which were listed among the Seven Wonders of the Ancient World. The burning question has always been where to search in

Babylon's extensive ruins. Curiously, the Greek historian Herodotus, who visited the city in the fifth century B.C., made no mention of the gardens. One early modern theory was that the large ziggurat he described in his *Histories* had originally borne the gardens but they had disappeared by his time. The noted German excavator Robert Koldewey later proposed that a structure scholars call the Vaulted Building was the Hanging Gardens. A more recent proposal, by University of London Assyriologist D.J. Wiseman, suggests that the gardens rested on some terraces atop an outer city wall near the Euphrates River. Insufficient evidence exists to prove any of these theories; so for the time being, the exact location of this renowned ancient architectural wonder remains uncertain.

SEE ALSO: Amytis; Babylon; Nebuchadnezzar II

Harran

An important city and trade center located several miles east of Carchemish in what is now southeastern Turkey. Harran's name came from the Akkadian word *hurranu*, meaning "road," which was fitting because the city lay in a strategic spot on the road leading westward from northern Assyria into Syria. (Later in antiquity the city also became known as Carrhae.) Thus, not only merchants from far and wide passed through but also armies on campaign. The Hittites captured Harran, as did the Assyrians later, in the eighth century B.C. After Nineveh was destroyed by the Babylonians and the Medes in 612 B.C., the last vestiges of the Assyrian court fled to Harran and made a last stand there until the Medes overran it. The town was also the site of later battles, including one fought in 53 B.C. between the Romans and the Parthians,

in which the Roman nobleman Marcus Crassus was defeated and killed. From a cultural standpoint, Harran was important as the home of the chief Mesopotamian temple of the moon god, Sin (or Nanna). Called the Ehulhul, or "House of Rejoicing," it was refurbished and expanded by a number of Assyrian and Babylonian kings. Harran is also mentioned in the biblical book of Genesis as the place where Terah, father of the prophet Abraham, lived after fleeing from Ur.

SEE ALSO: Parthian Empire; Romans; trade

Hatti

The kingdom, or nation, of the Hittites, at its height covering large sections of Anatolia.

SEE ALSO: Hattusas; Hittites; Mesopotamia, history of

Hattusas

The capital of the Hittite nation and empire, located in north-central Anatolia about 130 miles (209km) east of modern Ankara. The site of Hattusas (or Hattusa, modern Boghazköy or Bogazkale) was inhabited in the third millennium B.C. or earlier. But it did not become the Hittite capital until around 1750 B.C. It was located in a hilly region, presumably to make it more defensible, near a small, well-watered plain. Hattusas was divided into two major sections—the Lower City and Upper City. The older of the two was the Lower City, built on and around a royal acropolis, or fortified hill, featuring a palace and the temple of the principal Hittite deity, the Storm God, who was similar in many ways to the Mesopotamian god Adad, the Hebrew god Yahweh, and the Greek god Zeus. Much of the early city was destroyed circa 1380 B.C. Less than a century later extensive rebuilding programs took place, and the city expanded nearly 1 mile (1.6km) southward, forming the Upper City. Hattusas was destroyed again, circa 1190 B.C., and thereafter remained deserted for several centuries.

Excavations of the Upper City were undertaken in the twentieth century by a German team led by archaeologist Peter Neve. The work revealed twenty-six temples and thousands of clay tablets bearing the Hittite language expressed in Mesopotamian cuneiform characters. Excavators also uncovered a number of spectacular gates in the city's defensive walls, the most famous of which were the Lion's Gate, Sphinx's Gate, and King's Gate.

SEE ALSO: cuneiform; Hittites; languages

Herodotus
(ca. 485 B.C.–ca. 425 B.C.)

A noted Greek historian who wrote what modern scholars view as the world's first conventional history book, today called the *Histories*, which contains much valuable information about ancient Mesopotamia. The main subject of the work was the series of epic battles fought between the Persians and the Greeks in the early fifth century B.C. But Herodotus chose to go into voluminous detail about the backgrounds and cultures of the peoples involved, especially the Persians. He remains a major source of information about the Persians, Medes, Babylonians, Egyptians, Phoenicians, and some other Near Eastern peoples in the first millennium B.C. Herodotus's book is valuable partly because some sections are eyewitness accounts from his visits to Babylon, Palestine, and Egypt. He was a curious and observant

individual, as well as a gifted writer, and he jotted down priceless descriptions of numerous Mesopotamian artifacts and customs. Here is his well-meaning, if partly ill-informed, description of Europe, Libya (Africa), and Asia, the three great landmasses known in his day:

> I cannot help laughing at the absurdity of all the map-makers . . . who show Ocean running like a river round a perfectly circular Earth, with Asia and Europe of the same size. Let me spend a few words in giving a proper notion of the size and shape of these two continents. Persian territory extends southward to the Red Sea, as it is called. North of them are the Medes, then the Saspires, then the Colchians, who go as far as the northern sea [the Black Sea]. . . . These four nations fill the area between the Black Sea and the Persian Gulf. . . . This branch of the continent contains thirty different nations. The other starts from Persia, Assyria, and Arabia, and ends—or it is assumed to end—at the Arabian Gulf. . . . Asia is inhabited as far as India; farther east the country is uninhabited, and nobody knows what it is like. . . . Libya is part of the second branch I mentioned, for it adjoins Egypt. Egypt itself forms a narrow neck . . . but it soon broadens out, and what is known as Libya covers a very large area. . . . The three continents do, in fact, differ very greatly in size. Europe is as long as the other two put together. . . . As for Libya, we know that it is washed on all sides by the sea except where it joins Asia. (*Histories* 4.35–42)

SEE ALSO: Astyages; Babylon; Battle of Pelusium; bridges; clothing; Cyaxares II; Darius I; Deioces; Ecbatana; Magi; Median Empire; Persian Empire; roads; sacred prostitution; Semiramis; ships; Tower of Babel; transportation and travel; water supplies; weapons and warfare, naval and siege; Xerxes; Zoroastrianism

historical accounts

Constructing a complete, coherent, and accurate account of thousands of years of ancient Mesopotamian history is all but impossible, in part because none of the peoples of the region produced modern-style history books describing and dating the major figures and events of each historical period. The art of historical writing began with Greek writers—notably Herodotus and Thucydides—in the fifth century B.C., long after most of the major Mesopotamian civilizations had already risen and fallen. Modern scholars must therefore attempt to piece together information from a number of scattered sources, all of them incomplete and sketchy and most of them biased in one way or another. In general, the later ages of Mesopotamia, beginning with the Persian period, can be dated with fair accuracy. But the farther back one goes, the more uncertain the dating process becomes. For example, the often-cited date of 323 B.C. for the death of Alexander the Great in Babylon is likely correct within a margin of error of no more than one to five years. But experts estimate a margin of error of from 120 to 150 years for dates in the time of Babylonia's King Hammurabi, some fourteen centuries earlier. And dating events that occurred earlier than Hammurabi's reign is even more uncertain, resulting in considerable differences of opinion among scholars. Indeed, three separate possible Mesopotamian chronologies have evolved, usually referred to as the High, Middle, and Low chronologies. The Middle one (used in this book), which dates the start of Hammurabi's reign at circa 1792 B.C., is perhaps the most widely accepted.

Surviving King Lists Although the ancient Mesopotamians wrote no history books per se, they did leave behind various writings that can be very loosely termed *historical accounts*. Among these were the so-called king lists, compiled by royal scribes. As the name suggests, they are lists of rulers belonging to various dynasties, ranging from those of the Sumerians in the third millennium B.C. to those of the Parthians some two millennia later. These are by no means complete and accurate lists. For instance, the Sumerian King List, the most complete version of which dates from about 2125 B.C., attributes impossibly long reigns, some lasting tens of thousands of years, to several ancient rulers. Thus, though many of the names on this list may represent real rulers, it is impossible to know exactly when and how long they reigned.

Later king lists, such as those of the last few Assyrian and Babylonian kings, can be dated with considerably more accuracy, though many uncertainties remain. Also helpful sometimes are astronomical chronicles compiled by Babylonian priests and scribes, which record the movements of the planets and other heavenly bodies. In particular, the risings and settings of the planet Venus recorded during the reign of the Babylonian king Ammi-saduqa, in the seventeenth century B.C., have been helpful to scholars trying to establish ancient Mesopotamian chronologies. Also, sometimes the astronomical chronicles mention the death of a king, a plague, or some other noteworthy occurrence, and historians try to coordinate such observations with other ancient historical accounts.

Babylonian Chronicles Among the more valuable of these accounts are the Babylonian Chronicles and the annals of the Assyrian kings. The Babylonian Chronicles were composed by royal scribes between the eighth and second centuries B.C. and describe various political events during the reigns of a number of kings. The Assyrian annals consist of yearly reports of the major exploits of the kings. They take the form of carved scenes and inscriptions on the walls of palaces and temples, the bases of statues, and on cylinder seals and stelae (commemorative marker stones). The first important Assyrian annals were those of King Adad-nirari I in the thirteenth century B.C. Such annals were certainly not unbiased historical accounts in the modern sense. They were meant to glorify the rulers they described and so are filled with exaggerations and fabrications and make no mention of defeats, setbacks, or scandals.

The exploits of some of the Assyrian and Babylonian kings are also mentioned in various books of the Hebrew Old Testament. They include descriptions of the sieges of a number of Palestinian cities, the deportation of many Hebrews to Babylonia, and the fall of Assyria at the hands of the Medes and the Babylonians. Though valuable in some ways and often vivid, these accounts are anecdotal, highly selective, biased because they were written by the victims of Mesopotamian conquerors, and do not follow any chronological sequence.

The first-known Mesopotamian writer who tried to write a conventional, chronological, and largely unbiased history of the region was a Babylonian priest named Berossus in the third century B.C. His goal was to educate the Greeks, who then ruled Mesopotamia, about the civilizations that had come before in the area. He could read cuneiform and had access to many ancient records that are now lost. It is extremely regrettable, therefore, that his main work, the *Babylonaica*, survives only in fragments. Nevertheless, these fragments are sometimes helpful when coordinated with other sources.

For later Mesopotamian history, including the rulers and events of Neo-Babylonia, the Persian Empire, the Seleucid Empire, and the conquests of Alexander the Great, scholars rely heavily on Greek sources. In addition to Herodotus's *Histories*, which describes Babylon, the Medes, and the Persians in passing, though in some detail, fragments of a book by Ctesias have survived. The first Greek who wrote a conventional history of Mesopotamia, Ctesias spent considerable time at the court of Persia's King Artaxerxes II and had access to Persian historical chronicles that no longer exist. Also important are Xenophon's *Anabasis*, describing Cyrus the Younger's attempt to dethrone Artaxerxes II, and *Cyropaedia*, a sort of biography of Cyrus II, founder of the Persian Empire. The works of later Greek historians and writers, including Diodorus Siculus, Arrian, Strabo, and Plutarch, provide valuable information about Alexander's conquest of Persia and/or the Greek rulers who followed him in the region. Also valuable for the figures and events of this period are the writings of the first-century A.D. Jewish historian Josephus.

For the Parthian Empire, which followed the Seleucid realm in the region, no native Parthian historical accounts have survived, if they ever existed. Outside of scattered inscriptions on Parthian coins and pottery, most information about Parthia comes from Greek and Roman writers, whose works were decidedly biased and made no attempt to be comprehensive.

SEE ALSO: *Anabasis*; *Babylonaica*; Babylo-

An aerial view of Hittite ruins. © YANN ARTHUS-BERTRAND/CORBIS

nian Chronicles; Bible; Herodotus; Josephus; Xenophon

Hittites

An important ancient Near Eastern people who spoke an Indo-European language and established a powerful kingdom—called Hatti—centered in Anatolia in the early second millennium B.C. By the late eighteenth century B.C., the Hittites had built a capital city at Hattusas, in the highlands near the upper reaches of the Halys River. Under the leadership of King Mursilis I (reigned ca. 1620–1590 B.C.), they began campaigns of expansion toward the southeast. Mursilis conquered much of Syria, then suddenly followed the Euphrates southeastward and delivered a surprise attack on Babylon. It appears that the Hittites were aided in this venture by the Kassites, a tribal people who had entered Mesopotamia from the northeast

about a century or so before. Instead of consolidating their gains and trying to rule Babylonia, the Hittites departed, leaving the Kassites in control. It may be that Mursilis and other Hittite leaders felt they were too far from home and had too few soldiers to impose direct rule on Mesopotamia. In any case, the power vacuum thus created allowed the Hurrians, who originally hailed from the region near the Caspian Sea, to sweep through the area. The Hurrians established the kingdom of Mitanni, centered on the upper reaches of the Tigris and Euphrates rivers; the Mitannian state then acted as a sort of buffer between Hatti and Mesopotamia.

The largest imperial gains by the Hittites came about two centuries later. Under King Suppiluliumas I (reigned ca. 1370–1330 B.C.), they subdued most of northern Mitanni, created an alliance with the Kassite rulers of Babylonia, and imposed their will on a number of cities in Syria-Palestine. The latter intrusion raised the ire of the Egyptians, who had recently established their own influence in Syria-Palestine. Tensions between the two peoples came to a head in the Battle of Kadesh in Syria in 1274 B.C., in which the Hittite king Muwatallis II (reigned ca. 1295–1272 B.C.) fought the Egyptian pharaoh Ramesses II (ca. 1279–1213 B.C.) to an apparent draw. Shortly thereafter another Hittite ruler, Tuthaliyas (or Tudhaliya) IV (ca. 1237–1209 B.C.), further expanded the Hittite empire by conquering the Mediterranean island of Cyprus. Soon afterward, however, that empire collapsed suddenly and permanently, and Hattusas was destroyed. The reasons are still uncertain and disputed by scholars, but a large-scale invasion of Greece, Anatolia, and Syria-Palestine by tribal peoples migrating from the region west of the Black Sea seems probable.

SEE ALSO: Battle of Kadesh; Hattusas; Mesopotamia, history of

houses

Most houses in ancient Mesopotamia were one of two types—small huts made of bundled reeds and dried mud, or slightly more permanent dwellings composed of dried clay bricks. The reed huts were most common in the countryside, especially in marshy regions. Many stables and sheepfolds were also made of bundled reeds. Houses in cities were more often made of bricks, whenever possible with walls several feet thick to help insulate the interiors from the heat of the day. Whitewashing the exterior walls also served to reduce the amount of heat reaching the interior.

Heat was not the only thing that people wanted to prevent from entering their homes. They often painted their doors bright red in the belief that evil spirits would be repelled. And although there were few or no windows in brick houses, any windows usually had palm-wood gratings to help keep out unwanted pests. No matter what precautions were taken, however, it is probable that all Mesopotamian houses were at one time or another infested by rodents and/or insects and other pests. Scorpions were common, and snakes crawled into homes in search of rodents that made nests in the walls and ceilings. There were also ants, cockroaches, lizards, and beetles with which to contend.

Mud-brick homes varied in size. The smallest were often in the range of 8 by 18 feet (2.4 by 5.4m), but some were as large as 18 by 45 feet (5.4 by 13.7m), excluding those of the wealthy, which could be considerably larger. An average house featured a central courtyard with various rooms clustered around its perimeter. The kitchen was on the ground floor in two-story homes and sometimes opened into the courtyard, with a brick hearth on one wall. There was usually a living/family room and one or more small bedchambers. Well-to-do homes also had one or more rooms to house the family servants. Some houses also had small bathrooms with latrinelike toilets, from which wastes drained through baked clay channels to cesspools located just outside the house. The oil lamps used to light house interiors were also made of baked clay. To fuel their lamps, Mesopotamians generally used sesame seed oil as opposed to olive oil, which was common in Mediterranean cultures. Torches were also used for lighting in larger homes and palaces.

SEE ALSO: building materials and methods; furniture; palaces

hunting and fishing

Because Mesopotamian society was supported primarily by agriculture, hunting animals for food was rare. People hunted for the most part either to get rid of wild animals that posed a threat to herds, farms, and villages, or for sport. And sport hunting was generally a pastime of the rich, especially kings, who could afford to engage in elaborate expeditions involving horses, chariots, traps, corrals, wagons, and dozens of helpers. The main evidence of such royal hunts comes from the annals of several Assyrian kings. Tiglathpileser I (reigned 1115–1077) recorded the diverse kinds of creatures he hunted, among them lions, tigers, hyenas, bears, leopards, deer, bison, wild pigs, gazelle, lynx, onagers (wild asses), elephants, and ostriches. His inscriptions also mention a trip to the Mediterranean Sea, where he bagged a *nahiru*, which may have been a dolphin or a whale. (Tiglathpileser was clearly fascinated by animals, as he established several zoos.) Another Assyrian monarch, Ashurnasirpal II (884–859) bragged about killing 30 elephants, 257 wild oxen, and 370 lions. These numbers may be exaggerated, or they may reflect the fact that only some of the royal hunts consisted of the participants stalking animals in the wild. Many were staged affairs in which professional trappers gathered the creatures into enclosed areas, where the king and his nobles could dispatch their prey with a minimum of difficulty and danger.

Fishing, on the other hand, remained a source of food for many Mesopotamians even after the introduction of agriculture. In the marshlands near the confluence of the Tigris and Euphrates rivers, hunters in narrow reed boats used long poles with metal tips to spear fish. On the rivers or in the Persian Gulf, fishermen also used nets to catch carp and other varieties of fish as well as eels. Artificially stocked fish ponds were also employed in some places.

SEE ALSO: Ashurnasirpal II; farming; food and drink

Hurrians

A Mesopotamian people who seem to have come from the Caucasus region lying west of the Caspian Sea. Based on linguistic studies and other evidence, some scholars think that they may have been related to the Aryan peoples who eventually settled in India. Whatever their origins, by about 2200 B.C. bands of Hurrians had begun to settle in northeastern Mesopotamia and southeastern Anatolia. Subsequently, groups of Hurrians existed all over Mesopotamia and in other parts of the Near East. The only major kingdom they established was Mitanni, which played an important role in Mesopotamian political affairs between about 1500 and 1300 B.C.

SEE ALSO: Hittites; Mesopotamia, history of; Mitanni

Huwawa

A scary giant confronted by the heroes of the greatest of the Mesopotamian epic poems, the *Epic of Gilgamesh*. In the story, Huwawa (or Hawawa) inhabits the forests of the Cedar Mountain, lying west of the Mesopotamian plains. Gilgamesh, king of Uruk, and his faithful companion Enkidu journey to the Cedar Mountain and there, with the aid of the god Shamash, manage to slay Huwawa.

SEE ALSO: *Epic of Gilgamesh*

Iaggid-Lim
(reigned ca. 1830–1820 B.C.)

An Amorite leader who established a dynasty of rulers in the city of Mari, located on the upper reaches of the Euphrates River. Under Iaggid-Lim (or Yaggid-Lim), Mari grew highly prosperous, mainly through trade and local production of textiles. Apparently he got into a small-scale war with the ruler of a rival city, Ekallatum, who temporarily seized control of Mari. On his death, Iaggid-Lim was succeeded by his son, Iahdun-Lim.

SEE ALSO: Amorites; Iahdun-Lim; Mari

Iahdun-Lim
(reigned ca. 1820–1796 B.C.)

The second king of the Amorite dynasty established by Iaggid-Lim in Mari, and Iaggid-Lim's son. Like his father, Iahdun-Lim (or Yahdun-Lim) devoted much time and energy to keeping Mari safe and prosperous. The new king erected new defensive walls and constructed several irrigation canals to increase agricultural output. Iahdun-Lim also raised an army and tried to expand Mari's political power and territory. One campaign took him westward to the Mediterranean coast, where he forced some local towns to pay him tribute. Iahdun-Lim was eventually assassinated, perhaps by one of his own sons.

SEE ALSO: Iaggid-Lim; Iasmah-Adad; Mari

Iasmah-Adad
(reigned ca. 1796–1776 B.C.)

The fourth Amorite ruler of Mari and the son of the Amorite king of Assyria, Shamshi-Adad. The second Amorite king of Mari, Iahdun-Lim, was succeeded by one of his sons, Samu-Iamin, who may have obtained the throne by murdering his father. But Samu-Iamin himself was soon assassinated, after which Shamshi-Adad seized Mari and placed Iasmah-Adad (or Yasmah-Adad) on its throne. Several surviving letters exchanged between Shamshi-Adad and Iasmah-Adad, in which the father reprimands the son, show that the younger man was a mediocre ruler little interested in state affairs. When Shamshi-Adad died, another of Iahdun-Lim's sons, Zimri-Lim, pushed the ineffectual Iasmah-Adad aside and took Mari's throne.

SEE ALSO: Iahdun-Lim; Mari; Shamshi-Adad

Igigi

A collective name for a group of minor Mesopotamian deities who had no individual names of their own. Some scholars count as many as three hundred Igigi (or Igigu). In the famous myth about the hero Atrahasis, who builds an ark to survive a great flood sent by the gods, another group of minor gods, the Annunaki, compel the Igigi to do menial labor. But after a while the Igigi burn their tools, in effect going on strike. In an unintended development,

Part of the façade of the Eanna Temple of King Kara-indas in Uruk, which was dedicated to the city goddess Inanna. BILDARCHIV PREUSSISCHER KULTURBESITZ/ART RESOURCE, NY

the gods create humans to use as laborers and thereby ensure that the work gets done.

SEE ALSO: Annunaki; Atrahasis; religion

Inanna

A leading Sumerian goddess and the most popular deity in all of ancient Mesopotamia. Inanna (also Ishtar or Astarte) was known as the goddess of love and sexual passion, but she was also associated with war and was seen as a protector of kings and ruling dynasties. The great conqueror Sargon of Akkad, for instance, called on her to support him in battle. In addition, sometime in the third millennium B.C. she merged with a Semitic goddess, Ishtar, thereby becoming "queen of Heaven" and gaining an association with the planet Venus. As a result, one of her symbols was a star.

In her role as the sex goddess, Inanna was both selfish and inexhaustible, choosing, using, and discarding male lovers at will. Her chief lover, Dumuzi, for example, ended up spending half of his time in the dark reaches of the Underworld because of her, as told in the epic poem *The Descent of Inanna*. Not surprisingly, Inanna was a patron deity of prostitutes, and some of her priestesses may have served her as sacred prostitutes. Inanna had temples and shrines all across Mesopotamia, but her principal one was the Eanna, or "House of Heaven," at Uruk. Other important shrines were at Kish, also in Sumeria, and Nineveh, in Assyria.

Many hymns and other forms of written praise were composed for Inanna over the course of more than two millennia. The following example, phrased to make it sound as if the goddess herself is speaking, is Sumerian and dates from the late third millennium B.C.

I am Inanna! Which god compares with me? [The chief god] Enlil gave me the heavens and he gave me the Earth. I am Innana! He gave me lordship, and he gave me queenship. He gave me battles and he gave me fighting. He gave me the storm-wind and he gave me the dust cloud. He placed the heavens on my head as a crown. He put the earth at my feet as sandals. He wrapped [a] holy . . . garment around my body. He put the holy scepter in my hand. The [other] gods are [like] small birds, but I am the falcon. . . . When I enter the Ekur, the house of Enlil, the gate-keeper does not lift his hand against my breast; the minister does not tell me, "Rise!" The heavens are mine and the Earth is mine. I am heroic! Which god compares with me?

SEE ALSO: *Descent of Inanna, The*; Dumuzi; sacred prostitution

Indo-Europeans

Possibly the ancestors of a number of ancient peoples who inhabited Europe and western Asia, including Mesopotamia. The term *Indo-European* was initially mainly a linguistic one and referred to a proposed very ancient, ancestral language that may have given birth to many later languages. However, over time most scholars came to believe that there was also an ancestral Indo-European people, sometimes called the Proto-Indo-Europeans. If they did exist, the location of their original homeland is still a matter of considerable dispute. The two chief theories place that homeland either in southern Russia, just north and east of the Black Sea, or in Anatolia. Supposedly, sometime in the late Stone Age they spread outward in all directions and settled Europe, including Greece, Italy, and Germany; Anatolia; Armenia; Iran; and northern India. Noted University of Cambridge scholar Colin Renfrew recently suggested that the Indo-Europeans originated in Anatolia, where they invented agriculture and subsequently introduced it to neighboring peoples, including those who lived in the Fertile Crescent and later brought it to Mesopotamia. There may well be something to this idea. In the late 1990s Columbia University scientists William Ryan and Walter Pitman presented convincing evidence for a large-scale natural disaster in the Black Sea region north of Anatolia in the sixth millennium B.C. They believe that this catastrophe triggered the Indo-European migrations, including those into the Fertile Crescent. For the time being, however, the scholarly community as a whole remains uncertain about the origins of the Indo-Europeans.

SEE ALSO: Fertile Crescent; flood legends; languages

inscriptions

Written words or messages cut or scratched into stone, metal, or other durable materials, of which tens of thousands have survived from ancient Mesopotamia. The study of ancient inscriptions is called epigraphy.

SEE ALSO: Behistun Rock; cuneiform; epigraphy

Isaiah
(flourished mid-700s B.C.)

A Hebrew prophet and the name of the book of the Old Testament he is credited with writing. Isaiah may have been related to the royal family of the Jewish kingdom of Judah and advised some of the rulers of that realm. He witnessed the invasion of the other Jewish kingdom, Israel, by the Assyrian kings Tiglathpileser III and Shalmaneser V and was opposed to the pro-Assyrian stance taken by Judah's king, Ahaz. Isaiah advised Ahaz's successor, Hezekiah, to resist the Assyrians, which he did. The unfortunate result was an invasion of Judah by Assyria's King Sennacherib. These events are told in passing in the book of Isaiah as well in two other Old Testament books, Second Kings and Second Chronicles.

SEE ALSO: Bible; Judah; Israel

Ishbi-Erra
(reigned ca. 2017–1985 B.C.)

A ruler of the Sumerian city-state of Isin, whose rebellious activities helped to weaken and bring about the collapse of the empire now called the Third Dynasty of Ur. Ishbi-Erra started out as a soldier and army officer in the empire. He must have acquitted himself well because King Ibbi-Sin (reigned ca. 2026–2004 B.C.) soon placed him in charge of the city of Isin. But Ishbi-Erra then betrayed the king's trust. The realm was already faltering under the strain of Amorite tribes migrating from the northwest and raids by the Elamites from the east; and Ishbi-Erra took advantage of the situation by declaring Isin independent from Ur. He also took control of the city of Nippur and even made alliances with some of Ur's enemies. After the Elamites sacked Ur, causing the fall of its empire, Ishbi-Erra proclaimed himself the rightful heir to the Ur dynasts in the region; perhaps for this reason, the Sumerian King List lists him as the first monarch of a new line of rulers, the so-called First Dynasty of Isin.

SEE ALSO: Elam; Isin; Third Dynasty of Ur

Ishkur

A major weather god worshipped by the Sumerians, the Assyrians, and the Babylonians as well as by some Semitic peoples as far west as Syria. He was also known as Adad or Hadad. Supposedly a son of the chief god, Enlil, Ishkur was thought to have the power to unleash terrible storms on cities or lands that had fallen out of favor with the gods. In contrast, he sometimes brought gentle rains that watered the crops of lands that were on good terms with divine forces. His chief symbol was lightning, and his most sacred animal was the bull.

SEE ALSO: Enlil; religion

Ishme-Dagan
(reigned ca. 1780–1741 B.C.)

An early Amorite king of Assyria and the stronger and more capable of the two sons of King Shamshi-Adad. The latter placed Ishme-Dagan on the throne of the city-state of Ekallatum, and surviving letters exchanged between father and son suggest that Ishme-Dagan was an effective ruler and military leader. After Shamshi-Adad died, Ishme-Dagan inherited the Assyrian throne and wrote a letter to his brother, Iasmah-Adad, then ruling the city of Mari. "Say to Iasmah-Adad: Thus says Ishme-Dagan, your brother," the letter begins.

> I have ascended the throne of my father's house. This is why I have been extremely busy, and have not been

able to send you news of my well-being. . . . You must not be anxious. Your throne is and will remain your throne. The gods Adad and Shamash I hold in my hand. . . . Let us swear a binding oath to each other . . . [and] maintain brotherly relationships with each other for all time.

Unfortunately for the brothers, their remaining reigns were short. Iasmah-Adad was soon overthrown by the brother of a former ruler of Mari, and a few years later Ishme-Dagan's small Assyrian realm was absorbed by the Babylonians under King Hammurabi.

SEE ALSO: Assyrian Empire; Iasmah-Adad; Shamshi-Adad

Ishtar

Originally a local Semitic goddess associated with the planet Venus. Sometime in the third millennium B.C., the image of Ishtar (or Astarte) and her functions merged with those of the more important and popular Sumerian deity Inanna, goddess of love and sexual passion.

SEE ALSO: Inanna; religion; sacred prostitution

Isin

A Sumerian, and later Babylonian, city lying in the lowlands between the Tigris and Euphrates rivers in southern Mesopotamia, about 125 miles (200km) southeast of modern Baghdad. Isin (modern Ishan Bahriyat) was inhabited at least from the fifth millennium B.C., but it did not rise to prominence until the fall of the Third Dynasty of Ur, at the close of the third millennium B.C. The first dynasty of Isin was founded circa 2017 B.C. by a ruler named Ishbi-Erra. The city was most

famous for its cult center and temple dedicated to Gula (or Ninisina), goddess of healing, which occupied the highest point in Isin. Mesopotamians came there from far and wide in hopes of achieving some sort of miraculous cure. Meanwhile, during the first two centuries of the second millennium B.C., Isin engaged in a lively and sometimes warlike rivalry with the neighboring city of Larsa, until both were captured by Babylonia's King Hammurabi and absorbed into his empire. Eventually the marshes reclaimed the site of Isin, and the locals came to call it Ishan Bahriyat, the "Monument Drowned by the Sea."

SEE ALSO: Hammurabi; Ishbi-Erra; Larsa

Islam

The religion of the Muslims, based on the teachings of the prophet Muhammad and the holy book known as the Koran. Islam became the predominant faith of Mesopotamia following the Arab conquests of the region from A.D. 634 to 651.

SEE ALSO: Muslim period

Israel

One of two Hebrew (Jewish) kingdoms situated in ancient Palestine and conquered by Mesopotamian kings. According to the Old Testament, Abraham, the first prophet not only of the Jews but also of the Christians and the Muslims, lived sometime in the 1800s B.C. His son, Jacob, was later renamed Israel. Jacob's twelve sons became the chiefs of the twelve tribes of Israel. Many biblical scholars suggest that these and other stories about the early Hebrews, including their sojourn in Egypt, may be either mythical or only loosely based on fact. What seems more certain is that by the eleventh century B.C. the first kingdom of Israel was established in Palestine. Instrumental in its creation was a war leader named Saul and his successor, King David, who made Jerusalem the capital circa 1000 B.C. David's own successor, Solomon, supposedly erected the first great Jewish house of worship—the First Temple—in Jerusalem. Following Solomon's death in the tenth century B.C., the kingdom split into two Hebrew states—Israel in the north and Judah in the south. Judah retained Jerusalem as its capital, and Samaria became the capital of Israel. Unfortunately for the inhabitants of both of these kingdoms, the Assyrian Empire was rising to prominence in this period. In the 720s B.C. the Assyrians conquered Israel, captured Samaria, and carried away most or all of the local nobles and resettled them in Assyria. Judah managed to survive for a little more than a century before it too fell prey to Assyrian aggression.

SEE ALSO: Jerusalem; Judah; Palestine

Iter-Mer

The patron god of Mari, a city on the upper reaches of the Euphrates River that flourished in the early second millennium B.C. In ancient Akkadian, the language spoken by the Babylonians in that millennium, Iter-Mer translates as "Mer has Returned." *Mer* was the Sumerian word for "rain." So modern scholars assume that this deity was seen as the bringer of the seasonal rainfall essential for farming in the region.

SEE ALSO: farming; Mari; religion

Jarmo

An important archaeological site in northern Iraq, where modern excavators found the remains of a prehistoric agricultural village dating to the seventh millennium B.C. Located in the foothills of the upper Zagros Mountains, just east of the Assyrian plains, Jarmo (or Qalat Jarmo) appears to have been one of the early villages set up by the inhabitants of the Fertile Crescent as they made their way southward onto the Mesopotamian plains. Excavations undertaken between 1948 and 1955 by Robert and Linda Braidwood of Chicago's Oriental Institute revealed that the village measured about 300 by 450 feet (92 by 135m) and supported a population of from one to two hundred. The diggers found the remains of twenty primitive houses with walls made of packed mud, a technique predating that of dried clay bricks. The villagers raised barley, emmer wheat, peas, sheep, and goats. Small clay tokens of varying geometric shapes found in the ruins may have been used to count livestock and measure quantities of harvested crops.

SEE ALSO: farming; Fertile Crescent; Ubaidian culture

Jemdet Nasr

The name of the site of an early Sumerian town and of the last prehistoric period before the Sumerian cities entered their first great age of power and prosperity. Modern scholars usually date the Jemdet Nasr period to roughly 3200 to 3000 B.C. The site itself, located about 60 miles (97km) south of Baghdad, was first excavated in 1925 and again briefly in the late 1980s. Examples of pottery, cylinder seals, and clay tablets bearing cuneiform writing were found. The writing, dubbed proto-cuneiform by scholars, was used mainly for administrative purposes. Some tablets mention other Sumerian towns, including Ur, Larsa, Uruk, and Nippur, and evidence suggests that the Jemdet Nasr period was an era of cooperation among these cities.

SEE ALSO: cuneiform; pottery; Ur; Uruk

Jericho

An important early archaeological site in the Fertile Crescent and later a Hebrew town captured, along with the rest of Palestine, by the Assyrians. Located just north of the Dead Sea, Jericho (modern Tell-es-Sultan) occupied a strategic spot

A depiction of Jericho devastated by the Assyrians in the eighth century B.C. MARY EVANS PICTURE LIBRARY. REPRODUCED BY PERMISSION

along a trade route running from the deserts west of Mesopotamia to coastal Palestine. The town was among the early agricultural settlements in the Fertile Crescent, which stretched northeastward into Syria and then eastward across the northern rim of Mesopotamia. Archaeologists divide prehistoric Jericho into three levels of habitation: pre-agricultural, before 9000 B.C.; pre-pottery A, ninth and eighth millennia B.C.; and pre-pottery B, seventh and sixth millennia B.C. The second of these towns had a stone defensive wall with a stone tower and several round mud-brick houses. The people grew barley, emmer wheat, and lentils. Much later Jericho became part of ancient Israel until that kingdom was absorbed by Assyria in the eighth century B.C. The book of Joshua in the Old Testament describes how the early Hebrews laid siege to Jericho and brought down its walls by shouting and blasting trumpets. Partly because of its importance for studies of the prehistoric Near East and also because of its prominence as an early Hebrew city, Jericho has been excavated numerous times. The first digs there were conducted by Charles Warren in 1868. Then came Carl Watzinger (1907–1909), John Garstang (1930–1936), Kathleen Kenyon (1952–1958), and Lorenzo Nigro (1997).

SEE ALSO: farming; Fertile Crescent; Palestine

Jerusalem

An important Palestinian and Near Eastern city that, over the course of many centuries, fell under the control of numerous ancient conquerors, including several from Mesopotamia. According to the Old Testament, an early Hebrew king, David, made Jerusalem his capital around 1000 B.C. His successor, Solomon, erected the First Temple there, which became the principal focus of worship and religious and cultural identity for Jews in the region for many centuries to come. After early Israel split into two kingdoms—Israel and Judah—Jerusalem remained the capital of Judah. The Assyrian monarch Sennacherib besieged the city circa 701 B.C. but failed to take it. However, the Babylonians did manage to capture Jerusalem in about 597 B.C. and carried off King Jehoiachin and many other Jews into captivity. The Jews who remained in the city soon rebelled, and Babylonia's King Nebuchadnezzar II responded by destroying much of Jerusalem circa 587. Somewhat later Cyrus II, the Persian ruler who had defeated and absorbed Babylonia, allowed the Jews to return to Jerusalem, rebuild the walls, and erect the Second Temple. Subsequently, the city was ruled by Persians, Greeks, and finally, after a brief period of independence, the Romans, who installed a Jewish client king, Herod the Great. He renovated Jerusalem and embellished the Second Temple.

SEE ALSO: Israel; Judah; Sennacherib

jewelry

Both men and women wore jewelry in ancient Mesopotamia, and jewelry items were also used to decorate statues of gods, were exchanged as gifts between rulers, were given as wedding gifts, were included in dowries and inheritances, and, of course, were stolen as loot during military campaigns. One of the largest archaeological finds of Mesopotamian jewelry occurred when noted excavator Charles Leonard Woolley explored the royal cemetery at Ur between 1926 and 1932. He uncovered sixteen tombs dating to the period of about 2900 to 2350 B.C., all containing considerable quantities of jewelry. Particularly impressive were the jewelry items of Queen Puabi, including a crown made of gold and lapis lazuli; necklaces of gold, silver, lapis lazuli, and agate; and gold and silver pins for fastening clothes. All of the tombs contained finely made earrings. Another important Mesopotamian jewelry find was made during excavations in 1988 and 1989 by Iraqi archaeologist Mazahim Mahmud Hussein in the ruins of the Assyrian city of Nimrud (Kalhu). Three royal tombs yielded some fifteen hundred pieces of jewelry weighing a total of 100 pounds (45kg).

Precious stones such as gold and silver and semiprecious ones such as jasper, agate, lapis lazuli, and crystal were fairly scarce in Mesopotamia, so many were imported. Gold and silver came from Anatolia and northern Iran and lapis lazuli from Afghanistan, for example. Valuable metals, as well as finished jewelry pieces, were also seized during raids of foreign lands, especially by the Assyrian kings. Once they had the proper raw materials, Mesopotamian jewelers produced many finely crafted items for both men and women. From Akkadian times, the early third millennium B.C., on, men commonly wore strings of beads and bracelets. In the first millennium B.C. Assyrian men and women wore earrings, bracelets, and amulets. Earrings were typically shaped like rings, crescents, grape clusters, cones, and animal and human heads.

No actual jewelry shops have yet been found, but a jar containing the tools of a jeweler named Ilsu-Ibnisu was excavated at Larsa. Included were a small anvil, bronze tweezers, a stone for grinding and smoothing jewelry, and beads of silver and gold that had yet to be fashioned into jewelry. The name of another Mesopotamian jeweler is also known. A letter found in the royal archive at Mari was written by a local priestess to a jeweler named Ili-iddinam; she complained that she had not received the necklace he had promised her even though he had been paid in advance. From studying Mesopotamian jewelry, modern experts have concluded that Ili-iddinam and other jewelers made most gold and silver items by cutting thin sheets of gold or silver into small pieces and using hammers and other tools to shape them.

SEE ALSO: crafts and craftspeople; Ur; Woolley, Charles Leonard

Josephus
(ca. 37 A.D.–100 A.D.)

A noted Jewish historian whose works provide important supplemental material for the history of ancient Palestine, including its invasion by various Mesopotamian monarchs. Josephus was among the leaders of the great Jewish rebellion against Rome between A.D. 66 and 70. He was captured and brought to Rome, where he gained the respect and patronage of the emperor Vespasian. Josephus's *Antiquities of the Jews*, completed circa 93, ambitiously covers the history of his people from the creation of the world to the time of the Roman vassal Herod the Great. It includes a retelling of the great flood and accounts of how the prophet Abraham originated in Mesopotamia, how Saul and David organized the first state of Israel, how the Babylonians besieged Jerusalem and took away many Hebrews into captivity, how the Hebrews returned to Palestine, how Alexander the Great invaded the region, and how Herod rebuilt the temple in Jerusalem. Josephus was a serious and skilled historian. But he was only as good as his sources, and most of the book up to the Babylonian captivity is based on myths and hearsay, mainly from the Old Testament. The rest, however, is of some value to modern historians. For instance, the following is part of Josephus's account of how the first Persian king, Cyrus II, allowed the Hebrews living in captivity in Mesopotamia to return to Palestine:

> In the first year of the reign of Cyrus, which was the seventieth from the day that our people were removed out of their own land into Babylon . . . Cyrus called for the most eminent Jews that were in Babylon and said to them that he gave them leave to go back to their own country, and to rebuild their city Jerusalem and the Temple of God. For [these endeavors] he would be their assistant, and he would write to the rulers and governors that were in [Palestine] that they should contribute to them [the returning Hebrews] gold and silver for the building of the Temple. . . . Cyrus also sent back to them the [sacrificial] vessels of God which [the Babylonian] king Nebuchadnezzar II had pillaged out of the Temple and carried to Babylon. (*Antiquities of the Jews* 6.1.1–2)

SEE ALSO: historical accounts; Israel; Jerusalem

Judah

One of the two Hebrew (Jewish) kingdoms that flourished in ancient Palestine and were eventually attacked and absorbed by the Assyrians and the Babylonians. After King Solomon's death in the tenth century B.C., the first kingdom of Israel was divided into separate states—Israel in the north and Judah in the south. Jerusalem remained the capital of Judah. Judah survived the invasion of the Assyrians in the late 700s B.C. that brought about the destruction of Israel. But the Babylonians defeated Judah in 597 B.C. and deported its king and nobles to sites in Mesopotamia, marking the first stage of the Diaspora, the dispersion of Jews to areas outside of Palestine. In 537 B.C. the Persian king Cyrus II allowed the Jews to return to Judah, where they built the Second Temple between 520 and 515 B.C.. Judah was no longer an independent nation, however; it remained part of a Persian satrapy, or province, until Alexander the Great conquered the Persian Empire in the late fourth century B.C.

SEE ALSO: Israel; Jerusalem; Neo-Babylonian Empire

Kalhu

One of the leading ancient Assyrian cities and one of the capitals of the Assyrian Empire. For details about Kalhu, see its Arabic and more commonly used name, Nimrud.

SEE ALSO: Ashurnasirpal II; Assyrian Empire; Layard, Austen Henry

Kashtilash

The name of four rulers of the Kassite Babylonian dynasty (ca. 1729–1155 B.C.). The third member of the dynasty, Kashtilash (or Kastiliasu) I, who flourished during the early seventeenth century B.C., fought with Abi-esuh, grandson of Hammurabi, for control of Babylon. Little is known about Kashtilash II (late seventeenth century B.C.) and Kashtilash III (early sixteenth century B.C.). Kashtilash IV (mid-thirteenth century B.C.) attacked both Elam and Assyria but was unable to conquer either. The Assyrian king Tukulti-Ninurta I eventually ousted him and appointed three governors to rule Babylonia as an Assyrian dependency. The Kassites soon regained control of the region, however.

SEE ALSO: Elam; Kassites; Tukulti-Ninurta I

Kassites

An ancient Mesopotamian people of unknown origins who entered the region from the east, across the Zagros Mountains, in the early second millennium B.C.

Their native language was unrelated to any other known tongue and is still not well understood. Mentions of the Kassites first appear in Babylonian records in the late 1700s B.C. They seem to have settled somewhere near the city of Sippar, and for the next few generations they were viewed as a threat to the stability of the surrounding region. In the early years of this period the Kassites established a ruling dynasty that is variously dated from ca. 1595 to 1155 B.C. or from 1729 to 1155 B.C. if one counts the kings who ruled before the Kassite occupation of Babylon.

That 1595 B.C. occupation was accomplished by the Hittites with the aid of the Kassites, in ways that are unclear. The Hittites soon departed and left the Kassites in control of Babylonia. Wasting little time, the Kassite ruler Ulam-Buriash defeated the king of Sealand in southernmost Mesopotamia, near the Persian Gulf. The Kassites transformed the loosely organized Babylonian lands into a strongly centralized state. Under their rule the countryside became more densely populated, with the creation of many new small towns and villages. They also respected existing religious traditions and encouraged the use of the Babylonian dialect of Akkadian across Mesopotamia. The Kassite period was largely peaceful, as the rulers showed little interest in foreign conquests. The Kassites did have an army, though; they bred horses and developed a lighter, faster version of the chariot.

Eventually the Kassite Babylonians fell

prey to the Elamites, who launched several attacks on Babylon in the early twelfth century B.C. The Kassite dynasty was terminated in 1155 B.C., but the Kassites continued to exist as a distinct group in the region for several more centuries. Some served in high positions in the governments of various Mesopotamian kingdoms.

SEE ALSO: Babylon; chariots; Hittites

Khorsabad

The modern name for the ancient Assyrian city of Dur-Sharukkin. Modern scholars sometimes use the two names interchangeably. For details, see Dur-Sharukkin.

SEE ALSO: Assyrian Empire; Botta, Paul Emile

king lists

Lists compiled by various Mesopotamian scribes over the course of many centuries in an effort to record the many rulers of the various kingdoms of the region. Also included in some lists are the names of rulers of neighboring regions. The scribes not only listed individual names but also grouped names into ruling dynasties. There were several such lists, beginning with the Sumerian King List, of which a number of versions have survived. These record rulers' names beginning with the handover of kingship from the gods to the humans in the dim past to about 1800 B.C. The following excerpt from the opening section of one version of the Sumerian King List shows how the earliest monarchs were given ridiculously long reigns:

> After the kingship descended from heaven, the kingship was in Eridu. In Eridu, Alulim became king; he ruled for 28,800 years. Alaljar ruled for

The black Obelisk of Shalmaneser III, dating from 858–824 B.C., during the Neo-Assyrian era. HIP/ART RESOURCE, NY

> 36,000 years. Two kings, they ruled for [a total of] 64,800 years. Then Eridu fell and the kingship was taken to Bad-tibira. In Bad-tibira, Enmenluana ruled for 43,200 years. Enmengalana ruled for 28,800 years. Dumuzi, the shepherd [also a god], ruled for 36,000 years.

These impossibly long reigns are reminiscent of, though longer, than the centuries-long lifetimes cited for the early patriarchs in the Old Testament book of Genesis. The earliest ruler in the Sumerian lists whose existence has been verified by archaeology is Enmebaragesi, a king of Kish. Gilgamesh, the hero of the famous myth and epic poem, is listed as the fifth ruler of the first dynasty of Uruk; he may or may not have been a real person. There were also Babylonian and Assyrian king lists.

In general, the Mesopotamian king lists have both strengths and weaknesses from the standpoint of history and scholarship. On the one hand, those overly long reigns in the Sumerian lists make dating early Sumerian political events next to impossible. On the other hand, there are many gaps and errors in the lists. Also, the dynasties are listed one after another, as if they followed one another chronologically; whereas in reality they sometimes overlapped, with one dynasty ruling in one city-state while another dynasty ruled in a neighboring city-state. On the positive side, the king lists do show which rulers came first in each dynasty and how many years each king reigned. Combined with other evidence, especially archaeological finds, therefore, the lists can be helpful.

SEE ALSO: government; historical accounts; kingship

kingship

All of the city-states, kingdoms, and empires of ancient Mesopotamia were ruled by kings. Even when the Greeks, who had much experience with democracy, took over the region following the fall of the Persian Empire, they continued the local tradition of absolute monarchy. Going at least as far back as the third millennium B.C., kings justified their right to wield absolute power by citing one or another version of the myth of creation and how the institution of kingship was handed down from the gods. As told in the Babylonian *Epic of Creation*, for example, the ascendancy of the god Marduk as ruler of the universe and the other deities symbol-

ized the ascendancy of kings over their human subjects. Also, the Sumerian King List claimed that kingship was first handed down from the gods to humanity at Eridu.

To further reinforce this divine right to rule, Mesopotamian kings were often portrayed as somehow superhuman or semi-divine. Some ancient texts mention an aura or radiance surrounding the king's person, called the *melammu*, or "awe-inspiring luminosity." Also, it was common to refer to the king as the "son" of a certain god; to bestow on the king lofty, supernatural titles such as "king of heaven and Earth"; and to show the monarch standing with a god in artistic renderings.

However it was justified and reinforced, kingship brought with it duties and responsibilities as special and important as the king's titles and official images. Stemming from his unique relationship with the divine, he was often viewed as the highest of society's high priests. Among the words spoken during the crowning of an Assyrian king were these: "Before Ashur, your god, may your priesthood and the priesthood of your sons find favor." Although it varied from one time, place, and culture to another, a king's religious duties could include making sure that temples were built or maintained, appointing priests, leading various religious ceremonies and festivals, and consulting with official diviners and astrologers about the fate of the nation. The king was also the supreme commander of the army, with the authority to initiate wars at his will and to draw up plans for his military campaigns. In addition, he was the chief of state. In that capacity, he appointed government administrators and provincial governors, received and entertained foreign ambassadors, dispensed justice, and considered petitions from his subjects.

Most of these aspects of kingship in Mesopotamia were similar to those in many other places in the ancient world, from Egypt to Rome. There was one Mesopotamian royal custom that was unique and rather peculiar, however—that of the substitute king. In a number of Mesopotamian realms, if there seemed to be any sort of threat to the safety of the monarch, even an unfavorable omen, palace officials chose a temporary stand-in. The substitute, who had no real authority, was decked out in royal robes and was given quarters in the palace; meanwhile, the real king went into hiding. It was hoped that the stand-in would die in the king's place, thereby cheating fate. It appears that in some cases the substitute king was killed after the emergency had passed.

See Also: *Epic of Creation*; government; king lists

Kirkuk

The modern and more frequently used name for Arrapha, a Hurrian and Assyrian city located on the Hasa River about 155 miles (250km) north of modern Baghdad. The site of Arappha was occupied as early as the fifth millennium B.C. At some point in the second millennium B.C., migrating Hurrians established a small kingdom or city-state centered on Arrapha, which seems to have been subject to the larger Hurrian state of Mitanni, situated to its west. By the tenth century B.C. Arappha had been absorbed by the Assyrians and remained part of the Assyrian Empire for several centuries.

See Also: Assyrian Empire; Hurrians; Mitanni

Kish

One of the oldest and most venerable of the Sumerian cities and, according to the Sumerian King List, the place where the first royal dynasty arose following the great flood. Several mounds of ruins marking the site of ancient Kish lie about 8 miles (13km) east of the site of Babylon and some 85 miles (137km) south of modern Baghdad. The king list provides the names of many early kings of Kish, but Enmebaragesi and his son Agga were the first for whom archaeological evidence has been found. It appears that in the third millennium B.C. Kish was one of several prosperous and often competing Sumerian city-states, including Uruk, Ur, and Lagash; Kish may have enjoyed a brief period of dominance over the others around 2500 B.C. It is interesting that the king list gives credit for the establishment of the city's third and briefest dynasty (ca. 2450–2350 B.C.) to a woman named Kubaba since sole rule of Mesopotamian states by women was extremely rare. Kish also gained notoriety as the birthplace of the Akkadian conqueror Sargon in the late third millennium B.C. After the close of the Sumerian period, Kish remained an important center of learning. It was finally abandoned in the sixth century A.D.

Initial excavations at Kish were undertaken between 1912 and 1914 by a French team headed by Henri de Genouillac. An Anglo-American expedition under Stephen Langdon explored the site from 1923 to 1933. In addition to a royal cemetery similar to, but smaller than, the one found by Charles Leonard Woolley at Ur, they excavated the remains of a ziggurat dedicated to Kish's local warrior god, Zababa.

See Also: king lists; Ur; Woolley, Charles Leonard

Koldewey, Robert (1855–1925)

A German archaeologist best known for

his pioneering excavations of the ancient city of Babylon. An architect by trade, Koldewey taught himself the rudiments of archaeology and honed his skills on a series of expeditions to ancient sites in Greece, Italy, and Anatolia. He went to Iraq in the late 1890s and soon introduced a new, more efficient technique for excavating mud-brick structures. Koldewey began digging at Babylon in 1899 and continued there every season until the outbreak of World War I in 1914. He uncovered the foundation of the temple of Marduk, a ziggurat, parts of the city's defensive walls, and much more. He thought he had also found the remains of the Hanging Gardens of Babylon, but since that time a number of other scholars have voiced their doubts.

SEE ALSO: Assyriology; Babylon; Hanging Gardens of Babylon

Kramer, Samuel N. (1897–1990)

The twentieth century's leading archaeologist of Sumerian artifacts and translator of Sumerian documents. Long a scholar at the University of Pennsylvania, Kramer first began digging in Iraq in 1930. Over time he became increasingly adept at translating ancient Sumerian cuneiform texts and was particularly noted for his efforts to locate and translate neglected tablets lying in museums around the world. In one celebrated incident, he showed that pieces of a tablet in Istanbul, Turkey, were part of the same tablet to which pieces in Philadelphia belonged. He was also the first scholar to translate parts of the law code of Ur-Nammu, which predates the Babylonian king Hammurabi's law code. Kramer wrote many books, the most famous and influential of which is *History Begins at Sumer.*

SEE ALSO: languages; Sumerians; Ur-Nammu. And for one of Professor Kramer's translations, **see** farming

Kurigalzu

The name of two noted Kassite rulers of Babylonia. Kurigalzu I (reigned in the late fifteenth century B.C.) was the first of the Kassite rulers to declare himself divine. He established a new capital, Dur-Kurigalzu (modern Aqar Quf), at a site about 18 miles (29km) west of modern Baghdad, which became an administrative center. The first Kurigalzu expanded the kingdom's diplomatic contacts with foreign lands, including exchanges of gifts with Egypt. He also sent one of his daughters to become part of the harem of the Egyptian pharaoh Amenhotep III.

Kurigalzu II (reigned ca. 1332–1308 B.C.) was placed on the Babylonian throne by the Assyrians, who had recently helped the Kassite monarchy depose a usurper. Kurigalzu, who seems to have been more warlike than most other Kassite monarchs, proceeded to attack the Elamites and defeat them in battle. Later, he turned on and attacked the Assyrians, although he was unable to achieve victory against them. The second Kurigalzu also gained prestige for his building projects, including the restoration of the temple of Inanna at Uruk and the expansion of the new Kassite city of Dur-Kurigalzu.

SEE ALSO: Babylonia; Dur-Kurigalzu; Kassites

Lachish

An ancient Palestinian city captured by both the Assyrians and the Babylonians. By the early first millennium B.C. Lachish (modern Tell el-Duweir) was the second-most important town in the kingdom of Israel. As such it became a target of the Assyrian king Sennacherib, who took it in 701 B.C., although he failed to capture Jerusalem. Babylonia's King Nebuchadnezzar II seized Lachish circa 586 B.C.

SEE ALSO: Israel; Nebuchadnezzar II, weapons and warfare, siege

Lagash

One of the more important Sumerian cities in the late fourth millennium B.C. and all through the third millennium B.C. Located about 120 miles (193km) northwest of modern Basra, Iraq, the main urban center of Lagash (modern Tell al-Hibba) was large for its time, covering at least 2 square miles (5 sq. km). The city-state also included two smaller urban centers, Girsu and Nin-Sirara. Apparently Lagash underwent sporadic periods of expanding power and influence. One occurred under a ruler named Ur-Nanshe (reigned ca. 2494–2465 B.C.), who built tall defensive walls and numerous temples, and his grandson, Eannatum, who defeated the king of Ur, situated south of Lagash. Another period of expansion and prosperity was in the late third millennium B.C., especially under a ruler named Gudea (ca. 2141–2122 B.C.). In the early second millennium B.C., Lagash went into decline.

The main site of Lagash was discovered in 1877 by Frenchman Ernest de Sarzec. Principal excavations were undertaken between 1929 and 1933 under the direction of two other French scholars, Henri de Genouillac and André Parrot. These investigators uncovered more than thirty thousand cuneiform tablets. They also found that the city's main temple had been dismantled during the Greek Seleucid period in the late first millennium B.C. and the bricks had been used to erect a fortress.

SEE ALSO: Girsu; Gudea; Sumerians

Lama

A Sumerian goddess who was pictured in human form and thought to protect good, faithful people from harm. The term *lama* was also related to *lamassu*, the Assyrian term for the huge sculptures of winged bulls and lions placed at the entrances of Assyrian palaces. Like Lama, these images were thought to protect people, in this case those who lived and worked in the palaces.

SEE ALSO: palaces; sculpture

Lamashtu

In ancient Babylonian mythology and tradition, a terrifying female demon who stole fetuses from the wombs of pregnant women and relished committing other evil deeds. Ancient Mesopotamians usually attributed incidents of crib death to Lamashtu. To thwart this dangerous creature, it was customary to wear amulets—charms

A winged bull with a human face and a tiara, which represented protection to those in the palaces of Assyria. ERICH LESSING/ART RESOURCE, NY

thought to have magical powers—or to hang an amulet near the door of one's home.

SEE ALSO: amulets; religion

languages

Many languages were spoken over the course of the millennia in ancient Mesopotamia. The first widespread and important one was Sumerian, which modern experts have noted was unlike any other known tongue. Its original source remains uncertain, but sometime in the fourth millennium B.C. it replaced the existing language of southern Mesopotamia. That tongue, which scholars call Ubaidian and which was not written down, has survived in small part in the form of words adopted by the Sumerians; among them are the names of the great rivers—the Tigris and the Euphrates—along with the names of some cities and the words for *date* and *palm*. Sumerian was written down, of course, in cuneiform characters on clay tablets. And it was the official language of administration and correspondence in Mesopotamia in the late third millennium B.C. In the early years of the following millennium, use of Sumerian began to wane, and by about 1600 to 1500 B.C. it was no longer spoken. However, it was retained as a "classical" language used by scholars for many centuries to come, in the same way that Europeans still used Latin for scholarly and religious purposes long after it had ceased to be spoken. Sumerian was eventually largely deciphered thanks to the existence of ancient dictionaries, in which scribes listed Sumerian synonyms for words in their own languages. A series of modern scholars, including Francois Thureau-Dangin, Arno Poebel, Thorkild Jacobsen, and Samuel N. Kramer, used these dictionaries, along with much ingenuity and patience, to make the world's first important language understandable.

Among the languages that replaced Sumerian for everyday use were Semitic tongues that entered Mesopotamia from the west. The first of these was Akkadian, which appeared in the early third millennium B.C. and over time evolved into various dialects. The two main ones were Assyrian, spoken mainly in northern Mesopotamia, and Babylonian, used primarily in the south. Akkadian was very different in structure from Sumerian, although many Sumerian words were absorbed into Akkadian. By about 1450 B.C., Akkadian had become the chief language of diplomacy and correspondence in Mesopotamia. Meanwhile, two languages of unknown origin—Elamite and Hurrian—continued to be used in some areas. Elamite was spoken mainly in Elam, in the southern reaches of the Zagros range, and in eastern sections of Mesopotamia, and Hurrian was spoken primarily in Mitanni and northern Mesopotamia.

Among the other Semitic languages that entered Mesopotamia after Akkadian were Amorite and Aramaic. The latter became the most widely spoken and written language of the region and well beyond. In the words of H.W.F. Saggs, a leading expert of the ancient languages of the region:

> The trading activities of the Aramaeans spread their language over much of the Near East, so that by the time of the Persian Empire (from 539 B.C.) it had become the international language of diplomacy. Indeed, it was already beginning to take on that role more than two centuries earlier, for when the Assyrians were besieging Jerusalem in 701 B.C., the Judean authorities requested that the Assyrian general should conduct negotiations in Aramaic, which they as diplomats understood. ... Aramaic in its various dialects became the general language of much of the region from Palestine to Mesopotamia from the second half of the first millennium B.C. on, and had the same importance as a unifying force that was later enjoyed in the same region by Arabic, which displaced [Aramaic and other local languages] after the Islamic conquest in the seventh century A.D. (*Civilization Before Greece and Rome*, p. 18)

Meanwhile, in addition to Aramaic, some Indo-European languages were also used in Mesopotamia in the first millennium B.C. and early first millennium A.D. Notable among them were Old Persian and Greek, introduced after the conquests of Alexander the Great in the late fourth century B.C. But these never had the scope

or staying power of Aramaic, nor later of Arabic.

SEE ALSO: Aramaeans; Behistun Rock; Grotefend, Georg F.; Kramer, Samuel N., literature; Rawlinson, Henry C.; writing

Larsa

An important Sumerian, and later Babylonian, city in southern Mesopotamia, about 12 miles (20km) southeast of Uruk. Larsa (modern Tell Senkereh), which many scholars believe was the biblical city of Elassar, was continuously occupied from the fifth millennium B.C. to the third century A.D. Its heyday, however, was in the early second millennium B.C., when it engaged in a fierce rivalry with the city of Isin for control of southern Mesopotamia. By this time the rulers of both cities were Amorites, and Akkadian was in the process of replacing Sumerian as the main language of the area. The peak of Larsa's power came under a king named Gungunum (reigned ca. 1932–1906 B.C.), who defeated Isin, conquered Ur, and invaded Elam. The city's glory days were brief, though, as a later king, Rim-Sin (ca. 1822–1763 B.C.), was defeated by the Babylonian conqueror Hammurabi. Larsa was famous as a religious center. It housed a major temple and ziggurat of the sun god, Shamash (the Ebabbar, or "Shining House"), and shrines dedicated to the goddesses Inanna and Gula.

SEE ALSO: Gula; Hammurabi; Isin

laws and justice

Fortunately for interested modern observers, a number of legal codes, individual laws, and trial records have survived from ancient Mesopotamia. These laws did not cover every aspect of life by any means, but they were often surprisingly comprehensive, touching on matters of property rights, wage and price controls, inheritance, and crimes against people.

The earliest-known laws were issued by a Sumerian king, Uruinimgina of Lagash (reigned ca. 2351–2342 B.C.). These dealt with taxation, burial fees, treatment of women and orphans, and more. Another Sumerian ruler, Ur-Nammu (ca. 2113–2096, B.C.), founder of the Third Dynasty of Ur, also issued a set of laws, saying that he wanted "to free the land from thieves, robbers, and rebels." Ur-Nammu's legal system was noteworthy for making no distinctions regarding the wealth or status of the accused; all people were to be judged and punished equally. The justice system was also unusually liberal for the ancient world, or even for many countries in the modern world, as most offenses, including rape and assault, were punished by monetary fines. Still another Sumerian king, Lipit-Ishtar of Isin (ca. 1934–1923 B.C.) issued a law code that contained rules guiding work and workers and the institution of debt enslavement (becoming someone's slave to pay him back for a debt).

The most famous and comprehensive law code issued in ancient Mesopotamia was that of the Babylonian king Hammurabi (ca. 1792–1750 B.C.). Much of the 8-foot (2.4m), black stone stele on which his scribes carved the code has survived. Hammurabi gave a rationale for creating his laws as follows:

> In order that the strong might not oppress the weak, that justice be given to the orphan and the widow ... for the pronouncement of judgments in the land ... and to give justice to the oppressed, my weighty words I have written upon my monument. ... Let a man who has been wronged and has a cause, go before my stele ... and let him have my words inscribed on the monument read out. ... And may my monument enlighten him as to his cause and may he understand his case!

Of the 282 laws listed on the stele, some deal with property rights, money, and the regulation of wages and trade. Others cover family and marriage issues, adoption, medical malpractice, and personal injury. Among the latter are these:

> If a son strikes his father, they shall cut off his hand. If a man destroys the eye of another man, they shall destroy his eye. If he break another man's bone, they shall break his bone. If he destroy the eye of a client or break the bone of a client, he shall pay one mina of silver. If he destroy the eye of a man's slave or break the bone of a man's slave, he shall pay one-half his price [i.e., half the amount the owner paid for the slave]. If a man strike another man in a quarrel and wound him, he shall swear, "I struck him without intent," and he shall pay for the physician. If he die as a result of the blow, he shall swear (as above), and if the man was a free man, he shall pay one-half mina of silver.

As these samples show, most of Hammurabi's laws carried heavy penalties. Indeed, the death penalty was imposed for a conviction for kidnapping, receiving stolen goods, breaking and entering, and even for poor performance of a government job. Also, Hammurabi's laws, unlike those of Ur-Nammu, made distinctions for the wealth and status of the accused. Three general classes were treated differently—nobles and big landowners (*amelu*); everyday people (*muskinu*); and slaves (*ardu*, either captured in war or sold into slavery to satisfy a debt). Interestingly, the *amelu* paid stiffer penalties than members of the lower classes, perhaps because a higher degree of honesty and dignity was expected of upper-class persons.

The manner in which the laws were enforced and justice was handed out varied somewhat from place to place. Specific empires came and went, but Mesopotamia was at its heart a conglomeration of local towns and villages that endured for millennia, and in general most matters of justice were handled on the local level. Typically town officials or elders either served as judges or chose judges from among their ranks. (In the towns ruled by Ur-Nammu there were four judges in each court case, chosen from the professional ranks, such as scribes, respected merchants, city elders, and so forth. The judges were assisted by a court clerk, or *mashkim*, who kept careful records of the proceedings.) There were no juries or lawyers. Instead, the litigants (the person bringing the case and the person he charged with wrongdoing) pleaded their own cases and presented their own witnesses. Both litigants and witnesses first swore an oath to the gods that they would tell the truth. To further impress on all involved the importance of honesty, most trials were held on the grounds of temples, which must have made many people think twice about lying under oath. After the judges had handed down the verdict, it was recorded in writing. A number of such verdicts have survived on cuneiform tablets.

Some people seeking justice went further and appealed to a higher authority, sometimes the king himself. Such a plea, actually a follow-up to some earlier ones, was recorded in a letter written by an Assyrian man to King Ashurbanipal (ca. 668–627 B.C.):

How does it happen that I, who have

A painting depicting Austen Henry Layard, a 19th-century archaeologist who excavated several Assyrian sites. © BETTMANN/CORBIS

made several appeals to Your Majesty, have never been questioned by anybody? . . . I have not committed a crime against Your Majesty. . . . I merely conveyed an order of the king to [a man]. Although I said, "I am on business for the palace," he [took] my property away. He even arrested me and put me in fetters [chains], and that in front of all the people. . . . Ever since last year, nobody has given me anything to eat. . . . Your majesty should know that the same two men who took the gold jewelry from around my neck still go on planning to destroy me and to ruin me.

SEE ALSO: crime and punishment; Hammurabi; Ur-Nammu

Layard, Austen Henry (1817–1894)

A British diplomat and archaeologist who

was one of the major pioneers of Assyriology. While on an assignment in Iraq in 1845, Layard was drawn to the still largely unexplored ruins of ancient Assyrian cities. He later wrote:

These huge mounds of Assyria made a deep . . . impression on me. . . . A deep mystery hangs over Assyria, [and] Babylonia. . . . With these names are linked great nations and great cities dimly shadowed forth in history; mighty ruins in the midst of deserts, defying, by their very desolation and lack of definite form, the description of the traveler; the remnants of the mighty races still roving over the land; the fulfilling . . . of prophecies; the plains to which the Jew and the Gentile alike look as the cradle of their race. (*Nineveh and Its Remains*, vol. 1, pp. 2–3)

Layard first began digging at Nimrud, the site of the ancient Assyrian city of Kalhu. There he eventually unearthed nearly 2 miles (3.2km) of finely carved relief sculptures depicting the exploits of the Assyrian kings. One of the more exciting moments at Nimrud came when some of Layard's Arab workers discovered a huge carved stone head and were frightened because they thought they had dug up a mythical monster. "On reaching the ruins," Layard later recalled,

I descended into the newly opened trench, and found . . . an enormous human head. . . . [It was] the upper part of a figure, the remainder of which was still buried in the earth. I at once saw that the head must belong to a winged lion or bull. . . . I was not surprised that the Arabs had been amazed and terrified at this apparition. . . . This gigantic head . . . rising from the bowels of the earth, might well have belonged to one of those fearful beings which are described in

the traditions of the country as appearing to mortals, slowly ascending from the regions below. One of the workmen, on catching the first glimpse of the monster, had thrown down his basket and run [away] as fast as his legs could carry him. (*A Popular Account of Discoveries at Nineveh*, pp. 47–48)

Later, Layard excavated at the mound of Kuyunjik, near modern Mosul, site of ancient Nineveh, and discovered the library-archive of Assyria's King Ashurbanipal, including some twenty-four thousand cuneiform tablets. Also at Nineveh, he revealed the magnificent palace of King Sennacherib.

Over the course of the next few years, Layard sent thousands of sculptures and artifacts to London's British Museum, where they became the core of that institution's impressive Assyrian collection. He published several books about his adventures and discoveries, most notably *Nineveh and Its Remains* (1849) and *Discoveries in the Ruins of Nineveh and Babylon* (1853). In time, Layard went back into public service and served as Britain's ambassador to Constantinople beginning in 1877.

SEE ALSO: Assyriology; Nimrud; Nineveh; palaces; Palace Without Rival

letters

Some of the most important facts about political events and everyday life in ancient Mesopotamia have come from the contents of surviving letters. Unlike modern versions, these were not written on paper. Rather, the words were carved onto baked clay tablets, which explains why so many of them remain intact; if they had been written on paper they would have disintegrated long ago. The bulky clay letters were often placed within "envelopes," essentially carrying cases also made of baked clay, and delivered by servants or messengers. For the most part, letters were composed by scribes for kings, government officials, and members of the nobility. Most average people could not read and therefore had no use for letters, although there were undoubtedly occasional exceptions.

The setup of ancient Mesopotamian letters followed a standard, accepted formula, just as modern letters do. Today a typical letter begins with a salutation such as "Dear X" or "Dear Mr. X." The standard form for a Mesopotamian salutation was "X says the following: Tell Y that . . ." or words to that effect. After the salutation, the letter writer expressed wishes for the recipient's good health, then proceeded to get to the point of the letter. The social status of the correspondents also affected the style of the letter. If the letter writer belonged to a lower social class than the recipient, he took a subservient tone and used phrases such as "I grovel at your feet." If the two people were social equals, the letter writer addressed the recipient as "brother." If the letter writer was socially superior to the recipient, the tone of the letter might be very direct, even stern or cold.

There were numerous kinds of letters. One important category was royal correspondence—exchanges of letters between rulers. Hundreds of letters from the city of Mari, located on the upper Euphrates, dating to the early second millennium B.C. have survived, many of them written by King Zimri-Lim (reigned ca. 1775–1761 B.C.) and the early Assyrian monarch Shamshi-Adad (ca. 1813–1781 B.C.) and his sons. (For an example, see Ishme-Dagan.) Another important collection, the so-called *Amarna Letters*, consists of some

380 documents written in the 1300s B.C. by two Egyptian pharaohs to and from their royal counterparts in Hatti, Mitanni, Babylonia, and Assyria. Also, a number of later Assyrian letters were found in the ruins of the library of King Ashurbanipal at Nineveh.

Other common categories of letters included business correspondence, letters used as exercises for student scribes (generic letters copied and recopied), and those addressed to the gods. The latter were generally written by kings and were often read out loud before their assembled subjects. The ruler might thank the deity for sending divine aid or ask for guidance in a time of trouble. Letters were also written to praise the gods and thereby stay in their good graces, as in this example, addressed to the moon god, Nanna, from a Sumerian ruler:

> Say to Nanna . . . You, who are perfect in lordship and wear the legitimate headdress, the one with gleaming appearance and noble countenance, holy form endowed lavishly with beauty: Your greatness covers all countries. Your fearsome radiance overwhelms the holy sky. Your great awesomeness is imbued with terror. . . . You are indeed glorious from east to west. . . . You are the king of heaven and earth. It is you who decide their fate.

Some personal letters have also survived. The following example was written by a Babylonian student named Iddin-Sin to his mother, Zinu, in the eighteenth century B.C. It proves that modern students' concerns about looking fashionable in school are nothing new:

> Say to Zinu: Thus says Iddin-Sin. May the gods Shamash, Marduk, and Ilabrat preserve you safe and sound for my sake. The clothes of the other boys

[at my school] get better and better year by year. You let my clothes get plainer and plainer each year. By making my clothes plainer and fewer, you have enriched yourself. Although wool is used in our house like bread, you have made my clothes worse. Addad-iddinam's son ... [has just received] two new suits of clothes, but you are continually worried about merely one suit for me. While you actually brought me into the world, his mother adopted him. But the way in which his mother loves him, in such a way you do not by any means love me.

SEE ALSO: libraries; literature; Mari; writing

libraries

The ancient Mesopotamians did not have libraries in the modern sense—that is, public institutions where people could go to borrow books. A Mesopotamian library was more of an archive, a collection of clay tablets usually kept in one or more rooms in a temple or a palace. Such archives began as a way of retaining records of official administrative, economic, or religious business. Over time, however, other kinds of literature, including letters, historical accounts, and epic poems, were also stored in archives. Among the earliest Mesopotamian archives discovered to date are those in Ur and Nippur, compiled when these cities were part of the Third Dynasty of Ur in the late third millennium B.C. A larger archive was found in the ruins of Mari. Dating to the nineteenth century B.C., it contains thousands of documents, including many letters written to and from Zimri-Lim and other rulers of Mari.

The largest and best-preserved Mesopotamian library-archive is that of the Assyrian king Ashurbanipal (reigned ca. 668–627 B.C.) at Nineveh. It was discovered in 1849 by pioneer Assyriologist Austen Henry Layard. Of the more than twenty thousand tablets in the original collection, about five thousand proved to be in good enough condition to translate. Beginning with translations by German scholar Carl Bezold between 1889 and 1899, experts have revealed the contents of some fifteen hundred complete texts covering a wide range of subjects. Some evidence suggests that the archive was originally divided into several rooms, each devoted to a specific subject.

SEE ALSO: Ashurbanipal; Layard, Austen Henry; literature

literature

Thanks to the survival of thousands of clay tablets from many times and places in ancient Mesopotamia, it is clear that the civilizations of that region produced a large, varied, and rich collection of literature, some of it of high quality. Among the literary genres that developed were epic and other poetry, hymns and prayers, proverbs, social satires, laments, law codes, letters, astrological and divination texts, and historical accounts. Although examples of writing date back to the early third millennium B.C. or earlier in Mesopotamia, the earliest examples of literary texts date from about 2400 B.C. The Sumerians produced large amounts of literature. But few of the original versions have survived, and most of what exists today consists of later Babylonian and Assyrian copies. Particularly important are literary copies made by Kassite Babylonian scribes in the second half of the second millennium B.C.

Epic Poems The case of epic poetry is a clear example of this process. The Sumerians created several early epics, including the famous *Epic of Gilgamesh*. Babylonian and the divine. Besides the poems about Gilgamesh and Atrahasis, important epics included those about the goddess Inanna's descent into the Underworld, the romance between the deities Nergal and Ereshkigal, and the adventures of the heroes Adapa and Etana. The only Assyrian epic of which sections survive was the *Tukulti-Ninurta Epic*, which celebrates that Assyrian king's victory over the Babylonians in the thirteenth century B.C.

Mesopotamian poets also wrote shorter works, notably erotic poems that may have been intended as entertainment for royal courtiers at feasts, celebrations, and other gatherings. In one example, a man goes into a tavern and propositions a barmaid. The lyrics of these pieces are often sexually graphic. Yet their frequent use of similes and metaphors comparing lovers and their sexual organs to natural objects such as trees, wheat, and flowers make them literarily rich, even charming.

Hymns and Prayers Another important Mesopotamian literary genre consisted of hymns and prayers. This comes as no surprise since the people of the region were religiously devout, sometimes in the extreme. Most of the hymns were probably composed by priests and praised various gods. Consequently, modern scholars have learned much about these gods and the locations of their principal shrines by studying ancient hymns. This is part of a hymn to Inanna, goddess of love and sexual passion:

> The great-hearted mistress, the impetuous lady, proud among the gods and pre-eminent in all lands ... the magnificent lady who gathers up the divine powers of heaven and earth and rivals great An, is mightiest among the great gods. She makes their verdicts final. ... Her great awesomeness covers the great mountain and

This hexagonal prism from the reign of King Sansu-Iluna is inscribed with a hymn honoring a Sumerian god. ERICH LESSING/ART RESOURCE, NY

scribes later made copies of the original, which was subsequently lost. That original, like other written versions of epic poetry, was based on an oral tradition that likely stretched back to the period before the invention of writing. Just as Greek bards like Homer traveled around reciting stories about heroes, gods, and the Trojan War, early Mesopotamian poets told and retold tales about the heroes Gilgamesh, Enkidu, and Atrahasis and their encounters with the gods and fate. Epic poems were typically long, detailed, and dealt with universal, weighty themes, such as the meaning of life and death, the quest for immortality, and the relationship between humans levels the roads. At her loud cries, the gods of the Land become scared. . . . Wherever she [goes], cities become ruin mounds and haunted places, and shrines become waste land.

Other Mesopotamian hymns are like love songs and were probably recited in ceremonies in which kings enacted ritual marriages between themselves and Inanna. As Samuel N. Kramer and other noted scholars have pointed out, a number of such works resemble some of the psalms in the Old Testament; and indeed, the prevailing theory is that the writers of the biblical psalms were influenced to some degree by Mesopotamian models. Just as the psalms of the Hebrew king David were meant to be sung or recited to harp music, Mesopotamian hymns were likely accompanied by some kind of music. One striking example reads in part:

> Bridegroom, let me caress you, my precious caress is sweeter than honey. In the bed-chamber, honey-filled, let me enjoy your goodly beauty. . . . Your spirit, I know here to cheer your spirit. Bridegroom, sleep in our house until dawn. Your heart, I know where to gladden your heart. Lion, sleep in our house until dawn.

Proverbs and Laments Another popular category of literature in ancient Mesopotamia was the proverb, a short, wise saying passed from one generation to the next. Like poems, proverbs were at first preserved by word of mouth, but in the second millennium B.C. scribes began to collect them and write them down. Often they would give the same proverb in both Sumerian and Akkadian, which turned out to be helpful for modern scholars trying to translate Sumerian. The main reason that proverbs were so popular was that change occurred only very slowly in Meso-

potamian society; so most people felt that the wisdom of past generations could still be applied to their own. The following are among the most enduring of the Mesopotamian proverbs: "The poor men are the silent men in Sumer"; "Friendship lasts a day, kingship forever"; "If you take the field of an enemy, the enemy will come and take your field"; "Conceiving is nice, but pregnancy is irksome"; and "For a man's pleasure there is marriage, while on thinking it over, there is divorce."

Another literary genre that involved short but pointed statements about life was social satire, made up mainly of brief, humorous tales. Each involved everyday people and/or animals and commented in some way on common social injustices, especially the exploitation of the weak by the strong. In one story, for example, a simple, uneducated gardener shows that he is far wiser than a highly educated doctor. Many satires were animal fables like those of the Greek writer Aesop, with dogs (symbolic of average people) outwitting lions (representing royalty) and so forth. There were also fictional letters and contracts, including a contract for a worthless piece of land drawn up by a bird and witnessed by other birds.

On a more serious note, almost all Mesopotamians knew about the ravages of war and famine and the loss of loved ones in such times of crisis. The strong emotions aroused by such events were frequently expressed in laments, or lamentations. These were sad works in which the writer, speaking for the people of a city, described the ills that had befallen the city and expressed grief, sorrow, and asked the gods for forgiveness. The Mesopotamian laments directly inspired the ones in the biblical book of Lamentations, inspired by the fall of Jerusalem to the Babylonians, including:

> The Lord has scorned his altar. . . . He has delivered into the hands of the enemy the walls of her palaces. . . . Cry aloud to the Lord! O daughter of Zion [Israel]! Let tears stream down like a torrent day and night! Give yourself no rest, your eyes no respite! (Lamentations 2.7, 2.18)

For excerpts from a lament attributed to the goddess Ningal, the *Lamentation Over the Destruction of Ur*, **see also** Ningal; Third Dynasty of Ur. For an excerpt from the Assyrian *Tukulti-Ninurta Epic*, **see also** Tukulti-Ninurta I. And for details about other kinds of Mesopotamian literature, **see also** divination; historical accounts; laws and justice; letters.

SEE ALSO: Bible; languages; libraries; writing; and the names of individual epic poems

Lloyd, Seton
(1902–1996)

A noted English archaeologist who supervised a number of important excavations at ancient Mesopotamian sites in the twentieth century. Lloyd began his career in 1928 on an expedition that investigated Tell el-Amarna, site of the city built by the maverick Egyptian pharaoh Akhenaten. From 1930 to 1937 he led a team from Chicago's Oriental Institute in digs at several sites near the Diyala River in northern Mesopotamia, including Tell Asmar (Eshnunna), Tell Agrab, and Khafajah. Later he acted as adviser to Iraqi archaeologists exploring the early Sumerian ceremonial center of Eridu. A specialist in mud-brick excavations, Lloyd wrote a number of important books about ancient Mesopotamia, of which *Foundations in the Dust* (1947) is the most famous.

SEE ALSO: Assyriology; Eridu; Eshnunna

Loftus, William K.
(1820–1858)

An English geologist who became an early pioneer of Assyriology when he excavated the site of the ancient Sumerian city of Uruk. Like many other European intellectuals of his day, Loftus hoped that excavations of ancient Mesopotamian cities would reveal artifacts and information that would confirm the authenticity of statements made about the region in the Bible. Building on work already done in the area by Danish scholar Karsten Niebuhr, Frenchman Paul Emile Botta, and another Englishman, Austen Henry Layard, Loftus searched for the city of Uruk, called Erech in the Old Testament. Loftus suspected that Uruk lay beneath the surface at a site the local Arabs called Warka. Sure enough, Warka did prove to be ancient Uruk, where he uncovered the remains of the city's defensive walls, many still intact and rising to a height of 50 feet (15m). Loftus later excavated the ruins of another Sumerian city, Larsa. There he unearthed a temple of the god Shamash. He published *Travels and Researches in Chaldea and Susiana* in 1857, a year before his untimely death.

SEE ALSO: Botta, Paul Emile; Layard, Austen Henry; Niebuhr, Karsten

Lugalzagesi
(reigned ca. 2340–2316 B.C.)

A Sumerian king who conquered most of Sumer shortly before the rise of the Akkadian Empire. Lugalzagesi began as the ruler of Umma, a city situated northwest of Lagash. He captured Uruk and Lagash and apparently planned to push westward to the Mediterranean Sea. But his ambitions were cut short by a greater imperialist, Sargon of Akkad, who defeated Lugalzagesi and took him prisoner.

SEE ALSO: Lagash; Sargon of Akkad; Sumerians

Magi

A group or caste of religious experts in ancient Mesopotamia during the first millennium B.C. and perhaps later. According to Herodotus and other ancient Greek writers, the Magi (or Magians) originated under the Medes and were active in Zoroastrian worship during the years of the Persian Empire. The Greek geographer Strabo mentions Magi during the later Parthian period, and they existed in the Sassanian period, too. It appears that a Magus was not an ordinary priest but rather a special kind of priest who had expertise in interpreting omens and dreams and performing sacrifices involving fire. Herodotus writes about another peculiar Magian custom:

> There is a Persian practice concerning the burial of the dead, which is not spoken of openly and is something of a mystery. It is that a male Persian is never buried until the body has been torn by a bird or a dog. I know for certain that the Magians have this custom, for they are quite open about it. . . . [They] not only kill anything, except dogs and men, with their own hands but make a special point in doing so; ants, snakes, animals, birds—no matter what, they kill them indiscriminately. (*Histories* 1.140)

Today the Magi are remembered best in the traditional Christmas tale in which three of them, sometimes called wise men or kings, travel from Mesopotamia and visit the baby Jesus in Bethlehem.

SEE ALSO: Herodotus; Persian Empire; Zoroastrianism

magic

The people of ancient Mesopotamia did not make a clear distinction between magic and normal religious beliefs and rituals. It was thought that the gods had the power to wield magic, for both good and ill, and some gods, notably Enlil and Marduk, were seen as skilled sorcerers. Magic always acknowledged the existence of evil, which was seen as a palpable force that lurked on the fringes of human society and was capable of "infecting" anyone at any time. This infection could take the form of illness, accidents, bad fortune, or death and was supposedly caused by demons, witchcraft, or gods seeking to punish the wicked. Any and all of these negative forces could be viewed as forms of black magic. White, or positive, magic existed to counter the effects of black magic. White magic consisted of spells, incantations, and physical actions, including burning effigies representing demons or evil spirits, that drove away demons and other aspects of black magic. Rituals of white magic were usually performed by a diviner or a spiritual doctor (*ashipu*). The white magician first had to determine what kind of demon or other evil was affecting the victim. To this end, he could consult special texts, the *Surpu* and the *Maqlu*, which contained lists of the various ills that could afflict people and numerous spells and cures for these ills. The ultimate goal was to rid the person of evil, when necessary by performing an exorcism. Practicing black magic or witchcraft was a crime, and the law codes of ancient Mesopotamia provided statutes dealing with it. The statute in Hammurabi's code reads:

> If a man charge a man with sorcery, but cannot convict him, he who is charged with sorcery shall go to the sacred river, and he shall throw himself into the river. If the river overcomes him, his prosecutor shall take to himself his house. If the river shows that man innocent and he comes forth unharmed, he that charged him with sorcery shall be put to death. He who threw himself into the river shall take to himself the house of his accuser.

SEE ALSO: divination; doctors and medicine; exorcism

Mallowan, Max E.L. (1904–1978)

A renowned English archaeologist who significantly advanced modern studies of ancient Mesopotamia and the ancient cultures of neighboring regions. Mallowan received an education in classics at Oxford University and soon afterward launched his distinguished career by serving from 1925 to 1931 as an assistant to the great Charles Leonard Woolley in the groundbreaking excavations at the site of the major Sumerian city of Ur. It was while working at Ur that Mallowan met the famous English mystery writer Agatha Christie. Though she was fourteen years older than he, they fell in love and married. From 1932 to 1938, Mallowan directed excavations at several previously obscure ancient sites in Mesopotamia and then went on to work at the better-known ancient Assyrian site of Nimrud. Later,

between 1947 and 1961, he served as director of the prestigious British School of Archaeology. Mallowan was also knighted by the British queen in 1968. He wrote several important books, including *Twenty-Five Years of Mesopotamian Discovery* (1956).

SEE ALSO: Assyriology; Ur; Woolley, Charles Leonard

Mamitu

An ancient Mesopotamian goddess who protected the sanctity of truth, particularly oaths made by one person to another or by a human to a god. In fact, the name Mamitu (sometimes written as Mami or Mame for short) came from an Akkadian word meaning "oath." This deity was also thought to punish people who committed perjury in court.

SEE ALSO: crime and punishment; laws and justice; religion

map making

A number of maps have survived from ancient Mesopotamia. They were carved into clay tablets just as literary and other written texts were. Because it was difficult to carve rounded lines, most lines in maps were straight, even when denoting a road or boundary that actually curved. Maps were created to show the boundaries of estates and farms, the ground plans of temples and houses, the layout of cities or districts within cities, countries, and the world as a whole. All were drawn, like modern versions, as if looking down from above. Most maps were not drawn to scale; a notable exception is a map of the city of Nippur dating to the second millennium B.C., which is so accurate that it resembles the excavation charts prepared by modern

Babylonian tablet showing an ancient map of the world, most likely from Sippar, in modern-day southern Iraq, between 700–500 B.C. ERICH LESSING/ART RESOURCE, NY

archaeologists. Canals were sometimes drawn as parallel lines with wavy crests between them to indicate water, and cities and villages were designated by small rectangles or circles. Streets and roads were indicated by lines with street names etched beside the lines. A Babylonian world map dating from roughly 600 B.C. shows the city of Babylon resting in the center. Around it stretch the known lands, which rest on a round disk surrounded by a circular outer ocean or great river. An accompanying text describes the "seven islands," which are indicated by triangles pointing outward from the edges of the outer ocean. One passage mentions the "land where the Sun is not seen," suggesting that by this time the Mesopotamians knew about the arctic region lying far to the north. If so, the information likely came via thirdhand stories told by merchants who traded with the natives of what is now southern Russia.

SEE ALSO: Mesopotamia, geography of; Nippur; trade

Marduk

The chief god of the Babylonian religious pantheon. Marduk was originally a local deity, the patron god of the city of Babylon. He was possibly conceived as an agricultural god because one of his symbols was a hoe. Over time, however, Marduk's status and prestige increased. The circumstances of his rise to power over the universe and the other gods were laid out in the Babylonian myth expressed in writing as the *Epic of Creation*. In that tale, Marduk defeats Tiamat, goddess of saltwater, who helped spawn the race of gods. From the eighteenth century B.C. on in Babylonia, Marduk began to supplant the Sumerian deity Enlil as chief god, a process that was completed in the twelfth century B.C.

Temples of Marduk existed all over Babylonia. And shrines to him and his son, Nabu, were also erected in many Assyrian cities. Marduk's main temple, however, was the Esagila in Babylon. There rested his primary cult statue, which was stolen by the Elamites circa 1185 B.C. and also by the Assyrians in the seventh century B.C. It was seen as essential to win back this sacred image because the prestige and prosperity of Babylon and its realm were tied directly to worship and appeasement of Marduk. Among the numerous hymns and praises written to and for Marduk over the centuries was this one, which invokes the deity's blessings for a person to live a long and peaceful life:

May Marduk grant life! May he . . .

decree life for you! May he prolong your life, and may he let you keep it for everlasting days! May you live, and may you have peace! May it last forever! May life be your lot, and may a life of contentment be your share! When you lie down to sleep, may your dreams be propitious [promising], and when you rise, may your omens be favorable! Wherever you walk, may you be established in peace!

SEE ALSO: Babylon; *Epic of Creation*; Nabu

Marduk-nadin-ahhe
(reigned ca. 1100–1083 B.C.)

A Babylonian king who tried but failed to defeat the vigorous Assyrian king Tiglath-pileser I (reigned ca. 1115–1076 B.C.). The sixth ruler of the Second Dynasty of Isin, Marduk-nadin-ahhe was a younger brother of King Nebuchadnezzar I, who had recently become a national hero by rescuing the stolen statue of the god Marduk from Elam. Perhaps trying to match the military stature of his brother, Marduk-nadin-ahhe launched a large-scale attack on Assyria. For several years the Babylonian campaigns were successful, but eventually the forceful Tiglathpileser got the upper hand. Marduk-nadin-ahhe was defeated, and his ultimate fate is unknown.

SEE ALSO: Babylonia; Elam; Tiglathpileser I

Mari

Variously a city, city-state, and small kingdom situated along the upper reaches of the Euphrates River in what is now eastern Syria. The site of Mari (modern Tell al-Hariri) was occupied at least by the fourth millennium B.C., and a substantial town thrived there by the early third millennium B.C. In the late 2300s B.C. Sargon of Akkad used Mari as a base from which to launch some of his military campaigns. After the decline of Akkad, the city became subject to the Third Dynasty of Ur.

In the wake of the Third Dynasty of Ur's own decline at the close of the third millennium B.C., Amorites settled in Mari and ushered in its heyday of power and influence, spanning the period from about 2000 to 1800 B.C. During these years the city controlled one of the main trade routes leading from Mesopotamia into Syria-Palestine, and its kings had an effective army to enforce that control and to defend the city. Mari was also a center of art and culture in this period. Eventually Shamshi-Adad, an Amorite king of Assyria, captured Mari and installed his son, Iasmah-Adad, as king there. The last native king of Mari, Zimri-Lim (reigned ca. 1775–1761 B.C.), greatly expanded the local palace. But before he could expand the kingdom he was defeated by Babylonia's King Hammurabi, who burned and destroyed Mari.

The site of Mari then steadily faded from view until modern times. The city was rediscovered in 1933 by some Arab grave diggers, and soon a team of French archaeologists led by André Parrot began excavations. Another Frenchman, Jean-Claude Margueron, took over the digs in 1978. The excavators found that the fire set by Hammurabi's soldiers had preserved large sections of the city's mud-brick walls. The diggers also discovered more than twenty thousand clay tablets bearing writing in cuneiform, including many letters written by Zimri-Lim and other Marian rulers.

SEE ALSO: Iasmah-Adad; letters; Shamshi-Adad; Zimri-Lim

marriage and divorce

In ancient Mesopotamia marriage was

viewed as a bond between a man and a woman designed primarily to produce children to perpetuate society and its traditions and civic order. Marriage, along with female fertility, was therefore seen as crucial to maintaining a viable society. Men seeking brides accordingly prized healthy young women, especially virgins. Although romantic love may have occasionally played a part in the choosing of mates, most marriages were arranged by relatives when the prospective brides were in their teens and the prospective grooms were about ten years older.

Because considerations of love usually did not enter into the marriage equation, a marriage was viewed in large part as a business arrangement. As such, it required a legal contract to be binding. One of the statutes in Hammurabi's law code states, "If a man takes a wife and does not arrange a contract for her, that woman is not a wife." The groom and/or leading members of his family negotiated with the bride's family about the upcoming union, especially regarding money matters. The bride's father produced a dowry, which consisted of valuable items for her upkeep in the marriage. Typical dowry items included jewelry, cooking utensils and dinnerware, furniture, slaves, and bars of silver or other rare metals. If the wife died, the dowry legally became the property of the children produced in the marriage, although the husband could utilize the dowry items if he wanted to. The father of the groom often gave the bride's family money or valuables, called the bride-price. Both the dowry and the bride-price could be paid in installments until the first child was born, at which time payment in full was due. These and other details of the marriage contract were sometimes set down in writing, but verbal contracts were legal, too, and likely more common. The marriage was considered to officially begin at a feast held at the groom's father's house, although in some places and times it may not have been legal until the dowry and the bride-price were paid in full.

Marriage was usually monogamous. However, it was legal for a man to have another wife under certain special conditions. For example, when a wife could not bear children, her husband was allowed either to take a second wife or to father children with a female servant. Nevertheless, he remained legally bound to continue honoring and supporting his wife until her natural death, and a servant could not claim equality with the wife. One of Hammurabi's laws provided that if the servant "bears children and afterwards claims equal rank with her mistress," the wife "may not sell her," but "may reduce her to bondage and count her among the slaves."

Divorce was legal under a few circumstances, including abuse by the husband, the wife's infertility, or adultery on the part of the wife. Another of Hammurabi's laws stated, "If the wife of a man is caught lying with another man, they [the authorities] shall bind them and throw them into the water." It is unlikely, however, that husbands and local authorities resorted to such extreme punishments in all cases of adultery when divorce was a ready and more civilized option. Most scholars think that such harsh laws were meant to scare wives and thereby discourage them from having adultery. A divorce had to be approved in court by a judge. The judge made sure that the woman had some means of support after leaving her husband's house, and to that end the court might order the husband to give her back the dowry. The man also might have to

Clay tablet showing a calculation of the surface of a terrain at Umma, Mesopotamia, from 2100 B.C. ERICH LESSING/ART RESOURCE, NY

pay a fine. In Assyria, if a husband merely abandoned his wife and she had no living sons to support her, she was allowed to remarry after a waiting period of five years. If she did not wait the five years and had children by the second husband, the first husband could claim custody of those children.

SEE ALSO: laws and justice; women

Martu

Another name for Amurru, chief god of the early Amorites, a Semitic people who settled in Mesopotamia in the second millennium B.C.

SEE ALSO: Amorites; Amurru; religion

mathematics

The peoples of ancient Mesopotamia—particularly the Sumerians and the Babylonians—made important contributions to the early development of mathematics, and some of their mathematical ideas and systems are still used today. The early Sumerians had a simple decimal system, one based on the number 10, that they probably inherited from earlier peoples. That system used small clay tokens to indicate various numbers. One token stood for 1 sheep, 1 measure of grain, or, in the more general sense, the number 1. Another token stood for 10 sheep or the number 10. In this system, a number such as 23 was denoted by two number-10 tokens and three number-1 tokens.

Over time the Sumerians began writing numerical symbols on clay tablets, each symbol indicating a certain token and the number it represented. These symbols became very complex and are still not completely understood. By the last centuries of the third millennium B.C., however, the scribes had simplified the system, narrowing it down to just two symbols, a vertical wedge and a corner wedge. These had different meanings depending on their placement. In one configuration, they indicated 60 (6 x 10); in another, they stood for 3,600 (60 x 60), and so forth. All the multiples used either 6 or 10, which made it a rudimentary sexagesimal system (one based on the number 60). Everyday calculations, for commerce or construction, became somewhat less cumbersome when the Akkadians introduced the abacus in the late third millennium B.C.

Later, the Babylonians inherited and continued to use the Sumerian decimal system for counting, but only for numbers from 1 to 59. For higher numbers, the Babylonians expanded the Sumerian sexagesimal system into a more sophisticated version. Because the new system combined elements of decimal and sexagesimal schemes, it was rather clumsy in comparison to the simpler, strictly decimal version used in most of the world today. In Babylonia, for example, the number 3,832 was expressed as 1,3,52. Reading from right to left, the second number occupied an order of magnitude higher than the first, and the third an order higher than the second. Thus, the user understood that the 1 stood for 1×60^2 (or 3,600), the 3 for 3×60 (or 180), and the 52 for 52 single decimal

units. Adding the three numbers together therefore rendered 3,600 + 180 + 52 = 3,832. This shows that the Babylonians understood and used square roots. They also employed cube roots (for instance, $60^3 = 60 \times 60 \times 60 = 216,000$). The following is an actual surviving math problem from ancient Babylonia:

> Problem: If somebody asks you thus: As much as the side of the square which I made I dug deep, and I extracted one *musaru* [60^3] and a half of volume of earth. My base (ground) I made a square. How deep did I go? Solution: You, in your procedure, operate with 12. Take the reciprocal of 12 and multiply by 1,30,0,0 which is your volume. 7,30,0 you will see [i.e., will be the answer]. What is the cube root of 7,30,0? 30 is the cube root. Multiply 30 by 1, and 30 you [will] see. Multiply 30 by another 1, and 30 you [will] see. Multiply 30 by twelve, and 6,0 [360] you [will] see. 30 is the side of your square, and 6,0 [360] is your depth.

Some remnants of this sexagesimal system have survived. For instance, people still divide a circle into 360 degrees and count 60 seconds to a minute and 60 minutes to an hour in timekeeping, navigation, and astronomy.

The Babylonians also employed mathematical tables of various kinds to make some calculations easier. They had multiplication tables, tables of square roots and cube roots, and tables that listed monetary conversions, including the equivalents of the values of various goods to the value of given weights of silver. The Babylonians also developed a simple form of geometry for determining area and volume. This proved useful in constructing ziggurats and other large-scale buildings. Babylonian geometry eventually influenced early

Greek thinkers, who created a more sophisticated version by introducing provable theorems.

SEE ALSO: astrology and astronomy; weights and measures; writing materials

Medes

The inhabitants of Media, in the western part of Iran, who played a key role in Mesopotamian history in the first millennium B.C. The Medes, who spoke an Indo-European language, began as a group of loosely organized but culturally related tribes that migrated southward from central Asia into Iran around 1000 B.C. or shortly thereafter. The reasons these tribes began to unite into a sort of national unit are unclear; one major factor may have been raids into western Media conducted by the Assyrians, who were rising to power in the early first millennium B.C. In any case, by the mid-700s B.C. the Medes were strong enough to return the favor and pose a moderate threat to the Assyrians. The annals of Assyria's King Tiglathpileser III (reigned 744–727 B.C.) and King Sargon (reigned 721–705 B.C.) record campaigns against the Medes, including carved reliefs showing Median fortresses with high battlements. These reliefs also depict the early Medes themselves. They wore their hair short and sported short, curled beards, tunics covered by sheepskin coats, and high-laced boots. Their weapons included a long spear and a rectangular wicker shield as well as bows employed with great skill by archers on horseback. These effective warriors, who gained the respect of the warlike Assyrians, soon became instrumental in the rise of the Median Empire, which eventually overcame Assyria and laid the groundwork for the larger Persian Empire.

SEE ALSO: Ecbatana; Media; Persian Empire

Media

An ancient region and tribal kingdom that spanned the western and northwestern sectors of present-day Iran and bordered eastern Assyria. Media (Mada in Old Persian), which incorporated parts of the Zagros Mountains, was largely hilly but had several small, fertile plains as well. It was settled in the early first millennium B.C. by the Medes, an Indo-European-speaking group from farther north, and eventually became the focus of the short-lived but influential Median Empire, which helped bring about the fall of the Assyrian Empire in the seventh century B.C. Part of the reason that Media rose to prominence was that it controlled a major trade route running from Bactria and Parthia in the east, through Media, to Babylonia, Assyria, and Syria in the west. Even after the decline of the Median Empire, the region remained a populous, prosperous, and valuable part of the Persian, Seleucid, and Parthian realms that followed.

SEE ALSO: Medes; Median Empire; Persian Empire

Median Empire

A powerful but short-lived imperial realm created by the Medes in the seventh century B.C. and one of the leading factors in both the demise of Assyria and the rise of the Persian Empire. Perhaps because of threats from the Assyrians, who dwelled directly west of Media in western Iran, by the late 700s B.C. the Medes had become organized under a series of war leaders. Their identities and deeds are now largely shrouded in the mists of time. The Greek historian Herodotus claimed that the key early figures in the creation of the Median nation, its capital of Ecbatana, and its empire were Deioces and Phraortes. "The achievement of Deioces, who reigned for fifty years," Herodotus writes,

> was to unite under his rule the people of Media—Busae, Parataceni, Struchates, Arazanti, Budii, Magi; beyond these he did not extend his empire. His son Phraortes, however, who succeeded to the throne on his father's death, was not content to be king only of Media; he carried his military operations further afield, and the first country he attacked and brought into subjection was Persia [in Fars, in southern Iran]. (*Histories* 1.105)

Modern scholars think that Deioces and Phraortes, as described by Herodotus, may have been composite characters based on confused secondhand accounts of several early Median rulers. There is no doubt that Cyaxares II (reigned ca. 625–585 B.C.) was a real person, however. And it appears that he was a dynamic ruler who almost single-handedly created the Median Empire. He reorganized the military and enlisted recruits from minor Iranian peoples whom Media held as vassals, including the Persians. When Cyaxares was confident in the size and abilities of his forces, he attacked Assyria in about 614 B.C. He was aided by the Babylonians, with whom he had made an alliance. The great Assyrian city of Nineveh fell to the combined Median and Babylonian assault in 612, and the once-mighty Assyrian Empire rapidly fell to pieces. To cement and celebrate the alliance that had brought down the Assyrians, Cyaxares gave his daughter Amytis in marriage to Nebuchadnezzar II, king of Babylonia.

The rise of Media and elimination of Assyria created a new balance of power in the Near East. The region was now dominated by four nations of approximately the same strength: Media, Babylonia, Lydia in Anatolia, and Egypt. But Cyaxares was not content with maintaining this balance of power. He launched a series of conquests that gained Media an empire stretching from the southern shores of the Caspian Sea in the east to Armenia (Urartu) in the west. Then, circa 589 B.C., he turned to the northwest and invaded Lydia, but he failed to conquer it.

Having established the Median Empire, Cyaxares died and was succeeded by Astyages (reigned ca. 585–550 B.C.). Not only was Astyages a mediocre ruler, he also faced major logistical difficulties in holding together the huge Median realm, including communication and transportation of soldiers and supplies over long distances. The threat of rebellions by subject peoples was another problem. Most of these peoples were discontented with Median rule and had to be kept in line by the use of force. The fact that many of the Median nobles resented Astyages was another factor in the overall weakness and vulnerability of the realm. These and other factors made Media a tempting target for would-be imperialists. And in about 553 B.C. Cyrus II, ruler of the Persian region of Fars, led a rebellion that soon toppled Astyages from his throne.

Thanks to Cyrus's foresight, however, Media was not destroyed but instead was absorbed into the new Persian Empire. He actually honored the Medes, appointing a number of Median nobles as courtiers and army officers. He also made the Median homeland the first satrapy (province) of his own realm, calling it Mada, and kept Ecbatana intact as his second capital. Thereafter, people routinely referred to the Persian realm as the empire of the Medes and Persians.

SEE ALSO: Astyages; Cyaxares II; Ecbatana; Media

melammu

In the myths and lore associated with ancient Mesopotamian kingship, an aura or radiance surrounding the king's person. Sometimes translated as "awe-inspiring luminosity," *melammu* was an Akkadian word borrowed from the Sumerians. It is unknown where the concept came from, but it may have developed in the late fourth or early third millennia B.C. as a way of enhancing the image of kings by making them appear to be chosen or blessed by the gods. The Mesopotamian *melammu* was the partial basis for later artistic imagery of auras and halos surrounding the heads or bodies of Byzantine and Christian angels and saints.

SEE ALSO: kingship

Merodach-Baladan (reigned ca. 721–710 B.C.)

A Babylonian nobleman who became king of Babylonia but was unable to hold onto his throne in the face of Assyrian aggressions. Although Merodach-Baladan (or Marduk-apal-iddina) was the name assigned to him in the Hebrew Old Testament rather than his actual Babylonian name, the biblical version stuck and is the one used most often today. Shortly after Merodach-Baladan became king of Babylonia, Assyria's King Sargon II attacked and forced him to flee to Elam. Seven years later, with the aid of the Elamites, Merodach-Baladan made a comeback and once more sat on the Babylonian throne. But then Sargon's son and successor, Sennacherib, drove Merodach-Baladan away again. The deposed ruler, whom the Assyrians labeled a "terrorist" in their annals, soon launched a rebellion in hopes of regaining power; he was unsuccessful, and not long afterward he died in exile. The biblical book of Isaiah (39.1–4) tells how Merodach-Baladan tried to get Hezekiah, king of the Hebrew kingdom of Judah, to help him fight the Assyrians, which turned out to be another failed effort. Despite his bad image in Assyrian writings, the Babylonians remembered Merodach-Baladan as a good ruler who bravely tried to defend his country against outside aggression.

SEE ALSO: Babylonia; Elam; Judah

Mesopotamia, geography of

The geography of Mesopotamia—its topography, natural features and resources, and climate—and the geography of the regions surrounding Mesopotamia profoundly shaped the history of that ancient region and the lives of its inhabitants. First, Mesopotamia was located in the heart of what Europeans called the Near East (today referred to as the Middle East), centered mainly on what is now the nation of Iraq. The term *Mesopotamia* came from Greek words meaning "the Land Between the Rivers," a reference to the Tigris and Euphrates rivers, which run roughly from northwest to southeast through the region. In fact, much of that region consists of flat plains making up a vast river valley, and most of southwestern Mesopotamia was made up of the moist and marshy deltas of the two rivers. Today, the Tigris and the Euphrates join together at a point not far west of the Persian Gulf and then empty into the gulf. But in ancient times, the two rivers entered the gulf separately, forming two deltas that adjoined each other. That well-watered southeastern section of Mesopotamia was frequently referred to as Sumer because it is where the first major group of settlers, the Sumerians, erected the first cities in the region, and in the world. Later, after the decline of the Sumerians, the area was

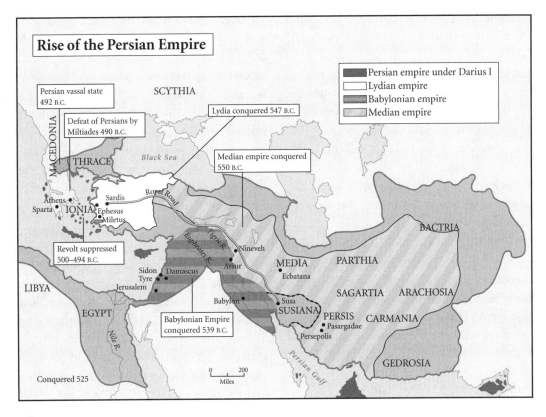

Rise of the Persian Empire

Persian vassal state
492 B.C.

SCYTHIA

Lydia conquered 547 B.C.

Defeat of Persians by
Miltiades 490 B.C.

Median empire conquered
550 B.C.

■ Persian empire under Darius I
□ Lydian empire
▧ Babylonian empire
▨ Median empire

MACEDONIA

THRACE

Black Sea

Royal Road

Athens
Sparta

Sardis

IONIA
Ephesus
Miletus

Revolt suppressed
500–494 B.C.

Euphrates R.

Tigris R.

Nineveh

BACTRIA

Assur

MEDIA
Ecbatana

PARTHIA

Sidon
Tyre
Jerusalem

Damascus

SAGARTIA

ARACHOSIA

LIBYA

EGYPT

Babylon

Susa

SUSIANA

PERSIS

Pasargadae
Persepolis

CARMANIA

Babylonian Empire
conquered 539 B.C.

Nile R.

Persian Gulf

GEDROSIA

Conquered 525

0   200
Miles

GALE

usually called Babylonia because the rulers of the city of Babylon often controlled it.

The section of Sumer/Babylonia that was situated closest to the Persian Gulf was appropriately called Sealand in ancient times. It should be noted that the original Sealand expanded in size over the centuries. In the heyday of the Sumerians, the gulf's coast lay more than 100 miles (161km) farther inland than it does now, so cities such as Ur and Eridu were almost seaports; over time, however, the coast receded southeastward, leaving these towns "high and dry," so to speak. In fact, there was usually less annual rainfall in Sumer than in other parts of Mesopotamia; average rainfall amounted to fewer than 10 inches (25cm) per year. And it was often very hot in the south, with temperatures reaching more than 100 degrees Fahrenheit

(38°C) fairly often. What made the area so fertile and tolerable was the presence of the rivers, with their rich network of tributaries and deltas. These were supplemented over time by many irrigation canals that the locals dug along the riverbanks.

Farther northwest, the moist alluvial plains of Sumer gave way to somewhat drier and slightly hillier plains. These so-called upper reaches of Mesopotamia were variously referred to collectively as Akkad, Assyria, and other names. Here, there was more annual rainfall, so the inhabitants needed fewer irrigation canals and relied more on wells for water. It was also somewhat less hot and in general more temperate in the northern parts of Mesopotamia. This made Assyria particularly suitable for growing grain. Most scholars think it was these northern plains that were first settled and exploited by early farmers who migrated southward and eastward from the region now known as the Fertile Crescent, stretching in an arc across the upper parts of Mesopotamia. The region of Assyria was also notable for the presence of some large tributaries of the Tigris, notably the Upper and Lower Zab rivers. Not surprisingly, most of the towns in the area were built on or very near these waterways.

Although the soil was rich in large parts of the Mesopotamian plains and there was plenty of water most of the time, the region possessed few other vital natural resources. There were very few trees, for instance, with the exception of occasional stands of date palms. Also, native stone suitable for building houses, defensive walls, palaces, temples, and so forth was scarce, especially in the south, in and around the river deltas. (In contrast, small amounts of gypsum, a soft, white or gray variety of stone, were available in selected places in Assyria.) It was because of this lack of building stone that the peoples of the region had to rely mostly on clay, or mud, to make bricks, which they dried in the sun or baked in ovens. Similarly, clay became the most common medium for making writing materials—in the form of dried-clay tablets. Mesopotamia also lacked sufficient quantities of metals, including copper and tin, which, when mixed together, made bronze; iron; silver; and gold. Thus, most timber, building stone, and metals had to be imported from neighboring lands.

Not surprisingly, therefore, the peoples of the region came to depend on trade; and many lucrative trade routes came to crisscross the plains. One exception to the general lack of natural resources in Meso-potamia—other than its soil and water—was bitumen, a material similar to asphalt or tar that seeped up from underground in certain spots. The ancients did not realize that this was a sign that enormous amounts of oil lay below the surface; indeed, today Iraq is one of the chief sources of oil in the world. The Mesopotamians used the bitumen to waterproof the hulls of boats and sometimes as a mortar for bricks.

Ancient Mesopotamia's land, climate, and resources should not be characterized solely in terms of its largely open plains, however. In antiquity, the region also encompassed small parts of what are now Syria in the west, Anatolia (modern-day Turkey) in the northwest, and southern Iran in the southeast. Much of eastern Syria was dry, even desertlike; and the vast, arid Arabian deserts stretched to the south of the central plains. Meanwhile, northern Assyria blended into the foothills of the rugged mountain chains of Armenia (called Urartu in ancient times) and southeastern Anatolia. In these foothills, the winters were mild and the summers dry and pleasant, and the locals grazed goats, sheep, and other livestock on the well-vegetated hillsides. A similar terrain and climate existed in the foothills of the Zagros range lying northeast of Sumer and east of Assyria.

Moving outside of Mesopotamia proper, one entered even higher, more rugged, and more forested terrain in the regions of southern Iran, Armenia, and Anatolia. These areas were also much richer in metals than Mesopotamia was. This is one of the major reasons that the empire builders of ancient Mesopotamia—the Akkadians, Assyrians, Babylonians, Persians, and others—so often tried to raid or conquer these neighboring regions. In

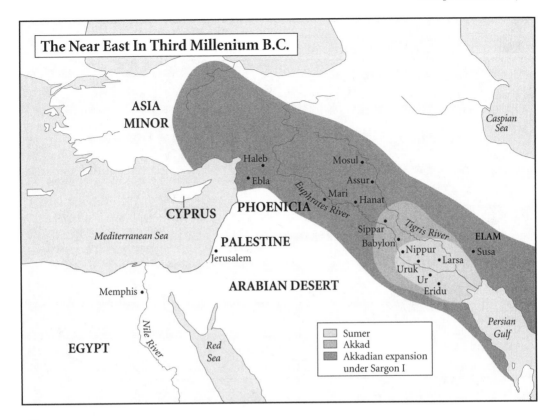

The Near East In Third Millenium B.C.

ASIA MINOR

Caspian Sea

Haleb
Ebla
Mosul
Assur
Mari
Hanat

CYPRUS

PHOENICIA

Mediterranean Sea

Sippar
Babylon
Nippur
Larsa
Uruk
Ur
Eridu

ELAM
Susa

PALESTINE
Jerusalem

Memphis

ARABIAN DESERT

Persian Gulf

EGYPT

Nile River

Red Sea

Sumer
Akkad
Akkadian expansion under Sargon I

GALE

short, they badly needed their natural resources. (They also frequently exploited their human resources by taxing their inhabitants or using them as soldiers or slaves.) Thus, it is impossible to discuss ancient Mesopotamia without considering the lands that bordered it and so often became incorporated into its political and cultural sphere.

SEE ALSO: Tigris and Euphrates; trade; transportation and travel

Mesopotamia, history of

The history and cultural legacy of ancient Mesopotamia is central to the history and development of humanity in general, especially Western societies and those of the Middle East, called the Near East when used to describe ancient or medieval

societies. This is partly because large-scale agriculture first developed in the Fertile Crescent, the arc-shaped region bordering Mesopotamia's northern rim sometime around 10,000 to 9000 B.C. Before this time there were likely no settled villages anywhere in the world. Historians generally refer to the long period of human culture before the advent of agriculture as the Paleolithic Age, or "Old Stone Age." The Neolithic Age, or "New Stone Age," when people in the area lived in villages but still used mainly stone tools and weapons, is usually dated from about 9000 to 6000 B.C. or somewhat later. Indeed, before farming began almost all people were nomads who moved from place to place, sustaining themselves through hunting, fishing, and gathering wild edible plants and fruits.

The Emergence of Towns and Cities Once

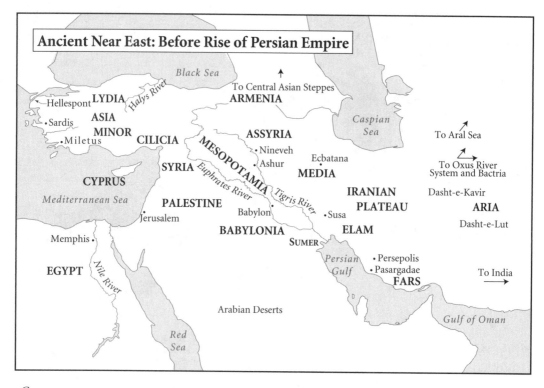

Ancient Near East: Before Rise of Persian Empire

farming began to develop in the Fertile Crescent, people settled into permanent villages; eventually, probably sometime between 6000 and 5000 B.C., some of them moved southward onto the Mesopotamian plains. There, agricultural villages were established. Some of these steadily grew into towns with populations of a few thousand people. Trade among these towns developed, stimulating increased cultural activities and still further expansion. Among the thriving communities were Tepe Gawra and Choga Mami, which featured the earliest-known irrigation canal, in northern Mesopotamia; and Ur, Eridu, Uruk, and Tell al-Ubaid in the south, near the Persian Gulf. Based on discoveries made at Tell al-Ubaid, modern scholars came to call the era lasting from roughly 5000 to 3500 B.C. the Ubaidian period.

Part of the importance of ancient Mesopotamia to world culture in general is the fact that these early villages and towns influenced people in neighboring regions to build similar settlements. In turn, the idea spread farther and farther, reaching many parts of Asia and Europe. Moreover, various logistical and cultural developments that originated in Mesopotamian towns—including artificial irrigation of crops, pottery making, and the erection of shrines and temples to honor the gods—also spread far and wide.

Meanwhile, within Mesopotamia itself, the march of civilization continued apace. Sometime in the late Ubaidian period, the first high culture arose in the southern part of the region, near the Persian Gulf. Its people, the Sumerians, may have been local Ubaidians who had reached a higher level of development; or they may have been outsiders who migrated into the region. Whatever their origins, they expanded some of their towns into full-fledged cities, some attaining populations in the tens of thousands. Though often referred to simply as cities, these were more accurately city-states, each consisting of a moderate-to-large expanse of farmland and villages controlled by a central urban area; the central city was usually surrounded by a large defensive wall made of dried mud-bricks. Among the leading Sumerian cities were Uruk, probably the first; Ur; Lagash; Sippar; and Nippur.

Each city-state thought of itself as a tiny nation. Other city-states, at the time mostly smaller, also emerged farther north, around the Tigris River and its tributaries. Each Mesopotamian city-state was ruled by a king who claimed to be somehow connected to or favored by the gods whom all Sumerians worshipped. These cities and their kings became quite territorial and frequently fought with one another. Fortunately for those involved, these early wars were not catastrophic and usually did not result in the complete destruction of population centers.

Meanwhile, when not fighting one another, these cities engaged in vigorous trade. Furthermore, commercial activities were not confined to Mesopotamia itself. Local merchants reached outward and either created or tapped into trade routes stretching far and wide. These routes were destined to keep the peoples of the Mesopotamian plains centrally connected, like the hub of a vast wheel, to a much greater world for many centuries to come. In the words of noted scholar A. Leo Oppenheim:

> During the nearly three millennia of its documented history, Mesopotamia was in continuous contact with adjacent civilizations and, at times, even with distant civilizations. The region with which Mesopotamia was in contact, either directly or through [middlemen], stretched from the Indus Valley [i.e., India], across and at times even beyond Iran, Armenia, and Anatolia to the Mediterranean coast and into Egypt, with the immense coastline of the Arabian peninsula and whatever civilization it may have harbored. (*Ancient Mesopotamia*, p. 63)

Modern scholars call the era in which the Sumerian cities exploited this vast trade network and reached their height of power and influence the Early Dynastic Period, lasting from about 3000 to 2350 B.C.

The First Empires It was perhaps inevitable that one of these early, burgeoning city-states would take the next step and try to conquer and rule most or all of its neighbors. The first Mesopotamian ruler to do so—in the process creating the world's first empire—was Sargon of Akkad (a town lying north of the cities of Babylon and Kish in central Mesopotamia). During his reign (ca. 2340–2284 B.C.) he seized most of the cities in the region one by one and absorbed them into his growing realm. For the first time in history, the lower and upper halves of Mesopotamia had been united into one large political unit ruled by a central administration. Sargon's realm was successful for a while because he and his immediate successors used what are often termed *strong-arm tactics*. Not only did they maintain a strong, well-trained army, but they also dismantled parts of the defensive walls of captured cities so that these places could no longer adequately defend themselves. Sargon and his heirs also placed their own trusted nobles and other operatives in positions of power in the subject cities to discourage feelings of independence and rebellions among the locals. In addition, the Akkadian monarchs took effective control of foreign trade in the region.

Despite these measures, the Akkadian Empire was fairly short-lived compared to many other ancient empires. In addition to various political instabilities that set in over time, a warlike people from the foothills of the Zagros Mountains lying east of the plains—the Guti—invaded. As Akkadian control disappeared, many of the old Sumerian cities became independent again, and soon they drove out the Guti. From among the rulers who led the campaigns against the Guti arose a ruler of Ur, Ur-Nammu (reigned ca. 2113–2094 B.C.). Under his guidance, Ur became the major power in the region and there emerged the second Mesopotamian empire, today referred to as the Third Dynasty of Ur, or "Ur-III" for short. That realm expanded outward under Ur-Nammu's successors; however, like the Akkadian Empire, it proved to be short-lived, lasting from circa 2113 to circa 2004 B.C. The Ur dynasts felt themselves pressed from the northeast by the Elamites, whose center of power lay in southwestern Iran; and from the northwest by the Amorites, a Semitic-speaking people who originated in the Syrian highlands. The Elamites eventually besieged and captured Ur, and the empire quickly dissolved.

In the two centuries following the fall of Ur-III, some large individual city-states vied for power in various parts of Mesopotamia. Among the most successful were Isin and Larsa in the south, located in the region still widely called Sumer; Mari, a prosperous trading city on the upper Euphrates; and Ashur and Eshnunna, which fought each other for control of northern Mesopotamia, generally called Akkad or Assyria. At one point, an early Assyrian king, Shamshi-Adad (reigned ca. 1813–1781 B.C.) captured Mari and installed his son as its ruler. This marked the beginning of the first and shortest of three periods of Assyrian expansion in the region. Eventually the rightful king of Mari, Zimri-Lim (ca. 1775–1761 B.C.) made a comeback. But he and the other local rulers in the region soon had a rude awakening. A dynasty of Amorite kings had established themselves in the large city of Babylon in about 1900 B.C. The sixth member of that dynasty, Hammurabi (ca. 1792–1750 B.C.), turned out to be an avid imperialist and conqueror who, like Sargon and Ur-Nammu before him, dreamed of ruling all of Mesopotamia. Hammurabi's troops swept across the plains, capturing cities and carving out an empire almost as large as the Akkadian realm.

Although this new Babylonian superstate was also short-lived, it and its ruler established important precedents for future generations of Mesopotamians. In particular, after Hammurabi's reign Babylon permanently became the most envied and coveted city in the region. As scholar Karen R. Nemet-Nejat puts it:

> Hammurabi's reign left a lasting impression on future generations of Babylonians, thus making him one of the major figures of Mesopotamian history. . . . Hammurabi's nation-state did not survive him, but he did make Babylon the recognized [major] seat of kingship, a position that remained uncontested until the Greeks [took control of the region later and] built [the city of] Seleucia. Babylon even survived as a [premiere Mesopotamian] religious center until the first century A.D. (*Daily Life in Ancient Mesopotamia*, p. 31)

Hatti, Mitanni, and Assyria Partly because of Babylon's ascendancy in these years, the period lasting from the fall of Ur-III, shortly before 2000 B.C. to roughly 1600 B.C. is often referred to as the Old Babylonian period. After Hammurabi's empire declined in the latter years of this period, a number of foreign peoples vied for control of parts of Mesopotamia. Among them were the Hurrians, the Kassites, and the Hittites. The Hurrians may have originated in the Asian region lying west of the Caspian Sea; the Kassites most likely entered Mesopotamia from the east, from or through the Zagros Mountains; and the land of the Hittites, called Hatti, was centered in Anatolia.

The Old Babylonian period ended when, in about 1595 B.C., the Hittites suddenly and boldly entered Mesopotamia, marched across the plains, and captured Babylon. For reasons that are still unclear, they did not follow up on this victory, however. Instead, they returned to Hatti, leaving a vacuum in central Mesopotamia that the Kassites swiftly filled. A Kassite dynasty now ruled Babylon and much of southern Mesopotamia from about 1595 to about 1155 B.C. The once culturally backward and unsophisticated Kassites very quickly adopted the local culture; like so many other Mesopotamian peoples over the course of time, they became "Babylonianized" in speech, dress, and political and religious customs.

Meanwhile, even as the Kassites were settling down in Babylon, many miles to the west the Hurrians were establishing their own strong foothold in the region. Located in the area lying between the upper reaches of the Tigris and Euphrates rivers, the new kingdom became known as Mitanni. The more well-to-do Mitannians raised horses and developed a formidable chariot corps, which they employed in their attempts to expand into southern

Syria. But these endeavors were largely fruitless. This is because the Mitannians increasingly found themselves part of a new and often dangerous political reality—an international balance of power in which at first four, and later five, major kingdoms vied for dominance in the Near East. In addition to Hatti to the north, Kassite Babylonia to the east, and Mitanni itself, there was Egypt, lying southwest of Palestine. The Egyptians had been invaded by a Near Eastern people of uncertain origins two centuries before, but they had expelled the intruders. And during Mitanni's formative years, Egypt was vigorously expanding its power and influence into the region of Syria-Palestine. This naturally brought the Egyptians into competition, and on occasion into armed conflict, with Hatti and Mitanni, both of which also had designs on Syria-Palestine. The climax of the Egyptian-Hittite rivalry was the great Battle of Kadesh, fought in Syria in about 1274 B.C.

The fifth member of the Near East's new major players, and the last to join the group, was Assyria. After the Babylonian king Hammurabi captured and absorbed the major towns of Assyria in the 1700s B.C., that area had fallen more or less into political obscurity. But the Assyrians were a proud and resilient people who retained their traditional culture during the centuries they were ruled by others. Under a strong and ambitious king, Ashur-uballit I (reigned ca. 1365–1330 B.C.), and his successors, they steadily began their second phase of expansion. By this time, Mitanni was already in decline, and some of its territories fell into Assyrian hands. Assyria also began moving into Armenia and developed a running rivalry with Babylonia, highlighted by the capture of Babylon by Assyria's King Tukulti-Ninurta I in the late 1200s B.C. In addition, the Assyrians launched many military expeditions into northern Syria.

The Neo-Assyrian and Neo-Babylonian Empires

The Assyrian dominance of Babylon initiated by Tukulti-Ninurta turned out to be brief. This was because the era of the Near East's "big five," so to speak, was finally ending. Kassite rulers managed to regain power in Babylon, but soon afterward they were defeated and their dynasty was extinguished by the Elamites, who attacked in about 1155 B.C. Not long before this, the Hittites and the Assyrians had brought Mitanni to its knees, aided partly by civil disputes within Mitanni itself, which had weakened it and left it vulnerable to foreign enemies. The Hittites, too, were suddenly eliminated from the corridors of Near Eastern power. Sometime in the early 1200s B.C. large groups of peoples from southeastern Europe, and perhaps other areas, launched a massive folk migration that swept across Greece, the Aegean Islands, Syria-Palestine, and Anatolia. The invaders, whom modern historians collectively call the Sea Peoples, burned numerous cities to the ground, including the capital and other major population centers of Hatti. The Sea Peoples attacked Egypt as well. And only with a great deal of difficulty were the local pharaoh, Ramesses III, and his soldiers, able to repel them.

Fortunately for the Assyrians, their homeland was located far enough inland from the Mediterranean to keep them largely insulated from the main thrust of the Sea Peoples. Thus, while large portions of the Near East had undergone unprecedented upheaval, most of Mesopotamia survived. Still, interruptions in the flow of trade and other factors caused Assyria to suffer a period of serious decline. Mean-while, in the years following Babylon's fall to the Elamites, Babylonia was equally hurt by disruptions in trade, as well as by internal political instability, and it, too, went into decline. Thus, by the early 900s B.C. all of Mesopotamia was politically fragmented and militarily weak. Historians sometimes call this Mesopotamia's "dark age."

As history has repeatedly demonstrated, such power vacuums in major centers of population and culture never last very long. Sure enough, before long a new imperial state rose to prominence in the already ancient Mesopotamian plains. Once more, it was the Assyrians who took the initiative. In their third and most successful period of expansion, they created the largest and most feared empire that Mesopotamia, and indeed the world, had witnessed to date. This realm is sometimes referred to as the Neo-Assyrian Empire to differentiate it from earlier phases of Assyrian empire building. The new drive for power began with two strong and ambitious kings—Ashur-dan II (reigned ca. 934–912 B.C.) and Adad-nirari II (ca. 911–891, B.C.). They and their successors seized all of Mesopotamia and many neighboring areas, including Babylonia, Elam, and parts of southern Iran, Armenia, southeastern Anatolia, Syria-Palestine, and eventually Egypt.

Particularly successful in their conquests were Ashurnasirpal II (reigned ca. 883–859 B.C.); his son, Shalmaneser III (ca. 858–824 B.C.); Tiglathpileser III (ca. 744–727 B.C.); and the four Sargonid rulers, so called because their dynasty was founded by the vigorous ruler Sargon II (ca. 721–705 B.C.). Sargon's son, Sennacherib (ca. 704–681 B.C.), was, like a number of Assyrian monarchs, both a ruthless conqueror and a great builder. When Babylon rebelled during his reign, Sennacherib swiftly and violently put down the insurrection and punished that city by laying waste to large sections of it, an act that people across the Near East remembered with horror for generations to come. Yet the same man who ordered this atrocity spent much time, effort, and money on domestic and cultural projects; most notably, he beautified the mighty Assyrian city of Nineveh and constructed a splendid new palace there. Sennacherib was succeeded by one of his sons, Esarhaddon (reigned ca. 680–669 B.C.), who, to the relief of the Babylonians, rebuilt much of Babylon. Then Esarhaddon's own son, Ashurbanipal (ca. 668–627 B.C.), brought Egypt into the Assyrian fold and defeated the Elamites, whose repeated attacks on Babylon and other cities on the plains had long plagued Mesopotamian rulers.

However, despite its strong start, Ashurbanipal's reign ended in abject failure. The last major ruler of the Assyrian Empire, he was defeated in the late 600s B.C. and his realm was torn asunder by a coalition of Babylonians and Medes, whose homeland was centered in western Iran. The Babylonians were led by a king named Nabopolassar; commanding the Medes was their talented ruler Cyaxares II.

The new empire established by Nabopolassar and expanded by his immediate successors is now often called the Neo-Babylonian Empire. Although it lasted less than a century—from about 626 to 539 B.C.—it was large and rich and witnessed Babylon's rise to a level of splendor and prestige greater than it had ever known or would ever know again. Nabopolassar's son, Nebuchadnezzar II (reigned ca. 605–562 B.C.), erected new palaces, temples, canals, and the famous Hanging Gardens of Babylon, built for his

wife. This sumptuous monument came to be listed among the Seven Wonders of the Ancient World.

Though these efforts may have been partially inspired by the king's love of culture and finery, they also had an underlying political dimension. Nebuchadnezzar recognized that the key to success for the new Babylonia was for it to become a worthy successor to the now-defunct Assyrian realm. Thus, he must appear to be an even greater builder than Sennacherib and other accomplished Assyrian builders. "The Assyrians had always deployed vast sums in building themselves new palaces and administrative capitals," scholar Gwendolyn Leick points out.

> But Babylonia . . . had suffered neglect during the centuries of [Elamite and Assyrian] occupation. Now was the time to make good the scars of Assyrian aggression and Babylon was to eclipse the former glory of Nineveh, now in ruins. . . . The new [Babylonian] dynasty was seen not only as the avenger of Babylon's humiliation [by the Assyrians], but as the rightful heir of Assyrian power. [Nebuchadnezzar's great works were designed] to demonstrate the unrivaled position of Babylon as the capital of a world power which had triumphed over its rivals. (*The Babylonians*, pp. 63–64)

The Sudden Rise of Persia Nebuchadnezzar seems to have envisioned his efforts as the groundwork for a powerful and magnificent imperial realm that would rule Mesopotamia for centuries, perhaps forever. In fact the realm outlived him by only twenty-three years. The last Neo-Babylonian king, Nabonidus (reigned 555–539 B.C.), was defeated by Cyrus II of Persia, an event that permanently ended Babylonia's status as an independent nation-state.

One of the most talented, ambitious, and successful men ever to rule Mesopotamia and neighboring regions, Cyrus had become ruler of the Persian region of Fars, in southern Iran, in about 559 B.C. At the time Fars was a province of the Median Empire, which had coexisted with the Neo-Babylonian realm in the period following the destruction of Assyria. Under Cyrus, the Persians, who before this had been a fairly obscure people, suddenly rose to prominence as masters of the known world. They easily overthrew the Medes and then proceeded to conquer Anatolia, including the kingdom of Lydia and the Greek cities on the peninsula's western coast. The Persians next seized the regions of what are now eastern Iran and Afghanistan; Babylonia and the rest of southern Mesopotamia; and most of Palestine. Cyrus also planned to absorb Egypt, but he died in 530 B.C., before this dream could be realized. So his son, Cambyses (cam-BEE-seez), took on the task of defeating the Egyptians.

Under Cyrus, Cambyses, and the next major Persian ruler, Darius I (reigned ca. 522–486 B.C.), the Persian army was widely respected and feared, much as the Assyrian military had once been. In fact, the Persians modeled their military organization in a number of ways on the Assyrian army. The Persians also copied many of the Assyrians' best political and administrative ideas. Like the Assyrian Empire, for example, the Persian Empire, the largest imperial realm in the world to date, was divided into provinces, each run by a local governor who answered to the king.

Because Cyrus, Cambyses, and Darius were strong, skilled rulers, the Persian realm got off to a good start and for a while promised to grow even larger and more powerful. Darius had designs on Europe, and in 512 B.C. he led an expedition into the forests and steppes lying north of Greece and west of the Black Sea. But eventually the Persian monarch came face-to-face with an obstacle that was to become his realm's biggest nemesis and the eventual instrument of its destruction. This obstacle was Greece, at the time consisting of a collection of many small city-states rather than a coherent, unified nation. (In fact, Greece never became a unified country in ancient times.) First, the Anatolian Greeks rebelled against Persian rule, and it took Darius more than five years to put down the revolt, which ended in 494 B.C. Four years later he sent a Persian army to destroy Athens, on the Greek mainland, to punish the city for helping the Anatolian Greek rebels. But the much smaller Athenian army crushed the Persian invaders at Marathon, located northeast of Athens. After Darius's death, his son, Xerxes (ZERK-seez), sought revenge for the Marathon debacle. In 480 B.C. the new Persian king led an enormous army into Greece, but in a series of epic battles the Greeks inflicted heavy casualties on the invaders and drove them away.

In retrospect, the failure to capture Greece and use it as a base from which to conquer Europe proved a major turning point for Persia. Xerxes turned out to be a mediocre ruler. After he was assassinated in 465 B.C., almost all of his successors proved to be no better; in fact, some were downright corrupt and/or ineffectual. They were unable to effectively reverse the empire's steady decline, caused partly by internal power struggles as well as by rebellions by subject peoples and the increasing menace of the militarily more formidable Greeks. The last Persian king, Darius III, whose reign began in 336 B.C., simply folded under these mounting

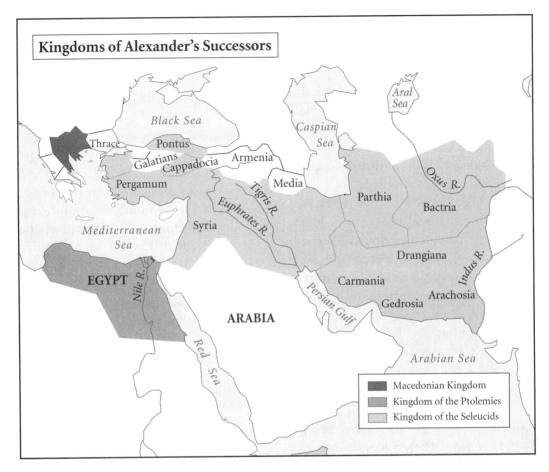

Kingdoms of Alexander's Successors

GALE

problems and pressures. Two years after he ascended the throne, Alexander III (later called "the Great"), the young king of Macedonia, a kingdom located in northern Greece, invaded Persia and swiftly defeated it. This initiated nearly two centuries of Greek rule in Mesopotamia and many of the lands on its borders.

The Seleucid Empire After the fall of Persia in the 320s B.C., Alexander's empire stretched from Greece in the west to the borders of India in the east, incorporating not only Iran, Mesopotamia, Syria-Palestine, and Anatolia but Egypt as well. However, Alexander died unexpectedly at age thirty-three, perhaps of alcohol poisoning, in Babylon in 323 B.C. His vast realm

quickly disintegrated as his leading generals (and some of their sons), the so-called Successors, vied with one another for its control. After many years of bloody warfare, most of the Successors were killed. The major survivors established three huge new Greek-ruled kingdoms: the Macedonian kingdom, centered in Greece; the Ptolemaic kingdom, centered in Egypt; and the Seleucid Empire, centered in Mesopotamia. The Seleucid realm also incorporated several other Near Eastern lands that had been part of the Persian Empire, including Syria and parts of Anatolia.

The founder of the Seleucid realm, Seleucus I (reigned 305–281 B.C.), and his successors worked hard to make Mesopotamia prosperous and successful in international relations. In particular, the Seleucids exploited all the old trade routes that ran through the region and attempted to open new ones. In this way, they became rich. They used the money partly to build new cities, the most important and splendid of which was Seleucia, located on the Tigris River not far north of Babylon. Due to its location, the city was sometimes literally called Seleucia-on-the-Tigris. Tens of thousands of administrators, soldiers, builders, artisans, and homesteaders migrated from Greece to Seleucia and other Mesopotamian cities and towns during these years. And Greeks came to form the upper crust of society on the plains. With a few exceptions, the local natives, especially those who could not speak Greek, were viewed and treated as inferiors.

Despite these successes, the Greeks were unable to maintain control of Mesopotamia and surrounding regions for very long. This was partly because the Seleucid rulers spent large portions of their great wealth on raising large armies, including many mercenary (hired) soldiers. These troops were used partly to prosecute costly border wars with the rulers of the Ptolemaic realm, mostly over possession of parts of Syria-Palestine. The Seleucid military was also used for defense because over time the realm came under increasing threats from outside powers. In the west, the Romans, masters of the Italian peninsula, conquered mainland Greece, the Aegean Islands, and most of Anatolia in the second century B.C. The Seleucid king Antiochus III (reigned 222–187 B.C.) was disastrously defeated by the Romans in western Anatolia. Meanwhile, in the east, the Parthians, who inhabited much of northern Iran, repeatedly attacked Seleucid towns and outposts, steadily capturing

and absorbing pieces of the empire. The Parthians also captured the main trade route that connected Mesopotamia to Afghanistan, India, and other eastern lands, a huge blow to the Seleucid economy.

The Parthian and Sassanian Realms Eventually the Seleucid rulers lost so much territory, wealth, and power that their realm—which, at the end, consisted only of parts of Syria—simply ceased to exist. Mesopotamia and parts of the rest of the former Seleucid Empire came under Parthian control. The Parthians, who spoke an Indo-European language, built a new capital, Ctesiphon, located on the Tigris near the old Seleucid capital of Seleucia. Yet they made no effort to suppress Greek commerce, or even the Greek language, in Seleucia and other Mesopotamian cities. In fact, in some ways the local Parthian and Greek cultures merged, even though the Parthians were firmly in charge.

Unlike the Greeks, Persians, and Assyrians before them, however, the Parthians did not maintain a strong central administration, nor even a national standing army. Instead, local nobles oversaw large estates or tiny vassal kingdoms; they gave their allegiance to the Parthian king, seen as the chief noble, and supported him when necessary with money, goods, and troops. This feudal society, which resembled the one that existed centuries later in medieval Europe, worked well enough within the confines of Mesopotamia and other parts of the Parthian realm. And for a while the Parthian lords were able to effectively pool their resources when attacked by foreign powers. Parthian armies soundly defeated two large Roman forces that invaded Mesopotamia in the first century B.C., for example. These forces were commanded by Marcus Crassus, who lost his life in his anti-Parthian campaign, and Marcus Antonius, or Mark Antony, who became the ally and lover of the last Ptolemaic ruler of Egypt, the famous Cleopatra VII. However, the Parthian realm's lack of a strong central organization eventually began working against it. In A.D. 116 the Roman emperor Trajan (reigned 98–117) invaded Mesopotamia and sacked Ctesiphon. Several later Roman rulers followed suit. In the year 224 a Parthian noble named Ardashir, who had charge of Fars, the old Persian homeland, led a rebellion. He defeated the weak Parthian king Artabanus IV and installed a new government.

This change of regime created what was in effect a new realm, which became known as the Sassanian Empire, named for an earlier local nobleman named Sassan. The Sassanian rulers were great admirers of the old Achaemenid Persian realm and its social, artistic, and religious customs. So the imperial state they administered became a kind of second Persian Empire. For this reason, some modern scholars have called the Sassanian Empire the Neo-Persian Empire. Like the Persians, and very much unlike the Parthians, the Sassanians maintained a strong central government that closely oversaw the affairs of its outlying provinces.

Also like the Persians, the Sassanians sought to expand their territory and influence through the use of force. Ardashir's son, Shapur I (reigned 241–272), invaded Roman-controlled Anatolia, Armenia, and Syria and sacked the prosperous Syrian city of Antioch. Shapur also defeated and captured the Roman emperor Valerian (reigned 253–260). Later, another Sassanian king, Shapur II (reigned 309–379), led military expeditions in the east, including parts of northern India and south-central Asia.

But as time went on, Sassanian rulers found it increasingly difficult to maintain their enormous realm. As has been the rule with all empires, no matter how great, throughout human history, theirs was doomed ultimately to collapse and make way for new rulers and peoples. During the reign of the last Sassanian king, Yazdgird III (632–651), Muslim armies from Arabia invaded southern Mesopotamia. In 651 the Muslim period of Mesopotamia began. The exact reasons for the decline and fall of the Sassanian Empire "are not clear," scholar John Curtis writes.

> However, one important factor must be that the Arabs had previously made inroads into Mesopotamia, but their potential threat was largely ignored. Also, by the mid-seventh century, the Sassanian state must have been exhausted by its long years of struggle with Rome and Byzantium [a strong state centered on the southern shores of the Black Sea]. And oppressive taxation, coupled with a rigid class system, would have made Islam seem an attractive alternative to many disaffected subjects of the ... [Sassanian] king. (*Ancient Persia*, p. 67)

The Cradle of Civilization Whatever the causes of the Sassanians' decline, their fall marked the end of ancient Mesopotamia, as reckoned by modern historians. For many millennia, that region had witnessed the rise and fall of seemingly countless cities, nations, peoples, and empires. And their societies had produced some of the most crucial cultural milestones in the human saga; these included the first implementation of large-scale agriculture, the first writing systems, the first cities, and the first empires. Certainly Western society would not have developed as it did without the profound cultural influences that Mesopotamian nations and cultures made on the Egyptians, Jews, Phoenicians, and especially the Greeks and Romans.

Meanwhile, the ruins of Sumerian, Babylonian, Assyrian, and Persian cities still dot the landscape of modern Iraq. On the one hand, they continue to beckon scholars and those fascinated by humanity's past. On the other, they serve as a constant reminder to the Iraqis and their neighbors that they are the shepherds and guardians of the precious remains of the cradle of civilization.

SEE ALSO: Akkadian Empire; Assyrian Empire; Parthian Empire; Persian Empire; Sassanian Empire; Seleucid Empire; Sumerians; Ubaidian culture

metalworking

Of all the crafts in ancient Mesopotamia, as well as in other parts of the ancient world, metalworking was arguably the most important and influential. Metalworking was essential to both agriculture, the mainstay of local economies, which came to rely on metal plow blades, and warfare, which could not be waged on a large scale without metal weapons and armor. Also, jewelry and other objects made of precious and semiprecious metals had great value for barter and as booty in military campaigns. Archaeologists have excavated a few workshops used by Mesopotamian metalsmiths, one in the ruins of Eshnunna. Other sites have yielded the remains of foundries and evidence of the crafting of metal weapons.

Most metals had to be imported into Mesopotamia, which had few native deposits. Copper came mainly from Anatolia, Palestine, and Iran, for instance. Copper was used widely for weapons, tools, utensils, and a host of other products in the fifth, fourth, and third millennia B.C.

Bronze, an alloy of copper and tin (or copper and lead), came into use in the Near East in the 4000s B.C. but did not achieve widespread use in Mesopotamia until about 3000 B.C. Like copper, bronze was commonly used for weapons and tools. It was also employed in making statues and other religious cult objects and for decorating city gates. In addition, brass, an alloy of copper and zinc, was used for some utensils and decorations. Gold, silver, and electrum, a mixture of gold and silver, were in wide use by the early 4000s B.C. for jewelry, cups, plates, and decorative inlays. Small pieces of iron, created as by-products of the copper-smelting process, made their way into Mesopotamia as early as the fifth millennium B.C. But true iron metallurgy did not begin until about 1200 B.C., after it was introduced by the Hittites. It remained small-scale until the Assyrians brought in large quantities of iron from Anatolia beginning in the eighth century B.C.

Metals such as copper came bound in ores and had to be refined before they could be made into useful products. Copper refining was referred to as washing. One method was to heat the metal until it was liquid, which settled to the bottom of the furnace, although considerable amounts of impurities remained. Most of these could be removed using a second method, smelting, in which the metal was heated along with small quantities of charcoal. At first artisans simply poured the liquid copper into molds of the desired shapes, but by the 3000s B.C. molding copper objects was supplemented by other techniques, including the lost-wax method. It consisted first of fashioning a wax model of the desired object and covering the wax with clay. When the artisan heated it in a kiln, the clay hardened, but the wax melted away, leaving hollow spaces inside the clay.

The artisan then poured liquid copper into the spaces, when the metal solidified, he removed the clay. The lost-wax method was also used to make bronze artifacts. Refining and molding iron was more difficult, partly because it requires much higher temperatures. Working the heated iron on a forge removed many of the carbon and other impurities, producing wrought iron, which was malleable enough to shape into sword blades and other objects.

SEE ALSO: crafts and craftspeople; trade; weapons and warfare, land

Mitanni

A kingdom established by the Hurrians in the 1500s B.C. in northern Syria and the lands lying between the upper Tigris and Euphrates rivers. Mitanni was called Hanigalbat by the Assyrians, Naharina by the Babylonians, and Naharin by the Egyptians. All of these peoples, along with the Hittites in Anatolia, shared with the Mitannians a sort of international balance of power in the Near East from about 1500 to 1300 B.C. During this period, all engaged in diplomacy and/or limited military disputes with one or more of the others.

Very little of a definite nature is known about Mitanni's leaders, internal history, and society. It appears that Mitannian society was dominated by a chariot-owning warrior class known as the *maryannu*, who owned large country estates and bred horses and sheep. Some or all of the members of this class may have been Indo-Europeans, suggesting some sort of cultural or political fusion of that group and the Hurrians in Mitanni. They established a capital at Wassukanni, the location of which remains unknown. The principal god of Mitanni was Teshub, a weather deity similar to the Storm God of the Hittites.

In the early 1400s the Mitannians tried to expand into southern Syria, which brought them into conflict with the Egyptians. Both sides soon recognized the threat of the Hittites, who also sought control of Syria. So the Mitannian king Sausatatar and the Egyptian pharaoh Thutmose III formed an anti-Hittite alliance in about 1460 B.C. In the century that followed, the Mitannian ruler Tushratta gave his daughter in marriage to the Egyptian pharaoh Amenhotep III.

It was not long after this royal marriage that Mitanni's fortunes started to wane. The exact events are uncertain, but evidently some kind of dynastic dispute or civil war took place within the country and the Hittites took advantage of the situation. The Hittite king Suppiluliumas I backed one side of the dispute against the other, then invaded northern Mitanni and captured Wassukanni. Mitanni still existed for a while longer, but only as a vassal state of the Hittites. Soon, however, the Assyrians challenged the Hittites by attacking Mitanni from the east. Sometime in the early 1200s B.C. the former Hurrian kingdom was transformed into the Assyrian province of Hanigalbat.

SEE ALSO: Hittites; Hurrians; Mesopotamia, history of

Mithridates I
(reigned 171–ca. 138 B.C.)

A Parthian king who made the Parthian Empire an independent and major Near Eastern power. Mithridates' brother Phraates (reigned 176–171 B.C.), who had ruled the Parthians before him, had paid tribute to the Greek rulers of the Seleucid Empire. But Mithridates aimed to make Parthia great at the Seleucids' expense. He conquered Media (the region now occupied by northwestern Iran) and Elam, then invaded Mesopotamia and took the Seleucid-controlled cities of Babylon and Seleucia (or Seleucia-on-the-Tigris). Having overrun much of the Seleucid Empire, he assumed the titles of the Persian kings and maintained many aspects of Greek culture, thereby creating a degree of continuity with the Seleucids.

SEE ALSO: Parthian Empire; Persian Empire; Seleucid Empire

money and banking

Coins were unknown in Mesopotamia until about forty years after their introduction in Lydia in western Anatolia circa 650 B.C. Before that, barter, or paying for goods with goods of equal value, was the main means of financial exchange. As early as the late third millennium B.C., Mesopotamian governments placed values on various commodities, including agricultural products like wheat and luxury goods sold by merchants. These values were based on the accepted existing value of silver, though it does not appear that silver actually exchanged hands during most financial transactions. (Large-scale transactions between merchants or between merchants and the palace might have been exceptions.) Instead, objects to be exchanged in barter were weighed and their values were computed based on given weights of silver. Then the bartering process proceeded. Palace and temple officials collected and stored the silver and oversaw its weighing and circulation, if any. The standard weights included the mina, weighing about 500 grams (17.5 ounces), the shekel (1/60 of a mina), and the talent (60 minas).

Even when coins were introduced into Mesopotamia in the last years of the seventh century B.C., they were probably exchanged mainly among merchants, shopkeepers, and other people who exchanged large quantities of goods. Coins did not become a widespread form of currency in the region until the Persian period, when King Darius I issued his silver "Darics." The Seleucid rulers who followed the Persian kings in Mesopotamia issued coins that varied in weight and value according to the whims of the individual monarchs.

The rapid spread of coins stimulated the rise of banking in Mesopotamia from the early 500s B.C. on. Bankers were individuals or groups of individuals who charged a fee for exchanging one form of currency for another and loaned people money, also for a fee (the interest on the loan). A few large families—notably the Egibi of Babylon, the Ea-iluta-bani of Borsippa, and the Murashu of Nippur—dominated the banking industry from the sixth century B.C. on. But individual lenders made loans, too. A banker drew up a contract consisting of a promissory note carved on a clay tablet. It listed the amount borrowed; the names of the lender and the borrower; the duration of the loan; how it would be paid back, including interest; and the type of collateral the borrower would provide. Finally, the document was signed, dated, and witnessed. When the debt was repaid, the banker gave the borrower the contract/tablet to acknowledge that he had fulfilled his obligation.

SEE ALSO: Nippur; trade; weights and measures

Morgan, Jacques de (1851–1924)

A French civil engineer, geologist, and archaeologist who made important contri-

A Persian gold coin from the 5th–4th century B.C.   Bildarchiv Preussischer Kulturbesitz/Art Resource, NY

butions to modern studies of ancient Mesopotamia, particularly that region's Persian period and culture. Morgan served as director of antiquities in Egypt before moving on to Mesopotamia. He excavated parts of two of the capitals of the Persian Empire—Persepolis and Susa, earlier an Elamite city. Morgan also discovered the black diorite stele bearing the famous law code of the Babylonian king Hammurabi.

See Also: Code of Hammurabi; Persepolis; Susa

mosaics

Few mosaics were created in Mesopotamia before the infusion of Greek and Roman artistic influences in the last few centuries B.C. The earliest mosaic-like technique in the region, introduced by the Sumerians, used small baked-clay cones. These were painted bright colors and were inserted into cracks in brick walls so that they formed simple geometric patterns, such as zigzags and triangles. Examples dating from circa 3200 B.C. were discovered in the ruins of the city of Uruk. The famous Royal Standard of Ur, dating from the third millennium B.C., is an outstanding example of a mosaic in a more conventional style. Depicting a military victory and celebration, it was made by pressing small pieces of blue lapis lazuli, shells, and pearl into wet tar and glue. This artifact was one of a kind, however, and does not seem to have had any influence on later native Mesopotamian art. Eventually the Greek Seleucids introduced richly ornamented mosaics for the floors and walls of well-to-do homes and some public buildings, a style widely imitated later by the Parthians and the Sassanians.

SEE ALSO: crafts and craftspeople; Greeks; Royal Standard of Ur

Mosul

In ancient times an important Assyrian city located about 250 miles (396km) northwest of modern Baghdad. The site of Mosul, on the right bank of the Tigris River, was inhabited as early as 6000 B.C. But it apparently remained a village until the Assyrians erected a fortress-citadel there to help guard their capital of Nineveh, which stood across the river. In the 500s B.C., following Nineveh's fall, Mosul grew into a prominent commercial center and remained a major city in the region thereafter. Muslim armies captured it in A.D. 637, and in the following century it became the capital of Muslim-controlled Mesopotamia. Today Mosul is Iraq's second-largest city after Baghdad, with a population of nearly 2 million. The ruins of both ancient Nineveh and ancient Mosul lie within the modern city's limits.

SEE ALSO: Assyrian Empire; Muslim period; Nineveh

music

At least from the beginning of the third millennium B.C., and likely considerably earlier, the Sumerians and other Mesopotamian peoples employed music in royal and/or religious festivals. Singers and dancers, both male and female, often accompanied by jesters and other entertainers, performed. Some of the compositions were upbeat and happy, to celebrate the crowning of a ruler or to give thanks to a god. Others consisted of laments, poems, and other literary works recited or sung to music. Archaeological evidence shows that the singers were frequently accompanied by musicians or sometimes played the instruments themselves. The instruments included lyres (small harps) and larger harps, wind instruments such as single and double pipes and small clay whistles, hand drums (tambourines) and larger kettle drums, and cymbals and bells. (Trumpets existed but were used to signal in battle rather than for music.) More evidence indicates the instruments were played both solo and in big orchestral ensembles. Musicians also marched with and played for soldiers during military campaigns.

Most ancient Mesopotamian music was not sung and played impromptu but rather followed written scores (collections of musical notes and symbols) by composers who understood music theory. Babylonian and Assyrian tablets dating from the second millennium B.C. name the harp's strings and depict scales of musical notes. The score of a hymn dedicated to the moon goddess, complete with lyrics for the singers, was found in the ancient Syrian city of Ugarit. Much later, in the Seleucid and Parthian periods, Greek-style wandering bards (minstrels who recited or sang heroic tales to the accompaniment of lyres and other instruments) became popular across Mesopotamia.

SEE ALSO: literature; religion; Ugarit

Muslim period

The era of Mesopotamia that began with the fall of the Sassanian Empire and the introduction of Islam into the region in the seventh century A.D., in a sense marking the transition from ancient to medieval Mesopotamia. The last Sassanian king, Yazdgird III (reigned 633–651), was an ineffective ruler, and during his reign the empire declined and fell partially into a feudal state. This left it vulnerable to attack by some opportunistic group. That group turned out to be the Muslims, who had recently risen to power to the south of Mesopotamia in Arabia.

The origins of Islam in Arabia began with the birth of a boy called al-Amin ("the Faithful"), a member of the Quraysh tribe, in about 571. His parents died when he was young, and he was raised by his grandfather and a slave woman. As a young man, al-Amin became a merchant. But soon he grew dissatisfied with his life and received a vision of the angel Gabriel. The latter's words to the young man became the basis of the Koran, the Muslim holy book, and the new faith of Islam. After being persecuted in Mecca in western Arabia, al-Amin traveled to Jerusalem and then to Medina, north of Mecca, where he adopted the name Muhammad and gained many converts. Islam soon spread to Mecca and other parts of Arabia.

Following Muhammad's death in 632, his successors began a series of campaigns to spread their faith and political control over neighboring regions. In 634 an Arab Muslim army led by Khalid Ibn al-Walid invaded the Sassanian Empire. Two years later the capital of Ctesiphon was taken, and by 651 all of Mesopotamia, Iran, Syria, and Palestine were in Muslim hands. The Arabic language replaced Persian, and Islam became the official religion. Ten years later the first Muslim dynasty—the Umayyad—assumed power and its members ruled from 661 to 750. The Muslim era that followed them is referred to as the Abbasid Caliphate (750–1258), which ended with the invasion of Mesopotamia by the Mongols, a warlike people from central Asia.

SEE ALSO: Mesopotamia, history of; Sassanian Empire

Nabonassar
(reigned ca. 747–734)

A Babylonian ruler who seems to have struck a deal with the Assyrian king Tiglathpileser III (reigned ca. 744–727 B.C.). Nabonassar (or Nabu-nasir) could reign unmolested by Assyria in exchange for recognition that Tiglathpileser was master of all of Mesopotamia. Not much is known about Nabonassar himself or his deeds. However, his reign is historically important because of something that happened much later. In the first century A.D. the Greek astronomer Claudius Ptolemy compiled a chronology of Babylonian history and began it with Nabonassar's accession to the throne. Ptolemy's chronology has helped modern historians date the reigns of the Babylonian kings following Nabonassar.

SEE ALSO: Assyrian Empire; historical accounts; Tiglathpileser III

Nabonidus
(reigned 555–539 B.C.)

The last native-born king of ancient Babylonia and the last ruler of the Neo-Babylonian dynasty. Nabonidus (or Nabunaid) was not of royal lineage; instead, he was a courtier and the son of a prominent priestess of the moon god. The exact manner in which he acquired the throne is unknown; it seems to have involved a palace plot to depose the recently crowned king, Labashi-Marduk, who was only a child. Better documented is the fact that, once in charge, Nabonidus launched military campaigns into Anatolia and Syria and used the proceeds from the booty he collected to repair temples across Babylonia. He also invaded northern Arabia in hopes of gaining control of the lucrative incense trade. For reasons unknown, he spent ten years at the Arabian oasis of Tema, leaving his son, Bel-shar-usur, in charge back in Babylon. This proved a mistake, for Bel-shar-usur did not pay serious enough heed to the growing threat of the Persian Empire recently founded in Iran by King Cyrus II. Nabonidus returned to Babylon in 539 B.C., but it was too late. Cyrus invaded, defeated him in battle, and claimed the Babylonian throne. Nabonidus was not killed, however; Cyrus assigned him to a government post in Iran, where the former Babylonian king died peacefully.

SEE ALSO: Babylonia; Cyrus II; Neo-Babylonian Empire

Nabopolassar
(reigned 626–605 B.C.)

The first king of the Neo-Babylonian, or Chaldean, dynasty, the last native-born ruling family of ancient Babylonia. Nabopolassar (or Nabu-apla-usur) began his career as an Assyrian-appointed government official in Sealand in southern Mesopotamia. After the death of Assyria's last strong king, Ashurbanipal, however, Nabopolassar felt confident enough to assert himself as ruler of Sealand and proceeded to fight the Assyrians stationed in

Babylonia. Then Nabopolassar wisely made an alliance with Cyaxares II, king of Media. Their combined armies ravaged Assyria and in 612 B.C. besieged and captured Nineveh. The fall of the Assyrian Empire allowed Nabopolassar to declare himself king of all Babylonia. He had only begun to deal with threats posed by the Egyptians in Syria-Palestine when he died, leaving the throne to his son, Nebuchadnezzar II.

SEE ALSO: Ashurbanipal; Cyaxares II; Nebuchadnezzar II; Neo-Babylonian Empire

Nabu

The Babylonian god of literacy and wisdom and the patron of scribes and the scribal arts. His main symbol was a stylus, the pointed tool used to inscribe clay tablets. Nabu, who rose to prominence in Babylonian religion in the early second millennium B.C., was at first called the scribe and minister of the chief Babylonian god, Marduk. But over time he came to be seen as Marduk's son. Nabu's main cult center was the Ezida temple in Borsippa, south of Babylon. There, people appeased him with offerings of elaborately inscribed tablets. His worship remained popular all through the first millennium B.C. and did not wane until the second century A.D. The Greeks who ruled Mesopotamia during the Seleucid period associated Nabu with their own god Apollo.

SEE ALSO: Borsippa; Marduk; scribe

Nabu-mukin-apli
(reigned ca. 977–942 B.C.)

A ruler of Babylonia who founded that realm's Eighth Dynasty. During his relatively long reign, Nabu-mukin-apli's main focus was on keeping the Aramaeans, tribal peoples from Syria and western Assyria,

from overrunning his realm. These intruders eventually settled in the region lying between the Tigris River and Elam.

SEE ALSO: Aramaeans; Babylonia

Nahum
(flourished late seventh century B.C.)

A resident of the Hebrew kingdom of Judah and a minor Hebrew prophet who penned a short narrative that later became one of the books of the Old Testament. Nahum's narrative consists of his account of the most momentous event of his time, the fall of the Assyrian Empire to the forces of Media and Babylonia. His description of the destruction of the Assyrian city of Nineveh is particularly vivid. Happy at the elimination of a warlike people who had long plagued the Hebrews and other Near Eastern peoples, Nahum concludes with these scathing words:

> There will the fire devour you, the sword will cut you off. It will devour you like the locust. . . . Your shepherds are asleep, O king of Assyria. Your nobles slumber. Your people are scattered on the mountains with none to gather them. . . . All who hear the news of [your fall] clap their hands over you. For upon whom has not come your unceasing evil? (Nahum 3.15, 18–19)

SEE ALSO: Assyrian Empire; Judah; Nineveh. And for Nahum's description of Nineveh's destruction, see Bible

Nammu

An early Sumerian mother goddess pictured as both a deity of freshwater and a creator goddess. In Sumerian creation stories Nammu (or Namma) supposedly was self-creating (i.e., she sprung into be-

A painting from 1830 depicts the fall of the Assyrian city of Nineveh in the 7th century B.C. ART RESOURCE, NY

ing on her own) and somehow brought about the existence of all things, including the other gods. Various versions and images of Nammu evolved over time, and other goddesses were either associated with her or replaced her in various religious narratives. For example, in the Babylonian creation epic, the *Enuma Elish*, her role is assumed by the goddess Tiamat, who unleashes monsters on the other gods and is defeated by the god Marduk.

SEE ALSO: *Epic of Creation*; Tiamat

Nanna

The Sumerian god of the moon, whom the Akkadians called Sin. Nanna (or Nannar), who was especially popular during the Third Dynasty of Ur in the late third millennium B.C., had his main temple—called the Ekishungal—in the city of Ur. Another important cult center of Nanna was at Harran in western Mesopotamia. Nanna appeared in numerous Mesopotamian myths, including those that called him the son of the chief god, Enlil; husband of the goddess Ningal; and father of Shamash, the sun god, and Inanna, goddess of sexual passion. In another myth, several gods get together and plot to steal the moonlight from Nanna, but Marduk (the Babylonian equivalent of Enlil) stops them. The people of Mesopotamia noted that the shape of the new moon resembled the horns of a bull, so they came to associate Nanna with the fertility of cattle.

SEE ALSO: Enlil; Inanna; Marduk

Naram-Sin
(reigned ca. 2260–2224 B.C.)

One of the kings of the Akkadian Empire and the grandson of its founder, Sargon.

Naram-Sin busied himself suppressing rebellions in cities across his realm. He also led campaigns that brought him into conflict with the Amorites in northwestern Mesopotamia and carried him to the shores of the Persian Gulf in the southeast. At some point he declared himself to be divine and emphasized it by adding *Sin*, the Akkadian version of the moon god, Nanna, to his name. One of Naram-Sin's stelae, now displayed in the Louvre Museum in Paris, shows him climbing a mountain in order to overshadow his enemies below.

SEE ALSO: Akkadian Empire; Nanna; Sargon of Akkad

Nebuchadnezzar I (reigned ca. 1124–1103 B.C.)

The fourth Babylonian king to rule his country after the fall of the Kassite dynasty in the mid-twelfth century B.C. Nebuchadnezzar (or Nabu-kudurru-usur or Nebuchadrezzar) is best known for his two military campaigns against Elam, the second of which was a great success. He defeated the Elamite king Hutteludush-Inshushinak and recovered the cult statue of the god Marduk, which the Elamites had earlier stolen from Babylon and taken to their capital of Susa. The restoration of the statue in Babylon, celebrated widely by the Babylonians, may have inspired the writing of the great Babylonian *Epic of Creation* (the *Enuma Elish*), of which Marduk was the hero. Nebuchadnezzar's younger brother, Marduk-nadin-ahhe, later became king of Babylonia.

SEE ALSO: Babylonia; Elam; *Epic of Creation*

Nebuchadnezzar II (reigned ca. 604–562 B.C.)

A prominent Babylonian king and the son of Nabopolassar, founder of the Neo-Babylonian Empire. Nebuchadnezzar (or Nabu-kudurru-usur or Nebuchadrezzar) defeated the Egyptians at Carchemish in northern Syria and extended Babylonian control over Syria and Palestine. He also besieged the Hebrew city of Jerusalem twice. After the second and successful siege in 586 B.C., he burned the great temple and deported the leading Hebrews to Babylonia during the so-called Babylonian captivity. Nebuchadnezzar also campaigned against the Elamites. Eventually he was able to sit back and collect huge revenues in taxes and tribute from his far-flung empire. He spent much of the money improving and beautifying Babylon, including building new defensive walls and a moat, erecting a bridge over the Euphrates, constructing new palaces, enlarging the temple of Marduk, and beginning a large, new ziggurat. Nebuchadnezzar married a Median princess, Amytis, and according to some ancient sources built for her the magnificent Hanging Gardens of Babylon. Frequent references to him in the Old Testament, especially in the book of Daniel, which describes his sacking of Jerusalem, have made him one of the most famous of all the ancient Mesopotamian kings.

SEE ALSO: Hanging Gardens of Babylon; Jerusalem; Neo-Babylonian Empire; ziggurat

Neo-Assyrian Empire

A term sometimes used by modern scholars to denote the third and last major phase of ancient Assyrian civilization, beginning in the mid-900s B.C. and ending with the fall of the last Assyrian royal stronghold, Harran, in about 610 B.C. During this period the Assyrian Empire reached its greatest extent under the Sargonids, consisting of Sargon II and his illustrious successors, Sennacherib, Esarhaddon, and Ashurbanipal. For an overview of the major figures and events of the period, **see also** Assyrian Empire.

SEE ALSO: Nineveh; Mesopotamia, history of

Neo-Babylonian Empire

A term coined by modern historians to denote the Babylonian realm ruled by the dynasty begun by King Nabopolassar (reigned 626–605 B.C.), accordingly referred to as the Neo-Babylonian dynasty (sometimes called the Chaldean dynasty). The Neo-Babylonian Empire lasted from 626 to 539 B.C. Though short-lived compared to most other ancient Mesopotamian empires, it witnessed much new construction of cities, palaces, temples, and bridges and is unusually well documented for a Mesopotamian realm.

The founder of the dynasty and empire, Nabopolassar, is remembered best for his destruction of the Assyrian Empire with the aid of the Medes, led by King Cyaxares II. After the Assyrian strongholds of Nineveh and Harran were taken, Cyaxares' daughter, Amytis, married Nabopolassar's son, Nebuchadnezzar II. The latter, who ruled from 605 to 562 B.C., defeated an Egyptian army that had been sent to help the ailing Assyrians. Nebuchadnezzar eventually reigned over all of Mesopotamia plus Syria, Palestine, and parts of Anatolia, a large realm that roughly approximated the extent of the now-defunct Assyrian Empire. He also launched dozens of construction projects in Babylon and elsewhere in Mesopotamia.

Nebuchadnezzar's reign marked the political height of the Neo-Babylonian Empire. After his death his son, Amel-Marduk, ruled only a few months before he was assassinated by his brother-in-law, Neriglissar. Neriglissar himself ruled only three years and was an ineffectual ruler. When he died, his son, Labashi-Marduk, who was still a child, became king, which opened the way for palace intrigues and a plot to usurp the throne. After only nine months, Nabonidus, the son of a local priestess of the moon god, was king. During his reign (555–539 B.C.) he invaded Arabia, where he spent ten years. During that time Cyrus II of Persia was building up his own forces, which he unleashed against Babylonia in 539, defeating Nabonidus and ending Babylonian independence. Thereafter, the Babylonians remained always subjects of other empires, including those of the Persians, Greeks, Parthians, and Sassanians.

SEE ALSO: Babylon; Mesopotamia, history of; Nebuchadnezzar II

Nergal

In Mesopotamian mythology, a god of death, disease epidemics, and war as well as a fertility deity. In astrology, Nergal (or Erra) was associated with the planet Mars. His chief function, however, was to rule the Land of No Return (the Underworld) with the goddess Ereshkigal. Their relationship is the subject of the epic poem titled *Nergal and Ereshkigal* (or *The Romance of Nergal and Ereshkigal*). Another Mesopotamian poem, *The Wrath of Erra* (or *The Erra Epic*), tells how Nergal rose from the depths and tried to destroy Babylon while its patron deity, Marduk, was away. Nergal's chief temple was the Meslam in the city of Kuthu, the exact location of which is still uncertain.

SEE ALSO: afterlife; Ereshkigal; *Nergal and Ereshkigal*; *Wrath of Erra, The*

Nergal and Ereshkigal

An ancient Mesopotamian myth and epic poem that tells how the god Nergal (or Erra) came to be Ereshkigal's husband and to share with her the rule of the Land of No Return (the Underworld). The tale begins with a banquet in heaven, overseen by An, father of the gods. An feels bad that Ereshkigal cannot leave her nether realm to join the party, so he sends a messenger to tell her that she is welcome to a portion of the food. Delighted, she sends her chief administrator, Namtar, up to collect the meal. But while in heaven Namtar is insulted by the god Nergal. The powerful god Ea (or Enki) tells Nergal that he must go down to the Underworld and apologize to Ereshkigal. But Ea is careful to warn him to avoid doing certain things during the visit, lest Ereshkigal become too attached to him. "From the moment they bring a chair to you, do not . . . sit upon it," Ea warns.

> When the baker brings you bread, do not . . . eat the bread. When the butcher brings you meat, do not eat the meat. When the brewer brings you beer, do not drink the beer. When they bring you a foot bath, do not wash your feet. When she (Ereshkigal) has been to the bath and dressed herself in a fine robe, allowing you to glimpse her body . . . you must not do that which men and women do.

Having reached the Underworld, Nergal is able to resist all of these temptations but one. Ereshkigal, who has up to now been a virgin, seduces him in her bath, and they make love for six days.

After his tryst with Ereshkigal, Nergal takes his leave. But just as Ea had warned, Ereshkigal has come to care for him and is not ready to let him go. Ereshkigal threatens that she will raise all the dead and al-low them to overrun Earth if the gods do not return Nergal to her. Eventually Nergal is compelled to reenter Ereshkigal's dark realm and in time agrees to become her husband and co-ruler.

SEE ALSO: Ereshkigal; literature; Nergal

Neribtum

A small ancient Mesopotamian city located about 10 miles (16km) east of modern Baghdad. Not much is known about the history of Neribtum (modern Tell Ishchali), but an expedition to the site in the 1930s by the University of Chicago's Oriental Institute uncovered a cult center, including a temple of Inanna, goddess of love and sexual passion. Inside the temple the archaeologists found a carved stone figurine of a monkey. Monkeys are not indigenous to Mesopotamia. So the existence of the figurine in the heart of that region suggests either that the sculptor had visited India or Egypt, where monkeys roamed, or that a trader had brought one or more monkeys to Mesopotamia.

SEE ALSO: Inanna; sculpture

Niebuhr, Karsten (1733–1815)

A German-born Danish mathematician, surveyor, and geographer who was instrumental in the modern discovery and understanding of ancient Mesopotamian cuneiform writing. In 1761, at age twenty-eight, Niebuhr joined an expedition sponsored by the king of Denmark. Its goal was to explore the ancient sites of Arabia, Mesopotamia, and other parts of the Near East, which at the time remained both mysterious and compelling to many Europeans. All of the other members of the expedition died of disease or other causes.

Niebuhr, the sole survivor, made it to Arabia as well as to Baghdad, Mosul, and the ruins of the ancient Persian capital of Persepolis. He also visited the Behistun Rock and was fascinated by the human figures and cuneiform inscriptions carved into it. Niebuhr made the first accurate copies of these carvings and published them in 1788, initiating the process by which cuneiform was eventually translated by Georg F. Grotefend, Henry C. Rawlinson, and others.

SEE ALSO: Behistun Rock; cuneiform; languages

Nimrud

The Arabic and more commonly used name for the ancient Assyrian city of Kalhu, located about 20 miles (32km) southeast of Mosul, Iraq. Although the site of Nimrud was occupied earlier, the first substantial city was erected there by the Assyrian monarch Shalmaneser I (reigned ca. 1274–1245 B.C.). Later, King Ashurnasirpal II (ca. 883–859 B.C.) made it his capital. Inscriptions found in the ruins claim that he celebrated its inauguration with a party attended by almost seventy thousand guests. Eventually Nimrud covered some 16 square miles (41 sq. km), had a defensive wall 4.5 miles (7.2km) long, and supported a population of a hundred thousand or more, making it a very large city for its time. It remained the Assyrian capital until King Sargon II moved it to Dur-Sharukkin about 150 years later. Nimrud remained important, however, because it contained several palaces as well as the tombs of many Assyrian queens. It was destroyed circa 612 B.C. by the Medes and the Babylonians during their conquest and destruction of Assyria.

Nimrud was first explored by pioneering Assyriologist Austen Henry Layard between 1845 and 1851. (Initially, he mistakenly thought it was the site of Nineveh.) A later British expedition excavated at Nimrud from 1949 to 1962 under the direction of Max E.L. Mallowan and David Oates; more recent work has been done by the Iraqi Department of Antiquities. Overall, the digs have yielded priceless treasures: the remains of the palaces of Ashurnasirpal II, Shalmaneser III, and Tiglathpileser III; the tombs of several Assyrian queens; temples of the gods Ninurta and Nabu; a ziggurat; and archives containing royal correspondence and administrative records.

SEE ALSO: Assyrian Empire; Dur-Sharukkin; Layard, Austen Henry

Nineveh

One of the most important cities of ancient Assyria and Mesopotamia, situated on the left bank of the Tigris River in the outskirts of the modern city of Mosul, Iraq. Most of ancient Nineveh (or Ninua) lies beneath two sprawling debris mounds—Tell Kuyunjik and Tell Nebi-Yunus. The site of Nineveh was first inhabited as early as the seventh millennium B.C. Sometime later in prehistoric times, a temple of the goddess Ishtar (later associated with Inanna) was erected there, a building that was subsequently rebuilt several times.

Nineveh's short but glorious heyday began when the Sargonid king Sennacherib (reigned ca. 704–681 B.C.) abandoned the capital of Dur-Sharukkin and made Nineveh his capital. Around Nineveh he erected a mighty double wall some 7.4 miles (12km) long and nearly 50 feet (15m) high, with fifteen large gates. Sennacherib also installed a series of canals and aqueducts to supply the city with

A reconstruction of the Palace Without Rival and other buildings at Nineveh before that city's destruction in the 7th century B.C. © BETTMANN/CORBIS

water and built a magnificent royal residence, the so-called Palace Without Rival. His successors, Esarhaddon and Ashurbanipal, also built palaces there, and Ashurbanipal created his famous library/archive of some twenty-four thousand clay tablets. The city also contained botanical gardens and a zoo. Nineveh was destroyed in 612 B.C. after a three-month-long siege conducted by the Medes and the Babylonians. A vivid account of the city's fall was penned by the Hebrew prophet Nahum in his narrative in the Old Testament.

Numerous archaeologists and other modern scholars have excavated at Nineveh. The first to explore its vast ruins were the noted early Assyriologists Paul Emile Botta; Austen Henry Layard, who found Sennacherib's palace and Ashurbanipal's library; William K. Loftus; and Hormuzd Rassam. Later a French team worked at the site, and then came an expedition in the early 1900s sponsored by the British Museum, a dig directed by L.W. King. Since World War II, various Iraqi teams have also excavated at Nineveh. For Nahum's account of Nineveh's destruction, **see** Bible.

SEE ALSO: Assyrian Empire; Botta, Paul Emile; Layard, Austen Henry; libraries; Nahum; palaces; Palace Without Rival

Ningal

A Sumerian goddess best known as the wife of the moon god, Nanna (or Sin), and mother of the sun god, Shamash. Ningal was also the deity of dream interpretation and a protector of the city of Ur, where her and Nanna's chief temple was located. Their other major cult center was at Harran in western Mesopotamia. A Sumerian myth, which has survived in the form of a lament (or lamentation), tells how Ningal tried but failed to persuade the gods An and Enlil not to destroy Ur:

> Truly, I myself mourned in front of [An and] Enlil: "May my city not be destroyed!" I said indeed to them. "May Ur not be destroyed!" I said indeed to them. "And may its people not be killed!" ... But An never bent towards those words, and Enlil never with an "It is pleasing, so be it!" did soothe my heart. Behold, they gave instructions that ... Ur be destroyed, and as its destiny decreed that its inhabitants be killed. ... The people mourn.

SEE ALSO: Enlil; literature; Nanna

Ningirsu

A Sumerian god whose name meant "Lord of Girsu," in reference to the city that housed his main cult temple, the Eninnu, and the greater city-state of Lagash, of which Girsu was a part. Ningirsu seems to have begun as a local protector of Girsu. He was also a deity of fertility and farming, as revealed by one of his symbols—the plow. Over time, however, his worship spread to other parts of Mesopotamia, and he adopted another symbol, the mythical bird Anzu, which stole the Tablet of Destiny in the epic poem *The Defeat of Anzu*. The building of the Eninnu in Girsu by Gudea, a noted ruler of the Sumerian city of Lagash, was commemorated by a long hymn, the title of which translates roughly as *The Building of Ningirsu's Temple*. In the following excerpt, Ningirsu visits Gudea in a dream and tells him how the god will furnish many of the materials needed for the temple's construction:

> When you, true shepherd Gudea, really set to work for me on ... the Eninnu, my royal house, I will call up to heaven for humid winds so that plenty comes down to you from heaven and the land will thrive under your reign in abundance. ... When you drive in my foundation pegs for me, when you really set to work for me on my house, I shall ... bring halub and nehan trees up from the south, and cedar, cypress and juniper together will be brought for you from the uplands. From the ebony mountains I will have ebony trees brought for you, in the mountains of stones I will have the great stones of the mountain ranges cut in slabs for you.

SEE ALSO: *Defeat of Anzu, The*; Girsu; Gudea

Ningishzida

A minor Sumerian god who, as the grandson of Ereshkigal, ruler of the Underworld, dwelled with her in that nether realm. Ningishzida's father was Ninazu, and his wife was Geshtinanna, who was compelled to spend half of each year with Ningishzida below and the other half on Earth. For his own reasons, a prominent king of the city of Lagash, Gudea, chose Ningishzida as his personal patron deity. That god's symbol was a dragon, and Mesopotamian astronomers envisioned him in the form of a dragon in one of the constellations in the night sky. Said constellation, still viewed as a dragon, now goes by its Greek name, Hydra.

SEE ALSO: Ereshkigal; Geshtinanna; Gudea

Ninisina

The Sumerian goddess of the healing arts, who, in Babylonian times, was called Gula.

SEE ALSO: Gula

Ninmah

A minor Sumerian goddess pictured as a divine midwife. In mythology, she helped deliver human beings while another goddess, Nammu, was creating them. Another myth tells how Ninmah and the god Enki got drunk on beer and played a game in which each tried to think of some alternate way to design human bodies. Enki won the game, but his final design was a poor one; this was the ancient Mesopotamian explanation for the many imperfections inherent in the human form.

SEE ALSO: Enki; Nammu; religion

Ninurta

The chief war god of the Assyrians and some other Mesopotamian peoples. Ninurta began as a Sumerian deity of agriculture and irrigation, and an early farmer's almanac was titled *The Instruction of Ninurta*. Over time, however, he took on more warlike characteristics, and by the end of the third millennium B.C. Ninurta had been transformed into a war god. Soon the Babylonians more or less replaced him with Marduk, who was seen as a heroic warrior as well as the chief god. But the Assyrian kings, perhaps the most aggressive of all the Mesopotamian monarchs, eagerly adopted Ninurta as an aid and protector on their many military campaigns. Ninurta's chief shrine, the Eshumesha, was at Nippur, and his wife was Gula, goddess of healing.

SEE ALSO: Assyrian Empire; Gula; Marduk

Ninurta and Agag

A Sumerian myth and minor epic poem about one of the martial exploits of the war god, Ninurta. The poem now exists only in fragments. The story begins when Agag, a nature spirit, leads an army of trees, vines, stones, and other natural objects in an invasion of Ninurta's territory. Rising to the challenge, the war god

uses rain—reflecting his roots as an early god of irrigation—to neutralize a great dust cloud raised by the intruders. After defeating them, the god assigns each stone a specific function as an inert, harmless mineral on Earth. Finally Enlil, leader of the gods, sings a hymn praising Ninurta, and Nidaba, goddess of writing, records the details of Ninurta's victory for posterity.

SEE ALSO: Enlil; literature; Ninurta

Nippur

One of the more important cities of ancient Sumeria, situated about 93 miles (150km) southeast of modern Baghdad. Nippur (modern Niffar) was one of the oldest Mesopotamian settlements, with habitations dating back to the late seventh or early sixth millennia B.C. And it remained inhabited longer than most other cities in the region—until circa A.D. 800, when it was a Muslim town with large Jewish and Christian quarters. During Sumerian and Babylonian times Nippur had no ruling dynasty of its own and usually remained politically neutral. So the rulers of many neighboring city-states used it as a religious center. In fact, in most cases no Mesopotamian king was thought to be legitimate unless he supported or made a pilgrimage to Nippur. The main cult of the god Enlil—the Ekur, or "Mountain House" —was there, as were important temples of Inanna and several other deities. The city endured a crisis in the 1700s B.C., when the Euphrates River, which had long flowed right through it, changed course. But the people of Nippur persevered, and in time the city regained its footing. In the Persian period, during the sixth through fourth centuries B.C., it was an important commercial center and headquarters of the influential Murashu family of bankers.

The first major modern excavations of Nippur were conducted by a team sponsored by the University of Pennsylvania from 1888 to 1900. From 1948 to the present, the site has been explored by Chicago's Oriental Institute, a project that remains ongoing. The site has revealed many important artifacts and a great deal of information about ancient Mesopotamia. Especially important was the discovery of a series of buildings dubbed Tablet Hill by the diggers, the remains of a large school or work area for scribes. So far, some sixty thousand cuneiform tablets have been found there, a treasure trove containing samples from every known ancient Mesopotamian literary work. Also found in the ruins was an unusually accurate ancient map of Nippur.

SEE ALSO: map making; money and banking; temples

Nusku

The Sumerian god of fire and light, who served as a key assistant to the chief god, Enlil. Nusku, whose symbol was quite appropriately an oil lamp, was a son of the moon god, Nanna (or Sin), and his own son, Gibil, was a fire god like himself. People invoked Nusku in prayers to condemn or punish the practice of evil sorcery. His cult survived in Syria, where devotees kept his sacred fire burning day and night, until the early centuries of the Christian era.

SEE ALSO: magic; Nanna; religion

Nuzu

An ancient Mesopotamian city located not far southwest of the modern city of Kirkuk in northern Iraq. Nuzu (or Nuzi) appears to have been first an Akkadian town called Gasur. In the early second millennium B.C. it was settled by Hurrians, who renamed it, and for a while it existed on the outskirts of the Hurrian kingdom of Mitanni as an important administrative center. After Mitanni's fall, Nuzu became an Assyrian city. The site was excavated from 1925 to 1931 by American archaeologists, who found thousands of cuneiform tablets dating to the city's Mitannian period. These tablets contain records of taxes, workers' salaries, and other data that have helped scholars better understand the workings of ancient Mesopotamian society. Also found in the ruins were several brass items, showing that brass, an alloy of copper and zinc, was already in use in the region in the second millennium B.C.

SEE ALSO: Akkadian Empire; metalworking; Mitanni

Old Babylonian period

A term often used by modern scholars to denote the era of ancient Mesopotamia lasting from about 2000 to 1600 B.C., directly following the decline of the Third Dynasty of Ur. The period was highlighted by a shift in political power from southern to northern Mesopotamia; the resultant rise of Babylonia, especially under King Hammurabi (reigned ca. 1792–1750 B.C.); and the replacement of the Sumerian language by Akkadian dialects, particularly Babylonian.

SEE ALSO: Babylonia; Mesopotamia, history of; Third Dynasty of Ur

omens

Divinely inspired signs of impending events, either good or bad.

SEE ALSO: divination; magic; religion

oracles

Persons thought to be mediums through which a god or gods could communicate messages to humanity, the messages themselves, or the temples or other places where the messages were conveyed. In general, oracles were not as important or revered in ancient Mesopotamia as they were in ancient Greece, home of the famous Delphic Oracle in the temple of the god Apollo. In Mesopotamian religion, the main form of communication between gods and humans was the omen, a natural sign that could be read by diviners and interpreted to have a divinely inspired meaning.

However, oracular activity did exist in Mesopotamia. It took two basic forms: prophecy, which could be delivered by almost any person who had the gift for it, and more formal oracular predictions made by priests. Male and female prophets, or "frenzied people," supposedly received unsolicited visits from gods, both in waking visions and in dreams. Often the visions or messages acquired by prophets were written down, but few prophetic texts have survived. More formal oracles received divine messages, too, sometimes without asking and other times as the result of directly questioning a god. The priest/oracle then communicated the message to the king. Like prophecies, such messages were frequently written down. The following surviving example was given to the Assyrian king Ashurbanipal in the seventh century B.C. and purports to be from the goddess Ishtar, who promises to help the king defeat his enemies, the Elamites:

> [When she spoke to me] the goddess Ishtar ... was holding a bow and her sword was drawn ready for battle. You [the king] were standing before her and she spoke to you like a real mother. ... She repeated her command to you as follows: "You will stay here where you belong. Eat, drink wine, [and] enjoy yourself ... while I go ... to help you achieve your heart's desire." ... Then she went out in a fearsome way to defeat your enemies, [namely the] king of Elam, with whom she is angry.

Assyrian relief depicting an oracular message written down by a prophet relating a promise from the goddess Ishtar to help King Ashurbanipal defeat the Elamites. The relief dates from the seventh century B.C. © WERNER FORMAN/CORBIS

Evidence shows that such oracular messages and other forms of divination were not always believed. For example, Ashurbanipal's father, King Esarhaddon, had a diviner killed when he suspected the man had made up the "sacred" information himself.

SEE ALSO: divination; religion

Orontes River

The chief river of Syria, used or crossed by numerous ancient armies, merchants, and travelers, including many from Mesopotamia. The Orontes (or Axius) rises in the Bekaa Valley, in what is now Lebanon, and empties into the Mediterranean Sea slightly northwest of the site of the ancient city of Antioch. Though not navigable by large ships, the river was used for travel by people in small boats and rafts. A number of ancient battles were fought along the banks of the Orontes; the most famous were Kadesh (ca. 1274 B.C.), fought between the Hittites and the Egyptians, and Karkar (ca. 853 B.C.), in which Assyria's King Shalmaneser III opposed an alliance of kings from Syria-Palestine.

SEE ALSO: Battle of Kadesh; Shalmaneser III; Syria

painting

Unlike the Greeks, who painted elaborate and often exquisite designs and pictures on their pottery, the ancient Mesopotamians rarely painted their ceramics. However, Mesopotamian artists did paint figurines and carved reliefs, as evidenced by tiny traces of the original paint found still clinging to their surfaces. The most numerous and impressive ancient Mesopotamian paintings, however, were wall murals, which graced the interiors of palaces, temples, and well-to-do homes.

The pigments for the paints were made mainly from mineral substances. Black pigment came from soot or tar, for instance; white from gypsum; red from iron oxide; blue from copper oxide or lapis lazuli; and green from malachite. The use of yellow seems to have been rare. The artist mixed the pigments with egg whites or milk solids, which acted as binding agents to make the paint adhere better to the wall surface. First, he treated that surface with a plaster or paste made from a mix of mud and lime or gypsum and let it dry. Then he used a pointed tool to sketch the outlines of his picture, and finally he applied the paint. This dry-surface technique was used in Sumeria and in early Babylonia and Assyria. In the late second millennium B.C., however, it became more common to apply the paint to the wet plaster, a method called fresco. An advantage of the fresco method was that the paint combined with the plaster as it dried, making the colors last longer; a disadvantage was that the artist had to work very fast to finish the work before the paint dried. The subjects of Mesopotamian paintings most often included religious ceremonies, royal processions, battles, hunting expeditions, and mythical beings and animals.

As for the survival of these paintings, examples in various states of preservation have been found at Nippur, Uruk, Nuzu, Dur-Sharukkin, and elsewhere. Among the best preserved of all are those from two sites on the upper Euphrates, Mari and Til Barsip. At Mari, the ruins of the palace of the eighteenth-century B.C. king Zimri-Lim have yielded twenty-six rooms of wall paintings, many of them in excellent condition. (When the soldiers of Babylonia's King Hammurabi attacked, they knocked the walls of the palace's upper story inward, thereby creating a barrier that protected the walls of the story below and preserved the paintings for posterity.) One particularly fine painting shows the king taking his oath of office in front of the goddess Ishtar (or Inanna). At Til Barsip, the Assyrian king Tiglathpileser III erected a palace whose wall paintings are still fairly vivid. There are scenes of warfare and hunting. And one outstanding 70-foot (21m) panel shows Tiglathpileser on his majestic throne, surrounded by soldiers and courtiers.

Another form of ancient Mesopotamian painting, less common but no less beautiful than the wall murals, consisted of paintings on enameled bricks. These were used on the exteriors of palaces, where the enamels resisted the corrosive effects of the weather. The artist mixed his pigments with melted silica, a kind of stone dust, to make a glaze or enamel that was applied directly to the surfaces of the bricks. Perhaps the best-known examples are the outer surfaces of Babylon's Ishtar Gate, created by the artists of King Nebuchadnezzar in the early 500s B.C. Pictured are bulls, lions, and dragons.

SEE ALSO: palaces; pottery; sculpture

Palace Without Rival

A magnificent palace erected in Nineveh by the Assyrian king Sennacherib (reigned 704–1681 B.C.). The structure had more than eighty rooms, many of which were lined with detailed stone relief sculptures showing the king's military victories. One panel has been of particular interest to modern historians, especially biblical scholars, because it depicts the Assyrian siege of the Hebrew town of Lachish, an event mentioned in the Old Testament (2 Kings 18.12–14). The palace also featured huge roofing beams and vertical columns made of cedar imported from Syria, as described by Sennacherib himself in one of the inscriptions found at the site:

> Beams of cedar, the product of mount Amanus [in northern Syria], which they [Sennacherib's loggers] dragged with difficulty out of these distant mountains, I stretched across their roofs. Great door-leaves of cypress, whose odor is pleasant as they are opened and closed, I bound with a band of shining copper and set them up in their doors. A portico [porch] patterned after a Hittite palace . . . I constructed inside for my lordly pleasure.

Some of the smaller upright columns in the palace were fashioned of solid bronze.

Meanwhile, most of the structure's many entrances were guarded by carved stone bulls weighing some 43 tons (39t) each. The palace was surrounded by parks in which several orchards were planted; to keep them well supplied with water from the nearby river, the king had a large canal built.

Sennacherib's great palace was wrecked in 612 B.C. during the horrific destruction of Nineveh by the Medes and the Babylonians. The ruins steadily faded from view under a great mound of debris until British archaeologist Austen Henry Layard brought parts of them back into the light in the 1840s. In the twentieth century the palace underwent more excavations under the guidance of L.W. King of the British Museum and later by several Iraqi teams. In the 1980s American scholar John M. Russell visited the site and recorded its layout in great detail. He also documented the unfortunate decay and recent looting of precious sculptures from the palace and recommended that excavators rebury such sites when they are finished studying them in order to keep them safe.

SEE ALSO: Cedars of Lebanon; Layard, Austen Henry; Nineveh; palaces

palaces

All of the great rulers of the ancient Mesopotamian kingdoms and empires had palaces. The earliest one whose remains have survived was erected in the city of Eridu, southwest of Ur, in the early third millennium B.C. Most palaces in Mesopotamia were not strictly residential mansions for the king and his family. They also functioned as administrative centers, storage facilities, and sometimes as manufacturing centers featuring workrooms for artisans of various types. Usually, these diverse functions were separated within a palace, each consisting of a number of rooms clustered around a central, unroofed courtyard. In many cases the throne room, meeting halls, and storage and work facilities were on the ground floor and the residential suites on the upper stories. Typically, for security purposes, the throne room could be reached only by walking through a series of twisting corridors and doors, all of which were heavily guarded by soldiers. The larger palaces in the region also featured gardens and parks; archives filled with cuneiform tablets, bearing both administrative records and literature; and sturdy defensive walls running around the perimeter.

One of the more impressive of the early royal Mesopotamian palaces was the one built at Mari in the eighteenth century B.C. by King Zimri-Lim. That it was well planned is evident from the ingenious complex of drainage channels beneath the floors. The structure had some three hundred rooms, several of which were devoted to an enormous archive of tablets. Many of these tablets contain letters exchanged by the monarchs of Zimri-Lim's day. The palace of the Assyrian king Sargon II at Dur-Sharukkin was notable for a massive spiral staircase that led to the roof, where the king and his astronomers could study the night sky. Another Assyrian city, Nineveh, featured several palaces, including those of Sennacherib (the so-called Palace Without Rival) and Ashurbanipal. Both had pairs of mammoth stone man-headed bulls guarding the entrances, a sight that must have struck visitors with awe and fear. Both palaces also had lengthy and elaborate panels of carved reliefs showing battles and hunting scenes; and Ashurbanipal's palace housed his famous library/archive containing thousands of baked-clay tablets.

Even larger and more sumptuous was the palace of the Babylonian king Nebuchadnezzar II. Erected in the early 500s B.C., it had at least six hundred rooms and was decorated by extensive sculptures coated with gold and lapis lazuli. After the fall of the Assyrian and Babylonian empires, the Persians adopted some of the same architectural styles and decorative motifs used in earlier Mesopotamian palaces, though Persian palaces also had some distinctive features of their own. The great terrace in the Persian capital of Persepolis supported three palaces—those of Darius I, Xerxes I, and Artaxerxes I—all situated close to an enormous audience hall (the *apadana*).

SEE ALSO: building materials and methods; Palace Without Rival; Pasargadae; Persepolis; sculpture

Palestine

In ancient times, the eastern Mediterranean coastal region lying south of Syria and north of the Egyptian-controlled Sinai Peninsula, an area fought over and conquered by many Mesopotamian and other Near Eastern rulers. Usually Palestine was considered to include the mostly fertile lands situated between the sea and the Jordan River as well as the more arid ones stretching eastward from the river. The term *Palestine* derives from the name of one of its peoples, the Philistines, famous opponents of the Hebrews in the Bible. The Egyptians called the Philistines the Peleset, and the Hebrews called them the Paleseth.

Palestine has been inhabited since Stone Age times. Parts of it belonged to the great curved swath of territory that modern scholars call the Fertile Crescent, where agriculture originated. One of Palestine's earliest towns, Jericho, existed before 9000 B.C., and many other prosperous settlements appeared in the region over the millennia that followed. The early inhabitants are generally referred to as Canaanites, after Canaan, the area lying immediately west of the Jordan.

It was probably inevitable that Palestine would become both coveted and invaded by many and diverse peoples. In ancient times the region occupied a highly strategic position, sandwiched between the populous and urbanized areas of Egypt, Mesopotamia, and Syria, whose rulers were often economic and military rivals. For the Egyptians, Palestine was a stepping stone to Syria; conversely, for the Mesopotamian kings Palestine was the corridor leading to both Egypt and the "great sea." Thus, although numerous independent city-states and kingdoms flourished in the region over the course of the centuries, Palestine was periodically and at times hotly contested by the great powers of the day.

Among the small Palestinian kingdoms of the late second and early first millennia B.C. were the southernmost Phoenician states, notably Tyre, on the coast of what is now Lebanon; the land of the Philistines, centered in the south near Gaza; and the Hebrew kingdoms of Israel and Judah. In the eighth century B.C. the Assyrians conquered Israel. And in 586 B.C. the Babylonian king Nebuchadnezzar overran Judah. Only a few decades later, however, the Persians captured and absorbed Palestine, which remained under the Persian yoke until Alexander the Great conquered Persia in the late fourth century B.C. Following Alexander's death, the Seleucid Empire, centered in Mesopotamia, and the Egyptian Ptolemaic realm vied for control of Palestine. Finally, in 63 B.C., the enterprising and aggressive Romans appeared on the scene and not long afterward the region became the Roman province of Judaea.

SEE ALSO: Fertile Crescent; Israel; Jericho; Judah; Phoenicians; Syria

Parthian Empire

A large realm that overcame and replaced the Greek-run Seleucid Empire in the second century B.C., bringing Mesopotamia under Parthian rule for nearly four centuries. The Parthians were originally a nomadic people from central Asia who spoke an Indo-European tongue and excelled at horse breeding and horsemanship. Sometime in the mid-first millennium B.C., bands of Parthians began migrating into northern Iran, then part of the Achaemenid Persian Empire. This region became known as Parthava. After the fall of Persia to the Greeks and the incorporation of much of its territory into the Seleucid Empire, more Parthian tribes entered Parthava, now a Seleucid province. But the people of the region became increasingly discontent with Seleucid rule. In 247 B.C. a local Parthian leader, Arsaces, declared himself king of the local Parthian tribes, marking the start of the Arsacid dynasty, named for him. Arsaces defeated the Seleucid governor of Parthava in battle in 238 B.C., thereby taking firm hold of northern Iran and launching the Parthian realm.

In the decades that followed, the Parthians steadily chipped away at the Seleucid state. They captured the Silk Road, an important trade route stretching eastward to India and China, thereby robbing the Seleucids of valuable revenues. Then, in 141 B.C., the Parthian ruler Mithridates I (reigned 171–ca. 138 B.C.) annexed Mesopotamia, including its two leading cities, Babylon and Seleucia. The Parthians

A coin depicting Arsaces, leader of the Parthian Empire in the 2nd century B.C. THE ART ARCHIVE/JAN VINCHON NUMISMATIST PARIS/DAGLI ORTI

proceeded to build a new capital, Ctesiphon, on the Tigris River not far from Seleucia. Highly tolerant of the beliefs and customs of other peoples, they allowed the Greek and Mesopotamian residents of Seleucia and other cities in the region to preserve their cultures. In fact, the Parthians admired Greek culture and appointed numerous Greeks to important administrative posts. The result was the rise of a sort of Greco-Iranian culture in

the region that over time reduced the importance of Persian traditions, including the old Persian Zoroastrian religion.

Though the Parthians had managed to gain control of large sectors of the Near East, they lacked the strong central organization needed to hold together such a large, diverse realm indefinitely. There was no overall, national army, for instance. Instead, small local armies commanded by individual chiefs (the heads of noble families) came together when necessary and supported the "head chief," the king. Thus, the Parthian Empire was in some ways a feudal state in which a number of vassal lords swore allegiance to the strongest of their number.

This loose political structure was viewed as weak by the Romans, who set out to incorporate the Parthian lands into their own empire. The Roman general Marcus Crassus invaded Mesopotamia in 53 B.C. but was defeated and killed at Carrhae (Harran). Later Roman forays into the region were more successful, however. In A.D. 116 the emperor Trajan (reigned 98–117) destroyed Ctesiphon and conquered large portions of Mesopotamia. Trajan's successor, Hadrian (117–138), gave up the captured territories, thinking them too difficult to rule from faraway Italy. But the emperor Marcus Aurelius (161–180) reversed this policy and seized northern Mesopotamia. Not long afterward, one of his own successors, Septimius Severus (193–211), recaptured Ctesiphon and looted much of the countryside.

The Parthians were unable to recover from this series of devastating onslaughts, and dissention steadily formed among the surviving Parthian vassal rulers. In 224 one of them, Ardashir, who ruled in the old Persian heartland of Fars, defeated the last Parthian king, Artabanus IV (reigned 216–224) and established a new Persian realm, the Sassanian Empire.

SEE ALSO: Ardashir I; Ctesiphon; Romans; Sassanian Empire

Pasargadae

The first capital of the Persian Empire. King Cyrus II began construction of Pasargadae, located some 50 miles (80km) northwest of Persepolis in the Persian heartland of Fars, in 547 B.C. The site had special significance to him, as it was there that he had defeated Astyages, king of Media, three years before. Much of the construction work was done by stonemasons from the Greek cities lying on Anatolia's western coast. The buildings featured a mix of architectural styles, including some pronounced Babylonian and Assyrian elements. For example, one of the city's two palace complexes, dubbed Palace P by modern archaeologists, was guarded by large stone bulls similar to those at the entrances of Assyrian palaces. Palace P also had a large *apadana* (audience hall), where Cyrus greeted courtiers and guests. Both this structure and the other palace, known as Palace S, utilized stone columns and baked mudbrick walls. Pasargadae later lost its status as the Persian capital when one of Cyrus's successors, Darius I, erected Persepolis; but Pasargadae retained ritual significance as the site where Persian kings were crowned. It also housed the simple but noble tomb of its builder, Cyrus, arguably Persia's greatest king.

SEE ALSO: Astyages; palaces; Persian Empire

Pazuzu

A terrifying demon recognized and revered by the Babylonians and Assyrians. The truly repellent Pazuzu had a scaly body, bulging eyes, four wings, and a snake-headed penis. Although he could cause harm to those who deserved punishment, he could also do good. He was believed to protect unborn babies when their pregnant mothers wore amulets featuring images of him. It was also thought that he kept foul winds from polluting Mesopotamian cities. An amulet and statue of Pazuzu appears prominently in the popular 1973 film *The Exorcist*.

SEE ALSO: exorcism; religion

Persepolis

From the time of King Darius I (reigned ca. 522–486 B.C.), one of the Persian Empire's three main capitals, along with Babylon and Susa. Work began on Persepolis in about 518 B.C., and additions were made to the city during the reigns of Darius's son, Xerxes, and later Persian kings. Darius chose a virgin site on the northern edge of a fertile plain in southern Iran about 43 miles (70km) northeast of the modern provincial capital of Shiraz. Building Persepolis was an unusually difficult task, partly because the site was in a remote area and the materials were shipped in from all parts of the known world. The bricks came from Babylonia, the cedar logs from Syria-Palestine, the gold from Anatolia, and the silver and ivory from Egypt and Ethiopia. The gigantic crew of workers included Mesopotamians and Anatolian Greeks as well as local Persians.

In its prime, Persepolis was dominated by an enormous terrace 1,640 feet (500m) long, 1,200 feet (366m) wide, and 50 feet (15m) high. Among the many structures on the terrace was an immense audience hall (*apadana*). It was accessed by a wide double staircase—which still survives largely intact—magnificently decorated with carved figures of people from all of Persia's subject nations. There was also a large throne room, the so-called Hall of a Hundred Columns, completed by Xerxes I and Artaxerxes I. Guarding the entrances to the hall were Assyrian-style carved stone bulls. Other structures on the terrace included the palaces of Darius, Xerxes, and Artaxerxes; a treasury; a harem complex with twenty-two separate apartments, each with a door leading into lush gardens; a council hall; workshops for artisans; and guardhouses for soldiers.

All of this splendor lasted fewer than two centuries. In 330 B.C. Alexander the Great burned Persepolis during his conquest of Persia. It was said that his men required twenty thousand mules and five thousand camels to cart away the treasures they looted from the great terrace. Although the terrace and surrounding city were devastated, in time materials from the site were used to erect a smaller, much less impressive town, Istakhr, nearby. The new town gained some prominence later under the Parthians, the Sassanians, and the Arabs until it was eventually abandoned. The site of Persepolis was excavated beginning in 1931 by a team from Chicago's Oriental Institute.

SEE ALSO: Darius I; palaces; Persian Empire

Persian Empire

The imperial realm that conquered and replaced those of the Medes and the Neo-Babylonians in Iran and Mesopotamia and territorially the largest native empire to ever encompass the lands of the ancient Near East. At its height, the Persian realm, ruled by members of the Achaemenid dynasty, stretched from the shores of the Mediterranean and Aegean seas in the west to the borders of India in the east. Nearly thirty separate nations and peoples fell under the authority of the Persian kings.

The Persians had originated as nomads from the central-Asian steppes who had descended into Iran in the late second millennium B.C. They identified themselves as Aryans, and the name *Iran* is derived from the word *aryanam*, meaning "land of the Aryans." One group of Persians became the Medes; the other, called the Parsua, settled in the region of Fars, just north of the Persian Gulf. For a long time the

Ruins of an ancient city known as Persepolis, which was built in the 6th century B.C. as one of the capitals in the Persian Empire. © LLOYD CLUFF/CORBIS

Persians remained more or less in the shadow of the great nations and empires of the Near East—those of the Assyrians, Babylonians, Elamites, Medes, and Egyptians.

Cyrus the Great In about 559 B.C. an Achaemenid nobleman ascended the throne of Fars, then a Median province, as Cyrus II. In a startlingly short span of time, he led his followers in a rebellion against the Medes, captured the Median capital of Ecbatana, deposed the Median ruler, Astyages, and established the Persian Empire. Recognizing that the Persians and the Medes shared the same ancestry, Cyrus showed deference to his conquered enemies, giving numerous Median nobles high positions in the Persian army and royal court. Media became a province, or satrapy, of the new empire, and Ecbatana

became a secondary Persian capital. (Cyrus's main capital was Pasargadae, in the hills of Fars.)

The Persians borrowed many Median customs, including a number of clothing styles. Cyrus and later Persian rulers and officials also wisely adopted ideas and customs of other formerly successful peoples in the region. Indeed, the Persians, like the later Romans, became highly adept at cultural borrowing. As the Greek historian Herodotus puts it, "No race is so ready to adopt foreign ways as the Persian; for instance, they wear the Median costume because they think it handsomer than their own, and their soldiers wear the Egyptian corselet." (*Histories* 1.136) Thus, Persian society became in many ways a fusion of the cultures of various earlier Mesopotamian and Iranian peoples. The upland Persians bred horses in imitation of earlier Iranian nomads; the lowland Persians farmed the Mesopotamian plains like the Babylonians; and Cyrus modeled his military in large degree on that of the Assyrians, although he improved on some of their ideas. The Assyrian Empire also inspired Cyrus's political organization. Like the Assyrian monarchs, he divided his own realm into provinces, each administered by a governor, called a satrap, who was subordinate to the king. A Persian satrap held considerable power. So Cyrus made sure his authority would not be threatened by having a satrap's secretary, financial officer, and chief military officer all report directly to Cyrus himself.

With the basics of an effective imperial government in place, Cyrus initiated a series of conquests designed to expand his new realm. Turning westward, he entered Anatolia and swiftly brought the kingdom of Lydia to its knees. In absorbing Anatolia, Cyrus also gained control of the Greek cities on that peninsula's western coast, including Miletus, Ephesus, and Halicarnassus (Herodotus's hometown). Next, Cyrus returned to Fars and began work on his new capital of Pasargadae. Then he marched his army eastward and conquered the peoples of what are now eastern Iran and Afghanistan, bringing him to the borders of distant India. Finally, Cyrus overran Babylonia and absorbed its lands, including all of southern Mesopotamia and most of Palestine. That left Egypt as the only one of the former great Near Eastern powers that had not yet fallen under the Persian yoke.

Cambyses and Darius I Before Cyrus could march on Egypt, however, he died in 530 B.C. and the responsibility of the Egyptian campaign fell to his son, Cambyses. After raising a huge new army, Cambyses attacked Egypt in 525 B.C. Near Pelusium,

located on the seacoast just east of the Nile delta, he soundly defeated the Egyptian military forces. Cambyses remained in Egypt for nearly three years and then died on the way back to Persia. In 522, after an impostor pretending to be Cambyses' brother, Bardiya, had ruled the empire for several months, a group of Persian nobles slew the usurper and placed another Achaemenid, Darius, on the throne. The new king found himself facing some major challenges. Hearing that the impostor had been removed, a number of provincial governors rebelled; Darius had to put down these revolts before he could address his own plans for the empire.

Those plans included more conquests like those of Cyrus and Cambyses. In 519 B.C. Darius led an expedition against the Saka, a people who inhabited the remote, rugged region northwest of India. After its fall to the Persians, the area became the empire's newest satrapy. The following year Darius initiated construction of a new city, Persepolis in Fars, which in time replaced Pasargadae as Persia's capital. Then he turned his attentions westward, seeing the absorption of Europe as a tempting goal. Darius sent out ships manned by scouts, who first cruised and mapped the Greek coasts and then pushed on to southern Italy. Though the king never gained a fully clear picture of the large size of the Mediterranean-European world, the data gathered by his scouts indicated that it was rich in natural and human resources and was ripe for the taking. So in 512 B.C. Darius crossed what is now the Bosporus Strait and entered Thrace, the rugged, sparsely inhabited region lying along the northern rim of the Aegean Sea. The Thracians submitted without a fight. But the Scythians, who lived farther north, employed a scorched-earth campaign and denied Darius a clear-cut victory. A few years after this initial and only partly successful Persian foray into Europe, the Anatolian Greeks rebelled against Persian rule. Darius was forced to expend time and resources to quash the revolt, which ended with a decisive Persian naval victory in the eastern Aegean Sea in 494 B.C.

Because some of the mainland Greeks had helped their Anatolian brethren during the rebellion, in 490 B.C. Darius ordered two of his generals, Datis and Artaphernes, to sail across the Aegean and sack the cities of Athens and Eretria. They captured Eretria, but soon afterward the Persian army was defeated on the plain of Marathon near Athens. Up to this time, the Greek military system, which relied on heavily armored infantrymen called hoplites, was untested in a large open battle with Persian troops, who had a reputation for fighting skill and ferocity that made them feared far and wide. Apparently Darius and his advisers thought the Athenian win was a fluke and prepared for a full-scale attack on Greece.

Second-Rate Rulers Darius died in 486 B.C. before he could mount his great expedition. His son, Xerxes, did so in 480 B.C., leading some two hundred thousand land troops and almost a thousand ships against the tiny Greek city-states. The superiority of the Greek military system now became clear as the Greeks crushed the invaders in a series of hard-fought battles that have since become the stuff of legend.

In the wake of his failure to penetrate Europe, Xerxes was forced to return to his homeland, and the remainder of his reign was largely undistinguished. In 465 B.C. he was assassinated by the captain of the palace guard and other conspirators, who placed the dead king's son, Artaxerxes, on the throne. The intrigue-filled reign of Ar-

taxerxes in many ways typified those of his successors, who were largely self-absorbed, second-rate leaders. They were unable to deal effectively with some of the serious problems the empire faced. These problems included the toll taken by frequent internal power struggles; mounting discontent among the empire's subject peoples, especially those far from the Persian heartland; more and more military use of paid Greek mercenaries, whose loyalty to Persia was practically nil; and a loss of interest in expanding the realm. Under these mediocre rulers the Persian Empire's political stability, structural integrity, and reputation as a great military power steadily deteriorated. And the degeneration of the high moral ideals of Cyrus and the first Darius continued.

When Artaxerxes died in 424 B.C., a new power struggle brought to the throne his son, Xerxes II, who lasted only a few months before he was murdered. Another of Artaxerxes' sons, Ochus, then became King Darius II, whose mediocre reign ended in 404 B.C., precipitating still another royal power struggle. Darius's eldest son, Arsaces, succeeded him as Artaxerxes II, much to the regret of the second son, Cyrus, usually called "Cyrus the Younger" to distinguish him from the founder of the empire. In 401 B.C. Cyrus launched a rebellion against Artaxerxes. Hiring thousands of Greek mercenaries to supplement his Persian troops, the would-be usurper fought his brother at Cunaxa in Mesopotamia and met with defeat and death. The Greeks then fought their way out of Mesopotamia, showing Greeks everywhere the damage that even a small Greek army could incur inside the decaying Persian colossus. Artaxerxes himself knew this better than anyone. He had witnessed firsthand the formidable charge of the Greek hoplites at Cunaxa and saw that he must do whatever was necessary to keep the Greeks out of his realm. Among other things, in 387 B.C. he concluded the Peace of Antalcidas, or King's Peace, with the major Greek states of the day. Artaxerxes agreed to recognize the sovereignty of these states and to stay out of their affairs, as long as they stayed out of his.

The Empire's Decline and Fall But the safety of the empire was an illusion, as the seeds of its destruction had already been planted by decades of internal corruption and decline. The central authority continued to weaken, rebellions increased in frequency, and in some cases the king had to resort to bribing the rebel leaders to get them to stop fighting. After Artaxerxes died in 358 B.C., his son, Artaxerxes III, managed to reconquer Egypt, which had rebelled, but only with great difficulty. And large parts of the empire remained independent of his control.

This was the sad state of affairs that the last Persian king, Darius III, faced when he ascended the throne in 336 B.C. In that same year, in faraway Greece the Macedonian king Philip II, who had recently brought most of the Greeks under his control, was assassinated. His son, Alexander III, then followed through with his father's plans to invade Persia. After Alexander's rapid capture of the eastern third of that realm, he and Darius faced each other in a huge battle fought in October 331 B.C. at Gaugamela, a few miles southeast of the ruins of the Assyrian city of Nineveh. Darius was defeated and fled the field. By the time Alexander had caught up with him, the Persian king was dead, having been murdered by his own followers. Alexander soon completed the conquest of Darius's realm, laying the groundwork for nearly two centuries of Greek

rule in Mesopotamia and much of the rest of the Near East.

SEE ALSO: Achaemenid dynasty; Alexander III ("the Great"); battles of Cunaxa and Gaugamela; Greeks; Median Empire; Persepolis; weapons and warfare, land and naval; and the names of individual Persian rulers

Persian Gulf

The large inland sea or bay situated between Iran and the Arabian Peninsula. The Persian Gulf, which is about 620 miles (1,000km) long and averages 230 miles (370km) in width, connects with the Gulf of Oman via the Strait of Hormuz in the south. In the northwestern sector of the Persian Gulf lies the delta of the Tigris and Euphrates rivers, which have supplied the civilizations of Mesopotamia with freshwater throughout history. It was in this delta and the fertile lands bordering it that the Sumerians built the world's first substantial cities.

SEE ALSO: Mesopotamia, geography of; Sumerians; Tigris and Euphrates

Persians

Historians variously use the term *Persian* in both a general and a more specific sense. In the general sense, the term denotes a group of Indo-European-speaking people who settled in Iran in the late second millennium B.C. They eventually separated into somewhat distinct groups. The two most important of these were the Medes, who made their capital at Ecbatana, and the Persians who dwelled in Fars, directly north of the Persian Gulf, who gave rise to the Achaemenid dynasty. Two other Iranian-based peoples who later controlled Iran and Mesopotamia—the Parthians and the Sassanians—are also frequently referred to as Persians. In the more specific sense, the term denotes the Achaemenid rulers (Cyrus II, Cambyses, Darius, etc.) and their subjects, the inhabitants of the Persian Empire.

SEE ALSO: Fars; Persepolis; Persian Empire; Sassanian Empire

Petrie, Flinders (1853–1942)

A pioneering English archaeologist whose methods for dating pottery came to be used in excavations all across the Near East, including Mesopotamia. The grandson of Matthew Flinders, a leading explorer of the coasts of Australia, Petrie studied surveying as a young man. In 1880 Petrie journeyed to Egypt to study and measure the Great Pyramid at Giza, and in the years that followed he became one of the leading excavators of ancient Egypt. For these efforts, he was knighted by the British queen in 1923, becoming Sir Flinders Petrie. In 1926, he decided it was time to tackle sites in the Near East and began excavations in Palestine. There, over the course of several years, he applied his effective new methods for dating ancient pottery. He also demonstrated how the cities and kingdoms of ancient Palestine, including ancient Israel and Judah, interacted with and were often integral parts of the great empires centered in ancient Mesopotamia, including the Assyrian, Babylonian, and Persian realms.

SEE ALSO: Egypt; Mesopotamia, history of; Palestine

Phoenicians

The inhabitants of Phoenicia, in ancient times a small region occupying the coastal strip of Syria and northern Palestine, roughly corresponding to modern Lebanon. The Phoenicians, who were renowned for their seafaring skills and mercantile endeavors, spoke a Semitic language and were of Canaanite stock. In fact, they called themselves Canaani, the term *Phoenician* deriving from the Greek name for them, Phoiniki. Although the Phoenicians existed as early as the third millennium B.C., their heyday was the period of about 1200 to about 800 B.C. During these years the Phoenician cities, including Tyre (the southernmost), Byblos, Sarepta, Sidon, and Berytus (modern Beirut), grew populous and prosperous and established colonies and trading posts across the Mediterranean world. They were important middlemen in the principal trade route connecting that world to Mesopotamia and Iran. In fact, most of the tin the Mesopotamians used to make their bronze came from the Phoenicians, who obtained the tin in Spain and northwestern Europe.

The relationship between the Phoenician cities and Mesopotamia became more personal when the Assyrian Empire captured most of them. Later, the Babylonians and the Persians exerted their own control over these cities. Later still, in the late 330s B.C., during his conquest of Persia, Alexander the Great conquered Phoenicia, successfully laying siege to Tyre. Finally, after Alexander's death, the Greek Seleucid rulers of Mesopotamia vied with the Greek Ptolemaic rulers of Egypt for possession of the Phoenician cities. By the first century B.C. Phoenicia had ceased to exist as a separate political and cultural sphere. Historically speaking, the Phoenicians' most important contribution was probably their alphabet, which the Greeks, Romans, and many other ancient peoples eventually adopted and transmitted to the modern world.

Phraortes
(reigned ca. 675–653 B.C.?)

The son of King Deioces and the second king of the united Median tribes. It remains somewhat unclear if Phraortes was a real person, as the Greek historian Herodotus is the principal surviving ancient source for him and Herodotus's information about the early Medes was second- or thirdhand. It is therefore difficult to date Phraortes' reign, if he did exist. Modern estimates include circa 675 to 653 B.C., circa 665 to 633 B.C., and circa 647 to 625 B.C. Herodotus said that Phraortes attacked the Assyrian city of Nineveh but failed to take it and died in the attempt. Phraortes' son, Herodotus added, was Cyaxares II. Definitely a real person, Cyaxares established the short-lived Median Empire.

poetry

The ancient Mesopotamians wrote both long epic poetry and shorter verses, including hymns, laments, and erotic poems. For general information, **see also** literature.

postal system

The ancient Mesopotamians did not have a complex, universal system of delivering letters and packages to and from ordinary people, by modern standards. However, the earliest precursors of modern postal systems do seem to have originated in Mesopotamia. Various ancient sources credit the Assyrians with instituting a post, which consisted of riders carrying messages from the king and/or his officials in the capital to the governors of imperial provinces. This system was the basis of a more sophisticated one established by the Persians in the wake of Assyria's decline. According to the Greek historian Xenophon, the first Persian king, Cyrus II, established the system. Other ancient sources claim that one of Cyrus's successors, Darius I (reigned 522–486 B.C.), created the Persian royal post, called the Barid. Essential to the system were some long "royal roads," including the one that stretched from Susa in southeastern Mesopotamia to Sardis in western Anatolia. Although the Persian post at first dealt only with official government mail, evidence suggests that over time the couriers carried limited amounts of business and personal correspondence as well, foreshadowing the more universal postal systems of the future.

pottery

Pottery (or ceramic) objects, both intact and broken, make up a large portion of the moundlike debris piles, or tells, found all over Mesopotamia. Indeed, vessels, figurines, and other artifacts of baked clay were the most common products manufactured by ancient Mesopotamian craftspeople. However, unlike the ancient Greeks, whose pottery was often an outlet for artistic expression and of high quality, with a few exceptions Mesopotamian potters produced pottery of largely uninspired, even crude design and execution. Thus, in Mesopotamia ceramics was a minor art at best, especially compared to native architecture and sculpture, which were often of superb quality. Nevertheless,

This ancient Mesopotamian pottery vessel was most likely used to pour water. © Gianni Dagli Orti/Corbis

study of the remains of pottery has greatly aided modern archaeologists in dating ancient sites in the region. This is because people usually made pottery objects featuring shapes, painted designs, and other characteristics that were distinct to their own time periods. The basics of dating Mesopotamian pottery were pioneered by British archaeologist Flinders Petrie (1853–1942) in the 1890s.

Pottery was in use at least as early as 7000 B.C. in Mesopotamia. The first pottery objects were shaped by hand and were baked in open fires. Hotter, more controlled firing was possible after the introduction of primitive kilns circa 6000 B.C., and subsequently kilns were made of fired brick and came in several different shapes and sizes. Due to a lack of oxygen in these kilns, during the firing process the reddish brown clay turned gray or black. In addition to hand shaping, early potters employed simple molds, into which they pressed the moist clay. A slow-turning, hand-operated potter's wheel appeared in Mesopotamia around 4000 B.C., making mass production of jars and other commonly used objects more feasible. A faster wheel came into use circa 2000 B.C. And Assyrian and Babylonian potters introduced ceramic items coated with colored glazes in the first millennium B.C. Pottery cooking pots, cups, plates, bowls, and jars continued to be made, but their quality was usually mediocre, as the well-to-do generally preferred metals such as bronze, silver, and gold for fine dinnerware and decorative vases.

SEE ALSO: crafts and craftspeople; sculpture; tell

priests and priestesses

To operate efficiently, ancient Mesopotamian temples required large staffs, including not only people who handled divine statues and other sacred objects but also those who interpreted omens, performed purification rites, ritually slaughtered sacrificial animals, advised kings on religious matters, and administered the temples and their rich estates. Any and all of these persons could be classified as priests, or priestesses in the case of women who performed such tasks. The most common word for high priest was *en* and for high priestess, *entu*. In most places and times in ancient Mesopotamia, high priests were the men who had seniority and political power in the temples and who performed the most sacred and delicate

rites. They and most other priests had to fulfill certain strict requirements before they could attain their coveted positions within the temple compounds. First and foremost, they had to be literate; and indeed, some priests began as scribes. They also had to be well educated, specially trained, and their bodies had to be free of physical deformities. In addition, once in the job a priest was required to maintain ritual purity by reciting special incantations on a regular basis.

For the most part in the priestly profession, males attended male gods, and females attended goddesses. However, there were some exceptions, notably the high priestess of the moon god, Nanna (or Sin). Whatever the status of women in general society, Mesopotamian priestesses commanded a high level of respect, as in the case of the famous Vestal Virgins in Rome. In some temples, notably those of the goddess Ishtar (Inanna), some of the priestesses may have taken part in a fertility ritual that featured sexual intercourse, usually referred to as sacred prostitution, although this remains controversial. In the Old Babylonian period (early second millennium B.C.), there were also female temple personnel, possibly priestesses, called *naditu*. Their religious duties are unclear, though some evidence suggests that they may have performed daily sacrifices and prayers. These women lived secluded lives in a cloisterlike structure called a *gagum* ("locked house") and were expected to remain chaste and childless. A group of *naditu* was prominent in the temple of the sun god, Shamash, at Sippar.

SEE ALSO: religion; sacred prostitution; temples

proskynesis

The Greek word for the act of prostrating

oneself before a social superior, a common practice in the ancient Near East, including Mesopotamia. The Greek historian Herodotus described the custom (*Histories* 1.135) among the Persians, indicating that members of the lower classes performed it when approaching members of the upper classes. But *proskynesis* was especially prevalent in the royal courts, where subjects prostrated themselves before their kings. Most Greeks who witnessed the custom viewed it as degrading and thought such a gesture should be used only to show reverence to a god. Nevertheless, in 327 B.C. following his conquest of Persia, Alexander the Great instituted *proskynesis* when holding court in Asia, which, not surprisingly, displeased his Greek followers. Alexander's ancient biographer Arrian quotes the comments of Callisthenes, one of Alexander's officers, on the subject:

> Do not forget that there is a difference between honoring a man and worshipping a god. The distinction between the two has been marked in many ways. . . . Yet of all these things not one is so important as this very

custom of prostration. Men greet each other with a kiss; but a god, far above us on his mysterious throne, it is not lawful for us to touch—and that is why we [pay] homage [by] bowing to the earth before him. . . . It is wrong, therefore, to ignore these distinctions; we ought not to make a man look bigger than he is by paying him excessive and extravagant honor, or . . . [by] putting [the gods] on the same level as men. (*Anabasis Alexandri* 4.11)

Alexander's move set a precedent; the Greek Seleucid rulers who followed him in Mesopotamia also demanded that their subjects prostrate themselves.

SEE ALSO: Alexander III ("the Great"); Persian Empire; Seleucid Empire

proverbs

Short, wise sayings or adages passed from one generation to another. The ancient Mesopotamians were fond of proverbs, and a number of Sumerian and Babylonian examples have survived.

SEE ALSO: literature

Rassam, Hormuzd (1826–1910)

A noted Iraqi-born archaeologist and Assyriologist who made significant discoveries in many parts of Mesopotamia in the nineteenth century. Rassam began as an assistant to the British scholar and pioneering Assyriologist Austen Henry Layard from 1845 to 1847. At Layard's urgings, he then went to England and studied at Oxford's Magdalen College. After completing his education, Rassam went back to Iraq under the auspices of the British Museum and excavated at several ancient Assyrian sites, including Nimrud. In a later expedition (1876–1882), Rassam explored the ruins of Nineveh and Babylon and discovered the site of the Babylonian city of Sippara. Among his other important finds were tablets containing the stories of the creation and great flood, the lion-hunt reliefs of Assyria's King Ashurbanipal, and the bronze gates of another Assyrian monarch, Shalmaneser II.

SEE ALSO: Assyriology; Layard, Austen Henry; Nineveh

Rawlinson, Henry C. (1810–1895)

A British soldier, diplomat, linguist, and one of the great pioneers of Near Eastern archaeology, Assyriology, and the decipherment of the ancient cuneiform writing system. While in Iran and Iraq on an official military assignment in the 1830s, Rawlinson was drawn to the mysterious cuneiform inscriptions that had recently been unearthed in the region. He visited and studied the Behistun Rock, bearing carved drawings and cuneiform inscriptions from the reign of Persia's King Darius I. A few years later he settled in Baghdad and made a complete transcription of the Behistun inscriptions. By 1851 Rawlinson was able to read some of the words, and in the years that followed, with the aid of other scholars, he deciphered most of the rest. Later in life he took a succession of diplomatic and political posts, including a stint in the British Parliament from 1865 to 1868. But his first love remained the study of ancient Mesopotamia and its languages. For his efforts in this area he is sometimes called "the Father of Assyriology." Rawlinson published a number of important books, including *The Persian Cuneiform Inscriptions at Behistun* (1846–1851) and *Outline of the History of Assyria* (1852).

SEE ALSO: Behistun Rock; cuneiform; languages

religion

Almost all ancient Mesopotamians were devoutly religious, and in one form or another various aspects of religion permeated their lives. From very early times, long before the introduction of writing and the building of large temples in the late fourth millennium B.C., people in the region envisioned that the world was alive with invisible spirits of various kinds. Good or evil spirits inhabited all aspects of nature,

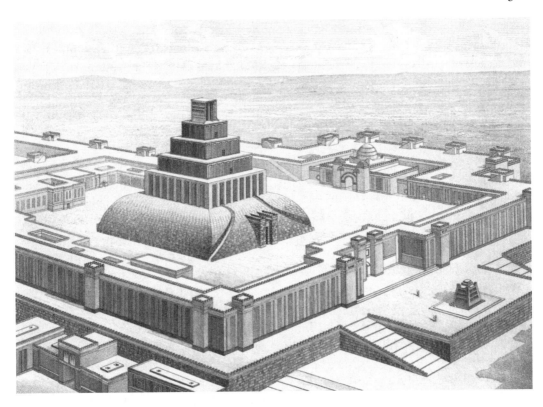

An illustration depicting an Assyrian temple. © Gianni Dagli Orti/Corbis

including the sky and the Sun, the Moon, and the planets; the mountains and forests; farmer's fields; and the waters of streams, rivers, and seas. In addition, it was thought that spirits were inherent within or guided human activities such as making fire, raising crops, writing literature, and healing the sick. Over time these spirits increasingly took on human form and exhibited humanlike characteristics, probably because this made it easier for people to relate to and worship them. But whether one saw the gods in abstract or in human form, the core belief was that the will and powers of these divinities guided the workings of both nature and humanity. Such guidance took the form of what might be called underlying rules of order that must be followed. The Sumerians referred to these rules collectively as *me*, and the

Babylonians and Assyrians called them *parsu*. In mythology, an important tangible artifact of this divine order was the so-called Tablet of Destiny, on which the fates of both gods and humans were recorded. Because of its great intrinsic powers, it was highly coveted, and several myths described attempts to steal it.

Personal and Temple Gods For the average person, the principal connection to the divine order was a personal god to whom the person could pray at any time and in any place. It is unknown how someone went about choosing a personal god, but certain gods were seen as protectors of groups, so that a farmer might pray to the patron of farmers and a soldier to a deity known to befriend soldiers. A personal god might also be the local patron deity of a town or a city. People thought that the patron deity took a special interest in that city and its people. Whoever the personal god was, when necessary the worshipper asked it to gain the assistance of a more powerful deity, one who transcended merely local affairs.

In fact, some local gods eventually gained national prominence. Sometimes this occurred through conquest, as when an invading people introduced its god to the inhabitants of the regions it captured. But even more often it was the result of cultural assimilation. It was very common for Sumerian deities to be passed on to, or adopted by, later Mesopotamian peoples, for instance. In the process, an older god's functions, duties, and physical image would be absorbed by the younger god, though the latter usually displayed some new attributes given to it by the later people. An obvious example is the way the Sumerian god Enlil gradually took on many of the attributes of the patriarchal, universal governor An. Later, the Babylonian divinity Marduk took on most of Enlil's powers and duties, as did the Assyrian god Ashur.

Although people continued to worship such gods on a private, informal level throughout Mesopotamian history, these deities were also worshipped on a more formal, organized, national level. The main focus of city, national, and imperial worship was the temple, of which a typical city had several. However, public worship did not take place inside the temple, as happens inside modern churches, synagogues, and mosques. In ancient times most people thought that a god or goddess actually dwelled inside the temple, so to respect his or her privacy, the congregation gathered outside. The ceremonies might take place in a special courtyard on the temple grounds, in a city square, or

somewhere else. The temple housed the god's cult image, or statue, which it was thought he actually inhabited. And it was common for priests to carry the statue out of the temple to the place where the main worship was taking place.

Festivals and Rituals Removing a god's cult image from its temple occurred only during religious festivals, special times of the year similar to modern religious holidays. The largest and most elaborate of these festivals was an agricultural celebration that the Sumerians called Akiti and the Babylonians and Assyrians Akitu. In some places it was held once a year, at harvest time (usually in March). This coincided with the New Year's celebration, making it doubly festive. In other places in Mesopotamia, the Akiti took place twice—during both harvest and planting times. In Babylonia from the second millennium B.C. on, the festival lasted twelve days and involved rituals including prayer and the sacrifice of animals; reciting the *Epic of Creation*, which describes how the chief god, Marduk, acquired universal power; formal processions in which people marched, sang, and carried the divine images; and large-scale as well as private feasts.

In addition to these more or less universal rituals, each Mesopotamian people or region had its peculiar local rituals during a given religious festival. A noteworthy example was a Babylonian ceremony that took place on the fifth day of the New Year's festival, dedicated to Marduk and his son, Nabu. Nabu's shrine was ritually cleansed and then covered with a golden embroidered canopy. Amid great pomp and solemnity, the king of Babylonia entered and the high priest removed his crown and other royal trappings. Then the priest slapped the king across the face, after which the monarch had to kneel before Nabu's image and swear that he had not abused the great powers and authority entrusted to him by the gods. These acts symbolized and emphasized the ultimate power of the divine order over humanity, including human kings. Later in the day, the priest returned the crown to the king and the two men prayed together to the planet Mercury, which was associated with Marduk.

Such prayers, sacrifices, festivals, and other physical acts of worship were performed to appease and show respect to the gods. But most Mesopotamians did not do these things simply out of fear, necessity, or as lip service to the divine. Following deep-seated traditions passed from generation to generation, religion was ingrained into society in such a way that most people had a strong sense of morality. They both understood basic concepts of right and wrong and felt obligated to strive toward what was right. The great Assyriologist Samuel N. Kramer perfectly sums it up this way:

> The Sumerians . . . cherished goodness and truth, law and order, justice and freedom . . . [and] mercy and compassion. And they abhorred evil and falsehood [and] lawlessness and disorder. . . . Kings and rulers constantly boasted . . . that they had established law and order in the land. . . . And practically all the major deities . . . are extolled in Sumerian hymns as lovers of the good and just, of truth and righteousness. (*History Begins at Sumer*, p. 101)

This does not mean that all Mesopotamians were just, always told the truth, and never committed crimes. However, society had strict ethical norms that many people at least tried to fulfill, and usually they were not driven to do so simply to ensure

they would be rewarded later with a comfortable residence in the afterlife. There was a strong sense of social conscience or humanity, which the Sumerians called *namlulu*, which in practical terms translated into such widespread acts as comforting the ill and protecting the weak and widows and orphans. These and other similar ethical acts were frequently expressed in and encouraged by the law codes issued by rulers such as Babylonia's Hammurabi. Thus, partly through religious devotion and rituals passed from one generation to another, the various peoples of Mesopotamia regulated themselves and strove to maintain a civil, just, and compassionate society. For more details about various aspects of religion and religious beliefs and customs, **see also** afterlife; burial customs; divination; magic; priests and priestesses; temples. For the religion of ancient Persia, **see also** Zoroastrianism.

SEE ALSO: the names of individual gods and goddesses

Rich, Claudius James (1787–1821)

An English scholar, linguist, traveler, and archaeologist who played a key role in educating the English and other Europeans about the then still largely mysterious ancient wonders of Mesopotamia. Rich early exhibited a gift for learning languages, and by the time he was a young man he was fluent in Latin, Greek, Hebrew, Persian, Syriac, Turkish, and others. On a journey to Egypt, he added Arabic to his growing repertoire. An important turning point for Rich was his move to the Iraqi city of Baghdad in 1808. He immediately became fascinated by the many mounds of ancient ruins in the region and was the first European to scientifically and methodically investigate the site of Babylon.

In 1815 he published his *Narrative of a Journey to the Site of Babylon in 1811*. Rich also visited and explored the sites of Nineveh and Persepolis and described his adventures in more books. In fact, his main contribution was, through these writings, to create public interest in Mesopotamia among Europeans, an effort that inspired later Assyriologists such as Austen Henry Layard.

SEE ALSO: Assyriology; languages; Layard, Austen Henry

Rim-Sin I (reigned ca. 1822–1763 B.C.)

A king who ruled the southern Mesopotamian city of Larsa for sixty years, the longest-known reign of any ancient Mesopotamian ruler. The Amorite dynasty of which Rim-Sin was a member came to power in Larsa following the collapse of the Third Dynasty of Ur, which had earlier ruled the region. The brother of the former ruler of Larsa, Warad-Sin, he carried on the already existing rivalry between the rulers of Larsa and the rulers of the city of Isin, which he captured circa 1796 B.C. Rim-Sin also defeated a coalition of nearby cities led by the king of Uruk. In this way, Larsa gained control of most of southern Babylonia, formerly Sumer. However, Rim-Sin was eventually himself defeated by Hammurabi, king of Babylon, in about 1764 B.C. and seems to have died in custody soon afterward. Several cuneiform documents about Rim-Sin have survived, most of them prayers addressed to various gods in his name. This excerpt is from one such prayer dedicated to the moon god, Nanna:

> Rim-Sin, king of abundance, august prince of rulers, may right and justice be your helpers. May they make a good [works] for you. ... Rim-Sin named with a name by [the great gods] An and Enlil, when you enter the Great Gate ... may the favorable protective god and the protective goddess of peace, gatekeepers of the Great Gate, shine upon you. May they bring you back an answer of life and peace ... to your greeting which they bring before Nanna. ... May they cause a good [future] that brings happiness, a mood of encouragement, to issue for you. ... May the gods of life of the Great Gate open the doors for you. May the gods of peace, guardians of the Great Gate, rejoice at your presence, and may their features light up at you.

SEE ALSO: Hammurabi; Larsa; Third Dynasty of Ur

roads

Long before any human-made roads were built in Mesopotamia, people used the rivers to travel long distances. If they had to journey overland, they used donkeys, and later camels and horses, and followed the routes that were physically easiest, keeping an eye on familiar landmarks along the way. Over time some of the routes became beaten-down dirt pathways, which long remained the main form of the roads in the region. Their obvious disadvantage was that they became muddy and in some places impassible during the rainy and flood season in the spring.

With the rise of larger empires in the region, however, the rulers of these entities began to see the need for expanding and better maintaining some of the ancient pathways. Better roads allowed more efficient communication between the capital and the provinces and quicker movement of supplies and soldiers from one place to another. The Assyrians were the first to approach this task in a major way. They built guard posts at intervals along the roads, dug wells to provide water for travelers and their animals, put up road signs to help people find their way, and established a postal system in which mounted messengers carried royal correspondence. These longer roads were mostly still dirt paths, though some were no doubt wider and better maintained than the previous versions. The Assyrians did have a few paved roads, but these were short, consisting mainly of processional ways leading from temple to temple inside cities or a few main streets in those cities. The paved surfaces were achieved by placing slabs of stone in a mortar of tar (bitumen), sometimes on a base of gravel.

Later, the Persians lengthened and improved many of the older Assyrian roads as well as built some new ones. The most famous of Persia's "royal roads" was the one King Darius I (reigned ca. 522–486 B.C.) built to connect Susa in eastern Mesopotamia to Sardis in western Anatolia. Incorporating sections of an earlier Assyrian road, it stretched some 1,500 miles (2,415km). The Greek historian Herodotus, who traveled this road during his visit to Mesopotamia in the fifth century B.C., gives this description:

> At intervals all along the road are recognized stations, with excellent inns, and the road itself is safe to travel by, as it never leaves inhabited country. In Lydia and Phrygia [in Anatolia], over a distance of . . . about 330 miles [530km]—there are 20 stations. . . . The total number of stations, or post-houses, on the road from Sardis to Susa is 111. . . . Traveling at the rate of 150 furlongs [18 miles (29km)] a day, a man will take just ninety days to make the journey. (*Histories* 5.52–53)

Darius's couriers, who periodically changed mounts at each road station and "slept in the saddle" (like the Pony Express riders in the American West), were able to make it from Sardis to Susa in just fifteen days; this was considered impressive, even astonishing, at the time. A similar royal road stretched eastward from Babylon to Ecbatana and from there northeastward into distant Bactria, joining with the major trade route known as the Silk Road. Later the Seleucids and the Parthians took full advantage of the roads the Assyrians and the Persians had left behind. Other roads, several of them well built and paved, were built across western portions of Mesopotamia by the Romans in the first and second centuries A.D.

SEE ALSO: Darius I; postal system; Romans; Sardis

Romans

The Romans, who rose to prominence in Italy and conquered the western Mediterranean sphere between about 600 and 200 B.C., at first had little interest in Mesopotamia, which they saw as a distant region on the fringes of the known world. But in the second and first centuries B.C. Rome conquered Greece, Anatolia, and Syria-Palestine; that greatly increased the size of its empire and widened the scope of its political ambitions in the East. By the first century B.C. Mesopotamia and other large tracts of the Near East were under the control of the Parthian Empire, which had recently supplanted the Seleucid Empire in the region. And for a long time the Parthians were the chief impediment to Roman penetration of Mesopotamia.

The first Roman notable to move against the Parthians was the real-estate tycoon and powerful politician Marcus Licinius Crassus, who had formed an impor-

A relief illustrating the victory of Shapur I over the Roman emperors Valerian and Philip the Arab. SEF/ART RESOURCE, NY

tant alliance with Julius Caesar in 60 B.C. While Caesar was away fighting in Gaul (now France), Crassus sought to distinguish himself militarily in the East. In 53 B.C. Crassus led some thirty thousand infantry and ten thousand cavalry through Armenia and attacked the Parthians at Carrhae (Harran) in western Mesopotamia. The ill-fated venture resulted in the loss of three-quarters of the Roman force, Crassus's death, and the embarrassing loss of the Roman eagles (standards of the legions, or battalions). Hoping to recover the eagles and earn glory for himself, another Roman general, Marcus Antonius (or Mark Antony), invaded Parthia in 36 B.C. His strategy was to capture the Parthian cities, but this became impossible when the enemy captured his siege devices. He ended up losing more than half his men and had to retreat. Though he planned to return and try again, Antonius was defeated by Caesar's adopted son, Octavian, in 31 B.C. during a Roman civil war and committed suicide the following year. Octavian soon took the name of Augustus and became the first of a long line of Roman emperors. He had no immediate designs on the East, so he signed a treaty with Parthia. It made Armenia a neutral buffer zone between Roman and Parthian lands and was the basis of a peace maintained between the two peoples for more than a century. Also, the Parthians returned the captured Roman eagles and prisoners that they had been holding.

In A.D. 114, however, one of Augustus's successors, the emperor Trajan (reigned 98–117), decided to attack Mesopotamia and bring it into the Roman fold. First Trajan overran Armenia. Then he captured the Parthian capital of Ctesiphon and marched to the Persian Gulf. The Parthians, whose decentralized political structure was unable to withstand this assault, sued for peace, and Rome now had a realistic chance of dismantling the rest of the Parthian Empire. However, Trajan's successor, Hadrian (117–138), gave up Mesopotamia, feeling that Rome could save many precious lives and resources by staying out of the area.

If the Parthians thought that the danger posed by Rome was over, however, they were mistaken. Several later emperors launched military campaigns into Mesopotamia, including Marcus Aurelius (161–180), Septimius Severus (193–211), and Caracalla (211–217), the last of whom died during his campaign. These attacks contributed to the steady decline of the Parthian realm and allowed the Sassanian Empire to rise in its place beginning in 224. The Romans were now in for a rude awakening. The Sassanians were more centrally organized than the Parthians had been, and the first Sassanian rulers created a strong, well-trained army that was a match for the Roman armies of the day. The Sassanian ruler Shapur I boldly attacked Roman territories in Syria. The emperor Valerian (253–260) responded with an army, but he suffered heavy casualties, both in battle and from a bout of plague that struck his forces. Valerian called for negotiations, which turned out to be a serious mistake. When he and Shapur met under a flag of truce, the Sassanians treacherously took Valerian prisoner, and he spent the rest of his life in the humiliating role of a foot servant to Shapur. Not long afterward the emperor Julian (361–363) entered Mesopotamia and tried to capture Ctesiphon, but it was too well fortified. During his march back to Syria, Julian died. Another Roman setback occurred when his successor, Jovian (363–364), signed a lopsided treaty with King Shapur II that forced the Romans to give up the sections of Mesopotamia they had recently taken.

Later, in 476, the western part of the Roman Empire ceased to exist thanks to a series of devastating incursions of tribal peoples from central and northern Europe. But the eastern sector of the realm, centered at Constantinople on the southern rim of the Black Sea, survived and steadily mutated into the Greek-speaking Byzantine Empire. In the 500s the Byzantine Romans clashed with the Sassanians in Syria, but no Roman army ever threatened Mesopotamia again.

SEE ALSO: Ctesiphon; Parthian Empire; Sassanian Empire

Royal Standard of Ur

A wooden box decorated in mosaics that constitutes one of the most important and beautiful of the Sumerian artifacts discovered to date in Mesopotamia. The Royal Standard of Ur, also called the Battle Standard of Ur or simply the Standard of Ur, was found in 1927 by the great British archaeologist Charles Leonard Woolley in the royal cemetery of the Sumerian city of Ur. The object measures about 8.5 by 19.5 inches (21 by 50cm) and is covered by inlaid mosaic fragments of shell, red limestone, and lapis lazuli. Estimates for the date of its manufacture range from about 3500 to 2500 B.C., with circa 2600

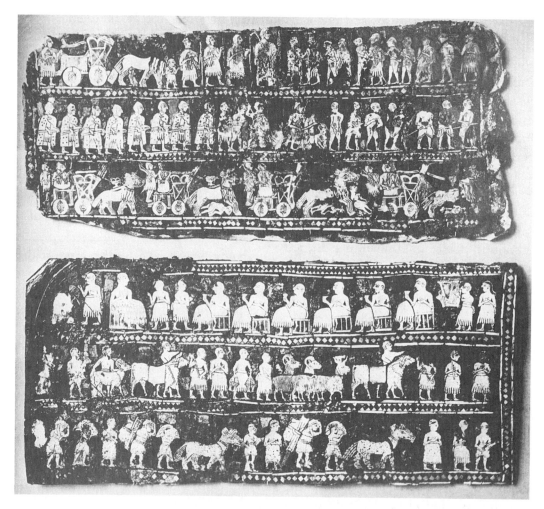

Pictured is the Standard of Ur, a wooden box decorated in a mosaic design. Among other things, it shows one of the kings of Ur, an army of Sumerians, and the king and his family at a feast. © Bettmann/Corbis

B.C. being the most likely date. Woolley suggested that the box was carried atop a pole as a military standard during parades or processions. However, a few other theories for its use have also been proposed, for instance that it was the sound box for a stringed musical instrument. One of the exquisitely rendered scenes on the box depicts the aftermath of a battle, with four-wheeled chariots drawn by onagers

(wild asses), spearmen, and soldiers carrying knives and axes. Some of the soldiers lead enemy prisoners. Another section shows a banquet scene, perhaps celebrating the victory achieved in the battle. The Standard of Ur is presently on display in the British Museum in London.

See Also: mosaics; Ur; weapons and warfare, land; Woolley, Charles Leonard

sacred prostitution

A Mesopotamian religious custom reported by several ancient Greek writers in which, supposedly, young women had sexual relations with male strangers inside temples of Ishtar (Inanna), goddess of love and sexual passion. Herodotus describes sacred prostitution, also called cultic prostitution, this way:

> There is one custom among these people which is wholly shameful. Every woman who is a native of the country must once in her life go and sit in the temple of [Ishtar] and there give herself to a strange man. Many of the rich women, who are too proud to mix with the rest, drive to the temple in covered carriages with a whole host of servants following behind, and there wait. Most, however, sit in the precinct [sanctuary, or holy grounds] of the temple with a band of plaited string round their heads—and a great crowd they are, what with some sitting there, others arriving, others going away—and through them all gangways are marked off running in every direction for the men to pass along and make their choice. Once a woman has taken her seat, she is not allowed to go home until a man has thrown a silver coin into her lap and taken her outside to lie with her. As he throws the coin, the man has to say, "In the name of the goddess [Ishtar]." The value of the coin is of no consequence. Once thrown, it becomes sacred, and the law forbids that it should ever be refused. The woman has no privilege of choice. She must go with the first man who throws her the money. When she has lain with him, her duty to the goddess is discharged and she may go home. . . . Tall, handsome women soon manage to get home again, but the ugly ones stay a long time before they can fulfill the condition which the law demands, some of them indeed, as much as three or four years. (*Histories* 1.199)

Modern scholars differ over how much of this account should be taken seriously. First, no ancient Mesopotamian sources make any mention of sacred prostitution; only Greek sources of the late first millennium B.C. and early millennium A.D., including the geographer Strabo and satirist Lucian, do so. Also, the idea of *every* young woman in the country being forced to have sex in the temple is far-fetched and sounds like a traveler's tale. Some scholars think that some form of sexual relations may have been part of the fertility rituals in Ishtar's temples. But if so, they say, it was likely confined to a few special priestesses. And in any case, if the act was part of the sacred rituals, it would probably not be accurate to call it prostitution.

SEE ALSO: Inanna; religion; temples

Samana

In the ancient Babylonian and Assyrian pantheon of gods, spirits, and other supernatural beings, a female demon who had the teeth of a dragon, the tail of a scorpion, and the claws of an eagle. Supposedly Samana attacked any human, male or female, but was particularly fond of hurting infants and prostitutes. Reciting certain incantations was thought to help keep Samana away.

SEE ALSO: divination; doctors and medicine

Samarra

A Mesopotamian city with an unusually long history. Located about 60 miles (125km) north of modern Baghdad, Iraq, Samarra began as a prehistoric farming community sometime in the seventh millennium B.C. Because rainfall in the area was scarce, the inhabitants built irrigation canals that channeled water from the nearby Tigris River into their fields. The town was notable for its distinctive pottery, appropriately dubbed Samarra ware by archaeologists. Its items feature regular geometric bands on the outside and pictures of people and insects on the inside.

Samarra remained a relatively insignificant town during the great ages of the ancient Mesopotamian empires. In the Muslim period, however, it gained sudden prominence, and in the ninth century A.D. it became the capital of the Abbasid Caliphate, which controlled the region from 750 to 1258. The newly expanded city featured a minaret (narrow tower usually accompanying a mosque and used for religious purposes) with a spiral ramp winding around it. Modern experts think this design was based on similar ramps encircling ancient Mesopotamian ziggurats. In any case, a number of medieval European painters used the Samarra minaret and its ramp as the inspiration for their renditions of the biblical Tower of Babel. The minaret still stands in Samarra, today one of the leading cities in Iraq.

SEE ALSO: Muslim period; pottery; Tower of Babel

Sardis

One of the more important cities in ancient Anatolia and a provincial capital of the Persian Empire. According to the Greek historian Herodotus, Sardis (or Sardes or Sardeis) was established by migrating Greeks sometime in the period of circa 1200 to 900 B.C., and remnants of early Greek pottery in the ruins seem to confirm this. Later the town was settled by the Cimmerians, an Indo-European people from the Black Sea area. By the early seventh century B.C. Sardis was the capital of the kingdom of Lydia, which issued the world's first-known coins. When the Achaemenid Persians, based in Iran and Iraq, conquered Lydia in the 500s B.C., they made Sardis the capital of their province of Sparda. A coalition of Anatolian and mainland Greeks burned the city in 498 during the anti-Persian revolt of the Anatolian Greeks; but the Persians soon recovered and rebuilt it. In 334 B.C., during the early stages of his conquest of Persia, Alexander the Great occupied Sardis and established one of his coin mints there. Later, after the wars of Alexander's generals, the city became part of the Seleucid Empire, centered in Mesopotamia. In the following century, however, Sardis came under the control of the kingdom of Pergamum in western Anatolia, and then it passed to the Romans, who absorbed much of Anatolia and made it their province of Asia.

SEE ALSO: Anatolia; Greeks; Persian Empire

Sargon II
(reigned ca.721–705 B.C.)

The founder of the Assyrian Sargonid dynasty and one of the more aggressive kings of Assyria during its last and greatest phase of expansion. The manner in which Sargon acquired the throne in the wake of the death of King Shalmaneser V is still somewhat unclear. What is more certain is that Sargon was an ardent imperialist and he spent almost his entire reign attacking neighboring regions and putting down rebellions within the empire itself. One of his most important foreign campaigns took him into central Anatolia, where he defeated a people called the Mushki, led by a king named Midas, perhaps the ruler who became famous in Greek mythology for his golden touch.

Thanks to surviving portions of Sargon's annals, including carved reliefs of his exploits, a fair amount is known about his efforts to stamp out rebels, especially in the regions bordering Urartu (Armenia). The king of Urartu, Ursa (or Rusas), had recently been stirring up insurrections among some of Assyria's vassal states. And Sargon felt compelled to put a stop to this activity by invading Urartu. In about 714 B.C. he marched his army northward into some hilly, forested territory, which is vividly described in his annals:

> I directed the line of march into the mountains. They were high mountains covered with all kinds of trees, whose surface was a jungle, whose passes were frightful, over whose area shadows stretch as in a cedar forest, the traveler of whose paths never sees the light of the Sun . . . on whose sides gorges and precipices yawn, to look at which with the eyes, inspires fear. Its road was too rough for chariots to mount, bad for horses, and too steep to march footsoldiers over. With [a] quick and keen understanding . . . I had my men carry mighty pickaxes . . . and they shattered the side of the high mountain . . . making a good road.

Eventually the Assyrians found King Ursa and his army in a sheltered valley, where a battle ensued. Sargon was victorious, and his men chased the enemy from the field:

> I cut down their army and broke up their organization. I defeated the armies of Urartu, the wicked enemy, and their allies. . . . I filled the gullies and gorges with their horses while they, like ants in distress, made their way over most difficult trails. In the heat of my terrible weapons I went up after them.

To discourage future rebellions in the region, Sargon ordered the burning of many of its towns, fields, and forests.

Having secured the northern flank of his empire, Sargon turned his attention to the south, where the Babylonians and the Elamites were causing trouble. Supported by Elam, a group of Babylonian rulers from the Sumerian plains in the south, near the Persian Gulf, had ousted the local Assyrian governor of Babylon and claimed its throne for themselves. In response, Sargon led an army against a combined force of Babylonians and Elamites near the foothills of the Zagros Mountains, but he was defeated. And one of the Babylonian usurpers, Merodach-Baladan, reigned in Babylon, in defiance of the Assyrians, for several years. In about 710 B.C., however, Sargon was able to dislodge Merodach-Baladan, who fled to Elam.

Although often busy fighting his enemies, Sargon managed to find the time to build a new capital city with a brand-new palace. In about 717 B.C. he began work on Dur-Sharukkin ("Sargon's Fortress"), later called Khorsabad, originally a virgin site about 15 miles (24km) northeast of Nineveh. His inauguration inscription, dating from several years later, reads, "For me, Sargon, who dwells in this palace, may he [the god Ashur] decree as my destiny, eternal life." Sargon's life proved far from eternal, however, because less than a year later he died trying to put down still another rebellion. His son, Sennacherib, and other immediate successors decided to abandon Dur-Sharukkin, which was sparsely inhabited for a time but then steadily fell into ruin.

SEE ALSO: Assyrian Empire; Dur-Sharukkin; Sennacherib

Sargon of Akkad (reigned ca. 2340–2284 B.C.)

The founder of the Akkadian dynasty of rulers and the Akkadian Empire, the first major imperial realm to rise in Mesopotamia. A number of later Mesopotamian accounts of Sargon and his exploits have survived. Unfortunately, most of these were written long after he died and portray him in legendary terms. He was said to have had a mysterious or miraculous birth, for instance, and to have survived as a baby in a basket on the river, the same way the Hebrew prophet Moses did in Egypt, as told in the Bible. In fact, some scholars think that the story of Moses's early experiences was inspired by the tale of the young Sargon.

Sargon's exploits as an adult are somewhat better documented. It seems that he began his political career as a courtier to the king of the Sumerian city of Kish. Somehow Sargon became a military general and defeated Lugalzagesi, who had recently taken control of most of Sumeria after capturing the cities of Uruk and Lagash. Thereafter, Sargon expanded his power and conquered northern Mesopotamia as well as Elam and Mari, making the town of Akkad, perhaps where he was born, his home base. Thus, he became the first Mesopotamian ruler to create a realm that combined both Sumeria (southern Mesopotamia) and Akkad (northern Mesopotamia). Sargon was also noted for his promotion of Akkadian, a Semitic tongue, to be used along with Sumerian throughout the region. His immediate successors maintained the empire he had created, with mixed success, for almost two centuries.

SEE ALSO: Akkadian Empire; Elam; Mari

Sargonid dynasty

The family line of rulers founded by the Assyrian king Sargon II (reigned ca. 721–705 B.C.) in about 721 B.C. It included his son, Sennacherib (ca. 704–681 B.C.); grandson Esarhaddon (ca. 680–669 B.C.), and great-grandson Ashurbanipal (ca. 668–627 B.C.). Under the Sargonids, the Assyrian Empire reached its height in size and power.

SEE ALSO: Assyrian Empire; and the names of the individual Sargonid rulers

Sassanian Empire

The large imperial realm that replaced the Parthian Empire in Mesopotamia, Iran, and other parts of the Near East in the early third century A.D. The Sassanian realm is also sometimes called the Neo-Persian Empire. Several centuries before, the Achaemenid Persian Empire had fallen to Alexander the Great, whose own realm was soon superseded by that of the Greek Seleucid rulers, who in turn were overcome by the Parthians. The latter had a fairly decentralized, feudal state in which local vassal rulers gave allegiance to an overall king. A number of old Persian religious and social customs and ideas still lingered

The relief sculpture carved into a rock face at Naksh-e Rustam, which dates from the Sassanid dynasty, depicts the investiture of Ardashir I, king of Persia in the early 3rd century. © CORBIS

in the region during the Parthian period. And the Parthian policy of welcoming and tolerating Greek and other foreign cultural influences was seen as decadent and corruptive by local traditionalists; this was especially true in Fars in southern Iran, the original homeland of the Achaemenid Persians. As a result, sometime in the late second century a man from Fars, Sassan (or Sasan), began calling for the overthrow

of the Parthians and a return to the "purer" Persian past. A number of legends have grown up about Sassan, and trying to sort out who he really was and what he really did is close to impossible. In one story he was a Zoroastrian priest; in another he was rebel leader who had to go into exile. Still another legend claimed he was a direct descendant of the last Achaemenid monarch, Darius III, a claim that was probably unprovable and designed to give legitimacy to his pro-Persian crusade.

Whoever Sassan really was, his grandson, or at least a man who claimed descent from him—Ardashir—rose to a position of prominence in Fars in the early 200s A.D. Ardashir led a rebellion against the Parthian king Artabanus IV and defeated him, after which the victor established the Sassanian dynasty, named for Sassan. Although Ardashir tried to expand the new realm he had inherited, his son, Shapur I (reigned 241–272), far surpassed him in this venture. Shapur brazenly attacked Roman territories in Anatolia, Armenia, and Syria, in the process plundering the Syrian city of Antioch, one of Rome's most important commercial centers. The Roman emperor Valerian (reigned 253–260) hastened to punish Shapur but was defeated by the Sassanian king at Edessa in southeastern Anatolia in 260. Shapur agreed to meet Valerian in a peace conference, but when the Roman delegation entered Shapur's camp, the Sassanians took Valerian prisoner. The emperor spent the rest of his life as Shapur's personal servant, forced to allow Shapur to step on his back when mounting his horse. After Valerian died, Shapur had the former emperor's body stuffed and hung on the gate of the capital, Ctesiphon, as a warning to his enemies.

Under Shapur and his successors, Mesopotamia, Iran, and other sectors of the realm at first became more organized under a strong, central, imperial administration located in Ctesiphon. These rulers also refurbished and expanded that city, opened new trade routes, cultivated more land than the Parthians had, and created a strong national army. In addition, the early Sassanians vigorously promoted the Zoroastrian faith, which had flourished in Achaemenid Persia, and made it the state religion. The Sassanian monarchs called themselves "Mazda-worshipping kings," meaning that they revered the Persian god Ahura-Mazda above all other deities. Under their rule the Magi, special Zoroastrian priests, were given many privileges and became judges and tax collectors as well as religious experts. At the same time, Christians and other non-Zoroastrians were persecuted. The prophet Mani, who had sought to combine the tenets of Christianity and Zoroastrianism, was crucified.

In the years that followed, the Sassanians continued to expand their realm. Shapur II (reigned 309–379), for example, pushed the western borders to the frontiers of China. And later King Khusrau II (reigned 590–628) captured parts of Syria, the city of Jerusalem, Egypt, and the Mediterranean island of Cyprus. But during these same years, new territories were often added at the expense of older ones. Mesopotamia suffered particular decline, partly because it remained the scene of numerous wars and battles among the Sassanians, the Romans, and other peoples. These conflicts caused a number of towns in the region to be destroyed and never rebuilt. Also, the later Sassanian rulers increasingly devoted their main attention and resources to the needs of the Iranian provinces and neglected the towns and fields of the Mesopotamian plains, which fell into disrepair.

These plains therefore became a tempting target for new enemies who threatened the Sassanians beginning in the reign of Khusrau II. The eastern Romans, who had morphed into the Byzantines, launched a large-scale attack on Mesopotamia in 628. When Khusrau tried to stop them, his army mutinied and he was murdered. Not long afterward, King Yazdgird III (reigned 632–651) ascended the Sassanian throne, not realizing at the time that he was destined to be the last ruler of his country. During his reign Muslim armies from Arabia swept into southern Mesopotamia and delivered the Sassanians a series of debilitating defeats from which they were unable to recover. In 651 the Sassanian Empire ceased to exist and the Muslim period of Mesopotamia began.

SEE ALSO: Ardashir I; Artabanus IV; Ctesiphon; Muslim period; Romans; Shapur I

satrapy

From the time of the Medes and the Persians on, a province within one of the ancient empires that spanned Mesopotamia and neighboring regions of the Near East. The ruler of a satrapy was called a satrap, a term derived from the Old Persian word *khshathrapava*, meaning "protector of the province." The Greek equivalent was *satrapes*. The Medes, who were culturally related to the Persians, organized the first imperial provinces in Iran, perhaps based on Assyrian models. After conquering the Medes, Persia's King Cyrus II also adopted the concept of satrapies. Yet whereas Median satraps were in effect local vassal kings who lent support to the principal, central king in Ecbatana, Persian satraps were mere governors, and closely controlled ones at that. A Persian satrap did have a number of powers on the local level, including governmental administration, tax collection, judging court cases, and putting down local rebellions. However, Cyrus and other Persian kings placed secretaries, financial officers, and military governors in each province, and these men oversaw the local satrap and made sure he did not overstep his authority. Cyrus cre-

ated twenty satrapies, and one of his distinguished successors, Darius I, added three more.

The Persian system of satrapies must have been either fairly efficient or widely perceived to be so because later imperialists in the region kept versions of it in place. For example, the Macedonian Greek king Alexander III ("the Great") retained the Persian satrapies after defeating King Darius III in the 320s B.C. And in the second century B.C., following Alexander's death and the wars of his leading generals, the Greek Seleucid rulers did the same. Under the Seleucids, a satrap was called a *strategos*, the Greek word for "military general." The Parthians, who supplanted the Seleucids in the area, also had satrapy-like provinces based on the older Persian versions. However, Parthian governors were, like Median ones, more like local vassal kings than mere governors. Then came the Sassanians, who followed the old Persian system more closely. Sassanian satraps were called *shahrabs*.

SEE ALSO: Cyrus II; Median Empire; Persian Empire

scribe

In ancient Mesopotamia, as well as in Egypt and several other ancient societies, an individual who possessed the ability to read and write and usually used these skills in some professional capacity. The Sumerian word for scribe was *dubsar*; the Akkadian (Babylonian and Assyrian) version was *tupsharru*. Mesopotamian scribes worked in administrative and other key positions in palaces, on temple estates, and in some private businesses as well. They had a wide range of functions and duties. One of the most important was accounting, which included keeping track of monies collected and spent; any and all supplies gathered and stored; profits and losses, if any; and the numbers and names of workers employed by the government or temple. But some Mesopotamian scribes did much more. From a modern viewpoint, these specialists can be thought of as "scholars." This is because they were the ancient equivalents of today's linguists, geographers, mathematicians, astronomers, and teachers. In addition, they were the keepers and classifiers of knowledge. They not only taught younger scribes to read and write but also wrote and copied books for use in learning. Like the Christian monks of the Middle Ages, they set down in writing the ancient myths, oral traditions, and proverbs of their culture, thereby transmitting them to future generations. Finally, scribes wrote and translated letters for kings, governors, and other high-placed people.

Not surprisingly, in a society in which most people were illiterate, individuals who could do these crucial things enjoyed widespread respect and high social status. In the political arena, scribes could also be highly influential as advisers to kings and generals, and from time to time a scribe might actually become such a leader; the Assyrian king Ashurbanipal was trained as a scribe, for instance. The social prominence of Mesopotamian scribes was reflected in their background and schooling. With perhaps occasional exceptions, most novice scribes were the sons of well-to-do or prominent members of the community. Evidence shows that a few women scribes existed, but the vast majority were males.

The trainees attended a school called a tablet house (*edubba* in Sumerian and *bit tuppi* in Akkadian). The remains of such schools have been found in Sippar, Nippur, and Ur. The students first learned how to make clay tablets and how to press wedge-shaped instruments into the wet clay to produce cuneiform letters. Simply learning the cuneiform writing system, with its hundreds of signs, must have taken a considerable amount of time. Then the students had to master multiple languages—not only Sumerian and Akkadian but also, depending on the time and place, sometimes Elamite, Hurrian, Persian, and others, too—in order to translate from one language to another. They also became familiar with the many Sumerian epic poems and traditional proverbs, perhaps in many cases memorizing them by heart.

Like a window into the past, a surviving text from a Sumerian *edubba* captures a teacher emphasizing to one of his students the importance of following the teacher's instructions as closely as possible. The passage also shows the high level of respect that scribes had for their teachers, men who had devoted their lives to becoming literate and transmitting knowledge to others.

> Like you, I was once a youth and had a mentor. The teacher assigned a task to me. It was a man's work. Like a springing reed, I leapt up and put myself to work. I did not depart from my teacher's instructions, and I did not start doing things on my own initiative. My mentor was delighted with my work on the assignment. He rejoiced that I was humble before him and he spoke in my favor. I just did whatever he outlined for me. . . . Only a fool would have deviated from his instructions. He guided my hand on the clay and kept me on the right path. He made me eloquent with words and gave me advice. He focused my eyes on the rules which guide a man with a task. . . . He did not vaunt [show off] his knowledge. His words were modest. If he had vaunted his knowledge, people would have frowned. Do not . . . reject the pleasur-

able company of a mentor or his assistant. Once you have come into contact with such great brains, you will make your own words more worthy. . . . There, I have recited to you what my teacher revealed, and you will not neglect it. You should pay attention. Taking it to heart will be to your benefit!

SEE ALSO: cuneiform; education; writing

sculpture

Ancient Mesopotamian sculpture took two principal forms: the free-standing, three-dimensional statue, figurine, or bust; and the relief, a carved scene raised partially from but still attached to a flat surface, such as a wall. Statues typically depicted gods, human rulers and worshippers, and/or mythical beings. Figurines and other small-scale sculpted works existed in the region well before the Sumerians built the first cities on the plains of southern Mesopotamia in the late fourth and early third millennia B.C. Because of the scarcity of stone in the area, many of these early sculptures were made of wood, although stone was used when and where it was available.

The Sumerians were the first people in the region to produce high-quality sculptures in large numbers. Many continued to be made of wood, but some had wooden cores covered with metal. One of the most famous surviving Sumerian sculptures—the sound box of a lyre (small harp), found at Ur—is a stunning bull's head; it consists of a wooden core covered by gold leaf and lapis lazuli. Statues were also sculpted from stone, much of which had to be imported from the mountains of Iran, Armenia, or elsewhere. Soft stones such as alabaster, limestone, and gypsum were common, but harder stones were also

sometimes employed. A set of twelve figurines found in 1932 at Eshnunna by noted archaeologists Seton Lloyd and Henri Frankfort were composed of gypsum, alabaster, and limestone. Dating from circa 2700 B.C., these statuettes, with their evocative oversized eyes, were votive gifts given to the gods by worshippers and represented the worshippers themselves. A later treasure trove of Sumerian statuary came from Lagash. One of its more famous rulers, Gudea (reigned ca. 2141–2122 B.C.), left behind about thirty sculpted stone images of himself of various sizes. And surviving from approximately the same period is a bronze bust of an Akkadian king, perhaps the famous Sargon of Akkad. The bust was discovered in the city dump at the Assyrian city of Nineveh, perhaps where vandals had thrown it during the city's destruction in 612 B.C. Now resting safely in a museum in the Iraqi city of Baghdad, the carved face realistically captures individual locks of hair and the subject's mustache. Unfortunately for interested modern observers, only a few such statues and busts of actual Mesopotamian rulers have survived. In fact, of the more than one hundred ancient Assyrian monarchs, sculptures exist of only two—King Ashurnasirpal II (reigned ca. 883–859 B.C.) and his son, Shalmaneser III (ca. 858–824 B.C.). On the other hand, a number of large-scale Assyrian statues of bulls and mythical creatures have survived. The most familiar and impressive are the huge human-headed bulls that guarded the entrances to many of the Assyrian palaces. Bearded and winged, these monstrous gargoyles weigh up to 20 tons (18t) or more each.

Considerably more plentiful, however, are the many surviving examples of Assyrian relief sculptures that adorned the walls

A bronze bust of an Akkadian king, which may be the famous Sargon of Akkad. © GIANNI DAGLI ORTI/CORBIS

of the same palaces guarded by the giant bull-monsters at Nimrud, Dur-Sharukkin, and Nineveh. The most outstanding artistic contributions made by Assyrian civiliza-tion, these carvings depict military cam-paigns and victories, major building projects, and other important activities sponsored by the Assyrian kings. They were intended as both decoration and propaganda and effectively achieved both goals. Most of the reliefs were made of gypsum, and because of its relative softness, they were confined primarily to interior corridors and rooms to prevent weathering by wind, rain, and sun. Also, the majority of the surviving reliefs date from the first half of the first millennium B.C., when the Assyrian Empire was rising to its political and cultural height. The sculptors had not yet developed the ability to show true perspective. So, to indicate that object A, for instance, lay behind object B, they placed object A above object B. Nevertheless, these relief panels are stunning in their realism and detail. Like the stelae (stone markers) erected by the Assyrian monarchs during their campaigns, the palace reliefs combined sculpted images with written texts to tell a narrative story, as described here by Seton Lloyd:

> The most-oft-repeated . . . subjects of the reliefs are detailed scenes of military conquest and the ruthless suppression of revolt. . . . The Assyrian army prepares for war. Led by the king, it crosses difficult country on the way to attack a walled city. . . . The city is taken, burned, and demolished. The enemy leaders are punished with ingenious brutality. A victory is then celebrated. In the inscriptions, the outcome of a minor campaign of this sort is recorded by the laconic comment, "So I came upon them and destroyed them utterly and turned their cities into forgotten mounds." . . . The scenes themselves are often arranged episodically—that is, they represent successive developments in the progress of a single action. . . . But what above all distinguishes the Assyrian sculptures is their stylistic vitality and fanciful detail. Horses in

particular are drawn with great understanding and expression. Even their movements in swimming seem the result of close observation. (*The Art of the Ancient Near East*, pp. 196–98)

The Assyrian carved reliefs proved highly influential, inspiring later peoples in the region, especially the Persians. Persian sculpted reliefs at Persepolis and elsewhere borrowed many of the themes and artistic styles of the Assyrian versions. However, Persian sculptures also showed considerable Greek influences since a number of the artisans who worked on the Persian palaces were imported from Greek Anatolia. Greek sculptors, both in Greece and in Persia, frequently tried to infuse a feeling of depth into the figures in reliefs; for instance, they portrayed some aspects of human anatomy beneath the clothes draping the carved figures. The Persian kings also had their sculptors carve large figures in low (shallow) relief on rock walls and cliff faces, perhaps the most famous example being the carvings of King Darius I (reigned ca. 522–486 B.C.) on the Behistun Rock, east of Babylon. Later, the Sassanians, who endeavored to revive Old Persian culture, produced a number of similar cliff carvings, some showing Sassanian kings fighting Romans, others portraying royal hunting scenes.

Both statues and reliefs in ancient Mesopotamia were often painted to make them more realistic and decorative. In many cases the original pigments wore off over the centuries, leaving the wood, stone, or metal surfaces plain, although traces of these paints still survive on some artifacts. Black was used for hair and beards; eyeballs were rendered in white; yellow paint represented gold jewelry; and vegetation was colored green.

See Also: Behistun Rock; crafts and crafts-people; cylinder seals; metalworking; painting; palaces; Persepolis

Sea Peoples

A general, collective name used by modern scholars to describe a group of peoples who underwent a major migration in about 1200 B.C., in the process attacking and destroying large parts of the eastern sector of the ancient Near East. The term *Sea Peoples* is somewhat misleading because not all of these migrants traveled and attacked via the sea. They seem to have originated in southeastern Europe, although exactly who they were, where they came from, and why they began migrating remains unclear. After ransacking and burning many cities in Greece, Anatolia, Syria-Palestine, and elsewhere, as well as causing the collapse of the Hittite Empire, many of the Sea Peoples settled down in areas they had assaulted. For example, one group ended up in southern Palestine and within a generation became the Philistines, a people famous in the Old Testament for their rivalry with the early Hebrews. For a more detailed account of the Sea Peoples, their migrations, and modern theories about them, **see also** Mesopotamia, history of.

See Also: Hittites; Syria; Ugarit

Sealand dynasties

Two lines of rulers who controlled Sealand, the southern, marshy area of Sumeria near the Persian Gulf, during the second millennium B.C. The dates and accomplishments of the members of both dynasties are now obscure, and little of a substantial nature is known about this region during these centuries. The first Sealand dynasty, which is sometimes also called the Second

Dynasty of Babylon, even though its rulers did not occupy that city, was founded by Iluma-ilum in about 1732 B.C. It appears that he challenged the power of Samsu-iluna, son of the great Babylonian lawgiver Hammurabi. In the three centuries that followed, eleven Sealanders ruled in the south, keeping much of the old region of Sumeria out of the hands of the kings in Babylon.

The second and much briefer Sealand dynasty lasted from about 1026 to 1006 B.C. It was established by a ruler named Simbar-shipak, who reigned from circa 1026 to 1010 B.C. He was succeeded by Ea-mukin-zeri (ca. 1009 B.C.) and Kashshu-nadin-ahi (ca. 1008–1006 B.C.). None of these rulers made any significant or lasting contribution to Mesopotamia, which during this period was, politically speaking, largely fragmented and stagnant.

See Also: Assyrian Empire; Babylonia; Hammurabi

Seleucid Empire

The large Greek-controlled imperial realm that replaced the short-lived empire of Alexander the Great in Mesopotamia and other sectors of the Near East in the late fourth century B.C. Soon after Alexander's untimely passing (caused perhaps by alcohol poisoning) in Babylon in 323 B.C., his leading generals and governors, who became known as the Diadochoi, or "Successors," fought a series of devastating wars for control of the Near East. In addition to Antigonus Monophthalmos; his colorful, adventurous son, Demetrius Poliorcetes, who became famous for besieging the island-state of Rhodes; and Antipater, who administered Greece for Alexander; these men included Ptolemy (TAW-luh-mee) and Seleucus. Ptolemy vigorously asserted himself in Egypt. There

A bust of Antiochus III the Great of Syria who reigned from 223–187 B.C. ERICH LESSING/ART RESOURCE, NY

he instituted a new dynasty, the Ptolemaic, which was destined to rule that land for a dozen generations and produce the famous Cleopatra VII.

Prosperity Under Seleucus Meanwhile, most of the remainder of the old Persian holdings in the Near East, including Mesopotamia, fell to Seleucus. Modern scholars refer to the Ptolemaic and Seleucid realms as Hellenistic, meaning "Greek-like," because their societies featured various Near Eastern languages, customs, and ideas overlaid by a flashy but ultimately thin coating of Greek ones. Numerous government administrators, army officers, merchants, and artisans migrated into the region from mainland Greece and other eastern Mediterranean areas. And these agents helped Seleucus establish a number of new cities in Mesopotamia that emphasized and celebrated Greek culture. The most prominent of these, Seleucia (or Seleucia-on-the-Tigris), situated somewhat northeast of Babylon, became the imperial capital. In the years that followed, the new city steadily drew both population and business away from Babylon, which went into decline. Still, on the whole Mesopotamia at first retained a high level of prosperity, especially commercially speaking. Seleucus and his immediate successors promoted the building and maintenance of irrigation canals, which kept up crop production; they also encouraged industry and trade by keeping open valuable trade routes or, when need be, seizing control of such routes from the Ptolemies and other Greeks who vied with them for control of the Near East. Also, banking flourished under the Seleucids, with huge amounts of capital (money borrowed, invested, earned, and repaid) exchanging hands at any given moment.

The principal downside of this initial prosperity was that only a privileged sector of society was able to fully reap its benefits. That fortunate sector was made up mostly of Greeks, and non-Greeks found it increasingly difficult to get ahead. Indeed, a decidedly classist society emerged in which Greeks enjoyed higher social status and business opportunities, and Greek became the language of administration and business, particularly in the cities. Other languages, notably Aramaic and Akkadian, remained prominent in the countryside and/or regions where fewer Greeks settled.

On the other hand, Seleucus and his successors wisely opted to maintain certain aspects of old Mesopotamian culture in order to make ruling this large and ancient land easier. In particular, the government spent large sums keeping up the temples and public worship of traditional Babylonian and other local gods, including Marduk, Nabu, Inanna, and others. To help promote royal authority, the Seleucids also created a ruler cult in which the reigning king was worshipped along with Marduk or other deities. In the major cities, the king took the title of *theos* (the Greek term for "god") and had his own high priest; the royal scribes were ordered to provide a divine genealogy that explained how the king was related to the traditional gods. Only later, in the second half of the empire's brief history, did this plan backfire. As the realm declined, the kings badly needed the huge revenues commanded by the temples; when they availed themselves of these funds, the priests and people strongly objected.

Decline and Warfare The reason why the Seleucid Empire, which started off with such vigor and promise, declined and eventually fell apart was in part due to the overall low quality of most members of the dynasty. The founder, Seleucus I, and some of his immediate successors were fairly strong rulers. But as time went on, incompetency and corruption set in, as somewhat amusingly but accurately captured here by noted classical historian Peter Green:

> If the word "degeneration" has any meaning at all, then the later Seleucids ... were selfish, greedy, murderous, weak, stupid, vicious, sensual, vengeful, and ... suffer[ed] from the effects of prolonged inbreeding. ... We also find the cumulative effect of centuries of ruthless exploitation: a foreign ruling elite, with no long-term economic insight, aiming at little more than immediate profits and dynastic self-perpetuation. (*Alexander to Actium: The Historical Evolution of the Hellenistic Age*, pp. 554–55)

The second major reason for the Seleucid realm's rapid decline was war related.

On the one hand, the Seleucid rulers frequently fought with the Ptolemies and other Hellenistic and Near Eastern rulers, draining valuable human and material resources. The most contested region in these wars was Syria-Palestine, which became a frequent battleground. On the other hand, the Seleucid kings found themselves increasingly beset by the onslaught of the Parthians, a seminomadic people who occupied large parts of northern Iran. In 238 B.C. a Parthian army commanded by Arsaces defeated the Seleucid governor of that region, and Arsaces proceeded to establish a dynasty of his own. The Arsacids/Parthians then began dismantling the Seleucid realm piece by piece. Aiding them in this endeavor was the growing weakness of the Seleucids themselves. For example, King Seleucus II (reigned ca. 246–225 B.C.) got involved in a power struggle with his brother and neglected the eastern provinces, to the decided benefit of the Parthians. His successor, Seleucus III (ca. 225–223 B.C.), was murdered by his own soldiers. And much larger setbacks occurred under the next Seleucid king, Antiochus III (ca. 223–187 B.C.). Although Antiochus managed to keep the Parthians more or less at bay in the east and defeated the Egyptians in 200 B.C., he suffered severe losses to the Romans, who had recently asserted themselves in mainland Greece. In a single battle against the Romans, Antiochus lost more than fifty thousand troops, forcing him to surrender immediately.

If Antiochus had been succeeded by a few strong, competent kings, the Seleucid Empire's downward slide might have been slowed or even halted. However, the reality was that his successors were even worse leaders than he was. Seleucus IV (reigned ca. 187–175 B.C.) was assassinated in a palace plot. And Antiochus IV (ca. 175–164 B.C.) was humiliated by the Romans and forced to withdraw from Egypt. The biggest single loss yet to the empire occurred in 141 B.C., when Mesopotamia was stripped away by the strong Parthian king Mithridates I (reigned 171–ca. 138 B.C.). From that time on, the Seleucids had no real chance to reconstitute their former holdings. The realm, which had at one time encompassed large portions of the great empires of the Achaemenid Persians and Alexander the Great, continued to shrink until it consisted only of parts of Syria. And the Seleucid Empire officially ceased to exist in about 64 to 63 B.C. The last, pathetic claimant to the once prestigious Seleucid throne was a youth named Antiochus XIII Asiaticus, who was ingloriously murdered by an Arab sheik.

SEE ALSO: Alexander III ("the Great"); Antiochus; Greeks; Romans; Seleucus I

Seleucus I
(ca. 385 B.C.– 281 B.C.)

One of the leading figures among the so-called Successors, the generals and governors of the Macedonian Greek conqueror Alexander the Great, and the founder of the Seleucid Empire. After Alexander died in Babylon in 323 B.C., Seleucus at first worked with Perdiccas, initially the most influential of the Successors, with both men professing their desire to keep Alexander's realm intact. But soon Seleucus took part in the plot to murder Perdiccas and became a full-time participant in the destructive wars of the Successors that ensued. For a while Seleucus's chief opponents in his quest to expand his Near Eastern holdings were Antigonus and his son Demetrius Poliorcetes. After the dynamic father and son duo was defeated at Ipsus in Anatolia in 301 B.C., Seleucus was able to seize much of Anatolia and all of Syria. Four years before, in 305 B.C., Seleucus had already taken the step of proclaiming himself king of Alexander's former empire. While continuing to fight other Successors, particularly Lysimachus, Seleucus promoted Greek culture and language in Mesopotamia and introduced a new dating system that his successors would follow in the region. Lysimachus was finally defeated at Corpedium in western Anatolia in 281 B.C., in effect bringing the wars of the Successors to an end. But before Seleucus could make any further gains, he was assassinated. The great realm he had carved out lasted fewer than two centuries before most of it was absorbed into the Parthian Empire.

SEE ALSO: Alexander III ("the Great"); Greeks; Seleucid Empire

Semiramis
(flourished late ninth century B.C.)

A noted Assyrian queen who was the wife of King Shamshi-Adad V (reigned ca. 823–811 B.C.) and mother of Adad-nirari III (ca. 810–783 B.C.). Semiramis (or Sammuramat) appears to have been very influential in the Assyrian royal court. She erected some of her own monuments in the city of Ashur and went with her husband on some of his campaigns, which was highly unusual for an Assyrian queen. Later, when Shamshi-Adad passed away, Semiramis served as regent for her son for a period of five years, during which time she seems to have virtually ruled the empire.

Perhaps because it was so unusual in this era for a woman to hold such power, a number of legends grew up about Semiramis, some of them plausible but others clearly outlandish. In one tall tale, for example, she created a vast empire that stretched to the borders of India and then turned into a dove when she died. Another story said that she had a different lover every night and killed each the next morning. One of these lovers was supposedly the Sun, who, after Semiramis had slain him, was restored to life by the goddess Ishtar. When he visited Babylon in the fifth century B.C., the Greek historian Herodotus heard other stories about the enterprising queen, including claims that she had completed some large-scale engineering projects. He writes that she "was responsible for certain remarkable embankments in the plain outside the city, built to control the river, which until then used to flood the whole countryside." (*Histories* 1.185) Fascination for Semiramis remained strong over the ages. In modern times she became the heroine of a number of poems and novels as well as the 1823 opera *Semiramide* by Italian composer Gioacchino Rossini (1792–1868).

SEE ALSO: Adad-nirari III; Babylon; Shamshi-Adad V

Semites

In ancient Mesopotamia and other parts of the ancient Near East, peoples who spoke Semitic languages. These tongues included Aramaic, Akkadian (Assyrian and Babylonian), Canaanite, Phoenician, Hebrew, and Arabic, along with their offshoots, as in the case of Carthaginian, an offshoot of Phoenician. The original Semitic tribes seem to have originated in the deserts of southern Syria and northwestern Arabia. Over time they spread throughout Palestine and Syria and migrated into and intermarried with the populations of Mesopotamia, Egypt, Armenia, and eastern Anatolia. Although the Jews are only one of many Semitic peoples

in history, today the term *anti-Semitic* refers mainly to hatred of Jews.

SEE ALSO: Akkadian Empire; Aramaeans; languages

Sennacherib
(reigned ca. 704–681 B.C.)

The son of the Assyrian king Sargon II and in his own right one of the more accomplished monarchs of the Assyrian Empire. From the very beginning of his reign Sennacherib found himself beset by rebellions and other unrest. Almost immediately following Sargon's death, the Egyptian pharaoh convinced the kings of Judah, Sidon, and other Palestinian states to launch insurrections against the Assyrians. One of Sennacherib's generals managed to put down these minor revolts. But then the Chaldean (Babylonian) usurper Merodach-Baladan organized an anti-Assyrian coalition of Babylonians, Arabs, Elamites, and others. Sennacherib drove Merodach-Baladan away, but three years later the Babylonian returned. Again Sennacherib asserted himself in Babylon, chasing away Merodach-Baladan, and this time he installed the Assyrian crown prince Ashur-nadin-shumi on the Babylonian throne. Still more trouble occurred in Babylonia in about 694 B.C., however, as the Elamites invaded and captured Babylon. Sennacherib besieged the city, and after he captured it he inflicted a severe punishment on its inhabitants, as a passage in his annals boasts:

> The city and its houses, from its foundation to its top, I destroyed, I devastated, I burned with fire. The wall and outer wall, temples and gods . . . I razed and dumped them into the Arahtu Canal. Through the midst of that city I dug canals, I flooded its site with water. . . . That in the days to

come the site of that city ... might not be remembered, I completely blotted it out.

One of Sennacherib's most famous exploits was his invasion of the Hebrew kingdom of Judah, described in the Bible:

> Sennacherib, king of Assyria, who was besieging Lachish [south of Jerusalem] with all his forces, sent his servants to Jerusalem to Hezekiah, king of Judah, and to all the people of Judah ... saying ... "On what are you relying, that you stand siege in Jerusalem? ... Do you not know what I and my fathers have done to all the peoples of other lands? Were the gods of the nations of those lands at all able to deliver their lands out of my hand? ... No god of any nation or kingdom has been able to deliver his people from my hand.... How much less will your god deliver you out of my hand?!" (2 Chronicles 32.9–15)

Sennacherib's siege of Lachish, mentioned in the above passage, was shown in considerable detail in some impressive relief sculptures found at Nineveh in the nineteenth century by noted Assyriologist Austen Henry Layard. The Assyrian sculptors who created these reliefs, which are now in the British Museum in London, worked from sketches made by Sennacherib's campaign artists, who watched the siege from a nearby hill. Further confirmation for the siege came from the excavations conducted from 1973 to 1987 at Lachish by Israeli archaeologist David Ussishkin. He found the remnants of the Assyrian siege ramp and large numbers of Assyrian weapons. Lachish eventually fell to Sennacherib. Fortunately for the Hebrews, however, Jerusalem survived and the Assyrians withdrew after Hezekiah agreed to pay a huge sum of money and other

valuables, including his harem and musicians, to Sennacherib.

Sennacherib also earned fame for enlarging and beautifying Nineveh. His so-called Palace Without Rival, which rose in the northern part of the city, was particularly noteworthy. Despite such positive domestic accomplishments, Sennacherib was hated by many in his own capital and even in his own family. In about 681 B.C. one of his sons assassinated him, and another son, Esarhaddon, succeeded to Assyria's throne.

SEE ALSO: Assyrian Empire; Bible; Jerusalem; Judah; Merodach-Baladan; Nineveh; Palace Without Rival; sculpture

serfs

Today mention of the word *serf* usually conjures visions of downtrodden medieval European peasants working in the fields for their noble lords, who dwell comfortably in their castles. Yet serflike workers existed in many other ancient and medieval places and times. In ancient Mesopotamia and other parts of the ancient Near East, these workers can be generally classified as agricultural laborers who were not slaves, and therefore could not be sold along with land, yet were closely dependent on the well-to-do persons who owned the land. In particular, serfs lived and worked on the large estates run by the palaces and temples.

In the Old Babylonian period (the first few centuries of the second millennium B.C.), Mesopotamian law codes began to recognize this special class of workers. The famous code of King Hammurabi (reigned ca. 1792–1750 B.C.), for example, divided the population into three general social classes: the *awilum*, the *mushkenum*, and the *wardum*. It seems that the *awilum* were members of Babylonia's traditional landowning class and that the *wardum* were slaves. In contrast, the *mushkenum*, from an Amorite term meaning "one who prostrates himself," were workers who lived on the land. Their exact situation is unclear, but they apparently kept for themselves a portion of the food they grew and turned the rest over to the landowners or their overseers.

By the end of the second millennium B.C., the legal distinctions between the *mushkenum* and other social groups had more or less disappeared. However, serflike laborers still existed. Some evidence suggests that they remained a common fixture of the agricultural systems of the Assyrian, Persian, and Parthian realms that followed in Mesopotamia. When the Parthians defeated the Roman notable Marcus Licinius Crassus in western Mesopotamia in 53 B.C., for instance, they resettled the ten thousand surviving Romans as agricultural serfs in Iran.

SEE ALSO: slaves and slavery; temples

Seven Counselors

In ancient Mesopotamian mythology and lore, seven wise men sent to Earth by the god Ea following the great flood to bring arts, crafts, and other aspects of civilization to human beings. The most famous of the Seven Counselors (or Seven Sages), who were collectively called the Apkallu, was Adapa (or Oannes). In a popular Sumerian myth and epic poem, he attempted but failed to acquire the secret of immortality from the gods. The other six Apkallu were Uandugga, Enmeduga, Enmegalanna, Enmebuluga, Anenlilda, and Utuabzu.

SEE ALSO: *Adapa*; flood legends

Shalmaneser I
(reigned ca. 1274–1245)

An Assyrian king credited with a number of successful military campaigns and victories that set the empire on the road to its first great period of expansion. Shalmaneser (or Shulmani-ashared) defeated Mitanni and appointed an Assyrian governor to administer the region. He also invaded Armenia (Urartu), where he beat a coalition of enemy forces that included large contingents of Hittite mercenaries. One of Shalmaneser's inscriptions brags:

> Shattuara, king of Hani, [and] the army of Hittites and Ahlamu with him, I surrounded. He cut off the passes and my water supply. Because of thirst and fatigue my army bravely advanced into the masses of their troops, and I fought a battle and accomplished their defeat. I killed countless number.... I cut down their hordes, [and] 14,400 of them I overthrew and took as living captives. Nine of his strongholds [and] his capital city I captured. ... The army of Hittites and Ahlami, his allies, I slaughtered like sheep.

Shalmaneser was also noted for building the city of Nimrud and making it his capital. He was succeeded by his son, Tikulti-Ninurta I.

SEE ALSO: Assyrian Empire; Mitanni; Tikulti-Ninurta I

Shalmaneser III
(reigned ca. 858–824 B.C.)

The son of Ashurnasirpal II and one of the more aggressive of Assyria's kings during the empire's third and greatest period of expansion. Shalmaneser led military campaigns on all three of Assyria's traditional fronts—the Babylonian-Sumerian

A basalt bas-relief dating from the 9th century B.C. depicting Jehu, king of Israel, prostrating himself before King Shalmaneser III of Assyria. ERICH LESSING/ ART RESOURCE, NY

plains in the south, the Zagros range in the east, and Palestine in the west; however, two factors kept him from adding much new territory to the empire. First, he often failed to follow up on his victories by setting up strong administrative bureaucracies among the peoples he conquered. He fought two Iranian peoples, the Medes and the Persians, for example, and in both cases seemed content just to sack their cities and collect tribute from them. The other factor frustrating Shalmaneser's efforts at expansion was that he faced much tougher opposition than his father and other ancestors had, especially in the west. In Syria, tough coalitions of small kingdoms formed to fight him. The most formidable of these alliances appeared in 853 B.C. Shalmaneser faced off with the rebels at Qarqar, located on the Orontes River some 120 miles (193km) north of Damascus, in one of the largest battles fought anywhere in the world up to that time. Each of the opposing armies may have numbered more than fifty thousand men; one of Shalmaneser's annals describes the enemy forces this way:

> 1,200 chariots, 1,200 cavalry, 20,000 soldiers, of Hadadezer [Ben-Hadad in the Bible] of Damascus; 700 chariots, 700 cavalry, 10,000 soldiers of Irhuleni of Hamath; 2,000 chariots, 10,000

soldiers of Ahab, the Israelite. . . . battled with them. From Qarqar, as far as the city of Gilzau, I routed them. 14,000 of their warriors I slew with the sword. . . . I scattered their corpses far and wide. . . . In that battle I took from them their chariots, their cavalry, their horses, broken to the yoke.

Despite these boasts of victory, in truth, the best Shalmaneser was able to obtain at Qarqar was a draw.

Shalmaneser was perhaps more successful on the domestic front. At Kalhu he erected a fortress, several temples, and a ziggurat. But then, in about 827 B.C., one of his sons, Ashur-dani-napli, rebelled and seized the cities of Ashur and Nineveh. Now a bitter old man, Shalmaneser remained largely in seclusion in his palace at Nimrud and delegated the task of fighting the civil war to another son, Shamshi-Adad V. The conflict was still ongoing when Shalmaneser died in 824 B.C.

SEE ALSO: Kalhu; Nimrud; Nineveh

Shalmaneser V (reigned ca. 726–722 B.C.)

The son and successor of the noted Assyrian monarch Tiglathpileser III. Evidently the son lacked the military, political, and diplomatic talents of his father. Shalmaneser's short and fairly obscure reign was marred by a rebellion during the course of which the king was killed and a much abler ruler, Sargon II, rose to power.

SEE ALSO: Sargon II; Tiglathpileser III

Shamash

The Babylonian sun god, who was closely associated with the older Sumerian solar deity, Utu, and whose symbol was the solar disk. Shamash's father was Nanna, god of the moon; his sister was Inanna, goddess of love and sexual passion; and his principal shrine was originally located at Larsa, northwest of Ur. In the Old Babylonian period, consisting of the early centuries of the second millennium B.C., Shamash became an important dispenser of justice, and for this reason the great Babylonian lawgiver Hammurabi depicted himself receiving his famous law code directly from Shamash. In these same years a new shrine to the god—the Ebabbar, or "Shining House"—was erected at Sippar and competed with Shamash's Larsa temple. Shamash was also a patron deity of soldiers, merchants, hunters, and other travelers, and a number of prayers and hymns reflecting that part of the god's personality have survived. A passage from one of these reads:

The feeble man calls you from the hollow of his mouth, the humble, the weak, the afflicted, the poor, she whose son is captive constantly and unceasingly confronts you. He whose family is remote, whose city is distant, the shepherd [amid] the terror of the steppe confronts you, the herdsman in warfare, the keeper of sheep among enemies. Shamash, there confronts you the caravan, those journeying in fear, the traveling merchant, the agent who is carrying capital. Shamash, there confronts you the fisherman with his net, the hunter, the bowman who drives the game, with his bird net the fowler confronts you.

SEE ALSO: Inanna; Larsa; Nanna

Shamash-shuma-ukin (reigned ca. 667–648 B.C.)

The Assyrian king of the city of Babylon during the early years of the reign of King

Ashurbanipal, ruler of the Assyrian Empire. Their father, Esarhaddon (reigned ca. 680–669 B.C.), had earlier decreed that Ashurbanipal would succeed him on the imperial throne, and Shamash-shuma-ukin would take charge of Babylon. The two brothers did not get along well, however. Ashurbanipal treated his older sibling with disdain, demanding that he swear the same loyalty oath that ordinary Assyrian vassals did. So Shamash-shuma-ukin sought support from the Elamites as well as from some Chaldean (local southern Babylonian) leaders. Eventually a full-fledged civil war ensued, and Ashurbanipal laid siege to Babylon for two years. Shamash-shuma-ukin died during the final assault in a palace fire that some rumors said he set himself.

SEE ALSO: Ashurbanipal; Babylon; Elam

Shamshi-Adad I
(reigned ca. 1813–1781 B.C.)

The first major king of Assyria during its initial phase of expansion in the early second millennium B.C. An Amorite, Shamshi-Adad seized the throne of Ashur and rapidly carved out an empire that stretched from the Zagros foothills in the east to the central valleys of Syria in the west and encompassed large swaths of northern Babylonia. He placed one of his sons, Ishme-Dagan (reigned ca. 1780–1741 B.C.), on the throne of Ekallatum and his other son, Iasmah-Adad, on the throne of Mari. It appears that the father and sons waged almost constant small-scale wars with their neighbors, in the process gaining Assyria many new territories. Most of the evidence for Shamshi-Adad consists of surviving letters found in the royal archive of Mari. These writings reveal him to be a forceful, often impatient man who demanded much from his sons. The follow-

ing excerpts concern troops movements and show how directly concerned these early Assyrian monarchs were with military details:

> Say to Iasmah-Adad: thus says Shamshi-Adad, your father. I have already written to you about the force of 500 men (from the troops) along the Euphrates, which it was suggested should be sent to Qatanum under the command of Zimri-ilu. Whether you have dispatched them, or whether you have not dispatched them, [I do not know], but as soon as you hear this my letter, you shall send off this force. Meanwhile I have also written to you about the force of 400 men (from the troops) along the Euphrates, which it is suggested should be sent to Qatanum together with the troops from the land of Dumatum and together with Sin-tiri's troops. These 400 men . . . will come to you. Do not send these 400 men away before the troops from the land of Dumatum and the troops under [the command of] Sin-dri have arrived. . . . Let them join these 400 men and send them to Qatanum.

SEE ALSO: Iasmah-Adad; Ishme-Dagan; letters; Mari

Shamshi-Adad V
(reigned ca. 823–811 B.C.)

The son and successor of the Assyrian king Shalmaneser III. While Shalmaneser was still living, Shamshi-Adad's brother, Ashur-dani-napli, launched a large-scale rebellion, and the two brothers continued to fight each other even after their father passed on. Shamshi-Adad was eventually victorious and succeeded Shalmaneser as king of Assyria. During the rebellion, the ruler of Babylonia aided Shamshi-Adad. But later, a new leader arose in Babylon,

Marduk-balassu-iqbi, who caused trouble for the Assyrians. Shamshi-Adad responded by invading Babylonia, burning many villages and crops, and capturing and skinning alive Marduk-balassu-iqbi and his chief assistants.

SEE ALSO: Assyrian Empire; Shalmaneser III

Shapur I
(reigned A.D. 241–272)

The son of the Sassanian king Ardashir I (reigned 226–241) and the second monarch of the Sassanian Empire. A capable war leader, Shapur raided a number of Roman towns. The Roman emperor Gordian III (reigned 238–244) defeated him in 242, but two years later the next Roman ruler, Philip the Arab (244–249), concluded a treaty with Shapur. Soon after that an eastern European people, the Goths, invaded some of Rome's eastern holdings, prompting Shapur to renew his attacks on the Romans. Growing increasingly bold, he assaulted Armenia and Syria, looting the large city of Antioch, one of Rome's most valuable commercial centers. Thousands of the city's inhabitants were deported to Mesopotamia and Iran. The emperor Valerian (253–260) tried to stop the Sassanians but met with disaster when Shapur took him prisoner during a peace negotiation. For the rest of his life, Valerian remained in captivity as the Sassanian king's personal servant. In a sculpted relief carved into a cliff in the valley of Istakhr, near Persepolis, Shapur sits in full armor, mounted proudly on his horse, while Valerian kneels before him, begging for mercy.

Despite these successes, Shapur suffered a significant setback when Septimius Odenathus, ruler of the rich trading city of Palmyra in eastern Syria and a Roman ally, attacked him. Odenathus took back some of the Syrian cities Shapur had recently overrun. Odenathus also besieged the major Sassanian city of Ctesiphon between 263 and 265.

In his domestic affairs, Shapur completed several large-scale construction projects. He built the town of Gundishapur, near the Persian capital of Susa. Shapur also befriended Persian Jews and showed toleration for other non-Zoroastrian religious groups.

SEE ALSO: Ardashir I; Ctesiphon; Sassanian Empire

ships

Though they possessed little in the way of seacoasts, the ancient Mesopotamians built a great many boats and ships. This was because the flat plains on which they farmed and fought were crisscrossed by numerous rivers and irrigation canals that were used as highways for travelers of all types. The first-known ships in the region were small models found by modern excavators in tombs and gravesites. Notable are a baked-clay sailboat from Eridu, dating to the late sixth millennium B.C., and a clay rowboat unearthed at Ur, dating from the early 2000s B.C. The sailboat depicts holes for a mast and rigging, and the rowboat features seven rowing benches, each of which would, in a full-size version, support a separate oarsman. These model boats may have been meant to be used by the dead in the afterlife, as was the case with miniature ships in many ancient Egyptian tombs. Or the Mesopotamian models might just as easily have been the work of hobbyists and/or people fascinated by boats.

In fact, real full-size boats were common and familiar artifacts across Mesopo-

A depiction of a bas-relief sculpture from the Palace of Sargon demonstrates the transport of wood in boats. © GIANNI DAGLI ORTI/CORBIS

tamia. In Sealand, near the shores of the Persian Gulf, and other marshy areas, poor folk built canoes out of tough river reeds, the same materials they used to erect their homes. These narrow boats were used for both hunting fish and water foul and for playing water sports. On the large rivers, meanwhile, small boats were employed as ferries for both people and supplies. Some of these craft moved on their own power, via sails or oars, but others were hauled along by ropes in the hands of people walking along the riverbanks. One common boat, the coracle, or "turnip," a version of which is still used in Iraq today, consisted of a round reed basket that was waterproofed on the bottom with a coat-

ing of bitumen, or tar. The law code of the eighteenth-century B.C. Babylonian ruler Hammurabi featured statutes demanding the proper calking of boats as well as penalties for boat builders who failed to provide proper calking.

The Greek historian Herodotus, who visited Mesopotamia in the fifth century B.C., describes another common small craft, the *kelek*, essentially a wooden frame with animal hides stretched over it:

> The thing which surprised me the most of all in this country, after Babylon itself [the sheer size of which astounded him] were the boats which ply down the Euphrates to the city. These boats are circular in shape and

made of [animal] hides. They build them in Armenia, to the northward of Assyria, where they cut tree branches to make the frames and then stretch skins taut on the underside for the body of the craft. ... The men fill them with straw, put the cargo on board—mostly wine in palm-wood casks—and let the current take them downstream. They are controlled by two men. Each has a paddle which he works standing up. (*Histories* 1.194)

One advantage of *keleks* was their portability. Most were dismantled after being used for one downstream trip, and the hides were saved to make a new boat later upstream. *Keleks* and other kinds of boats were also sometimes made of inflatable goatskins, which helped them float.

For trade in the Persian Gulf and larger waterways beyond, people needed bigger boats. The trade route from that gulf to the Red Sea and the Indian Ocean was in use at least by 3000 B.C., although the extent of the trade is unclear. Also uncertain is the design of the ships that made these daring voyages. Some apparently had rudders for steering, but others used one big oar to steer. And such larger boats were also sometimes lashed together and connected by wooden or reed gangways to make artificial pontoon bridges across bays and channels.

On the opposite flank of Mesopotamia—along the coast of the Mediterranean Sea—Mesopotamian rulers long had no need of navies made up of full-size warships. In fact, evidence suggests that the first Assyrian ruler who built such a fleet was Sennacherib, in the early 600s B.C.; it was launched in the Persian Gulf to disrupt Elamite trade and military strategies. The kings of Achaemenid Persia were the first Mesopotamian rulers who required large Mediterranean fleets. And for a long time

they made do by requisitioning the seagoing ships of their Phoenician, Canaanite, and Greek subjects in the region. The warships that fought for King Darius and his son, King Xerxes, in their invasions of Greece in the early fifth century B.C. were almost all Phoenician and Greek. The manner in which Phoenician vessels— traders and warships alike—predominated in eastern Mediterranean shipping for centuries is captured well in the biblical book of Ezekiel:

The inhabitants of [the Phoenician cities of] Sidon and Arvad were your rowers; skilled men of Zemer were within you, they were your pilots. The elders of Gebal and its artisans were within you, caulking your seams; all the ships of the sea with their mariners were within you, to barter for your wares. ... Your mighty warriors; they hung shield and helmet in you; they gave you splendor. ... Tarshish [Spain?] did business with you out of the abundance of your great wealth; silver, iron, tin, and lead they exchanged for your wares. Javan [Greece], [and] Tubal [in Anatolia] traded with you. ... Judah and the land of Israel traded with you; Damascus [in Syria] traded with you for your abundant goods. ... Arabia and all the princes of Kedar were your favored dealers in lambs, rams, and goats. ... These traded with you in choice garments, in clothes of blue and embroidered work, and in carpets of colored material. ... So you were filled and heavily laden in the heart of the seas. Your rowers have brought you into the high seas. ... Your riches, your wares, your merchandise, your mariners and your pilots, your caulkers, your dealers in merchandise, and all your warriors within you ... all the company that is with you. ... At the sound of the cry of your pilots the countryside shakes, and down from their ships come all that handle the oar. (Ezekiel 27.8–29)

SEE ALSO: Greeks; Phoenicians; trade; transportation and travel; weapons and warfare, naval

Shubat-Enlil

A town on the upper reaches of the Tigris River that the Amorite Assyrian king Shamshi-Adad I (reigned ca. 1813–1781 B.C.) chose as his capital circa 1800 B.C. Originally inhabited around 5000 B.C., Shubat-Enlil (or Shekhna) long remained of minimal importance until Shamshi-Adad expressed an interest in the site. The city became not only his administrative capital but also his center of beer production. In about 1726 B.C. the Babylonians destroyed the town, and it remained abandoned until it was rediscovered in the 1980s by an archaeological team from Yale University.

SEE ALSO: Shamshi-Adad I

Shulgi
(reigned ca. 2094–2047 B.C.)

The second ruler of the Third Dynasty of Ur and son of the dynasty's founder, Ur-Nammu (reigned ca. 2113–2096 B.C.). The main accomplishments of Shulgi (or Culgi) included setting up a strong central administration for the empire and creating an efficient standing army with which to defend it. The new king also concentrated on building up a core group of trained scribes to keep official state records, all of which were written in Sumerian. To help ensure that the individual Sumerian cities in the realm showed allegiance to the central government, Shulgi elevated the image of the king to semidivine status, calling himself the "brother" of Utu (later

Shamash), the sun god, and the "husband" of Inanna, the widely popular goddess of love. Many hymns of praise were written to inflate his image, several of which have survived. Part of one reads:

> I am the king, a wild bull of acknowledged strength, a lion with wide-open jaws! I am Shulgi. . . . I am a great storm let loose from heaven, sending its splendor far and wide! I am good stock, with brindled body, engendered [sired] by a breed-bull! I am a king born from a cow, resting amid butter and milk! I am the calf of a thick-necked white cow, reared in the cowpen! Dressed in a . . . royal robe and holding out a scepter, I am perfect for . . . I am also the good shepherd who takes joy in justice, the scourge and stick of all evil! Strength of lions, hero of battle—I have no rivals! . . . I am a hero! Let them appropriately acknowledge my fame! . . . Let them repeatedly bless me in prayer according to the heavenly stars! Let them tell in song a perfect recital of all my praiseworthy deeds!

Shulgi's foreign policy was accordingly vigorous. He conquered the region of Anshan in western Iran and negotiated several treaties, strengthening them with dynastic marriages. It appears that he died during a rebellion that broke out in his palace. Shulgi was succeeded by his son Amar-Sin.

SEE ALSO: Third Dynasty of Ur; Ur-Nammu

Shutruk-Nahhunte I
(reigned ca. 1185–1155 B.C.)

A prominent king of the ancient nation-state of Elam, which bordered the Mesopotamian plains in the east. It appears that Shutruk-Nahhunte established the Sutrukid dynasty of Elam. Like many Elamite rulers before him, he disliked the

Babylonians and wished to see much of southern Mesopotamia come under Elam's control. To that end, in 1155 B.C. he led a large military force in a lightning campaign, capturing the cities of Kish, Sippar, and the much-coveted Babylon. In the latter, Shutruk-Nahhunte removed the last Kassite Babylonian ruler, Zababa-shum-iddina, and seized an enormous amount of booty. Among the precious artifacts the Elamites carried back to Susa were the black diorite stele containing Hammurabi's famous law code and sacred statues of Marduk and other Babylonian gods. These thefts greatly angered and insulted the Babylonian people, many of whom cursed Elam and its king to the gods. Those who did so must have thought these curses were successful, for soon after he put his own son, Kudur-Nahhunte, on the Babylonian throne, Shutruk-Nahhunte suddenly died of unknown causes.

SEE ALSO: Babylon; Elam; Kassites

Sidon

One of the most important, and maybe the oldest, of the ancient Phoenician cities. Located on the Mediterranean coast about 25 miles (40km) north of another major Phoenician port, Tyre, Sidon was Tyre's mother city as well as the founder of other Phoenician colonies. The famous Greek poet Homer praised Sidon for its talented craftsmen, including glassmakers and purple-dye makers; and there is no doubt that the city was a major commercial center in the first half of the first millennium B.C. Sidon also boasted a thriving bronze-making quarter and a community of scholars versed in mathematics, astronomy, and navigation. All of these qualities made the city a tempting prize for a long series of foreign conquerors, including several from Mesopotamia. The Assyrians, Babylonians, and Persians all captured Sidon in the first millennium B.C., and other intruders included Philistines, Egyptians, Greeks, and Romans. The city was frequently mentioned in the Bible: for its arts and commerce (1 Kings 5.6; 1 Chronicles 22.4; Ezekiel 27.8); relations with ancient Israel (Judges 10.12); and visits by Jesus (Matthew 15.21; Mark 7.24). Sidon survived ancient times only to be destroyed in the Middle Ages, first in 1249 during the Crusades and again in 1260 by the invading Mongols. Modern Sidon is one of Lebanon's three biggest cities.

SEE ALSO: Assyrian Empire; Bible; Phoenicians

Simbar-shipak (reigned ca. 1024–1007 B.C.)

The founder of the second of the two brief Sealand dynasties that controlled southeastern Mesopotamia in the late second millennium B.C. Almost nothing is known about his reign other than that he attempted to achieve popularity with his people by supporting traditional religious activities.

SEE ALSO: Sealand dynasties

Sin

The Sumerian moon god, whom the Babylonians called Nanna. For details about Sin (or Suen), **see also** Nanna.

SEE ALSO: Inanna; religion; Ur

Sippar

According to both Sumerian and later more general Mesopotamian mythology, one of the five special cities chosen by the gods to rule the land of Sumer following the ravages of the great flood. Located about 16 miles (26km) south of modern Baghdad, Sippar (modern Tell Abu Habah) was called Zimbir by the Sumerians and Sippar or Sippara by the Akkadians (Assyrians and Babylonians). It was first excavated by pioneering archaeologist Hormuzd Rassam in 1881.

Rassam and other experts found a number of artifacts that seemed to confirm the city's legendary status as the major sacred home of the Sumerian sun god, Utu, whom the Assyrians and the Babylonians called Shamash. First, there were the ruins of Utu's White Temple, called the Ebabbar in Sumerian and the Bit-Un in Semitic tongues. Excavators also discovered a series of two-room houses aligned along parallel streets not far from the temple. The prevailing theory is that these were the residences of Utu's priestesses, the daughters of well-to-do Mesopotamian families sent to Sippar to serve the god. In addition, tens of thousands of cuneiform tablets were found in the temple's ruins, records of that holy institution.

SEE ALSO: cuneiform; Rassam, Hormuzd; Shamash

slaves and slavery

Slaves, known as *wardum* in the Babylonian dialect of Akkadian, existed in all of the societies of ancient Mesopotamia. However, slavery did not play the kind of major social and commercial role that it did later in classical (Greco-Roman) societies, particularly that of Rome, which was heavily dependent on slave labor at all levels. In Mesopotamia, by contrast, slaves were an important but not necessarily essential element of domestic life and public institutions.

Slavery was well established in Mesopotamia at least by the early third millen-

Relief showing the daily life of Assyrian slaves, created around 705–681 B.C. © WERNER FORMAN/CORBIS

nium B.C. At first the vast majority of slaves were captives taken during raids into the mountains lying along the northern and northeastern rims of the plains. Hence, the earliest word or cuneiform sign for a slave translated literally as "man from the mountains." Many of these captured people were put to work on state building projects, such as palaces, temples, canals, defensive walls, and so forth. They often lived in barracks erected near the worksites, and their names, ages, and lands of origin were recorded by scribes on cuneiform tablets. Nevertheless, though some of these "public" slaves existed across the region for many centuries to come, in general they merely supplemented free workers. As was the case in ancient Egypt, in the third millennium B.C., and probably later, a majority of large-scale public labor in Mesopotamia was performed by free people, especially farmers, who worked on government projects on a part-time basis. As for the public slaves, over time many became workers of various kinds on the large estates run by the palaces and temples. They did jobs as diverse as ditch digging, cleaning, tending animals, planting and harvesting, and assisting craftsmen and scribes.

Also over time, another group of Mesopotamian slaves became domestic workers in private homes. The numbers of slaves in an average home remains unclear. But evidence suggests that poor people had no slaves at all because they lacked the resources to buy and maintain them; an average household in Babylonia or Assyria in the first millennium B.C. had perhaps two to four slaves; and a well-to-do household in the same period had maybe forty or more slaves. The typical work done by these domestic slaves included cleaning, cooking, taking care of the family children, and running errands. Some slaves worked in the owner's fields. However, evidence shows that in Babylonia in the second millennium B.C. it was cheaper for a farmer to hire a free farmhand for two or three years than to buy and feed a slave to do the same work during those years. Thus, a large proportion of the agricultural workforce remained free. On the other hand, some private owners employed their slaves, particularly those who showed intelligence, skill, and initiative, in workshops—making textiles, for example—or as clerks or secretaries. That means that some slaves were taught to read and write, even if on a rudimentary level. Slaves in such positions of responsibility must have had a somewhat higher status than those who performed only menial labor.

Slavery in the Law Codes The status of slaves within society, along with rules and customs pertaining to slavery, was often addressed in the various law codes created in ancient Mesopotamia, including the most famous one—that of Babylonia's King Hammurabi (reigned ca. 1792–1750 B.C.). These legal codes make clear that not all slaves were war captives. Over time other avenues for enslavement developed. For instance, by the late third millennium and early second millennium B.C., it was common for some people to sell either themselves, their children, or even the whole family into slavery to repay a debt. Various laws stipulated the terms and periods of enslavement involved in debt slavery, such as this one from Hammurabi's code:

> If any one fail to meet a claim for debt, and sell himself, his wife, his son, and daughter for money or give them away to forced labor, they shall work for three years in the house of the man who bought them, or the proprietor, and in the fourth year they shall be set free.

Thus, some people in Mesopotamia were slaves only on a temporary basis and reverted to free status once their debts were paid. Perhaps at times the practice of debt slavery got a bit out of hand and produced what society, or at least the authorities, viewed as too many ordinary people reduced to slavery. This is suggested by the fact that from time to time kings declared amnesties in which all debt slaves were freed. In Babylonia in the early second millennium B.C., such a royal decree of amnesty was called a *mesharum*, literally translated as "justice" or "righteousness."

Another way that people became slaves was by being born into the slavery institution. As property, slaves could be passed along by their owners from one generation to another; and a child born of a slave mother and slave father was a slave, too. However, the legal status of the child was different if one of his or her parents was a free person. Another of Hammurabi's laws states, "If a state [i.e., public] slave or the slave of a free man marry the daughter of a free man, and children are born, the master of the slave shall have no right to enslave the children of the free." Laws or customs such as this one probably had the effect of helping to keep the number of slaves in society more or less at a minimum.

However a person may have become a slave, other laws and customs affected the slave's treatment and the master's rights and responsibilities. The law often protected the master, for example, even during the initial purchasing process. One of Hammurabi's laws says that if a person bought a slave, he had what was in effect a thirty-day warranty on the slave; in other words, if the slave contracted a disease during the thirty days following the purchase, the new master could return the slave and get his money back in full. The law also addressed both master and slave when an escape occurred. The frequency of slaves running away from their masters in ancient Mesopotamia is unknown, but modern scholars think it was a fairly rare occurrence. This may have been partly because the penalties for escape were severe; also, an escaped slave essentially had no where to go and no one to help or shelter him or her. In Mesopotamian society, as in all other ancient societies, slavery was viewed as a natural and inevitable condition, one sanctioned by the gods, so there was no sympathy for the escapee. In addition, a person who aided a runaway slave was himself severely pun-

ished, sometimes with the death penalty. For instance, a barber who shaved off the long lock of hair that often designated slave status in Mesopotamia could have his own hand cut off. However, when an escape did happen, it is probable that the runaway slave was rarely, if ever, killed. This is because the slave, despite his or her rebellious nature, was a valuable piece of property; it was cheaper for the owner to punish the slave in hopes of deterring future escape attempts than to slay the slave and buy a new one. A runaway was perhaps beaten or starved. He or she also had a symbol or word standing for "escaped slave" branded onto his or her forehead, a practice also used later by the Romans.

The fact that slaves, even runaways, had financial value is also reflected in laws that protected masters for "damages" suffered by their slaves. According to another of Hammurabi's statutes, "If [a free person] puts out the eye of a man's slave, or breaks the bone of a man's slave, he shall pay [the owner] one-half of [the slave's] value." Similarly, the law protected the master against "malpractice" by doctors who might treat an injured slave. "If a physician makes a large incision in the slave of a free man, and kill him," Hammurabi decreed, "he shall replace the slave with another slave."

Despite their lowly condition, however, slaves did have a few rights and privileges that masters and society in general were forced to recognize and uphold. First, as in ancient Greece and Rome, household slaves in Mesopotamia often developed close relationships with the master and his family members; sometimes, if the master had no children of his own, or if his children had died, he might legally adopt one or more of his more trusted slaves. By doing so, he could be assured that there would be someone around to care for him in his old age. On the other hand, if the master's wife was physically unable to bear children, a slave woman might be selected to bear the master's child. That child would, of course, be a free person. It is likely that in many such situations the child's biological mother was freed as a reward for the services she had rendered the family. In addition, slaves could take part in commerce, usually in a business owned by the master, and receive wages for such work. Some evidence suggests that at least a few slaves accumulated considerable "savings" this way. As for whether they could use this money to buy their freedom, modern scholars are divided; some think that Mesopotamian slaves (debt slaves aside) could buy their freedom, but others feel there is not yet enough evidence to support this contention.

SEE ALSO: crafts and craftspeople; laws and justice; women

Smith, George
(1840–1876)

An English scholar and leading Assyriologist who produced the first English translation of the ancient "great flood" story contained in the famous *Epic of Gilgamesh*. As a young man studying to be a bank engraver, Smith took a keen interest in the archaeological finds of Austen Henry Layard and Henry C. Rawlinson in Mesopotamia. Smith diligently studied the cuneiform texts these early Assyriologists had found and put on display in London's British Museum. Eventually Rawlinson himself noticed Smith, got to know him, and allowed him to use his private museum office, where many other ancient tablets were waiting to be translated. In 1867 Smith was appointed to the position of assistant

Assyriologist; four years later he published his own translation of the known historical records of one of Assyria's most famous kings, *The Annals of Ashurbanipal*.

Smith's greatest achievement came in 1872, when he translated the flood account in the Babylonian version of the Gilgamesh epic. At the time, about fifteen of the lines in the account were missing. Because the discovery of any ancient texts relating to the Bible was big news, a London newspaper, the *Daily Telegraph*, offered to back an expedition to Iraq in hopes of finding a tablet containing the missing lines. Incredibly, after only a few weeks of digging, Smith himself found just such a tablet and was able to insert the missing fragments into his translation of the flood story. He later described the great discovery:

> On the 14th of May ... I sat down to examine the store of fragments of cuneiform inscriptions from the day's digging, taking out and brushing off the earth from the fragments to read their contents. On cleaning one of them I found to my surprise and gratification that it contained the greater portion of seventeen lines of inscription belonging to the first column of the Chaldean [Babylonian] account of the Deluge [great flood], and fitting into the only place where there was a serious blank in the story. When I had first published the account of this tablet I had conjectured that there were about fifteen lines wanting [lacking] in this part of the story, and now with this portion I was enabled to make it nearly complete.

In 1875 Smith published *Assyrian Discoveries*, an account of his work and exploits up to that time, which became a seminal work in Middle Eastern archaeology. He died the following year in Mesopotamia in the

The Royal Game of Ur was a popular board game in Ur, located in modern-day southern Iraq, dating from the third millennium B.C. HIP/ART RESOURCE, NY

midst of another expedition to dig up the lost secrets of the past.

SEE ALSO: Assyriology; cuneiform; *Epic of Gilgamesh*; flood legends

sports and games

The people of ancient Mesopotamia played a wide variety of games and sports, many of which are still avidly played by people around the world today. The use of dice and board games by the Sumerians, Babylonians, Persians, and other Mesopotamians is a clear-cut example. As is true today, dice were employed in various forms of gambling. There were some differences between these and modern versions. For example, Mesopotamian dice throwers did not necessarily reckon the numbers of their throws in combinations that added

up to seven, and some Mesopotamian dice had four triangular-shaped surfaces rather than six square-shaped surfaces.

Board Games Board games, some that used dice and others that did not, were particularly popular in ancient Mesopotamia. In the early twentieth century the great English archaeologist Charles Leonard Woolley found the remains of a Sumerian board game while excavating the royal cemetery at Ur. The game was similar in some ways to the ancient Egyptian game called *senet*, only nearly a thousand years older, dating to the early third millennium B.C. The board Woolley found is made of wood covered by layers of chips of dark blue lapis lazuli, white shell, and red limestone. It measures about 5 by 11 inches (13 by 28cm) and has twenty-one squares, a large rectangular zone, a small rectangular zone, and a narrow bridge connecting the two zones. Each player had seven playing pieces, or tokens. The rules of the game remain unclear. Apparently the object was for a player somehow to move tokens from one end of the board to the other while keeping his or her opponent from moving tokens across the bridge. Experts think that some of the squares encountered along the way were special ones, as in many modern board games, that allowed the player to take an extra turn or advance an extra number of squares.

Other board games more familiar to modern observers were played by the ancient Persians and likely by other Mesopotamian peoples as well. The Persians played an early form of chess, for instance, which they called *shatrang*. The board was similar to a modern chess board, and the playing pieces represented military men and war devices. In the same vein, the moves were meant to mimic military strategy and tactics, as indeed some of the moves of modern chess still do ("capturing" the opponent's knight or king, for example). The Persians also played a form of backgammon, called *nard*, which featured two dice.

Polo and Falconry More physically demanding games, which people today generally refer to as sports, were also widely popular across ancient Mesopotamia. A good example is polo, the oldest-known team sport. The Persians were playing it at least as early as 600 B.C.; and it is possible that they copied it from a similar game played by earlier peoples in the area, perhaps the Medes or the Elamites. King Darius I (reigned ca. 522–486 B.C.) refined the rules and used the sport to help train his cavalrymen. In his day there were up to one hundred players on each team, and the style was what might be termed *no holds barred*, meaning that it was very rough and often resulted in serious injuries, occasionally even death. Later modifications in the game resulted in smaller teams and stricter rules, which made it much less dangerous, so kings and their nobles adopted the sport. Even Persian queens and their ladies-in-waiting played, sometimes against one another and other times against the king and his all-male team. Persian kings also engaged in the sport of falconry, in which they raised and exploited large birds of prey. Persian men of all classes—but especially soldiers—engaged in contests of weight lifting, swimming, chariot racing, horse racing, and archery, the latter performed while seated on a galloping horse. Evidence attests that the Assyrians and the Babylonians also practiced racing and archery as sports.

The Assyrian kings also fired arrows for sport from chariots during large-scale hunting parties. Surviving carved stone reliefs from the Assyrian city of Nineveh, for instance, show King Ashurbanipal (reigned ca. 668–627 B.C.) hunting in his royal chariot. According to scholar Arthur Cotterell:

> He [Ashurbanipal] can be seen firing his bow from a heavy chariot during a lion hunt. One sculpture shows the king shooting ahead, while two guards ward off with spears a wounded lion attacking the chariot from the rear. The heroic encounter is somewhat undercut by another relief, which reveals a gamekeeper about to release from a cage a captured lion. As the monarch reserved to himself the right to kill lions, they were collected in the wild and taken to the palace for royal sport. (*Chariot*, p. 240)

Wrestling In addition, all of the peoples of Mesopotamia—from the Sumerians and the Babylonians to the Persians, Greeks, and Sassanians—took part in the most popular of all ancient sports: wrestling. It is likely, in fact, that wrestling is the world's oldest sport. Many modern scholars think it originated in Stone Age times because it was already well developed by the time that the earliest civilizations—in Egypt, Mesopotamia, and China—first began keeping records. For example, archaeologists digging in Iraq in the 1930s found artifacts depicting Sumerian wrestling matches dating from about 3000 B.C. These finds include a small bronze sculpture showing two wrestlers gripping either each other's hips or the wrestling belts they wore around their hips. Wrestling belts were common among most ancient peoples and are still used by wrestlers in a number of countries today. By grasping and then pulling or twisting on an opponent's belt, a wrestler tries to throw the other person off balance and gain the advantage.

Another clear indication of the popularity of wrestling among the ancient Sumerians and Babylonians is literary in nature. The title character of the famous *Epic of Gilgamesh* is a champion wrestler and is frequently called "Gilgamesh the wrestler" in ancient Mesopotamian writings. In the story contained in the epic poem, Gilgamesh faces off with his nemesis and later friend, Enkidu, in a huge, sprawling match in the city streets. The fact that the text describes the two men using their fists and tossing each other into walls suggests that a catch-as-catch-can style, similar to modern professional wrestling, was common and popular. However, various sculptures and other forms of evidence show that other styles of wrestling, with more structured rules, existed as well. It appears that the Babylonians and the Assyrians used wrestling moves similar, and indeed often identical, to those of their ancient Egyptian counterparts. A series of about four hundred paintings of sparring wrestlers, dating from roughly 1900 B.C., were found at Beni Hasan, located on the Nile River in central Egypt. The wrestlers depicted use many of the same moves and holds employed today in both amateur and professional wrestling, including headlocks, armlocks, trips, and shoulder throws. Also shown are wrestlers choking each other. It remains unclear whether choking was considered legal in ancient Egypt and Mesopotamia.

SEE ALSO: chariots; *Epic of Gilgamesh*; Woolley, Charles Leonard

stele

A common form of monument used across the ancient world, including the nation-states and empires of Mesopotamia, to commemorate an important event, ruler, or decree. A typical stele (or stela) consisted of a slab of stone, or occasionally metal, covered by written inscriptions, images sculpted in relief, or both.

Akkadian, Assyrian, and Babylonian rulers often set up stelae to mark the farthest extent of their conquests or to commemorate their military victories. But many other stelae celebrated peacetime events or accomplishments. One of the more famous of these is a 4-ton (3.6t) stele of black diorite (a hard stone) on which the Babylonian king Hammurabi carved his law code. At the top of the slab a sculpted relief shows Hammurabi facing, and supposedly receiving the laws from, Shamash, the sun god. Below these figures the laws are inscribed in some thirty-five hundred lines of Babylonian cuneiform.

Another well-known stele was erected in the 2500s B.C. by a ruler of the Sumerian city of Lagash—Ur-Nanshe—to commemorate his establishment of a new temple. (Ur-Nanshe's stele is presently on display in the Louvre Museum in Paris.) The Assyrian ruler Ashurnasirpal erected a large stele to celebrate the completion of his palace in about 879 B.C., a monument that also records a huge banquet the king held for his builders and architects. Still another famous Mesopotamian stele is the so-called Stele of the Vultures (also in the Louvre), which shows soldiers from Lagash defeating troops from the rival city of Umma.

SEE ALSO: Code of Hammurabi; Stele of the Vultures; writing materials

Stele of the Vultures

An ancient Sumerian stone marker, of which a large fragment was discovered at the ancient site of Lagash by French excavator Ernest de Sarzec in the late 1800s. The monument, now on display in Paris's Louvre Museum, earned the name "Stele of the Vultures" because one section of it depicts dead soldiers being picked at by vultures. The stele was erected circa 2525 B.C. by King Eannatum of Lagash to celebrate his military victory over King Enakalle of Umma, a rival city lying about 18 miles (29km) northwest of Lagash.

Modern scholars attach major importance to the stele as a crucial early depiction of Sumerian and, in a more general sense, Mesopotamian warfare. The artifact shows a large group of armored foot soldiers from Lagash marching in a tightly packed formation over the bodies of their slain enemies from Umma. The men in the front rank hold up their shields, creating a protective barrier, and some of the men behind them point their spears for-

ward through the spaces between the shields, making the unit even more formidable. Such a formation was designed either to mow down or to scare off enemy forces. Many modern scholars point out the similarities this battlefield unit bears to the phalanx formation developed by the Greeks much later, in the early centuries of the first millennium B.C. (Ironically, the Greek phalanx, as modified by Macedonia's Philip II and his son, Alexander the Great, became a major factor in the Greek conquest of Mesopotamia in the fourth century B.C., when the area was part of the Persian Empire). In a lower part of the stele, King Eannatum is seen holding a battle-ax and riding in a wheeled cart drawn by four onagers (wild asses); this was the early Sumerian version of the war chariot. In this respect, the stele contains the earliest-known depiction of the military application of the wheel. The Stele of the Vultures is also notable for having the earliest-known depiction of soldiers wearing metal helmets.

SEE ALSO: chariots; Lagash; Umma; weapons and warfare, land

Strabo
(ca. 64 B.C.–25 A.D.)

An important ancient Greek traveler, geographer, and historian whose book on geography covered most parts of the known world of his day, including the plains of Mesopotamia and the surrounding territories. Strabo, who was born in Anatolia, moved to Rome in 44 B.C., where he studied philosophy and geography, and then he traveled extensively. In addition to Greece and other parts of the Mediterranean world, he visited Egypt. During these travels, Strabo wrote down detailed descriptions of the mountain ranges, valleys, plants, animals, cities, and peoples he

A relief depicting boats that are made out of reeds and coated with plaster to make them strong and durable in the water. THE ART ARCHIVE/MUSEE DU LOUVRE PARIS/DAGLI ORTI

encountered. He also interviewed the locals about their histories and customs, information that makes up large sections of his *Geography.* Because he saw these lands and peoples in person, his data about them, especially the sections about Greece, Anatolia, and Egypt, is very enlightening and useful to modern historians.

However, Strabo did not travel in person to Mesopotamia nor to most of the lands adjoining the Mesopotamian plains. For that reason, his descriptions of these regions are based solely on his researches of existing Greek sources, a number of which are now lost. Especially important to him in this respect were the writings of two Greek geographer-astronomers who flourished in Alexandria, Egypt, Eratosthenes and Hipparchus. Thus, Strabo perpetuated whatever mistakes their works already contained. Another of his faults was to disregard the historical and geographical information in the famous book of his Greek predecessor, Herodotus, who had traveled to Babylon and other parts of Mesopotamia in person. Nevertheless, a good deal of the information that

Strabo provided about Mesopotamia was accurate and valuable to one degree or another, given a careful and cautious analysis by modern researchers. The following example is his description of the petroleum found beneath the surface of the Mesopotamian plains, a resource still much valued and fought over today. It shows that he made no pretensions about having seen the oil himself, which is called both asphalt and naphtha in this translation, but instead he openly and honestly credits his sources. (Note that, despite his tendency to dismiss Herodotus's data, Strabo here corroborates Herodotus's description of river boats coated with petroleum tar to make them waterproof.)

> Babylon produces also great quantities of asphalt, concerning which Eratosthenes states that the liquid kind, which is called naphtha, is found in Susa [here meaning Elam], but the dry kind, which can be solidified, in Babylonia; and that there is a fountain of this latter asphalt near the Euphrates River; and that when this river is at its flood at the time of the melting of the snows, the fountain of

asphalt is also filled and overflows into the river; and that there large clods of asphalt are formed which are suitable for buildings constructed of baked bricks. Other writers say that the liquid kind also is found in Babylonia. Now writers state in particular the great usefulness of the dry kind in the construction of buildings, but they say also that boats are woven with reeds and, when plastered with asphalt, are impervious to water. . . . If the naphtha is brought near fire it catches the fire; and if you smear a body with it and bring it near to the fire, the body bursts into flames; and it is impossible to quench these flames with water (for they burn more violently), unless a great amount is used, though they can be smothered and quenched with mud, vinegar, alum, and bird-lime. . . . [The Greek writer] Poseidonius says of the springs of naphtha in Babylonia, that some send forth white naphtha and others black; and that some of these, I mean those that send forth white naphtha, consist of liquid sulphur (and it is these that attract the flames), whereas the others send forth black naphtha, liquid asphalt, which is burnt in lamps instead of oil. (*Geography* 16.1.15)

SEE ALSO: Greeks; Mesopotamia, geography of; ships

Sumer

An ancient Babylonian name for the region encompassing southeastern Mesopotamia, the largely flat plains and marshes stretching from the shores of the Persian Gulf to the area of Babylon itself. Sumer was never a unified nation or empire. Rather, it was the heartland of the civilization that came to be called Sumerian (also a Babylonian term), although this was not the term the Sumerians themselves used. They called the region Kengir, meaning

"Civilized Land." Long after the decline of Sumerian civilization, the peoples of Mesopotamia continued often to refer to the region as Sumer.

SEE ALSO: Babylonians; Sumerians; and the names of individual Sumerian cities

Sumerians

The first important ancient people to inhabit Mesopotamia, specifically the flatlands of southeastern Mesopotamia near the Persian Gulf, the region called Sumer by the Babylonians. The Sumerians were well entrenched in the area by the fourth millennium B.C. and began to build large-scale cities there in the last few centuries of that millennium.

The Sumerian Problem Modern scholars are still unsure who the Sumerians were and where they originated. These questions lie at the core of what has come to be called the Sumerian problem. Some scholars argue that the Sumerians were the descendants of the original hill peoples who migrated onto the plains beginning in the sixth millennium B.C. That would mean that they were part of the pre-literate culture in the region, often referred to as Ubaidian, and that the Sumerians introduced the first examples of writing, using cuneiform symbols. Other experts think that the Sumerians were not indigenous to the region. According to this view, they migrated into the Near East and onto the plains of Mesopotamia in the fourth millennium from the east, possibly from India. If that is true, the Sumerians displaced and/or intermarried with the indigenous Ubaidians and used and improved upon a writing system that was already in place.

One strong argument for the second theory is the fact that the Sumerian language was different from the one originally spoken in Mesopotamia. Numerous important place names in the region, such as Ur, Eridu, and Uruk, are not Sumerian. In fact, Sumerian is unlike any other known tongue, living or dead. Some scholars suggest that the Sumerian language may be remotely related to the Dravidian languages of India, which are themselves related to Elamite, the early language of southern Iran, the region adjacent to eastern Sumer.

Language aside, from a racial and ethnic standpoint the Sumerians were not a separate, distinct social group. Like the Akkadians, Babylonians, Assyrians, and many of the other Mesopotamian peoples who succeeded them, the Sumerians were part of a large racial and ethnic melting pot. There was a general culture with many similar religious and social customs, and new groups entering the area were usually assimilated. A convenient modern analogy would be that the various peoples who inhabited the cities and regions of southern Mesopotamia from about 3300 to 2200 B.C. shared a common culture called Sumerian, just as people of various races and ethnic backgrounds living in U.S. cities share a common culture called American.

The First Cities The later peoples of Mesopotamia absorbed many aspects of Sumerian culture largely because, as the creators of the first major civilization in the region, the Sumerians established a number of important cultural and logistic precedents and models. Among the most important of these was the construction of the first major cities and city-states shortly before the dawn of what modern scholars call the Early Dynastic Period, lasting from about 3000 to 2350 B.C. The first true city may have been Eridu, then located very near the shore of the Persian Gulf, which

has since that time receded about 125 miles (201km) southeastward. Another possibility is that Uruk, located northwest of Eridu, was the first actual urban center supporting a large population, and Eridu served mainly as a ceremonial center. In any case, the Sumerians believed that Eridu was the home of the first king and the first civilized arts and works, a situation that scholars refer to as the "Eridu genesis." According to the Sumerian King List, which dates from about 2125 B.C., the first earthly king ruled Eridu for thousands of years. Only later, the Sumerians held, did the main seat of kingship move to other Sumerian cities, including Kish, Ur, and Lagash.

These and other early Sumerian cities, also including Adab, Larsa, Nippur, Larak, Umma, and Sippar, began as small villages covering only a few dozen acres. But by the start of the Early Dynastic Period, each had several thousand inhabitants. That growth continued apace. Between 3000 and 2700 B.C., for example, Uruk grew into a city of several tens of thousands of people, whose houses, shops, and temples were surrounded by a defensive wall 6 miles (9.7km) in circumference.

It is important to emphasize that these early cities were not dependent units within a larger Sumerian nation. Instead, they were independent city-states, each in a sense a tiny national unit in its own right. In the third millennium B.C. a typical Sumerian and, in a more general sense, Mesopotamian city-state consisted of a densely populated central town surrounded by dependent villages and farmland. There was trade between the cities and also with regions outside of Mesopotamia. But in an earnest effort to maintain self-sufficiency and independence, each city planted a wide variety of crops and built irrigation canals to make sure the fields had sufficient moisture. The farmlands and outer villages of a city-state were tightly organized and controlled. Nippur, for example, was eventually surrounded by as many as two hundred dependent villages, all distributed along five large irrigation canals and about sixty smaller canals. The ruler of the city-state's urban center, as well as his advisers and leading nobles, ordained how much each farm or farming area was expected to produce and oversaw maintenance of the canals. The urban centers themselves were also closely organized and overseen by the state. Most of these central cities probably looked much like Uruk. About a third of that city was composed of private homes and shops; another third was made up of gardens and other open lands administered by the government; and the last third consisted of temples and the sanctuaries (sacred territories or properties) surrounding them.

As separate political states and entities, the Sumerian cities often became rivals for power, resources, territory, or all of these things. And from time to time, they fought among themselves. In about 2600 B.C., for instance, Uruk defeated Kish. Soon afterward, Ur also defeated Kish. But by circa 2500 B.C., Kish had regained its lost power and held sway in the region surrounding it. In the same period, Lagash and Umma sparred with each other repeatedly, as highlighted in the victory of Lagash over Umma depicted in the famous Stele of the Vultures. Numerous other such contests among the Sumerian cities occurred. At times one city-state would amass an unusual amount of power and prestige and dominate most of the others for a generation or a century or so. When this happened, the defeated cities were vassals of the city in power, which means that their leaders were required to show allegiance to the king of the most powerful city. Then the balance of power would shift and another city or group of cities would rise to prominence. Yet all of the players remained steadfastly Sumerian in language and culture and made no attempt to eradicate the gods, temples, social customs, laws, or other major facets of the defeated cities. As scholar Norman B. Hunt puts it:

> The balance of power [in ancient Sumeria] was continually shifting from one dynasty to another, and with that the center of power moved between city-states, but there is little [evidence] to suggest that there were any cultural or ideological [political or religious] shifts. We do not, for instance, see the wholesale displacement of city-state deities, which remained as they were even under the control of a different dynasty. And it is unlikely that local populations saw change that significantly altered their daily lives. (*Historical Atlas of Ancient Mesopotamia*, p. 43)

Kingship and the First Empires These repeated rivalries and wars among the Sumerian city-states required a great deal of central organization and political and logistical control on the part of local governments. In other words, strong leadership was needed for any given city to remain a viable player in the rough-and-tumble world of Sumerian affairs. As a natural result, therefore, the institution of kingship grew stronger over time. And this, in turn, stimulated even more wars since the more powerful the kings became, the more likely it was that they would desire to expand the power and prestige of their individual cities. In this way, as the great Assyriologist Samuel N. Kramer explains:

The story of Sumer is largely a tale of warfare, as the rulers of its dozen or so city-states, which were bound only by a common language and culture, vied for mastery of the entire region. . . . The Tigris-Euphrates plain became the scene of constant battle, a broad stage across which marched a pageant of ancient armies led by warrior-kings with exotic names. (*Cradle of Civilization*, p. 35)

In this stormy situation, it was only a matter of time before one strong ruler, from either Sumer or Mesopotamia's northern portion, variously called Akkad, Assyria, and other names, would manage to conquer the entire region and create the world's first empire. As it turned out, this feat was accomplished by Sargon of Akkad (reigned ca. 2340–2284 B.C.). He swiftly captured the Sumerian cities, and by incorporating them into his empire, with its highly centralized government, he caused the old Sumerian city-state system more or less to collapse.

Sargon's imperial state, ruled by himself and a few successors, lasted for just over a century. When it fell apart, the Sumerian cities were still very much intact. But now they fell under the sway of other imperialists: at first, and briefly, an invading hill people, the Guti, and then the dynasty of Ur-Nammu (reigned ca. 2113–2096 B.C.), the empire known as the Third Dynasty of Ur. Following the decline of the Third Dynasty of Ur came the Old Babylonian period, roughly encompassing the first four centuries of the second millennium B.C. This era witnessed the rise of new empires, including those of the Babylonians and the Assyrians. Once more, the older Sumerian cities became incorporated into larger imperial units. As a result, by about 1800 B.C. the inhabitants of these cities no longer thought of themselves as Sumerians; and by about 1600 B.C., or perhaps earlier, the Sumerian language ceased to be spoken by the public on an everyday basis. However, Babylonian and other Mesopotamian scribes, scholars, and priests kept that language intact for some sacred and official purposes. And many Sumerian ideas, customs, gods, and so forth remained integral facets of the Mesopotamian cultures that followed.

SEE ALSO: Eridu; king lists; languages; Third Dynasty of Ur; Ubaidian culture; writing

Suppiluliumas I (reigned ca. 1370–1330 B.C.)

A considerable amount is known about the reign of this Hittite King because his son, Mursilis II, later compiled a chronicle of his exploits, the *Deeds of Suppiluliumas*, which fortunately survives. Suppiluliumas (or Suppiluliuma) was the son of the strong, ambitious Hittite ruler King Tudhaliya III, and in young adulthood he acted as his father's chief adviser as well as accompanied the king on his military campaigns. Despite the closeness of father and son, however, Tudhaliya ordained that he should be succeeded, following his death, by an older son, usually referred to as Tudhaliya the Younger. For reasons that are uncertain, this did not sit well with Suppiluliumas, nor with the leading Hittite nobles and generals. Not long after Tudhaliya the Younger ascended the throne, Suppiluliumas took it from him. According to Mursilis' chronicle:

> When my father revolted against Tudhaliya [the Younger], on the departure from [the Hittite capital of] Hattusas the princes, the lords, the military chiefs, and the nobles were all ranged alongside my father, and

An aerial view of the Elamite ruins in Susa, Iran. © ROGER WOOD/CORBIS

the conspirators seized Tudhaliya and they killed [him].

King Suppiluliumas distinguished himself as an ambitious and politically astute imperialist. He led military campaigns that expanded Hittite power into northern Mesopotamia and Syria. But his greatest accomplishment was an invasion of Mitanni, then ruled by King Tushratta, which brought the once-powerful kingdom to its knees. Suppiluliumas's army swept into Mitanni and sacked its capital, Wassukanni. Afterward the Hittites turned what was left of Mitanni into a vassal state whose leaders were expected to do the bidding of Suppiluliumas. In the "treaty" ending hostilities between the Hittites and the Mitannians, he states, "I, the great king, the king of Hatti, I conquered the Mitanni lands. . . . I established the Euphrates River in my rear and Mt. Niblani as my boundaries. All of the cities of the land . . . of Mitanni . . . I allotted to my son, Piyassili."

After subduing Mitanni, Suppiluliumas attacked the Syrian cities of Aleppo, Alalakh, and Amuru. He also negotiated a peace treaty with the king of Babylonia and sealed the deal by marrying that ruler's daughter. Suppiluliumas eventually died of a serious disease, probably bubonic plague brought to Hattusas by infected prisoners of war. But he left behind the legacy of having turned Hatti, at least for the moment, into the most powerful kingdom in the Near East; later generations of Hittites, as well as modern historians, came to see him as the greatest of the Hittite kings.

SEE ALSO: Hattusas; Hittites; Mittani

Suppiluliumas II (reigned ca. 1207 B.C. –?)

A ruler who had the distinction of being the last Hittite king. (The dates of Suppiluliumas's death and his kingdom's fall are uncertain.) Various surviving tablets and other documents show that by this time Hatti was in decline, partly because of food shortages and also because of both internal rebellions and insurrections of subject peoples. Suppiluliumas tried hard to hold the kingdom together. He managed to put down some of the rebellions; and there are surviving records of some sea battles—the only known naval engagements fought by the Hittites—over control of Alasiya, the Hittite name for the large Mediterranean island of Cyprus. But the king's efforts came to naught. Sometime in the early twelfth century B.C., Hatti, along with Greece, Syria, and several other sectors of the eastern Mediterranean region, was overrun by swarms of invaders from southeastern Europe, usually referred to as the Sea Peoples, though only some of them actually attacked in boats.

SEE ALSO: Hittites, Sea Peoples

Susa

One of the leading cities of the ancient Near East and a capital of several nations and empires that controlled that region. Archaeological finds indicate that the site of Susa (modern Shush), located in southwestern Iran about 150 miles (241km) east of the Tigris River, was inhabited, probably as an agricultural village, as early as 7000 B.C. By the late fourth millennium B.C. it had become a city and served as the capital of Elam. The Elamites called it Susan.

Because there was frequent warfare between Elam and the kingdoms of neighboring Mesopotamia, Susa came under attack numerous times by the Babylonians and the Assyrians. The most devastating of these assaults occurred in the late seventh century B.C., when the warlike Assyrian ruler Ashurbanipal (reigned ca. 668–627 B.C.) sacked the city. In a cuneiform tablet discovered by famed Assyriologist Austen Henry Layard, Ashurbanipal boasts:

> Susa, the great holy city, abode of their [the Elamites'] Gods, seat of their mysteries, I conquered. I entered its palaces, I opened their treasuries where silver and gold, goods and wealth were amassed. . . . I destroyed the ziggurat of Susa. I smashed its shining copper horns. I reduced the temples of Elam to naught; their gods and goddesses I scattered to the winds. The tombs of their ancient and recent kings I devastated, I exposed to the sun, and I carried away their bones toward the land of Ashur. I devastated the provinces of Elam and on their lands I sowed salt.

The Assyrian Empire soon fell, however, and Susa was rebuilt. The Neo-Babylonians controlled it for a while in the sixth century B.C. During this period, a Babylonian army transported large numbers of

Hebrews from Judah to Mesopotamia (the so-called Babylonian captivity), and some of these captives were resettled in Susa. According to the Old Testament books of Esther, Nehemiah, and Daniel, the title characters of these books dwelled in Susa, called Shushan by the Hebrews. Esther became the wife of the local ruler:

> When Esther was taken to King Ahasuerus in his royal palace . . . the king loved Esther more than all the [local] women, and she found grace and favor in his sight more than all the virgins, so that he set the royal crown [of the city] on her head and made her queen. (Esther 2.16–17)

The Hebrews were allowed to return to their homeland in Palestine under the next rulers of Susa, the Persians. The first Persian king, Cyrus II, captured the city in about 538 B.C. Susa became one of Persia's three capitals under Cyrus's son, Cambyses. The city retained that lofty status for about two centuries, and then the Macedonian Greek conqueror Alexander the Great took Susa and demoted it in importance. However, under the Parthians, who wrested Iran and Mesopotamia from the Greeks, Susa became a capital once again. The Parthian kings summered in their western capital of Ctesiphon and wintered in their eastern capital of Susa. In A.D. 116 the Roman emperor Trajan captured Susa but was unable to maintain control of it for long. It became a Sassanian city in the following century. Finally, after a long and distinguished existence as a city, Susa was destroyed by an invading Muslim army in the year 638.

SEE ALSO: Assyrian Empire; Elam; Persian Empire

Syria

The region located along the eastern Mediterranean coast and bordered by southeastern Anatolia in the north, northern Palestine in the south, and northwestern Mesopotamia in the east. This remarkably strategic location made Syria a busy and influential crossroads of trade, commerce, folk migrations, artistic and literary developments, and military conquests throughout ancient times. In the area of trade alone, the region was pivotal because it connected the commercial centers of Mesopotamia and Iran to European-Mediterranean markets. And all the great Near Eastern powers of the third, second, and first centuries B.C., including the Assyrians, Babylonians, Hittites, and Egyptians, coveted and vigorously fought for possession and control of Syria.

Syria's importance as a good place for human habitation and commerce was established very early. Its warm, pleasant climate, dense forests, rich soil, and long seacoast attracted settlers in the Stone Age. The area around Damascus, near the border with Palestine, and other sites in Syria supported thriving agricultural villages at least by 9000 B.C.. The region was part of the so-called Fertile Crescent, where many basic farming techniques first developed. In the centuries that followed, the inhabitants of Syria made increasingly extensive contacts with peoples living in Anatolia and Palestine, and a number of Syrian towns grew larger, richer, and culturally more sophisticated.

These trends culminated in the emergence of a small but prosperous and influential Syrian nation-state in the third millennium B.C. It was centered on the city of Ebla (modern Tell Mardikh) in northern Syria. The locals, who spoke an early Semitic tongue, engaged in lucrative trade with towns in Anatolia in the north and Akkad and Sumer in the east and southeast. The Ebla state was overrun by the Akkadians circa 2250 B.C., but it rose to prominence again in the mid-second millennium B.C.

Meanwhile, that millennium witnessed increased attempts by various Near Eastern states to exploit and, when possible, control Syria's location and resources. The Canaanites of Palestine and the Phoenicians, vigorous traders who established thriving towns on the coasts of Syria and Palestine, became middlemen in far-reaching trade for Syrian timber, cattle, and other valuable products. The cedar forests of the Syrian hills were particularly sought after by the Mesopotamians and the Egyptians, who had few native woodlands. In an effort to exploit these resources, in about 1800 B.C. the Assyrians established the town of Shubat-Enlil (now Tell Leilan) in northeastern Syria. Assyrian influence in the area soon declined, however, as Babylonia's King Hammurabi brought large parts of Syria into his own empire in the 1700s B.C. Not long afterward, in the late 1500s B.C., many of the same portions of Syria that Hammurabi had occupied were seized by migrating Hurrians and became part of the kingdom of Mitanni.

Thus, in the second half of the second millennium B.C., Syria found itself ringed, and in a sense hemmed in, by a group of competing great powers. These included the Hittites, who had become masters of most of Anatolia, in the north; the Egyptians in the south; and the Mitannians, Assyrians, and Babylonians in the east and southeast. The Egyptians eventually decided that mere trade for Syrian products was not enough for them, and they launched military expeditions into Syria, turning a number of the city-states there into vassals. The rival Hittites did the same, which brought them into conflict with the Egyptians. The climax of this rivalry was the Battle of Kadesh, fought circa 1274 B.C. near that important Syrian city. Both sides claimed victory, but in truth the outcome was indecisive, and Syria remained a bone of contention for the great powers.

Then a watershed event abruptly changed the fortunes of both Syria and the great powers. In the early twelfth century B.C., much of the eastern Mediterranean region, including Syria and Anatolia, underwent destructive upheavals; the culprits appear to have been swarms of invaders from southeastern Europe, often called the Sea Peoples, who defeated local military garrisons and sacked city after city. Only the Egyptians and the Assyrians escaped the disaster relatively unscathed. That allowed the Assyrians to overrun large parts of Syria in the centuries that followed. After the fall of the Assyrian Empire in the late seventh century B.C., the Neo-Babylonians briefly controlled Syria. But shortly afterward they were supplanted by the Persians, who had conquered most of the Near East, including Mesopotamia, Egypt, and Anatolia, by the late 500s B.C.

The next great historical watershed for Syria came in the 330s and 320s B.C., when the Macedonian Greek king Alexander III, later called "the Great," swiftly conquered the Persian Empire. It was in northern Syria, at Issus, that Alexander first defeated the last Persian king, Darius III. Thus began Syria's long and largely prosperous Greco-Roman phase. Following Alexander's death in 323 B.C., one of his generals, Seleucus, transformed large sections of the Near East, including Syria, into the Seleucid Empire. Seleucus established a new city, Antioch, located near Syria's coast, which rapidly grew into the third most populous and prosperous city in the Mediterranean world (after Rome in Italy and Alexandria in Egypt). Antioch became the central depot for trade between Europe and the Near East. The city was so rich and Syria's commercial and strategic importance was so great that another Greek-ruled kingdom, Ptolemaic Egypt, frequently tried to take the region away from the Seleucids. It was Rome, however, that eventually benefited from this incessant infighting among the Greeks. Having decisively defeated the Seleucids and reduced Egypt to a third-rate power, in 64 B.C. the Romans occupied Syria and turned the region into a province of their empire. The Romans built roads, temples, bathhouses, stadiums, and other structures across Syria, which became increasingly populous and richer than ever before. In the centuries that followed Rome drew large numbers of soldiers, as well as slaves, from the region.

It was also during the early years of Syria's Roman period that Christianity began to take root in nearby Palestine. In the 40s and 50s A.D. the early Christians—then a group of Jews called the People of the Way—set up communities in Syria, including at Damascus and Antioch. It was on the road to Damascus that, according to the Old Testament, Saul of Tarsus, later called St. Paul, had a vision of Jesus Christ and converted to the faith. Paul and the Syrian branch of the church became instrumental in spreading Christianity to Gentiles (non-Jews), thereby ensuring that the faith would survive and grow.

When western Rome fell to "barbarian" tribes in the late fifth century, the eastern Roman realm centered at Constantinople, which became the Byzantine Empire, held onto Syria for a while. But then the region was overrun by Muslim Arab armies in the 630s, ending Syria's ancient history and bringing it into what modern observers call medieval times.

SEE ALSO: Battle of Kadesh; Ebla; Egypt; Hittites; Mitanni; Palestine; Phoenicians; Romans; Seleucid Empire

taxation

Evidence shows that some form of taxation existed in Mesopotamia and neighboring regions of the Near East at the time that written records appeared in the late fourth and early third millennia B.C. So it is safe to assume that at least some people in these areas paid taxes even earlier. Whenever taxation began in Mesopotamia, it was long based on a core principle relating both to religious faith and the inherent powers of local rulers. This principle stated that the land and soil, forests and marshes, and rivers and lakes were created by the gods; and the gods had entrusted the maintenance of these resources to their earthly representatives, the kings and high priests. With the consent of the gods, the kings and priests had the right to tax ordinary people for using these resources. Thus, no matter what kind or burden of taxes a ruler chose to inflict on his subjects, he could always fall back on the argument that the system was not of his making; rather, it was sanctioned by the gods and therefore was an inevitable part of the natural order.

As for the forms of taxation imposed, during much of ancient times coins did not yet exist. (Coins first appeared in Lydia in western Anatolia during the mid-first millennium B.C.) Also, most people did not have the means of acquiring large quantities of silver and other precious metals with which to pay their taxes. So for a long time most taxes took the form of goods and services. The most common form of goods used to pay taxes were crops and livestock, of which a farmer often paid the government 10 percent of what he raised. The services used to pay off a tax burden included military service and labor on state-sponsored construction projects. Some men were obliged to assemble, go on campaigns, and fight when the king announced his need for soldiers. Other people, both men and women, worked on construction gangs or as artisans for new canals, temples, palaces, city walls, and so forth. Modern scholars call this form of work, which fulfilled a person's tax obligations to the state, corvée labor. (Though some construction work was performed by slaves, the bulk of it was usually accomplished by free laborers.) In addition, merchants often paid extra taxes, in the form of duties or tolls, when they passed with their goods through pivotal cities or regions. The rate of these duties varied from place to place and from era to era, but it seems most often to have been about 10 percent or somewhat more.

With the rise of empires from the late third millennium B.C. on, by sheer necessity tax collection became a huge task that required hundreds or thousands of government officials and tax collectors. The first imperialists in Mesopotamia, the Akkadians, introduced the idea of the central government imposing taxes on its outlying provinces. Taxes were levied, often in kind, on crops, animals, trade goods, and various craft products. Later the Assyrians used a similar system, but they often hired people, in a sense as subcontractors, to go out and collect the taxes. The subcontractors were expected to provide the central government with a certain minimal amount of revenue, but the manner in which the taxes were gathered was left to the collectors. This quite naturally led to corruption, as the subcontractors often extorted far more than was fair from the impoverished masses and kept the extra revenues for themselves. This corrupt system led to widespread fear of tax collectors, hatred of the government, and likely contributed over time to the decline of the Assyrian Empire.

Under the Persians, who controlled Mesopotamia and other parts of the Near East after the fall of Assyria, taxation was somewhat different. Persian citizens were exempt from taxation. And the burden of taxes fell on the inhabitants of foreign lands conquered by the Persian kings. During the reign of King Darius I (ca. 522–486 B.C.), almost half of the entire revenues needed to run the empire came from taxes collected in Egypt and western India. Over time, however, some regions of the Persian realm fell into what is often termed *tax debt*. In such situations, residents or local rulers were unable to pay their taxes in full and tried to make up the shortfall by borrowing money or goods, usually at high interest rates. In many cases this only plunged them further into debt. Tax debt was one of the reasons that on occasion Near Eastern rulers declared tax moratoriums, essentially allowing people to erase their debts. The reasoning behind such a moratorium was that it was necessary in order to keep large sectors of society from falling so far into debt that they hurt overall national prosperity.

SEE ALSO: government; money and banking; slaves and slavery

tell

An Arabic word denoting a mound or hill made up largely of accumulated layers of ruins and debris from centuries of human habitation. (The Persian word for *tell* was *tepe*; the Turkish word is *höyük*.) During medieval times, when the Arabs controlled large parts of the Near East, the Mesopotamian plains were littered with tells of different ages and in various states of preservation or disintegration. For a long time these sites were known only by their "tell" names, such as Tell Asmar or Tell Halaf. In the modern era, however, with the rise of the science of archaeology, these sites were investigated, and scholars learned that certain tells were the remains of specific and once-important ancient cities. Tell Asmar turned out to be the site of the Sumerian city of Eshnunna; Tell Halaf is the remains of the northern Mesopotamian city of Guzana; and Tell al-Hibba is the site of the important Sumerian city of Lagash. The ancient names of a few of the ancient Mesopotamian cities unearthed from tells remain unknown. So they are still called by their "tell" names, as in the case of the Sumerian city of Tell al-Ubaid, near Ur.

SEE ALSO: Tell al-Ubaid; and the names of individual Mesopotamian cities

Tell al-Ubaid

The site of a prosperous Sumerian town lying on the Euphrates River about 4 miles (6km) northwest of the larger city of Ur. English archaeologist H.R. Hall discovered Tell al-Ubaid in 1918 and began rudimentary excavations there the following year. More thorough investigation of the site was undertaken by the great Assyriologist Charles Leonard Woolley from 1923 to 1924, during the same period in which he

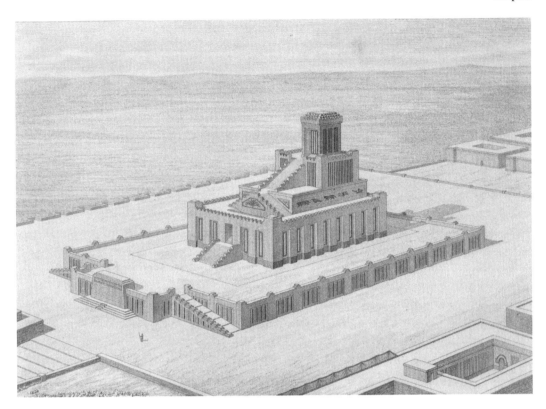

A reconstruction of a Babylonian temple. © Gianni Dagli Orti/Corbis

was first exploring nearby Ur. The main discovery at Tell al-Ubaid was a beautiful temple dedicated to Ninhursag, the Sumerian goddess of childbirth and divine protector of wild animals. Erected in about 2500 B.C., when the Sumerian cities were nearing their height of power and influence, the temple featured eight large copper-sheathed lions guarding its entrance. The insides of the structure were decorated with elegant reliefs inlaid with red limestone and mother-of-pearl.

Hall and Woolley also found the remains of a number of simple private houses at Tell al-Ubaid. Some were of sundried clay bricks and dated from Sumerian times, but in the lower levels of the tell they found smaller houses made from reeds that dated from an earlier period. Woolley found similar huts, along with

primitive pottery, at the lowest levels of the Ur site. This led him and fellow archaeologists to the conclusion that Sumerian culture was directly preceded in the region by a less sophisticated one, probably made up of the first people to settle and grow crops on the southern Mesopotamian plain. Appropriately, they coined the term *Ubaidian*, after Tell al-Ubaid, to describe this culture.

SEE ALSO: Ubaidian culture; Ur; Woolley, Charles Leonard

temples

Every ancient Mesopotamian city had at least one temple, and it was common for a city to have several. Each was dedicated to a specific god, but the largest and most splendid temple in a given city was usually that of its patron, the divinity thought to watch over the town and give it special protection. Thus, the main temple in the Sumerian city of Ur was dedicated to the local patron, the moon god, Nanna; and the largest temple in Babylon was that of Babylonia's chief god, Marduk. Marduk's temple complex in Babylon covered some 60 acres (24ha), nearly .10 square miles (.26 sq. km).

Unlike modern churches, ancient Mesopotamian temples were not intended as meeting places for worshippers. Instead, a temple was the dwelling place of the god's sacred image, or cult statue; the residence of his or her priests and attendants; and the storehouse of the valuables given to the god by worshippers. Ordinary worshippers congregated outside the temple primarily on holy days, although sometimes they were allowed to stand in the first inner courtyard of the temple complex. Never, however, was the public allowed to enter the inner enclosures of the temple, where the cult statue and treasures were located. Only the king and priests or priestesses could enter these inner sanctums.

The evolution of the structural design of Mesopotamian temples can be seen at the site of the ancient Sumerian ceremonial city of Eridu. There, archaeologists found the oldest-known temple of the region, dating to the 4000s B.C., the so-called Ubaidian period. This temple consisted of a single room measuring roughly 12 by 15 feet (3.6 by 4.5m) and featured a table in the center for offerings given by worshippers. A niche in one wall held an altar and the cult statue. Because that statue is missing, experts remain unsure of the identity of the god to which the structure was dedicated. Another temple at Eridu, which dates from the fourth millennium B.C., is much larger. It featured a spacious central hall with rooms running off of each side, somewhat like the nave and anterooms in a modern Christian church. The hall and side room of the Eridu temple sat on a raised terrace that one approached by a staircase, and the corners of the main building pointed to the four cardinal directions (north, south, east, and west). In general, with occasional small differences and modifications, this was the standard design of Sumerian and other Mesopotamian temples thereafter. Some of the platforms supporting these structures reached heights of 40 feet (12m) or more, making them landmarks that could be seen for long distances above stretches of ordinary houses and shops. Some temples in the larger cities were adjoined by a ziggurat, a pyramid-like structure with a small chapel built on top.

The temples and their sanctuaries (sacred grounds) were deemed so important and played such a major role in society that they often made up as much as a fourth or even a third of the space inside the defensive walls of a Mesopotamian urban center. Also, a number of towns and cities had an extra temple located outside the city walls. They were called *bit akitu* in Akkadian (Babylonian and Assyrian). Typically priests and worshippers marched in a sacred procession from the urban center to the outer temple to celebrate the New Year's festival, the biggest annual religious observance. In addition, many temples owned extensive tracts of farmland—the temple estates. Temple personnel ran these estates, planting and harvesting crops and raising livestock, as well as workshops that produced textiles, pottery, and other products. This made a temple a thriving economic enterprise as well as a religious institution. Another economic function of many temples was, like a bank, to lend money to people in need, possibly at lower interest rates than those charged by bankers. Temples could do this because they were usually very rich from their vast accumulation of offerings and government support.

Regarding that support, a special relationship developed between kings and local temples in Mesopotamian cities. First, it was seen as a sacred duty of the king to support, maintain, and, when necessary, help rebuild the temples. The king also often appointed the temple's leading priests and derived large measures of prestige by fighting wars and erecting new buildings in the god's name. In return, the government was allowed to tax the temples, money that helped maintain the palace and government. The Assyrians and the Babylonians exploited this special relationship between church and state by building temples alongside and even connected to royal palaces. This emphasized in the eyes of the people the king's role as the earthly representative of the god.

Finally, Mesopotamian temples were, like medieval European monasteries, centers of learning. Scribes, both priests and laypersons, worked on the temple staffs. And at least one building in a temple complex was devoted to teaching scribes to read and write and keeping temple records on cuneiform tablets.

SEE ALSO: money and banking; priests and priestesses; religion; sacred prostitution

Ten Thousand, the

A term commonly used both in ancient and modern times to describe the group of Greek mercenary soldiers who followed the Persian prince Cyrus the Younger in his bid to topple his brother, Artaxerxes II, from the throne. In 401 B.C. Cyrus and Ar-

taxerxes faced off at Cunaxa in central Mesopotamia. The would-be usurper was defeated and killed. As described in the *Anabasis* by the Greek writer Xenophon, who was among the Ten Thousand, the surviving Greeks had to fight their way out of western Asia to reach their homes.

SEE ALSO: *Anabasis*; Battle of Cunaxa; Xenophon

Tepe Gawra

An ancient town in northern Mesopotamia, situated about 15 miles (24km) northeast of modern Mosul, and one of the most important archaeological sites in the Near East. (The term *tepe* is the Persian and Kurdish equivalent of the Arabic word *tell* and describes a mound of debris built up over time by successive layers of human habitation.) Polish-born American archaeologist Ephraim Speiser discovered the site in 1927 and subsequently published an enlightening two-volume description of his digs there, entitled *Excavations at Tepe Gawra*. He found that the first town on the site rose around 6000 B.C. or so. Between that time and about 1800 B.C., during the Old Babylonian period, Tepe Gawra supported twenty-four layers of habitation, each representing a new town or village erected atop the ruins of the older ones. Thus, the site provides scholars with a steady progression of evidence about the development of agriculture and other aspects of local culture from the prehistoric Halaf and Ubaidian periods through the historic Sumerian centuries.

Among the more important discoveries Speiser made at Tepe Gawra was a series of graves containing human remains. A number of the bodies wore fine jewelry, including necklaces, bracelets, and other items made of jade, ivory, shell, turquoise, gold, silver, and electrum, an alloy of gold and silver. One tomb alone yielded some twenty-five thousand assorted jewelry beads. These finds suggest that the local nobility were very well-to-do. The excavators also unearthed three temples and a large round house that may have been used as a community center and weapons storage.

SEE ALSO: Halaf culture; Ubaidian culture

Terqua

An ancient Near Eastern city located on the Euphrates River in what is now Syria, about 42 miles (67km) northwest of the site of ancient Mari. Terqua (modern Tell Ashara) probably had close ties with and for a time may have been dependent on Mari, which was conquered by the early Assyrian king Shamshi-Adad I (reigned ca. 1813–1781 B.C.). Following Mari's fall at the hands of Babylonia's King Hammurabi around 1761 B.C., Terqua and its surrounding villages became a small independent kingdom. Terqua had at least two temples. One was dedicated to Dagan, an important god of the weather and a protector of grain. There was also a temple of Ninkarrak, goddess of good health. Her traditional companion/symbol was a dog; and excavators found the skeleton of a dog buried beside the temple's altar. In addition, Terqua had a small school for scribes, who fashioned their own cuneiform tablets.

SEE ALSO: Dagan; Hammurabi; Mari

Third Dynasty of Ur

The name given by modern scholars to both a powerful dynasty of Sumerian rulers and the empire they ruled in the late third millennium B.C., from circa 2113 to circa 2004 B.C. Scholars sometimes abbrevi-

ate this name as "Ur-III." The second empire to rise in Mesopotamia and the Near East, after that of the dynasty of Sargon of Akkad (reigned ca. 2340–2284 B.C.), Ur-III represented an earnest and for a while successful attempt to reestablish lost Sumerian power. The Akkadians under Sargon and his heirs had earlier absorbed the once independent Sumerian cities. In the late 2200s B.C. the Guti, a fierce mountain people, descended onto the plains, brought about the end of the declining Akkadian realm, and began harassing several of these cities. Finally, a coalition of Sumerian rulers defeated the Guti.

Taking a leading role in the elimination of the Gutian menace was the ruler of Ur, Ur-Nammu (reigned ca. 2113–2094 B.C.). An ambitious man, a talented military leader, and a gifted administrator, he quickly asserted Ur's power over neighboring Sumerian cities, creating a small but strong empire. That realm expanded further under his successors. Ur-Nammu's son, Shulgi (ca. 2094–2047 B.C.) captured parts of southwestern Iran, including Susa and its environs, for instance. Shulgi appointed military generals as governors of outlying provinces. He also continued to expand on his father's strong administrative system and instituted standard weights and measures for use across the empire, thereby making trade and commerce more efficient. These efforts have been revealed by thousands of cuneiform tablets found in Ur's ruins. More expansion occurred under Shulgi's son, Amar-Sin (ca. 2046–2038 B.C.), who overran large parts of Assyria (northern Mesopotamia).

Even during Shulgi's and Amar-Sin's reigns, however, the security of the new empire was threatened on both of its main flanks. The Elamites raided in the northeast, and Semitic-speaking Amorites intruded into Mesopotamia from the northwest. Hoping to stave off the Amorites, Shulgi built a massive wall across part of the plain. It had several ancient names, among them "the wall in front of the mountains" and "the wall of the land." Amar-Sin's brother, Shu-Sin (ca. 2037–2027 B.C.), who succeeded him on the throne, also built a wall to keep the Amorites out. But these efforts were in vain, as the Amorites continued to settle on the plains. Meanwhile, the Elamites grew increasingly powerful, and during the reign of Shu-Sin's son, Ibbi-Sin (ca. 2026–2004 B.C.), they launched an all-out attack on Ur. After a long siege, the city fell and the invaders captured the king and slaughtered the rest of the inhabitants. The administrative structure of the empire then swiftly fell apart, marking the effective end of Sumerian political power in ancient Mesopotamia.

The fall of Ur-III was widely seen as a watershed event and was long remembered in the poem the *Lamentation over the Destruction of Ur*, composed by an unknown scribe shortly after the event. In the poem, Ningal, divine wife of Ur's patron, Nanna, the moon god, pleads with the gods Enlil and An to spare the city and empire. But they turn a cold shoulder, and the grim destruction begins:

> (Behold,) they gave instruction that . . . Ur be destroyed, and as its destiny decreed that its inhabitants be killed. Enlil called the storm. The people mourn. . . . He called the storm that annihilates the land. . . . He called disastrous winds . . . the (great) hurricane of heaven . . . the (blinding) hurricane howling across the skies . . . the tempest . . . breaks through levees, beats down upon, devours the city's ships, (all these) he gathered at the base of heaven. The people mourn. (Great) fires he lit that heralded the storm . . . and lit on either flank of furious winds the searing heat of the desert. Like flaming heat of noon this fire scorched. The storm ordered by Enlil in hate . . . covered Ur like a cloth, veiled it like a linen sheet. On that day . . . that city was a ruin. O father Nanna, that town was left a ruin. . . . Its people's corpses . . . littered the approaches. The walls were gaping. . . . The roads were piled with dead. In the wide streets, where feasting crowds (once) gathered, jumbled they lay. In all the streets and roadways bodies lay. In open fields that used to fill with dancers, the people lay in heaps. The country's blood now filled its holes, like metal in a mold; bodies dissolved like butter left in the sun.

SEE ALSO: Akkadian Empire; Elam; Shulgi; Ur; Ur-Nammu

Tiglathpileser I (reigned ca. 1115–1077 B.C.)

One of the strongest and most ambitious kings of Assyria's second period of imperial expansion, spanning the last few centuries of the second millennium B.C. Tiglathpileser (or Tukuti-apil-Eshara) pushed the empire's borders outward farther than any other ruler of that era, thereby fulfilling what he and other Assyrians thought was a sacred duty to the Assyrian gods. He expressed this divine obligation in one of many cuneiform texts surviving from his reign:

> Ashur and the great gods, who have made my kingdom great, and who have bestowed might and power as a gift, commanded that I should extend the boundary of their land, and they entrusted to my hand their mighty weapons, the storm of battle. Lands, mountains, cities, and princes, the enemies of Ashur, I have brought

under my sway, and have subdued their territories. ... Unto Assyria I added land, unto her peoples, peoples. I enlarged the frontier of my land, and all their lands I brought under my sway.

This and the other texts make up Tiglathpileser's annals. In fact, he was the first Assyrian ruler to systematically record his exploits and victories in this fashion, which has been a boon for modern historians studying that period of Mesopotamian history.

Though the quoted passage may appear overly vain and exaggerated, as many such ancient kingly texts tend to be, it is in fact fairly accurate. A vigorous military campaigner, during his long reign Tiglathpileser led one expedition after another against enemies on all three of Assyria's traditional main frontiers. In the north, he swept into eastern Anatolia and defeated a number of local peoples. In the west, he marched to the shores of the Mediterranean Sea in Syria-Palestine; and among the records of that expedition is a description of a fishing trip in which he caught a large swordfish or perhaps a dolphin. In the south, Tiglathpileser attacked Assyria's frequent foe, Babylonia, defeated King Nebuchadnezzar I, and captured Babylon.

Tiglathpileser was no mere warmonger and destroyer, however. His annals also show that he approached domestic affairs with equal vitality. He ordered the codification of all existing Assyrian laws, and in his capital city of Ashur he built a library, which he stocked with tablets his agents collected from far and wide. In addition, he planted large parks filled with fruit and shade trees. Still another tablet describing his exploits tells how he went on hunting expeditions, killing a total of 920 lions, most of them using a bow while standing

Assyrian limestone bas-relief of the head of Tiglathpileser III from Nimrud, Mesopotamia, dating from the 8th century B.C. ERICH LESSING/ART RESOURCE, NY

in his royal chariot. In the thirty-ninth year of his reign, Tiglathpileser was murdered by a group of aristocratic conspirators, one of whom ascended the throne as King Ashared-apil-Ekur and ruled less than a year.

SEE ALSO: Ashur, 1 and 2; Assyrian Empire; Babylon

Tiglathpileser III (reigned ca. 744–727 B.C.)

One of the leading kings and imperialists of the Assyrian Empire during its last major phase of expansion, spanning the first half of the first millennium B.C. Tiglathpileser (or Tukuti-apil-Eshara) came to the throne after a period of roughly fifty years during which the realm had stagnated due to weak leadership and internal instability. He succeeded an ineffectual king, Ashur-nirari V, maybe in a palace coup in the capital of Kalhu (modern Nimrud). An energetic, thoughtful leader, Tiglathpileser saw that the empire could not long survive without major administrative and military reforms. In this respect, his strategy was to increase the authority of the central government over both the nobles and the provinces. He both created new provinces and appointed a handpicked governor (*shaknu*) for each province. He also set up an efficient system of communication, made up of swift messengers on horseback, between the royal court and the provinces. At the same time, the new king bolstered his own power by reducing that of the chief nobles, partly by decreasing the size of their sprawling estates. As for Tiglathpileser's military reforms, he overhauled the existing army. In place of large numbers of Assyrian men who were drafted and served on a temporary basis, he created a permanent professional force consisting mostly of foreigners from the provinces. Likewise, he increased the number of troops on active duty.

Tiglathpileser put this new and improved military organization to good use. Like his first earlier namesake, Tiglathpileser I, he was a relentless campaigner; in fact, Tiglathpileser III led a large-scale military expedition every year but one during his seventeen-year-long reign. In the north, he entered Anatolia, where he built a number of fortresses to maintain the northern frontier. He also attacked and subdued Urartu (Armenia), the pivotal region lying between Assyria and Anatolia. In the west, Tiglathpileser marched into Syria, where he compelled most of the local rulers to pay him tribute (regular payments acknowledging submission). But soon a group of these rulers, led by Ra-khianu of Damascus, combined forces to resist the Assyrians. After a long series of campaigns, Tiglathpileser defeated these "rebels" and seized Damascus and half the kingdom of Israel. He also campaigned in the east, where he forced the peoples of the western Zagros range to pay him tribute. Finally, the vigorous Assyrian monarch seized Babylon, a favorite target of Assyrian imperialists. Tiglathpileser died in 727 B.C., leaving behind a revitalized Assyrian state, a militarily strong and administratively sound foundation on which Sargon II and his dynastic successors would bring the empire to its zenith.

SEE ALSO: Assyrian Empire; Israel; Tiglath-pileser I

Tigris and Euphrates

The two principal rivers of Mesopotamia, which defined the name of that region ("the Land Between the Rivers"). The Tigris, which the Sumerians called the Indigra and the Persians the Tigr (or Tigra), rises in the mountains of eastern Turkey and Armenia and then flows southeastward onto the Mesopotamian plains. After some 1,150 miles (1,800km), it joins with its sister river, the Euphrates, at modern Al Quirna in southern Iraq. The combined rivers form the Shatt al-Arab waterway, which flows directly into the Persian Gulf. The major cities situated along the Tigris include ancient Nineveh, Ashur, Nimrud, Ctesiphon, and Seleucia, as well as modern Baghdad.

The Euphrates also rises in the highlands of Armenia and neighboring regions, and after an initial jog toward the Mediterranean coast, it curves southeastward and flows onto the plains, roughly parallel to the Tigris. *Euphrates* is the Greek name for the river that the Sumerians called the Buranun, the Akkadians the Purattu, and the Persians the Ufrat. It flows for a distance of about 1,730 miles (2,780km) before uniting with the Tigris at Al Quirna. Among the major ancient cities on the banks of the Euphrates were Mari, Sippar, Nippur, Uruk, Ur, and Eridu.

The courses and annual floods of the Tigris and Euphrates rivers profoundly affected patterns of settlement, farming, military campaigns, trade, and many aspects of everyday life in ancient Mesopotamia. First, because large portions of the region are arid, people tended to build towns and cities on or near the rivers in order to ensure sufficient supplies of water for drinking, cooking, bathing, and watering crops. Also, it was nearly impossible for merchants, soldiers, messengers, or migrants to travel across Mesopotamia without fording at least one of these rivers and often several of their tributaries, of which the Diyala and Upper and Lower Zab are the largest.

More importantly, the people of ancient Mesopotamia had to deal with the fact that the two great rivers, though lifegiving, were also unpredictable and sometimes destructive. In this respect, the neighboring Egyptians were more fortunate. The Nile flooded annually, and usually remarkably slowly and gently, on a schedule that only rarely varied. In contrast, when the snows in the mountains of Armenia and Turkey melted, they made the waters of the Tigris and Euphrates rise in ways that were impossible to predict. Flood season could come at any time between April and June, usually too late for farmers to use for their winter crops. Also, these waters, particularly those of the Tigris, could be violent enough to sweep away crops and sometimes even homes and entire villages. The Tigris flows faster than the Euphrates, and the Tigris is usu-

ally the first of the two to flood. Shallower and slower moving, the Euphrates was and remains the gentler river, and for that reason a larger portion of Mesopotamian irrigation canals were dug along its banks rather than along the banks of the Tigris.

Another significant aspect of the water flow of the rivers was the fact that both move from north to south; also, the prevailing winds in the region blow in the same direction. With the exception of short trips in some areas, therefore, boats could travel only southward. People who wanted to travel northward had to walk, ride donkeys or other animals, or use ropes to pull their boats upriver.

SEE ALSO: farming; ships; transportation and travel; water supplies; Zab rivers

tombs

As was the case in other ancient civilizations, the peoples of ancient Mesopotamia interred their dead in graves or tombs of varying size and splendor. They also placed grave goods, such as food, clothes, tools, weapons, and musical instruments, in tombs, believing that the deceased would need these in the afterlife.

SEE ALSO: afterlife; burial customs

Tower of Babel

A famous Mesopotamian structure mentioned in the Bible, a description that modern scholars believe was based on memories of a ziggurat erected in Babylon during the rule of its Neo-Babylonian dynasty. According to Genesis 11, all people originally spoke a single language. Large numbers of them attempted to build a great city with an unusually high tower in the land of Shinar, the Hebrew word for Sumer, or southern Mesopotamia. See-

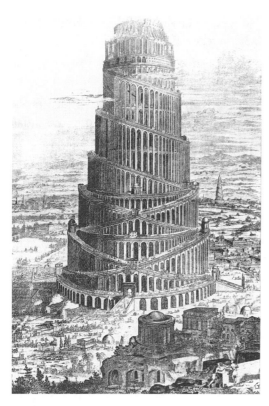

A picture depicting the infamous Tower of Babel. According to Genesis 11, God halted the production of the tower by making all people speak a different language so no one could communicate and properly construct the tower. AKG-IMAGES, LONDON.

ing this, God did not want that tall structure to approach Heaven, and he halted construction by causing the people to begin speaking many different languages, so that they could no longer properly coordinate their work. The passage reads in part:

> Now the entire Earth was of one language and uniform words. And it came to pass when they . . . found a valley in the land of Shinar and settled there. And they said to one another, "Come, let us . . . build ourselves a city and a tower with its top in the heavens." . . . And the Lord descended to see the city and the tower that the

sons of man had built. And the Lord said, "Lo! . . . They all have one language, and this is what they have commenced to do. . . . Let us descend and confuse their language, so that one will not understand the language of his companion." And . . . they ceased building the city. Therefore, He named it Babel, for there the Lord confused the language of the entire earth, and from there the Lord scattered them upon the face of the entire earth. (Genesis 11.1–9)

Most modern scholars see evidence that this biblical story was based on both mythical and real aspects of Mesopotamian culture at a time when the Hebrews were in close contact with Babylonian society. First, biblical scholars believe that the book of Genesis was compiled from a variety of sources only a century or so following the Babylonian captivity. This was the deportation of large numbers of Hebrews from the defeated kingdom of Judah in Palestine to Babylonia in the early sixth century B.C. In Babylonia, the scholars point out, the Hebrews would have been exposed to Mesopotamian culture, including local myths. One well-known Sumerian myth, called "Enmerkar and the Lord of Aratta," told how there was once just a single human language and how the gods Enki and Enlil purposely caused people to begin speaking a multitude of tongues.

More importantly, these scholars say, the captive Hebrews worked on local Babylonian construction projects, and it appears that one of these was a large ziggurat raised in Babylon by the king who had brought the Hebrews to that city, Nebuchadnezzar II (reigned ca. 605–562 B.C.). This structure—the great ziggurat of Etemenanki, dedicated to the god Marduk—had been initiated by Nebuchadnezzar's predecessor, Nabopolassar (ca. 626–605 B.C.), but had been left unfinished. Using a large workforce that included several subject peoples, including the Hebrews, Nebuchadnezzar completed the ziggurat. Evidence shows that it had a core of clay held in place by an outer shell of sun-dried clay bricks some 50 feet (15m) thick. For added strength, bitumen (tar) was used as mortar. The building featured eight levels: seven tall layers of brick, each slightly smaller than the one below it, and a temple at the top. Each level was connected to the others by staircases that wound around the perimeter. According to Nebuchad-nezzar's description of the project, the temple at the apex had blue glazed tiles on the outside, a cedar roof, and gold-plated walls studded with lapis lazuli on the inside. The authenticity of the king's inscriptions are corroborated by a description of the structure by the Greek historian Herodotus, who saw it with his own eyes in the century after its completion:

> It [the temple complex] has a solid central tower, one furlong [about 656 feet (200m)] square, with a second erected on top of it, and then a third, and so on up to eight. All eight [levels] can be climbed by a spiral way running around the outside, and about half way up there are seats for those who make the ascent to rest on. On the summit of the topmost [level] stands a great temple with a fine couch in it, richly covered, and a golden table beside it. (*Histories* 1.181)

Thus, the prevailing theory is that the biblical account of the Tower of Babel is based on a real Babylonian building that some Hebrews helped construct and later generations of Hebrews, among them the authors of Genesis, remembered.

See Also: Babylon; Bible; Marduk; Nebuchadnezzar II; ziggurat

trade

Wide-ranging and intensive trade, especially foreign trade, was absolutely essential to the prosperity and success of the ancient Mesopotamian cultures. This was because Mesopotamia was—and still is—deficient in many important natural resources. In particular, the region lacks metals, including copper and tin, the ingredients of bronze, which the ancients used for a wide variety of everyday objects; it also lacks forests for wood products and large deposits of stone for building projects. These deficiencies were already troublesome to the natives well before the rise of cities in Mesopotamia. But with the rapid urbanization of the region under the Sumerians in the late fourth and early third millennia B.C., existing crafts became more specialized, and this increased the demand for imported raw materials, especially metals, wood, and stone. In addition, the rise of cities stimulated an increase in wealth among a hard core of aristocrats, who wanted and demanded more and more luxury goods; many of these goods, or at least the raw materials needed to make them, had to be imported. Thus, for example, early Sumerian sources mention the importation of gold and lapis lazuli from eastern Iran and Afghanistan.

Imperial Governments Encourage Trade

Subsequently, the rise of empires in Mesopotamia, beginning with the Akkadian realm and the Third Dynasty of Ur in the late third millennium B.C., further increased the demand for foreign goods and raw materials. The governments of these empires saw the need to encourage trade and both to regulate it and to provide merchants with financial help and incentives.

This government aid included financing for the building of ships, warehouses, roads, and rest houses for merchants. In the Old Babylonian period, the early second millennium B.C., the Babylonian government created a high official called the chief trader, perhaps equivalent to the secretary of commerce in many modern nations. However, it appears that his job was mostly to regulate and support international, and maybe also domestic, trade. Most of the major financing for trading ventures appears to have come from private parties, including wealthy nobles or merchants or loans from rich temple estates.

Kinds of Merchants The merchants who facilitated these ventures were of three basic kinds. First, there were the traders who took part in caravans and expeditions to foreign lands, where they exchanged Mesopotamian goods for foreign goods. A second group of merchants were those who ran the import-export businesses inside Mesopotamia. The third group of merchants were the shopkeepers who bought the imported goods from the merchants in the second group and sold them in the towns and cities. Mesopotamian merchants eventually formed their own guildlike organizations, each called a *karum*. These groups provided mutual aid for merchants, including added security to guard caravans from bandits; helped to find sources of financing for trading expeditions; and dealt with state officials in matters such as trade regulation and taxation of merchants and trade goods.

Evidence suggests that at least some merchants existed before the rise of the Sumerian city-states. However, major mercantile activity, including vigorous foreign trade, became large-scale only with the urbanization of the region and the large demand for imported goods it created. Mesopotamian traders were sailing cargo ships in the Persian Gulf and the Red Sea as early as 3000 B.C., in the initial stages of the city-building era. Because of its close proximity to the Persian Gulf, the city of Ur took the lead and long remained the most active trading city in Sumeria. Traders from Ur and other city-states sailed out of the gulf and reached the delta of the Indus River in India, the coasts of the Arabian Peninsula, and the eastern coast of Africa. Eastern Africa, including Egypt, was also accessed via the Red Sea. Over time Sumerian and later other Mesopotamian traders also exchanged goods with towns and cities in Syria, which became a major crossroads of commerce by the mid-second millennium B.C.; Anatolia; the Mediterranean island of Cyprus; Greece; and other areas. Some of this trade was conducted by sea, but much of it was done by land. The land journeys were long and arduous. For instance, it could take a trader two to three months to transport his goods via a donkey train from Anatolia to Babylon. Meanwhile, internal trade within Mesopotamia was conducted, whenever possible, using boats on the Tigris and Euphrates rivers and their tributaries.

A Wide Range of Goods Traded The goods exchanged with these foreign lands were diverse and show what both the Mesopotamians and the peoples they traded with viewed as essential or important. From Anatolia came tin and later iron. Tin also came from Iran. From Arabia and lands along the eastern African coast, the Mesopotamians got copper, gold, ivory, pearls, diorite (a very hard stone), and various semiprecious stones. The African coast also provided ebony wood for building fine furniture. From Syria-Palestine came timber, especially cedar, and aromatic oils. The Indus Valley was a source of semiprecious stones, as Afghanistan was for lapis lazuli, which was always highly popular in Mesopotamia. And Cyprus and Greece were important sources of wine and fine pottery. In exchange for these and other foreign goods, the peoples of Mesopotamia traded their own domestic products, chief among them grain, sesame seeds, dates, textiles, embroidered garments, leather goods, bronze weapons, and jewelry. Bronze weapons and jewelry were major examples of Mesopotamian commercial enterprise. Local craftsmen imported foreign copper and tin, used it to create bronze, fashioned the bronze into weapons, and then exported the weapons in exchange for valuable imports. Similarly, they imported gold, lapis lazuli, and other valuable metals and semiprecious stones, turned them into jewelry, and then exported the finished products.

Such international trade existed throughout ancient times in Mesopotamia. Sometimes it was more intense and lucrative than other times, however; and from one age to another certain peoples or groups temporarily dominated international trade in the Near East. In the third millennium B.C., for example, foreign and domestic trade flourished in the region. With the fall of the Third Dynasty of Ur around 2000 B.C., however, the volume of trade decreased briefly. It then increased significantly during the Old Babylonian period. For several centuries the Babylonians dominated trade in the Near East and were probably the most vigorous traders in the world. They were nearly matched by the Hittites, whose kingdom was in Anatolia, who were very active traders in Syria, Palestine, Cyprus, and elsewhere. A major reduction in foreign trade occurred

after the disruptions caused by the invasions of the Sea Peoples in the early twelfth century B.C. But by the early ninth century B.C., with the third and final rise of the Assyrian realm and the concurrent rise of the Phoenician cities on the Syrian coast, the volume of trade expanded again. The Phoenicians became the most prolific traders in the known world. Following the fall of Assyria in the late seventh century B.C., they became both subjects of the Persian Empire and the chief middlemen in trade between Persian-controlled Mesopotamia and the Mediterranean-European sphere.

Trade During the Seleucid and Parthian Periods Following the conquest of Persia by the Greeks in the fourth century B.C., Mesopotamian trade continued to flourish and even expanded. This was partly because both the Persians and Alexander the Great had opened or expanded markets in the Far East, especially trade routes coming out of India; it was also due to the high emphasis placed on international trade by the Greek rulers of the Seleucid Empire. As noted classical scholar Michael Grant explains:

> Although agriculture was important to the Seleucids, it was not as important as international trade, which they elevated to unprecedented dimensions. Every Seleucid king was a tycoon on an enormous scale, making millions from the great trade routes from the Mediterranean to central Asia, India, and Arabia, routes which passed through their empire and were served by a network of good roads. Trading was also facilitated by the creation of an impressive unified coinage, which the rulers issued themselves and made the basic currency of the whole of their huge territories, speeding up the process, begun by the Persians, of transforming an economy of kind [bartered goods] onto a mon-

etary basis. (*From Alexander to Cleopatra*, p. 56)

Among the trade routes Grant mentions, one of the most lucrative for the Seleucids was the one running along the western shores of the Persian Gulf. There, in the mid-to-late first millennium B.C., thrived a well-organized Arab state known as Gerrha. The rich Gerrhaean sheiks enjoyed commercial relations with the tribes of southern and western Arabia as well as with western and southern India and southern Mesopotamia. To keep the Gerrhaeans from capturing and looting their own merchant ships, the Seleucids maintained a small fleet of warships in the Persian Gulf. The Seleucid monarchs also used diplomacy, as well as threats of military intervention when necessary, to maintain trade relations with Gerrha. This was vital because a large proportion of the valuable goods (especially spices) that the Seleucids got from India and Arabia came from the Gerrhaean middlemen. Some of these goods made it all the way to Syria, Greece, and beyond.

After the Parthians supplanted the Seleucids in Mesopotamia and surrounding areas, they avidly tried to maintain the existing trade routes. One difference, however, was that the Parthians placed a higher degree of importance on the land routes running through the region, particularly the so-called Silk Road that connected India and other Far Eastern lands to the Mediterranean world via the Near East. Conversely, unlike the Greeks and those who preceded them in Mesopotamia, the Parthians showed little interest in and actually neglected the sea trade that utilized the Persian Gulf and the Red Sea. This was a major reason that the prosperous Arab state of Gerrha went into major decline in the Parthian period.

The most important Mesopotamian outpost on the Silk Road in Parthian times was Hatra, a fortified town in what is now northwestern Iraq. A cosmopolitan city, Hatra hosted traders from far and wide and supported local communities of Greek, Persian, Arab, and other merchants and craftsmen as well as Parthians. This important city became a frequent target of Roman armies that invaded Parthia and was finally sacked and then abandoned by the Sassanians following their takeover of the Parthian Empire. However, the old Silk Road remained open under the Sassanians, as well as under the Arab Muslims who controlled Mesopotamia during the early medieval period.

SEE ALSO: money and banking; Phoenicians; Seleucid Empire; transportation and travel

Trajan
(reigned A.D. 98–117)

One of the most accomplished of the early Roman emperors, who successfully conquered Mesopotamia, although Roman control of that region turned out to be only temporary. Trajan (Marcus Ulpius Trajanus) was born in A.D. 53 in Spain, making him the first emperor born outside of Italy. After a successful military career as a young man, he was adopted by the emperor Nerva in 97 and ascended the throne after Nerva's death the following year. Trajan soon showed that he was a constructive ruler by launching large-scale building programs and running the realm's economy honestly and effectively. In fact, later generations of Romans and other Europeans came to see him as one of Rome's "five good emperors," the other four being his predecessor Nerva and his successors Hadrian, Antoninus Pius, and Marcus Aurelius. Trajan also showed that

The Roman Emperor Trajan (reigned A.D. 98–117) meets with an Armenian king. MARY EVANS PICTURE LIBRARY. REPRODUCED BY PERMISSION.

he was a strong and ambitious emperor by leading military expeditions designed to expand Rome's borders. He overran Dacia in eastern Europe between 101 and 106 and turned the area into a Roman province.

Then Trajan set his sights on the Near East and Parthian-controlled Mesopotamia. The Romans had installed a friendly client king in Armenia, lying north of the Mesopotamian plains, giving them an indirect foothold in the region. In the year 114 Trajan used the charge that the Parthians had forced that client ruler out of power as an excuse to invade Parthian territory. At the head of eleven legions (some sixty thousand troops), he marched southward from Armenia into Mesopotamia. The Romans swiftly captured the Parthian capital of Ctesiphon and in less than a year were in control of all of Mesopotamia. Perhaps to emphasize the extent of his achievement, Trajan marched to the shores of the Persian Gulf, a symbolic demonstration of power that had been enacted in the past by numerous Mesopotamian conquerors. At this point in time, thanks to Trajan's recent conquests, the Roman Empire had reached its largest extent ever—a total of some 3.5 million square miles (9.1 million sq. km).

The main reason for Trajan's success in Mesopotamia was the inability of the Parthians to mount a credible counteroffensive. This was partly because their realm was feudal and decentralized; most military contingents were under the command of local lords and governors, who had been slow to mount a coordinated defensive. So the Parthian king, Osroes I (reigned 109–129), was eager to end hostilities and sign a peace treaty with the Roman leader.

Trajan did not maintain the upper hand long, however. Late in 116, people across Mesopotamia rose in revolt against the Roman occupiers, and in the following year Trajan was unable to capture the well-defended Parthian city of Hatra. In fact, the emperor narrowly escaped death by a Parthian arrow while prosecuting the failed siege. He eventually decided it would be prudent to withdraw some of his forces; and on the way back to Rome in 117 he suffered a debilitating stroke and died. Ironically, all of Trajan's warlike endeavors in Mesopotamia came to nothing in the end. His successor, Hadrian (reigned 117–138), felt that Rome had overextended itself and gave Mesopotamia back to the Parthians.

SEE ALSO: Mesopotamia, history of; Parthian Empire; Romans

transportation and travel

In the fourth millennium B.C. and before, the inhabitants of Mesopotamia and surrounding regions had to rely on very basic forms of transportation, such as walking, riding donkeys, and riding in small boats on the local rivers. Around 3000 B.C., however, shipbuilders managed to construct large seaworthy vessels that could navigate in open waterways like the Persian Gulf and the Red Sea. This allowed for faster travel to and trade with distant lands, including India and Egypt; expanded opportunities for fishermen; and more expansive travel and trade in general.

The First Wagons and Chariots During the same period, probably sometime between 3500 and 3000 B.C., the widespread practical application of the wheel resulted in the appearance of the first wagons and carts in Sumeria. These early wheels were solid—consisting of two half disks of wood nailed together to form a circle—and were therefore quite heavy and bulky. Noted scholar Lionel Casson comments on what he calls

> heavy wagons with a box-like body borne on four solid wheels and drawn by teams either of oxen or onagers, a type of wild ass. Some remains dating back [to] about 2500 B.C. have been excavated, and these all belong to wagons that were quite small, the bodies only twenty inches [51cm] or so broad and the wheels twenty to forty inches [51 to 102cm] in diameter. This may have been the size that the onagers pulled, since any larger wagon of so massive a style would be too much for them. Indeed, pictures [paintings and sculpted reliefs] of the age more often than not show the beasts hitched in teams of four rather than just two. (*Travel in the Ancient World*, p. 23).

Another disadvantage of these early solid, wooden wheels was that the edges of the wood tended to crack, fray, and rapidly wear out under heavy loads. Centuries later, in the second millennium B.C., the Assyrians added sheets of metal—at first copper or bronze and later iron—to the wheel rims, which made them much more durable. Another advance in the second millennium B.C. was the ability to bend strips of wood to form the wheel rims; this allowed for the attachment of spokes running from the rim on the outside to a hub in the center. The result was a much lighter wheel, which in turn made the vehicles faster. In the same era, this advance also made possible the development of faster, more maneuverable chariots, which developed from two-wheeled carts that had appeared somewhat later than the four-wheeled variety.

Beasts of Burden The earliest wagons and chariots were pulled not only by oxen and onagers but also by donkeys and mules. It was not until circa 2300 B.C. that horses began to be used as draft animals in Mesopotamia; this remained on a limited scale for some time because horses were expensive to raise and were not much larger than donkeys. Also, the harnesses used for horses in this era rested and pushed on their throats rather than on their shoulders, which severely limited the amount of weight they could pull without choking. Horses were not effectively used to pull wagons and chariots until the mid-second millennium B.C. And horses were not used for riding (by soldiers, messengers, traders, and travelers) with any frequency until at least the ninth century B.C. Even then, the absence of stirrups, which had not yet been invented, made it difficult to maintain one's balance on a horse.

Another beast used for transportation

and travel in ancient Mesopotamia, the camel, appeared relatively late compared to other animals used for pulling vehicles, carrying loads, and riding. There were actually two broad types of camel employed in the Near East. One, the two-humped, or Bactrian, camel originated in central Asia, was comfortable in cool climates, and was used exclusively as a pack animal. The single-humped dromedary camel was first tamed in Arabia, thrived in hot climates, and was used both for carrying loads and for riding and fighting. Both types were imported into Mesopotamia by the Assyrians sometime between about 1000 and 900 B.C.

The Assyrians recognized the value of the Bactrian camel as a beast of burden for traders and travelers heading into the mountainous areas lying north, northwest, and east of Mesopotamia. A single camel could carry up to five times as much as a donkey and needed to drink far less often than a donkey. Also, the Bactrian camel was well suited to hilly terrain and the cooler temperatures in such regions. The Assyrians, and to an even greater degree the Persians who followed them in Mesopotamia, also were the first to take advantage of dromedaries as pack animals in desert regions. The earlier peoples of the Tigris-Euphrates valley had tended to avoid the arid, scorching deserts of eastern Syria and northern Arabia when traveling or transporting goods toward the west. This naturally made land trips to the Mediterranean coast, Palestine, and Egypt a good deal longer because travelers had to follow a wide, curving arc around the edges of the desert. But the dromedary made it possible for both traders and soldiers to cross these deserts with more ease and frequency. The Assyrians and the Persians also employed the dromedary in

battle. The Greek historian Herodotus tells how, in the sixth century B.C., Persia's King Cyrus II (reigned ca. 559–530 B.C.) surprised Lydia's King Croesus by unleashing a regiment of camel-riding cavalrymen, which helped the Persians attain victory:

> [Cyrus] ordered them to advance as the first line of attack against the cavalry of Croesus, with the infantry following and his own cavalry [horsemen] bringing up the rear. . . . The reason for confronting the Lydian cavalry with camels was the instinctive fear which they inspire in horses. No horse can endure the sight or smell of a camel. . . . The ruse succeeded, for when the battle began, the [Lydian] horses turned tail the moment they smelled and saw the camels, and Croesus's chief ground of confidence [his cavalry] was cut from under him. (*Histories* 1.80–82)

Hostels and Other Conveniences The Assyrians and Persians also helped pioneer systems of major roads for use by travelers, traders, messengers, and armies. These roads were generally few in number, but some were long and well maintained, in particular the Persian royal road that ran from Mesopotamia northwestward into Anatolia and ended at Sardis, near the Aegean coast. This road could accommodate not only draft animals and wagons loaded with goods but also what was perhaps the largest and most luxurious traveling conveyance ever used in the Near East. The Greeks called it a *harmamaxa*, roughly translated as "chariot-wagon." In essence, it was a very large wagon with four or more huge wheels, a roof, and hanging curtains on the sides to provide privacy for those who rode inside the padded, comfortable interior. Mostly it was used for transporting noblemen and their families or members of a king's harem.

Whatever mode of transportation one used, the Persian government set up hostels at intervals on the chief roads so that messengers could change horses and traders and other travelers could rest, find food and water, and in some cases stay overnight. The idea of such hostels was not new. They had been introduced, though probably in much smaller numbers, by the Sumerians in the late third millennium B.C. Surviving cuneiform tablets describe how Shulgi (reigned ca. 2094–2047 B.C.), the second king of the Third Dynasty of Ur, set up a system of hostels, making travel within his realm more amenable:

> I enlarged the footpaths, straightened the highways of the land, I made secure travel, built there "big houses," planted gardens alongside of them, established resting places, settled there friendly folk, so that who[ever] comes from below [i.e., the south], [or] who[ever] comes from above [the north], might refresh themselves. . . . The wayfarer who travels the highway at night might find refuge there like in a well-built city.

The phrase "who travels the highway at night" is a reference to the fact that in the summertime many travelers set out after dark in order to avoid the extreme heat of the day. No traces of these or other ancient Mesopotamian traveling accommodations have survived. However, later peoples who inhabited the region, including the Greeks and the Romans, built hostels and inns there, along with new and better roads. And the Sumerian, Assyrian, and Persian hostels likely closely resembled the later Greco-Roman versions. Archaeologists have excavated a few of these inns. Typically they were one- or two-story structures about 70 feet (21m) long and 40 feet (12m) wide. There was a small courtyard,

sometimes with a roof, to store wagons and a stable that could hold perhaps eight to twelve animals. Also on the premises was a blackmith shop for fixing wagon wheels and axles, a kitchen, a dining room, and a few small bedchambers for travelers staying overnight.

SEE ALSO: bridges; chariots; postal system; roads; ships; Shulgi; trade

Tukulti-Ninurta I (reigned ca. 1244–1208 B.C.)

The son of Assyria's King Shalmaneser I and one of the stronger and more ambitious Assyrian monarchs of Assyria's second, or middle, period of imperial expansion, which spanned the last few centuries of the second millennium B.C. Tukulti-Ninurta was known for his harsh treatment of rebels and enemies, including a coalition of Anatolian rulers he decisively defeated. He also subdued the region around Lake Van in Armenia and parts of the western Zagros range. Tukulti-Ninurta's major accomplishment was the defeat of the Kassite Babylonian king Kashtilash IV, marking the first instance of direct Assyrian rule over Babylon. In that city Tukulti-Ninurta erected a new palace for himself, called, the Kar-Tukulti-Ninurta. He also celebrated his victory over the Babylonians by commissioning an epic poem—today called the *Tukulti-Ninurta Epic* —the only Assyrian epic that has survived. In this excerpt, the Assyrian king addresses Shamash, the sun god, and points out how Tikulti-Ninurta has shown the god respect, whereas the Kassite ruler Kashtilash has not:

> O Shamash . . . lord, I respected your oath, I feared your greatness. He who

A base from the Ishtar Temple in Ashur depicting King Tukulti-Ninurta I, dating from 1220 B.C. BILDARCHIV PREUSSISCHER KULTURBESITZ/ART RESOURCE, NY

does not ... transgressed before your [authority?] ... but I observed your ordinance. When our fathers made a pact before your divinity, they swore an oath between them and invoked your greatness. You are the hero, the valiant one, who from old was [the] unalterable judge of our fathers, and you are the god who sets [things] right, who sees now our loyalty. Why has the king of the Kassites [i.e., Kashtilash] from of old invalidated your plan and your ordinance? He had no fear of your oath, he transgressed your command, he schemed an act of malice. He made his crimes enormous before you, judge me, O Shamash!

It appears that Tukulti-Ninurta was murdered in his new palace by a group of conspirators led by his son, Ashur-nadin-apli, who took the throne and ruled from circa 1207 to 1204 B.C.

SEE ALSO: Assyrian Empire; Kashtilash; Shalmaneser I

Tukulti-Ninurta II (reigned ca. 890–884 B.C.)

The son and successor of King Adad-nirari II, who initiated the third and most successful period of Assyrian expansion, which spanned the first four centuries of the first millennium B.C. Tukulti-Ninurta carried on his father's policy of rapid military and territorial expansion. The new king forced Aramaean tribes in northern Mesopotamia to pay him tribute, built fortresses on the frontiers of his realm, and rebuilt the defensive walls around his capital of Ashur.

SEE ALSO: Adad-nirari II; Ashur; Assyrian Empire

Tushratta
(reigned middle to late 1300s B.C.)

The son of the Mitannian king Shuttarna II and the last major ruler of the Hurrian kingdom of Mitanni. The surviving *Amarna Letters*, exchanged between the Egyptian pharaohs Amenhotep III and Amenhotep IV, better known as Akhenaten, and a number of other Near Eastern rulers, show that Tushratta (or Tusratta) desired closer relations with Egypt. This was likely because hostile feelings were mounting between Mitanni and Hatti, and the Mitannian king hoped that an alliance with powerful Egypt would make the Hittites think twice about attacking him. Tushratta's eagerness for friendship with the Egyptian royal house is more than plain in this gushing letter addressed to Queen Tiye, wife of Amenhotep III and mother of Akhenaten:

> To Tiye, Lady of Egypt. Thus speaks Tushratta, King of Mitanni Everything is well with me. May everything be well with you. May everything go well for your house. . . . You are the one who knows that I have always felt friendship for Amenhotep, your husband, and that . . . your husband . . . always felt friendship for me. And the things that I wrote and told . . . your husband, and the things that [he] told me incessantly, were known to you.

> . . . But it is you who knows better than anybody, the things we have told each other. . . . You should continue sending joyful embassies, one after another. Do not suppress them. I shall not forget the friendship [I have] with . . . your husband. At this moment and more than ever, I have ten times more friendship for your son, Akhenaten. (*Amarna Letters* EA 26)

To foster this friendship, Tushratta sent his daughter, Tadukhipa, to Egypt to become a member of Amenhotep III's harem. By the time she arrived, however, the pharaoh was dead. So she ended up marrying his successor, Akhenaten, and may have become the Egyptian queen Kiya. The sudden passing of Amenhotep, probably coupled with Akhenaten's obsession with religious matters and neglect of foreign policy, turned out to be unfortunate for Tushratta and his kingdom. The Hittite king Suppiluliumas I invaded Mitanni in at least two campaigns. No Egyptian aid, which apparently Tushratta had been counting on, was forthcoming.

Part of Suppiluliumas's success was due to the fact that Mitanni was wracked by civil dissent during Tushratta's reign. And Tushratta met his end at the hands of one of his own sons, perhaps in revenge for not being chosen as the royal successor. The rightful heir to the throne, Tushratta's other son, Shattiwaza, fled to Babylon and eventually to Hatti, which had by that time turned Mitanni into a Hittite vassal state. For an excerpt from another of the *Amarna Letters*, **see** Burnaburiash II.

SEE ALSO: Hittites; Mitanni; Suppiluliumas I

Tyre

A leading Phoenician city located about 20 miles (32km) south of another major

Phoenician city, Sidon, on the coast of what is now Lebanon. Tyre (modern Sur), which the Phoenicians themselves called Sur, meaning "Rock," was called Surru by the Assyrians and the Babylonians, who both coveted it, and Tyros by the Greeks. The reference to a rock likely came from the fact that the city, which may have been founded as early as the late third millennium B.C., was originally built around a fortress atop a rocky knoll on the shore. Over time the inhabitants constructed a quay that joined the old city to a newer section on an island lying about .5 miles (.8km) offshore. This also created two excellent harbors, from which the Tyrians launched their famous colonizing and trading expeditions. Tyre established colonies in the Aegean Sea; North Africa, including Carthage; Sicily; Spain; and elsewhere in the Mediterranean basin. The Tyrians also vigorously traded a number of products, the most desirable of which was a purple dye called Tyrian purple, imported by royal houses far and wide because purple was viewed as the signature color of royalty in ancient times.

Owing to its strategic location, wealth, influence, and excellent fleets, Tyre became a prize fought over by the Egyptians, Assyrians, Babylonians, Persians, Greeks, and other ancient peoples. The strong Assyrian king Shalmaneser III (reigned ca. 858–824 B.C.) besieged the city for five years; later, Babylonia's Nebuchadnezzar II (ca. 605–562 B.C.) spent up to thirteen years trying to take the city. Both of these sieges ultimately failed, although in the end the Tyrians did agree to pay the Babylonians tribute. The city was unable to withstand the onslaught of the Greeks under Alexander the Great during his conquest of Persia, however. In 332 B.C. he attacked the island portion of Tyre for seven months and eventually captured it. Following Alexander's death in 323 B.C., Tyre became part of the Greek-ruled Ptolemaic Empire, but in time the Seleucid Empire, centered in Mesopotamia, took possession of the city. Finally, in the first century B.C., the Romans seized control of Tyre and made it part of their new province of Syria.

SEE ALSO: Alexander III ("the Great"); Phoenicians; trade

Ubaidian culture

The name given by modern scholars to the culture, or civilization, that occupied Mesopotamia (especially in the south) immediately before the rise of the Sumerians and their creation of the first cities. The term was coined after Tell al-Ubaid, a site not far from Ur, which began as a Ubaidian settlement and later became a Sumerian town. The Ubaidian ruins at Tell al-Ubaid and Ur were first excavated by H.R. Hall and Charles Leonard Woolley in the 1920s. Later major investigations of Ubaidian culture were undertaken by noted archaeologists Seton Lloyd and Fuad Safar.

The term *Ubaidian* is also used to denote the historical period in which the Ubaidian culture thrived. All scholars agree that this period should be seen as a subdivision of the larger Chalcolithic period, lasting roughly from 6000 to 3500 B.C. The Chalcolithic has been nicknamed the copper-bronze-stone era of Mesopotamia because it was a transitional phase in which people were still using stone tools and weapons but at the same time developing crude copper and bronze ones. However, there is little agreement on the exact dating of the Ubaidian period, which overlapped somewhat with the earlier Halaf period of northeastern Syria and northern Mesopotamia. Estimates by various experts include circa 5500 to 4000 B.C., circa 4500 to 3500 B.C., and circa 5000 to 4000 B.C., among others.

Whatever the proper dating of the culture may be, it is clear that the Ubaidians were among the first people to settle on the alluvial plains of Mesopotamia, particularly along the lower Euphrates River near the Persian Gulf. For that reason, some scholars refer to the Ubaidians as Proto-Euphrateans. The exact origins of the Ubaidians are unknown, but it is probable that they either were migrants from the Fertile Crescent (the highlands lying along the northern rim of Mesopotamia) or were a mix of these migrants and peoples from other nearby regions. Archaeologists have established that, with a single-known exception, all of the Ubaidian villages occupied sites that had never before been built on.

The Ubaidians maintained largely a village culture, which is evident by the fact that most of their settlements remained villages throughout the period; still, a few did attain populations of perhaps five thousand by the fourth millennium B.C., thereby qualifying them as small towns. Each village consisted of a group of small houses made from hard-packed earth and/or reeds. Toward the end of the period, sun-dried mud bricks began to be used along with the cruder materials. These homes lined narrow, unpaved alleyways. A typical village also featured a few larger structures, including storage facilities for grain and other foodstuffs. There was also sometimes a central earthen mound with a small building at its summit. Scholars think the building was a

An excavation site at Tepe Gawra, an Ubaidian settlement in northern Mesopotamia. AKG-IMAGES. LONDON.

primitive temple and that the combination of mound and temple was an early form of the ziggurat, later a common feature of Mesopotamian cities. Three such early temples were discovered at Tepe Gawra in northern Mesopotamia.

Although it is doubtful that the Ubaidian villages had any centralized authority, archaeological evidence, including pottery and other products, shows that they traded with one another, as did the Halaf villages. Ubaidian pottery went through two main phases. In the first, the bowls, cups, figurines and other items were highly decorated with hand-painted geometric patterns in brown and black; later, however, pottery was simpler, less decorated, and more utilitarian. Meanwhile, the Ubaidians sustained themselves by grow-

ing wheat, barley, and lentils and raising livestock, including sheep, goats, and cattle. Nothing substantial is known about their social structure or customs.

It is also unclear how some of the Ubaidian sites became Sumerian cities. Some scholars think that the local Ubaidians simply became the more sophisticated Sumerians over time; others suggest that the Sumerians were outsiders who arrived in the area in the fourth millennium B.C. and steadily and swiftly absorbed the native population. Whichever of these scenarios is closer to the truth, the Sumerian sites of Ur, Larsa, Nippur, Lagash, Adab, Eridu, and Kish all began as Ubaidian villages and later grew into full-fledged Sumerian cities. And the cultural influence of the Ubaidians on the Sumerians was significant to say the least. As Yale University scholar Karen R. Nemet-Nejat points out:

> The Sumerians borrowed from them the names for occupations such as farmer, herdsman, fisherman, potter, carpenter, metalworker, leather worker, mason, weaver, basket maker, merchant, and priest. Other non-Sumerian words [that the Sumerians borrowed from the Ubaidians] include those for plow, furrow, palm, and date. Clearly, the development of these skills can be credited to these early settlers. (*Daily Life in Ancient Mesopotamia*, pp. 13–14)

SEE ALSO: farming; Fertile Crescent; Halaf culture; pottery; Sumerians; Tell al-Ubaid; Woolley, Charles Leonard

Ugarit

An important Near Eastern port city that, before the rise of the Phoenicians, constituted a principal trade link between the peoples of the Mesopotamian plains and the peoples of the eastern Mediterranean region. Ugarit (modern Ras Shamra) was located on the coast of northern Syria a few miles north of the modern town of Latakia. Adjoining the Fertile Crescent, the site of Ugarit was inhabited at least as early as 6000 B.C. and probably earlier. In the centuries and millennia that followed, the town flourished, mainly because of its strategic location as a trading post. Pottery and/or writing tablets from many surrounding cultures have been found in Ugarit, including examples from Sumeria, Babylonia, Assyria, Palestine, Egypt, Anatolia, Cyprus, Crete, and Greece. In the second millennium B.C. the city came under the influence of the Egyptians, who periodically campaigned in Syria. Later it appears that Hurrians controlled Ugarit, which may actually have become part of the Hurrian kingdom of Mitanni for an undetermined period. If so, Ugarit became independent after Mitanni's fall in the fourteenth century B.C. It was during this period, lasting roughly from 1450 to 1200 B.C., that the city reached its height of wealth and power. Its fall at the close of this period was both sudden and unexpected. Ugarit was one of the cities sacked and destroyed during the upheavals brought about by the invasions of the so-called Sea Peoples in the early twelfth century B.C.

Following its destruction, the site of Ugarit was eventually overgrown by soil and vegetation and was forgotten. Then, in 1928, a local Syrian farmer accidentally uncovered part of a Ugaritian cemetery while plowing his field. Soon, the French, who controlled Syria at the time, sent archaeologist Claude Shaeffer, from a museum in the French city of Strasbourg, to begin investigating the site. Considered to be among the most important ancient excavations in the Near East, the digs at Ugarit subsequently yielded a vast treasure trove of artifacts and information relating not only to the city itself but also to Mesopotamia and other neighboring regions. Shaeffer and other excavators unearthed a palace containing some ninety rooms arranged around eight courtyards. They also found libraries filled with well-preserved clay tablets. Because Ugarit was a thriving trading center, the writings on the tablets are in several languages, among them Sumerian, Akkadian (the language of the Babylonians and the Assyrians), Hurrian, and the local tongue, dubbed Ugaritic by scholars. Some tablets also feature ancient symbols and scripts from Egypt, Cyprus, and Crete. Another important discovery was that of a Ugaritic alphabet with thirty

A ziggurat from the city of Ur, which was inhabited around 4500 B.C. © Dean Conger/Corbis

letters based on sounds. Like their Phoenician counterparts, the scribes of Ugarit were experimenting with a way to simplify the existing, complex cuneiform and hieroglyphic writing systems. It remains uncertain whether the Ugaritic alphabet developed before or after the Phoenician one, which was subsequently adopted by the Greeks and other European cultures.

See Also: Hurrians; languages; trade; writing

Umma

A Sumerian city in southern Mesopotamia, situated a few miles northeast of Lagash. Umma (modern Djokha) rested within a network of canals that connected to the Tigris and Euphrates rivers. Its patron god, Shara, was a warrior deity, which in retrospect seems quite appropriate. During the Early Dynastic Period (ca. 3000–2350 B.C.), when the city flourished,

its rulers were frequently at war with the kings of Lagash and other neighboring cities. The now-famous Stele of the Vultures depicts a victory by King Eannatum of Lagash over King Enakalle of Umma in the 2500s B.C. Umma's day in the sun, so to speak, occurred when one of its kings, Lugalzagesi (reigned ca. 2340–2316 B.C.), captured Uruk and Lagash and began to plan further expansion toward the west. He was eventually defeated, however, by Sargon of Akkad and Umma was absorbed into the Akkadian Empire.

See Also: Lagash; Lugalzagesi; Stele of the Vultures

Ur

One of the most important cities of ancient Sumeria and Mesopotamia, both in its own time and to modern archaeologists and historians. Ur (modern Tell al-Muqayyar) was originally located on the

Euphrates River in what is now southeastern Iraq, quite close to the shores of the Persian Gulf. (Later, however, both the river and gulf moved away from the city.) Inhabited at least by 4500 B.C., in the Ubaidian period, Ur became one of the twelve or so major Sumerian cities that emerged in the late fourth and early third millennia B.C. The city's main rise to prominence began in about 2750 B.C., and two of its early kings, Mesannepadda and his son Aannepadda, initiated an expansionist policy. Ur defeated Lagash and Kish and eventually came to control large sections of southern Mesopotamia. The city acquired great wealth, not only through conquest but also through trade. Its location on the Persian Gulf stimulated its traders to venture out into the Indian Ocean sphere; and the well-to-do classes at Ur enjoyed an influx of foreign luxury goods.

Ur's initial period of power and prosperity ended when the imperialist Sargon of Akkad (reigned ca. 2340–2284 B.C.) created the first Mesopotamian empire and absorbed the Sumerian cities, including Ur. Little is known about Ur during the century or so it owed allegiance to the Akkadians. After the fall of the Akkadian Empire, however, the city's second and most notable and splendid period began with the rule of Ur-Nammu (reigned ca. 2113–2094 B.C.). He and his immediate successors (Shulgi, Amar-Sin, Shu-Sin, and Ibbi-Sin) created and administered the second Mesopotamian empire, the so-called Third Dynasty of Ur (or Ur-III). Like the Akkadian realm that preceded it, Ur-III's existence was spectacular but relatively brief. Pressure from the Amorites in the northwest and the Elamites in the northeast mounted, and in the last years of the third millennium B.C. the Elamites

sacked Ur. This major event was commemorated soon afterward in a dirge known as the *Lamentation over the Destruction of Ur*. (For excerpts from the work, see Ningal and Third Dynasty of Ur.)

In the years that followed, Ur remained populated but its people no longer aspired to acquire political power and territory. During the Old Babylonian period, spanning the first few centuries of the second millennium B.C., the city was largely a quiet center of learning and religious observance. Religious pilgrims from across Mesopotamia periodically visited the local temple of Ur's patron deity, Nanna (or Sin), the moon god. And Babylonia's Kassite and Neo-Babylonian rulers maintained this and other temples in Ur to curry favor with both their subjects and the gods. Steadily, however, the city declined. In large part this was due to factors beyond human control. Over time the coast of the Persian Gulf receded away from Ur toward the southeast; also, the Euphrates changed course, moving northward. (Today, the river lies 9 miles [14.5km] north of the city.) As a result, Ur's agricultural base and trade network became increasingly difficult to maintain. By about 450 B.C. the city was largely abandoned.

As the succeeding ages passed, most of Ur was covered over by dirt and vegetation and became part of a large tell, although a few of the larger buildings remained visible above the surface. Major modern excavation of the ancient city began with the epic digs of Charles Leonard Woolley, considered to be among the most important and revealing in Mesopotamia and indeed in the world. Between 1922 and 1934 Woolley led an expedition sponsored by the British Museum and the University of Pennsylvania

Museum. The items uncovered in Ur during these years now rest in these institutions as well as in the Iraqi Museum.

The crowning achievement of Woolley's expedition came early on, when he uncovered a series of what appear to be royal graves and tombs. In all, the burial sites of sixteen kings and queens of the third millennium B.C. came to light in the very same year (1922) that noted archaeologist Howard Carter excavated the tomb of Tutankhamun, or King Tut, in Egypt. Counting the graves of less prestigious people, Woolley and his associates brought to light an astounding 1,850 burial sites in Ur. In the tomb of the Sumerian warlord Meskalamdug, Woolley found that ruler's skeleton along with his golden helmet, featuring ear holes on the sides; a golden dagger; a lapis lazuli whetstone to sharpen the blade; a grooming kit containing golden tweezers; and the remains of several guards and nine women—possibly part of Meskalamdug's harem—who wore earrings in the shape of the crescent moon. On the tomb's ramp Woolley's team uncovered two four-wheeled wagons. Another tomb, that of Queen Puabi (or Shub-ad), yielded an elegant board game, a small harp covered in gold foil, and golden straw to allow the queen to sip drinks in the afterlife. In the largest of the tombs, dubbed the Great Death Pit, Woolley found the remains of six warriors; two chariot-wagons, each with three bodies, perhaps a groom and two drivers; and the bodies of thirty-eight serving maids with ribbons of silver and gold in their hair.

The royal tombs and other grave sites were not the only treasures Woolley and his team unearthed at Ur. They also found what became known as the Royal Standard of Ur, consisting of panels of inlaid mosaics depicting a military victory and the celebration that followed it. Woolley also investigated the great ziggurat of Ur. The best-preserved ziggurat in Mesopotamia, portions of it had always remained aboveground. He found that the structure, dedicated to the god Nanna, was some 240 feet (73m) high and that it had been rebuilt twice in antiquity—once in the late third millennium B.C. and again in Neo-Babylonian times. In addition, Woolley found an 8-foot (2.4m) layer of mud and sand lodged between two layers of human habitation debris. This led him to believe that he had found evidence of Noah's flood, mentioned in the biblical book of Genesis. However, scholars now think that the mud layer Woolley found came from a more localized flood.

Another important connection between Ur and the Bible was the fact that the patriarch and prophet Abraham was supposedly a native of that city. A passage from Genesis states:

> Terah took Abraham, his son, and Lot, the son of Haran, his grandson . . . and they went forth together from Ur of the Chaldeans [a name used to describe the Babylonians during the period when Genesis was written] to go into the land of Canaan. (Genesis 11.31)

Yet many modern scholars are doubtful that Abraham hailed from Ur. They suggest that he came instead from Ura, a smaller town with a similar name in northern Mesopotamia.

SEE ALSO: Bible; burial customs; flood legends; Shulgi; Sumerians; Third Dynasty of Ur; Ubaidian culture; Ur-Nammu; Woolley, Charles Leonard

Urartu

The ancient name for the region now encompassed by Armenia, lying directly north of the Mesopotamian plains. The name of its highest point, Mt. Ararat—supposedly where the biblical Noah's ark came to rest—is a mangled Hebrew version of Urartu.

SEE ALSO: Armenia

Ur-Nammu
(reigned ca. 2113–2094 B.C.)

An important and accomplished ruler of the Sumerian city of Ur and the founder of the ruling family and empire known today as the Third Dynasty of Ur, or Ur-III. Ur-Nammu began as governor of Ur under Uruk's ruler and would-be imperialist, Utuhegal. But after they successfully drove away the Guti, a hill people from the Zagros range, Ur-Nammu declared his and Ur's independence and began asserting control over other Sumerian cities, including Lagash. As his empire grew, he created a central administration that oversaw outlying provinces run by governors. He also instituted building programs, including work on the great ziggurat at Ur, new canals, improvements in Ur's defensive walls, and the planting of large orchards of date palms. Ur-Nammu eventually died from wounds sustained in battle with the Guti, who remained a menace throughout his reign. His death and burial were commemorated in a hymn, large parts of which survive, including the following passage:

> The wise shepherd . . . does not give orders any more . . . in battle and combat. The king, the advocate of Sumer, the ornament of the assembly, Ur-Nammu . . . the leader of Sumer, lies sick. His hands, which used to grasp, cannot grasp any more, [because] he lies sick. His feet . . . cannot step any more. He lies sick. Ur-Nammu, he who was beloved by the

troops, could not raise his neck any more. The wise one lay down; [and soon] silence descended. As he, who was the vigor of the land, had fallen, the land became demolished like a mountain; like a cypress forest it was stripped, its appearance changed. As if he were a boxwood tree, they put axes against him in his joyous dwelling place [i.e., his tomb]. As if he were a sappy cedar tree, he was uprooted in the palace where he used to sleep. . . . His appointed time had arrived, and he passed away in his prime. After . . . ten days had passed, lamenting for Sumer overwhelmed . . . Ur-Nammu. My king's heart was full of tears. . . . He could not complete the wall of Urim. He could no longer enjoy the new palace he had built. . . . He could no longer bring pleasure to his wife with his embrace; he could not bring up his sons on his knees.

SEE ALSO: Guti; Lagash; Third Dynasty of Ur

Uruk

An important Sumerian city that seems to have been the first large urban center in Mesopotamia and the world. Uruk (modern Tell al-Warka), from whose name the modern name *Iraq* may have derived, lies within the city limits of Warka, an Iraqi city situated some 140 miles (225km) southeast of modern Baghdad. *Warka* is the Arabic name for the site; the Sumerian name for Uruk was *Unug*, and in the Old Testament it is called *Erech*.

According to legend, Uruk was established by a king named Meskiaggasher in the dim past. Evidence uncovered by archaeologists suggests that the site was occupied by about 5000 B.C., near the beginning of the Ubaidian period. The town's great heyday, however, came later, in the fourth millennium B.C., when it underwent spectacular growth. For a while it was the world's only and largest city, covering an area of up to 2 square miles (5.2 sq. km). A number of temples were erected during this period, including the Eanna (House of An), dedicated to Inanna, goddess of love and sexual passion. It also appears that Uruk's scribes invented the art of writing using cuneiform symbols etched onto clay tablets. In the early third millennium B.C., according to the Sumerian King List, a king named Gilgamesh ruled Uruk. Assuming he was a real person, he is credited with extending and finishing the city's outer defensive wall, which reached 6 miles (10km) in circumference. Gilgamesh, or at least an exaggerated, romanticized memory of him, also later became the subject of the most famous piece of ancient Mesopotamian literature, the *Epic of Gilgamesh*.

Later in the same millennium, King Lugalzagesi of Umma captured Uruk. But he was soon defeated by the great imperialist Sargon of Akkad, and Uruk became part of the Akkadian Empire. The Akkadians continued to construct temples in Uruk, as did the rulers of the empire that superceded the Akkadian realm, the Third Dynasty of Ur. After the latter's fall in about 2004 B.C., Uruk went into decline. It revived somewhat in the first millennium B.C. and remained prosperous during the Persian, Seleucid, Parthian, and Sassanian periods that followed. Finally, during the early years of the Muslim period, which began in the A.D. 630s, Uruk was abandoned.

The first modern investigation of Uruk began in 1912, when a German team led by Julius Jordan arrived on the site. Work was suspended during World War I, but it resumed in 1928. Excavations, mostly by other German groups, have been continu-

ous almost ever since. Still, only about one-fifth of the city's huge expanse has been explored in depth to date.

Uruk is also the name given by modern scholars to the Mesopotamian historical period following the Ubaidian period; various estimates for the span of the Uruk period, in which Uruk became a true city, include circa 4000 to 3200 B.C. and circa 3700 to 3100 B.C. Scholars further break down the period into Early, Middle, and Late phases, based on pottery and other artifacts uncovered in the eighteen layers of human habitation found in Uruk.

SEE ALSO: *Epic of Gilgamesh*; Lugalzagesi; Third Dynasty of Ur; Utuhegal; writing

Utnapishtim

A character in the famous Mesopotamian epic poem the *Epic of Gilgamesh*, who survived a great flood sent by the gods by constructing a large boat. Gilgamesh, a Sumerian king, undergoes an arduous journey to a remote island in the Mediterranean Sea where Utnapishtim makes his home. The traveler is looking for the secret of eternal life, the whereabouts of which the other man supposedly knows. But before Utnapishtim reveals the secret, he tells Gilgamesh the story of how he and his family escaped death during the great flood. Modern scholars believe that Utnapishtim and his flood tale were, along with other similar Mesopotamian flood stories, the basis for the version in Genesis, the first book of the Old Testament, in which Noah survives a great flood by building an ark.

SEE ALSO: Bible; *Epic of Gilgamesh*; flood legends

Utu

The Sumerian name for the sun god, called

Shamash by the Babylonians and some other later Mesopotamian peoples.

SEE ALSO: Shamash

Utuhegal
(reigned ca. 2123–2113 B.C.)

A king of the Sumerian city of Uruk during the period following the decline of the Akkadian Empire, when Uruk enjoyed a brief period of considerable power in southern Mesopotamia. Utuhegal became famous for playing a major role in a coalition of local rulers who drove out the Guti, tribal marauders from the Zagros Mountains who had been harassing several of the Sumerian cities. Not long afterward, however, one of his associates, perhaps a general he commanded—Ur-Nammu—usurped his authority and established the dynasty and empire now referred to as the Third Dynasty of Ur, or Ur-III. Some evidence suggests that Utuhegal eventually met his end in a drowning accident while he was supervising the building of an irrigation canal.

SEE ALSO: Guti; Third Dynasty of Ur; Ur-Nammu

Warad-Sin
(reigned ca. 1834–1823 B.C.)

A king of the Amorite dynasty of the southern Mesopotamian city of Larsa, which flourished in the two centuries following the fall of the Third Dynasty of Ur (ca. 2004–1741 B.C.). Warad-Sin came to power after his father, Kudur-Mabuk, a powerful local tribal leader, slew the reigning king, Silli-Adad, in battle and placed his own son on the throne. As king, Warad-Sin tried to maintain popular support by renovating local temples and improving the fortifications of the towns controlled by Larsa. He was succeeded on the throne by his brother, Rim-Sin I (ca. 1822–1763 B.C.), who had the longest reign of any ancient Mesopotamian ruler.

SEE ALSO: Larsa; Rim-Sin I; Third Dynasty of Ur

Warka

The Arabic name for the ancient Sumerian city of Uruk, called Erech in the Old Testament. The modern Iraqi city that incorporates the site of ancient Uruk still bears the name Warka.

SEE ALSO: Uruk

water supplies

In the Stone Age, when people first began settling on the alluvial plains of Mesopotamia, perhaps their single most immediate concern was finding reliable sources of freshwater for drinking and watering their crops and animals. At first, the Tigris and Euphrates rivers and their tributaries, including the Upper and Lower Zab, offered the most obvious and convenient water supplies. And this is why so many of the early Ubaidian and Sumerian villages and cities were built on or very near the rivers. However, though they were important sources of life-giving water, the rivers, especially the Tigris, could be unpredictable and at times produced destructive spring floods. Periodic attempts were made to erect levees and dams to control the rivers, but ultimately the soft soil of southern Mesopotamia allowed these barriers to erode rapidly. Also, as populations grew, some people desired to build settlements in areas lying a few or even tens of miles from the nearest river. And the need to supply these new settlements with water presented another major challenge.

Canals To overcome these challenges, the early inhabitants of Mesopotamia steadily learned to supplement the direct tapping of the rivers with other water sources and supplies, including artificial canals, wells, and aqueducts. Canals—water channels dug on the surface of the ground—distributed water efficiently and safely and became vital to sustaining life in the region throughout ancient times. Their importance is reflected in a much-repeated ancient Mesopotamian curse: "May your canal become choked with debris!" By necessity, therefore, kings and other rulers made digging and maintaining canals a major priority. Any ruler who neglected

A stone bas-relief depicting the Elamite city of Madaktu surrounded by canals, dating from the 7th century B.C. ERICH LESSING/ART RESOURCE, NY

the existing canals was certain to become unpopular and risk inciting unrest or even rebellion. It is not surprising, therefore, that the famous Babylonian king Hammurabi spent the better part of the last nine years of his reign (ca. 1792–1750 B.C.) building irrigation canals. Because constructing a canal was a massive undertaking, a ruler like Hammurabi called on large numbers of his subjects to do the job. In some times and places, slaves did some of the work; however, most of the laborers on such projects were free people who were working off part of their tax obligations to the government.

In the actual construction of such ir-rigation canals, the main challenge was making sure that the bed of the waterway had the proper slope. The channel had to slope downward slightly as it moved away from the river to take advantage of gravity and thereby make the water flow. If the slope was too little, the water would stagnate from a buildup of silt; by contrast, if the slope was too great, the water would flow too fast and erode the channel's bed. Even when the slope was just right, silt slowly but inevitably built up, and the beds and banks of the waterway slowly but surely deteriorated. Thus, regular maintenance was required. The first-century B.C. Greek geographer Strabo describes it this way:

There is need of much labor to keep them [the Mesopotamian canals] up, for the soil is so deep and soft and yielding that it is easily swept out by the streams, and the plains are laid bare, and the canals are easily filled, and their mouths choked, by the silt. . . . The aid required is this: to prevent most of the overflowing [and] filling up effected by the silt . . . by keeping the canals cleared and the mouths opened up. . . . [It] requires the work of many hands; for, since the earth readily gives in and is soft, it does not support the silt that is brought upon it, but yields to the silt, and draws it on, along with itself, and makes the mouth hard to dam. (*Geography* 16.1.10)

Once the canal had been dug, a sluice gate constructed on the bank of the river controlled the volume and flow of the water into the artificial channel. When deemed necessary, the gate was opened or closed the desired amount, thereby increasing or decreasing the water's flow.

Such a sluice gate was only effective, however, when the level of water in the river was normal. At those times when the level dropped below that of the gate, the flow of water into the canal stopped. To overcome this problem, some bright, anonymous ancient Ubaidian or Sumerian got the idea for a device that the Arabs later called a *shaduf*. It consisted of a long pole with a bucket attached to one end; there was a counterweight attached to the other end of the pole, the center of which rested on a fulcrum, such as a rock or a block of wood. Depending on the size of the *shaduf*, one or more people operated the device by swinging the pole on the fulcrum so that the bucket dipped into the river and filled. Next, they swung the device up and over the bank of the canal and emptied it into the canal. The *shaduf*

was also used to move water from one canal to another. The Greek historian Herodotus saw this device in action when he visited Babylonia in the fifth century B.C. "The rainfall . . . is slight," he reports,

and provides enough moisture only to burst the seed and start the root growing, but to swell the grain and bring it to maturity, artificial irrigation is used, not, as in Egypt, by the natural flooding of the river, but by hand-worked [*shadufs*]. Like Egypt, the whole country [i.e., region of Mesopotamia] is intersected by [canals and] dykes. The largest of them has to be crossed in boats and runs in a southeasterly direction from the Euphrates until it joins another river, the Tigris. (*Histories* 1.193)

Wells Hand-dug wells were another important source of freshwater in ancient Mesopotamia, especially in the northern plains where the Tigris River was more difficult to control and the soil was denser. At first a typical well was simply a deep vertical hole in the ground; a person lowered a bucket on a rope, dipped the bucket in the water at the bottom, and pulled it up. This process was made easier by the introduction of the pulley in about 1500 B.C. or slightly earlier. Another improvement came in the reign of the Neo-Babylonian king Nebuchadnezzar II (ca. 605–562 B.C.). His engineers attached many pulleys and buckets to a long chain connected to a winch, and when the winch was turned the chain carried the buckets out of the well, over a basin where the water poured out, and back to the well, all in a continuous loop.

Aqueducts Aqueducts were still another source of water in Mesopotamia. An aqueduct is an artificial channel that carries water from one location to another, usually underground. Herodotus told the story of a sixth-century B.C. Arabian ruler who made such a water channel out of animal skins. Supposedly it was 300 miles (483km) long. Although this smacks of fable, or at least is surely exaggerated, that technique was used to transport water for short distances in some parts of the ancient Near East. A more stable and durable kind of aqueduct consisted of a tunnel excavated belowground. As in the case of irrigation canals, the proper slope of an aqueduct was the key to its success. It had to tilt enough so that water flowed away from its source (a river, stream, or lake), but not too much, or else the water would flow too fast and erode the channel. The first underground aqueducts in Mesopotamia were built during the reign of the Assyrian king Sargon II (ca. 721–705 B.C.). Sargon invaded Armenia (Urartu) and there saw a system of aqueducts the locals had constructed. He destroyed these, but on his return home he ordered similar water channels to be dug in Assyria.

After Assyria's fall, the Persians adopted and expanded the Assyrian system of aqueducts. These were located mainly in northern Mesopotamia, where the ground is reasonably firm; the alluvial soil in southern Mesopotamia was too soft to make underground aqueducts practical. The Persians called an aqueduct a *kariz*, but the later Arabic term *qanat* became much more common and remains in use today.

Later the Romans became famous for building similar but better-constructed and more extensive aqueducts in many parts of the ancient world. One major reason that the Roman versions were superior to those of Mesopotamia was that the Romans had access to large quantities of solid, durable stone to line the channels. They also used the stone to build special bridges, called arcades, to carry the water channels aboveground when it was necessary to ford streams or ravines. Lacking significant supplies of stone, the Mesopotamians were unable to erect such arcades. The only known exception was a bridge erected by Sargon's son, Sennacherib (reigned ca. 704–681 B.C.), to carry a water channel across a small river valley near Nineveh.

The Fate of Mesopotamia's Water Supplies
These water suppliers and conveyors—canals, wells, and aqueducts—combined to create huge amounts of freshwater for use across many parts of ancient Mesopotamia. This allowed local cities to support large populations and increased the size of arable lands, which resulted in the production of enormous quantities of crops. In the best times, southern Mesopotamia alone had an estimated 12,000 square miles (31,000 sq. km) of irrigated farmland. This may seem incredible when one looks at modern Iraq, which has far less arable land and must import much of its food. The question naturally arises: What happened to the complex and far-reaching water supplies that the ancient Mesopotamians spent millennia developing and maintaining?

One part of the answer is neglect. The Greek Seleucids carefully maintained the old canals and aqueducts. But the Parthians, with their decentralized, feudal administrative system, left such maintenance up to local lords, and many of them allowed the canals under their care to deteriorate. The next group of rulers who inherited the region, the Sassanians, spent most of their resources maintaining Iran and tended to neglect the Mesopotamian plains overall; so in this period the canals

Relief detail from the temple of Ishtar in Mari, Syria, from 2400 B.C. *depicting a victory parade of Mesopotamian soldiers carrying battle-axes.* ERICH LESSING/ART RESOURCE, NY

and aqueducts suffered further disintegration. Purposeful destruction also took a toll, as various foreign conquerors destroyed the canals, as Sargon had wrecked the Armenian ones, in an effort to defeat the local Mesopotamians. The worst offenders were the Mongols, a tribal people from central Asia who invaded Mesopotamia in the thirteenth century A.D.

Finally, nature slowly but surely acted to erase Mesopotamia's ancient waterworks. The region's rivers occasionally changed course; silt and vegetation clogged sluice gates, canals, and *qanats*; and salt deposits from evaporation of lakes and parts of the Persian Gulf made it increasingly difficult to germinate seeds even in the remaining well-irrigated regions. Ironically, cameras aboard modern satellites have revealed the locations of many of Mesopotamia's ancient water channels that are dried up and no longer visible at ground level.

SEE ALSO: farming; Sennacherib; taxation; Tigris and Euphrates; Zab rivers

weapons and warfare, land

Mesopotamia was not only the site of the world's first cities, but also of humanity's first major land armies and wars. Archaeological evidence shows that small-scale fighting among tribes and villages was an inevitable phenomenon across the globe in the Stone Age. But in the fourth, third, and second millennia B.C., the Mesopotamian city-states and empires were able to field armies consisting of thousands and at times tens of thousands of soldiers. They

A relief depicting soldiers manufacturing weapons in an Assyrian army camp. © GIANNI DA-GLI ORTI/CORBIS

also introduced major new military innovations, which in turn spread to Syria, Palestine, Egypt, Anatolia, and the eastern Mediterranean sphere. Some of these innovations, such as the composite bow and the horse, had filtered into Mesopotamia from central Asia; but the Mesopotamian state war machines had the resources to improve on them and applied them on a much larger and more organized scale than ever before. New military weapons, ideas, and tactics continued to originate in or to enter Mesopotamia over the centuries. And each major new culture or imperial state, such as the Akkadian and Assyrian empires as well as the Persians, Greek Seleucids, and Parthians, developed its own specialized approaches to land warfare

while maintaining many or most of the basic military ideas used in the region in the past.

Modern scholars have been able to piece together a fairly reliable picture of Mesopotamian warfare from a variety of sources. These include stelae, including the famous Stele of the Vultures from the mid-third millennium B.C.; carvings on cylinder seals; paintings and mosaics, such as the Royal Standard of Ur, also from the third millennium B.C.; relief sculptures depicting military campaigns and battles, especially those from the Assyrian palaces; royal inscriptions, or annals, describing such campaigns and battles; and archaeological finds of weapons, armor, coins commemorating battles, and other items relating to warfare.

Early Weapons These sources, especially archaeological finds, show that the first major military development in Mesopotamia and neighboring regions was the transition from stone to metal weapons. This was not a sudden development. Rather, even after the introduction of metal-smelting techniques, Stone Age versions of some weapons, particularly maces, or clubs, remained in use for a long time. Over the course of centuries, stone knife and ax blades, spearheads, and arrowheads were replaced by versions made of copper, bronze, and eventually iron. The rate at which this transition took place and the quality of the weapons produced depended on how effective the metalworking techniques were in a given region and era. The development of metal swords is a useful example. In Mesopotamia in the early fourth millennium B.C., swords had serious limitations. This was because copper was still the only metal widely used for weapons, but copper is relatively soft; if a long copper blade is swung in a slashing or hacking motion, it can easily break. Thus, at first swords were secondary weapons used only occasionally in battle.

The main early Mesopotamian weapons remained maces, axes, spears, and bows. Many of the maces had stone heads made of the hardest kinds of rock available in a given region. Often the Mesopotamian city-states had to import hard stone, including diorite, from foreign lands. Over time some local armies switched to copper mace heads. For fighting at close quarters, the mace was used to break skulls and other bones, but soldiers also needed a weapon with a large blade that could chop off an enemy's hand or leg or slice through enemy shields. (Many soldiers now carried shields, usually made

of wooden frames covered by animal hide.) Early sword blades were not only too soft but also too thin for the job. The battle-ax, in contrast, had a much wider and therefore stronger blade, even when it was made of copper. Metal battle-axes were employed all across Mesopotamia and the Near East for at least three thousand years.

The early peoples of Mesopotamia also developed most of the basic missile weapons that appeared independently at various times in cultures around the world. These included the metal-tipped throwing spear, or javelin, which was in use on the Mesopotamian plains by the end of the fourth millennium B.C. It consisted of a long wooden staff topped by a leaf-shaped blade of copper or bronze tied to the shaft by cords. Another early missile weapon used in the region—the bow—was little different from Stone Age versions. The most common type, called the "self" or "simple" bow, was constructed of a wooden shaft ranging from 3.5 to 7 feet (1 to 2m) in length, strung with a cord made of tightly twisted animal gut. The only major innovation in the weapon during this period was the transition from stone- to metal-tipped arrowheads. For the moment, therefore, the bow remained the least revolutionary weapon in the region and did only minimal damage to enemies protected by shields.

Early Battlefield Tactics and Military Customs The degree of damage these early weapons inflicted of course depended in large degree on how military leaders and their troops used them in battle. They could be employed either in single combat between two opponents or in larger battlefield formations involving clashing armies. The following passage from a surviving Near Eastern document describes a fight between an ancient Syrian warrior and a foreign opponent. Their use of bows, battle-axes, and javelins probably closely mirrors the manner in which these weapons were employed by individual Sumerian, Akkadian, and early Babylonian soldiers.

> A mighty man of Retenu [Syria] came, that he might challenge me in my own camp. He was a hero without peer, and he had [beaten all opponents in his land]. . . . During the night I strung my bow and shot my arrows [in a practice session] . . . and I polished my weapons. When day broke . . . he came to me as I was waiting. . . . Every heart burned for me; women and men groaned. . . . Then he took his shield and his battle ax and his armful of javelins. Now after I had let his weapons issue forth [without doing me any damage] . . . he charged me and I shot him, my arrow sticking in his neck. He cried out and fell on his nose. I [finished him off] with his own battle ax and raised my cry of victory . . . while every Asiatic roared. . . . Then I carried off his goods and plundered his cattle.

These same weapons and some of the same hand-to-hand tactics were used by the soldiers of opposing armies in Mesopotamia during the third and second millennia B.C. The difference was that the individual fighters were organized by their generals into formations, mainly blocks, lines, and columns. These were intended to make both attack or defense more effective and thereby, if possible, achieve victory. Evidence suggests that the Sumerians pioneered many formations and tactics used later throughout the region and beyond. At least by 2500 B.C. they used both light and heavy infantry (foot soldiers), for example. The terms *light* and *heavy* refer to the use of armor. The soldiers making up light infantry wore little or no armor, and heavy infantry wore body armor and helmets. Surviving sculptures show, for instance, that Sumerian light infantry wore no protective armor and carried no shields. Each man held a javelin and a battle-ax. It appears that a line of these troops approached the enemy, at a given signal hurled their javelins, and then closed with the enemy lines and fought hand-to-hand with their axes.

The heavy infantrymen, in contrast, had metal helmets; heavy leather cloaks, sometimes studded with metal disks; and wielded long spears and large shields stretching from shoulder to ankle. The Stele of the Vultures, dating from the 2500s B.C., shows a tightly packed formation of heavy infantry from the Sumerian city of Lagash marching over the bodies of enemy troops from the rival city of Umma. The soldiers in the formation's front rank hold up their shields, creating a protective barrier. Meanwhile, the men behind them project their spears forward through the spaces between the shields, making the unit even more formidable. Such a formation was designed either to mow down or to scare off enemy forces. To maneuver with any effectiveness, much less fight, in such a tight, organized formation requires a great deal of drill and practice. So at least some of the Mesopotamian soldiers of the third millennium B.C. must have made up a hard core of full-time professionals. The rest were called up for temporary service when needed.

The use of heavy infantry in effective battlefield arrays was not the only military innovation introduced by the Sumerians. They also invented the war chariot—at first consisting of a heavy wagon drawn by donkeys or wild asses—which was destined later to revolutionize warfare in Mesopotamia and neighboring lands. Sumerian and early Babylonian generals increasingly designed the formations and tactics of ordinary foot soldiers around those of central strike forces made up of chariots. Still another important military innovation was the composite bow, used with devastating effect by chariot warriors but also employed by some foot archers. Rudimentary versions of the composite bow, which combines several different materials to produce a more powerful spring, had been known for centuries, especially in parts of central Asia. Some technical breakthrough that still eludes modern scholars occurred in Mesopotamia that made composite bows significantly more powerful and practical. What seems certain is that the four primary materials of this more advanced missile-firing weapon were wood, animal horn, sinew, and glue. Even the wooden portions were often made up of two to four kinds of wood, each having certain desired elastic properties. The weapon could fire an arrow up to 400 yards (364m) or more. However, even the best archers could not achieve effective accuracy beyond 150 yards (137m). Still, the new bow could fire arrows faster and at higher velocities than the traditional simple bow. Skilled archers standing in chariots could do more damage to enemy lines, even when the opposing troops had shields.

Regarding the foot archers, some of whom wielded composite bows and others traditional simple bows, over time a new tactical field unit built around these fighters developed. Appropriately, it became known as the archer pair. The typical archer pair consisted of two men, one of whom held a large shield to protect against incoming arrows and other missiles. The other man, who carried the bow, hid with his companion behind the shield and fired off one arrow after another. Rows of hundreds or thousands of these pairs moved forward in unison during a battle, doing varying amounts of damage to enemy lines.

Although chariots and archer pairs were often the centerpiece of an army on the attack in Mesopotamia in the second millennium B.C., these units were also frequently part of a larger, integrated military force. In other words, they acted in concert with large numbers of light infantrymen armed in various ways. Their weapons were a combination of old and new. By this time the mace had finally been phased out in most parts of the Near East, mainly because it could not penetrate the metal helmets now worn by a majority of soldiers. Battle-axes remained standard, however, as did spears, javelins, and daggers. Meanwhile, the increasing production of better-quality bronze made sword blades stronger, which in turn made swords more common on the battlefield. One particularly useful sword, the *khopesh*, was in wide use across the Near East by 1600 B.C. Its curved blade resembled those of sickles used to cut wheat, and like a sickle it was very effective for slashing in a horizontal or curving stroke.

One military element that the Sumerians and other early Mesopotamian peoples lacked was units of effective cavalrymen—that is, warriors mounted on horses rather than chariots. Partly because horses were fairly scarce and very expensive to breed and train, they were used sparingly in warfare in the second millennium B.C., and cavalry units of any consequence did not come into use until the early years of the first millennium B.C. Even when small groups of early cavalrymen were employed in warfare, their effectiveness remained only marginal due to a number of technical limitations. So most of the horsemen ended up dismounting in the midst of battle and joining the infantrymen. As historian Arthur Cotterell explains:

> Fighting on horseback in ancient [Mesopotamian] armies usually ended as fighting on foot. . . . Without stirrups [which were not invented until many centuries later], it was impossible for horsemen to fight man to man, as both riders would be knocked off their mounts. Cavalry engagements usually began with a gallop towards the enemy, which slowed at javelin range so that the missile could be safely hurled. This might occur several times before riders dismounted and fought like foot soldiers. . . . [As for mounted archers,] their accuracy of fire . . . was less than an archer on the platform of a chariot. Apart from bouncing around on a horse's back, the mounted archer had to carry his quiver [arrow case] on his shoulder, and twist around whenever he needed another arrow. He also had to let go of the reins when shooting. (*Chariot*, pp. 254–55)

It is not completely clear how these early, primitive cavalrymen, along with infantrymen and foot archers, worked in conjunction with chariots in the second millennium B.C. It is likely that the integration of these forces varied from one place, time, and military commander to another. The most common approach may have been for the foot archers to soften up the enemy and then retire toward the rear of their army to make way for the chariot charge. Right behind the chariots came groups of light infantry, called "runners." Their jobs were to clear the field of capsized chariots, capture or kill fallen enemy foot soldiers and archers, and rescue their own fallen infantrymen. An army's foot soldiers and any horsemen it had on hand also chased down escaping enemy troops.

Ancient Mesopotamian military customs involving weapons, armor, chariots, horses, and battlefield tactics were well integrated into more general religious, political, and economic customs and practices of ancient warfare. For example, the Sumerians, and later the Babylonians, the Assyrians, and others, believed (or at least their rulers claimed) that the god of war or a city's patron god accompanied an army into battle. If that army won the day, it was seen as a confirmation that the deity continued to favor that city and its people. On the other hand, if the army lost the battle, the defeat was interpreted as a sign of the god's displeasure, perhaps a punishment for some offense by the city or its rulers. It was also customary for the victors of a battle or a siege to pillage the town and farms of the defeated people. The treatment of captured enemy soldiers by the Sumerians, the Akkadians, and especially the Assyrians in later centuries, was frequently harsh, as summarized by Yale University scholar Karen R. Nemet-Nejat:

> [Male prisoners] were often killed, tortured, or mutilated. . . . Official propaganda of the third millennium B.C. described piling up enemy corpses into heaps and burying them in large mounds, thereby ensuring that they would harass their descendents as restless ghosts. Sometimes women and children were included as part of the general massacre, but usually they became slaves. . . . Prisoners of war were often taken on long marches. Often naked, they were put in neckstocks, their hands bound behind their backs. . . . [They] were often blinded [to make it hard for them to escape or cause trouble]. . . . At the end of a war, prisoners were brought

to the victor's land. Some prisoners were incarcerated and used as bargaining chips in political negotiations. Other prisoners were held hostage for ransom. (*Daily Life in Ancient Mesopotamia*, pp. 236–37)

Sometimes treaties, a few of which have survived, were drawn up. These treaties redrew boundaries of the warring states and might call on the defeated state to pay the victors tribute. Large portions of the spoils of war and tribute were traditionally deposited in local temples to please the gods; however, some of this wealth almost surely ended up in the royal treasury and/or the pockets of local nobles. Both sides swore by the gods to obey the terms of a treaty, based on the belief that the side that broke the agreement would surely endure divine retribution.

Assyrian Military Organization In the battles and wars waged by the city-states, kingdoms, and empires of ancient Mesopotamia, it was only natural that the opponent who had the largest number of trained soldiers and the superior battle plan and tactics possessed a clear advantage. To put large numbers of well-armed, well-trained troops in the field at one time, however, was (and remains even today) an expensive and difficult undertaking. Early commanders learned that they could reduce confusion, disorder, and cost, and at the same time increase speed and efficiency, by organizing their armies into manageable units of varying sizes.

In this regard, the Assyrians, principally during the fourteenth through twelfth centuries B.C. and the early centuries of the first millennium B.C., are the most notable example. Their army was better organized and more lethal than the armies fielded by earlier Mesopotamian peoples. The breakdown of Assyrian army units was likely based to some degree on that of earlier military organizations in the region, harkening back to the Sumerians. But the Assyrians kept the best military ideas and customs, altered those that were less effective, and introduced a number of new ones, including the use of moderate-size cavalry units on the battlefield. The Assyrian king was the army's commander in chief, and his assistant, or field marshal, was in charge of moving the army from place to place and preparing it for battle. Under the field marshal were lesser officers, each in command of a unit of troops. The units were composed of one thousand, two hundred, one hundred, fifty, and ten men each. So, for each commander of one thousand there were five subcommanders of two hundred, ten of one hundred, twenty of fifty, and a hundred of ten. Scholar Norman B. Hunt provides detail about the types of troops and other personnel in these units:

> The bulk of the army consisted of bowmen, slingsmen [who used slingshots to hurl small stones great distances], swordsmen, pike-bearers, and light and heavy infantry, as well as permanent units of charioteers and cavalry. Ethic regiments [from the foreign lands Assyria had conquered] retained their traditional weapons and the dress of their own region; thus, there might be a contingent of bowmen from one specific area. There was also a section [of the army] which dealt exclusively with the logistics of transporting military equipment and basic provisions. (*Historical Atlas of Ancient Mesopotamia*, p. 104)

Many of Assyria's best and full-time soldiers lived and trained on a large military base called the *ekal masharti*, located in Kalhu (Nimrud). It featured a large field for drilling and practicing maneuvers, several large barracks to house the troops, and vast storage areas for weapons and other war materials. Thus, when the king decided to initiate a military campaign, the personnel of this and other smaller military bases were prepared to enter action almost immediately. The traditional season for warfare, supposedly as ordained by the war god, Ninurta, was the summer, after the farmers had harvested their crops. Once the army had reached the target region, a typical tactic was to surround an enemy city and demand its surrender. The king and his officers, and perhaps many of the ordinary soldiers, would hurl insults and threats to intimidate their opponents and convince them that resistance was useless. If the enemy refused to surrender, the Assyrians attacked and, if necessary, laid siege to the town. Assyrian armies tried to avoid large pitched battles in the open, probably because such affairs were costly in lost lives and materials; but when necessary they did fight such battles and only rarely lost. Common customs following a victory included severing the hands of fallen enemies, skinning the bodies of rebel leaders, and deporting local populations to chosen remote spots in Mesopotamia.

The Persians and the Seleucids The Assyrian military was so effective and feared that some of its customs and tactics were widely copied by other Near Eastern peoples. In Mesopotamia itself, the Persians, who came to power in the region not long after Assyria's fall, fashioned their own military in large degree around Assyrian models. Still, the Persians, especially under their first and greatest king, Cyrus II, modified and improved on the older system. Take the example of an Assyrian battlefield mainstay, the archer pair. The Persians called these tactical units *sparabara*, or "shield bearers," after their term for a shield, *spara*. Usually, the Assyrians had lined up their archer pairs side by side, forming a single row of shield carriers backed by a single row of archers. Cyrus wisely increased the depth of the formation and also the number of archers per shield, producing a heavier concentration of arrow shot.

As was the case in the Assyrian army, the organization of these and other early Persian infantrymen followed the decimal system. A Persian unit of a thousand men was called a *hazarabam*. Each *hazarabam* was commanded by an officer known as a *hazarapatis* and was subdivided into ten *sataba*, units of a hundred men each. Each *satabam* broke down into ten *dathaba* of ten men each. The use of the decimal system continued for units bigger than regiments because it was common for the Persians to field armies containing ten, twenty, or more *hazaraba* (i.e., ten thousand, twenty thousand, or more men). The Persian name for these larger groups has been lost, but the Greeks called them *myriads*. The most important of the Persian myriads was the elite group that formed the king's personal bodyguard. The best soldiers in the army, they became known as the *Amrtaka*, or "Immortals," a name based on their practice of immediately replacing any of their number who died. The Immortals were probably the finest troops in the Near East in Persia's heyday. But they were no match for Greek heavy infantrymen; during the famous Battle of Thermopylae, fought against the Greeks in 480 B.C., a unit containing thousands of Immortals was repulsed with heavy casualties by a mere few hundred Greek soldiers.

Cyrus utilized other kinds of tactical units besides infantry. For his cavalry, at first he relied on regiments of Medians, the most highly skilled horsemen in the

Near East in the early-to-mid first millennium B.C. As time went on, he developed an elite corps of mounted warriors drawn from the Persian nobility. He also employed war chariots, introducing several improvements in their construction to make them more formidable in direct frontal assaults on enemy lines. In general, members of the infantry, cavalry, and chariotry were drawn, to one degree or another, from both the nobility and the commoners, for military service was compulsory for all Persian men. Every male between the ages of twenty and twenty-four was expected to train and/or fight, and many stayed in the service longer, sometimes until they were as old as fifty.

The Persian military system more often than not served the needs of the kings and the empire and was, at least at first, widely respected, even feared, in the ancient world. But in the long run, it was unable to stand up to the Greek system. The first indication of this fact was the impressive showing made by Greek infantry against the Persian armies that tried to invade Greece in the fifth century B.C. The final test between the two systems proved that these Greek successes were no mere fluke. When Alexander the Great invaded the Persian Empire in the 330s and 320s B.C., he utilized a much smaller army than the ones sent against him by the Persian monarch, Darius III. However, Alexander's combined Macedonian and allied Greek forces were superior in armor, training, discipline, and, most of all, in strategy and tactics. The core of these forces was the so-called Macedonian phalanx. A variant of the normal Greek phalanx, the Macedonian version had been developed by Alexander's father, Philip II. It consisted of a solid block of soldiers arranged in ranks (lines), one behind another. This was in some ways very similar to the tightly packed Sumerian formation shown in the Stele of the Vultures. The men in the front rank of the phalanx created a sturdy shield wall. And all the men in the formation brandished pikes (very long spears), many of which projected outward from the front of the phalanx. This created a veritable forest of spear points, an impenetrable barrier that struck terror into the hearts of opposing troops. As the phalanx marched forward, its members acting in disciplined unison, Greek cavalry units both supported it and acted on their own. Philip and Alexander had made significant improvements in battlefield cavalry that allowed units of horsemen to make devastating charges directly into enemy infantry. Once these riders had opened fatal holes in the opposing ranks, the mighty phalanx plowed into the openings and wreaked havoc. These and related weapons systems and tactics are what allowed Alexander to defeat the largest empire in the world so swiftly.

In the post-Alexander age, when Mesopotamia was ruled by the Greek Seleucid monarchy, the Macedonian phalanx, supported by cavalry, remained the mainstay of armies in the region. These core units were supported by archers, slingers, and other "specialist" units drawn from the Seleucid Empire's subject peoples. Although some of the infantry and cavalry units were manned by local citizens, the Seleucids made increasing use of mercenaries, or hired troops from other lands. The rulers of the other great Greek kingdoms of the age—namely, Ptolemaic Egypt and the Macedonian kingdom—had similar armies, which frequently clashed with those of the Seleucids. A significant new tactic for the Greeks in this period was the use of war elephants, an idea borrowed from India. Siege warfare also underwent major developments and improvements.

The Parthians and the Sassanians Eventually, however, the reign of the Greek phalanx in warfare ended in the Near East and elsewhere. Though highly effective in its heyday, this formation had some serious inherent limitations. First, it could operate with efficiency only in flat areas having few or no rocks, trees, and other obstacles; and it was not very good at scaling and descending hills. Also, the phalanx was very rigid. And its members were not trained to fight effectively on their own, either individually or in smaller units. The Romans were the first to defeat the Greek phalanxes by outmaneuvering them with smaller, more mobile and flexible battlefield units.

Later the Parthians, who sought to oust the Seleucids from Mesopotamia and surrounding regions, also defeated Greek armies on a number of occasions. The Parthian Empire was at heart feudal in nature. So there was no national standing army; instead, soldiers were raised and maintained by local lords, vassals of the Parthian king who ruled from the capital, Ctesiphon. Also, the Parthian army had few foot soldiers, no chariots, and no siege devices. Most of the soldiers were cavalrymen who rode some of the finest horses in the ancient world. Parthian horses became so widely admired that even the Romans, longtime enemies of Parthia, tried, when possible, to acquire them for themselves.

The Parthian horsemen were divided into two main groups—light and heavy cavalry. The light cavalrymen wore no armor and carried as little weight as possible while mounted. Their only weapon was a double-recurved composite bow about 3 feet (1m) long. Parthian generals used these horsemen for hit-and-run tactics to wear down an opposing army and for flanking maneuvers, or attempts to ride around the sides of an enemy formation and attack its rear. The Parthian light cavalrymen became world famous for their agility while in the saddle, particularly their execution of a difficult move in which they turned and shot toward the rear while riding forward; this maneuver became known, appropriately, as the Parthian shot. In contrast, Parthian heavy cavalrymen, called *cataphracts*, wore protective armor, usually consisting of small metal plates or disks sewn onto a leather jerkin. Even their horses were decked out in similar armor. These horsemen carried long lances, with which they stabbed at enemy soldiers.

Typically, the lines of Parthian horsemen marched into battle to the sound of massed kettle drums, which at the least must have unsettled the opposing troops. As the battle commenced, the light cavalry struck first, harassing the enemy soldiers, trying to disrupt their lines, and in general wearing them down. Then, as the light cavalry retired, the heavy cavalry entered the fray and charged directly into the opposing ranks. Finally, as the battle raged on, the Parthian light cavalry returned and struck at the enemy's weak points.

Mesopotamia and neighboring regions witnessed still another military revolution when the Sassanians wrested control of the area from the Parthians in the third century A.D. First, the Sassanian rulers eliminated the feudal system and took the control of horses and cavalry units away from local lords. The more centralized Sassanian state created a large standing army—called the *spah*—based in many ways on the old Assyrian-Persian model. Still, Parthian-style heavy cavalry, its members drawn from the nobility, remained the core of the army. These horsemen carried lances, swords, axes, and bows, and the most outstanding of their number joined an elite group of ten thousand called the Immortals. Like their earlier Persian counterparts who were foot soldiers rather than horsemen, they were expected never to retreat, no matter how difficult the circumstances. In some ways, the Sassanian Immortals resembled medieval European knights.

Unlike the Parthians, the Sassanians also employed large units of infantrymen, both archers and men who carried spears and shields. These troops were drawn mainly from the peasantry, and it is questionable how much training they had. Nevertheless, when used in concert with the Sassanian cavalry, they helped the Sassanian kings win many battles. During a battle, the king typically sat atop an elephant so that he could get a better view of the battlefield, and he was surrounded and guarded by a large core of expert archers.

The Sassanian armies were the last to maintain control of the Mesopotamian plains in ancient times, as the Arab Muslim conquests of the seventh century A.D. brought that long and eventful era to a close.

SEE ALSO: Alexander III ("the Great"); battles of Cunaxa, Gaugamela, Kadesh, and Pelusium; cavalry; chariots; Romans; Stele of the Vultures; weapons and warfare, naval and siege

weapons and warfare, naval

No naval warfare of any consequence occurred within the confines of ancient Mesopotamia, mainly because the region itself contained no large open bodies of water and the local inhabitants were mainly landlubbers, except for their travel on the rivers in small boats. The only major waterway that bordered Mesopotamia was the Persian Gulf, and no major enemies with war fleets ever materialized on its shores. So there was no need for the Sumerians, Akkadians, Babylonians, and Assyrians to build large numbers of warships of their own. Nevertheless, two of the empires that controlled Mesopotamia—the Persians and the Seleucids—had larger political designs that sometimes carried their armies into the eastern Mediterranean region. Inevitably, the Persian and Seleucid kings were compelled to use ships to transport troops and supplies for land battles as well as to fight sea battles against the Greeks and the Romans. Though these naval encounters, which were largely provoked by Mesopotamian rulers, were few in number, their consequences were often huge. If Persia's king Xerxes I had won, rather than lost, the Battle of Salamis in 480 B.C. against the Greeks, for example, he may have gone on to conquer much or all of Europe. Also, Seleucid naval losses to the Romans contributed to the decline of Seleucid power in the Near East.

Because the Persians were largely a land power with their capitals situated far from the Mediterranean, they did not view it as cost effective to build and maintain large fleets of warships of their own. So they adopted the practice of commandeering vessels from those of their subject peoples who already had Mediterranean fleets. In particular, Persian admirals—or foreign admirals answering to the Persian king—used Phoenician and Greek ships. The breakdown of Persian vessels that fought in the empire's first major naval battle illustrates this policy in action. In 499 B.C. most of the Greek cities situated

The Greeks defeat the Persians in the huge naval battle fought in the Salamis Strait in 480 B.C. TIME LIFE PICTURES/MANSELL/TIME LIFE PICTURES/GETTY IMAGES

along the western coast of Anatolia rebelled against King Darius I. In 494 the allied rebel forces faced a Persian fleet at Lade, near the Greek city of Miletus in southwestern Anatolia. According to the Greek historian Herodotus, who was born at about this time, the Persian squadron had some 600 ships. Most of these were Phoenician, but there were also contingents from Caria in southern Anatolia, Cyprus, and Egypt, all regions then subject to Persia. In contrast, the Greeks had about 350 vessels.

The ships on both sides were mostly triremes. The chief warship of the mid-first millennium B.C., the trireme (*trieres*) was typically about 130 feet (40m) long, 18 feet (6m) wide, and carried a crew of about 200, 170 of whom were rowers. The rest were sailors and marines (fighters, including archers and men armed with spears and swords). The main battle strategy and tactics these crews employed were naturally intended to sink or board enemy vessels. The most common tactic was the ramming run, which utilized a metal-covered wooden ram, often called a "beak," mounted on a ship's prow. Various tactics developed to outmaneuver opposing vessels and make it easier to ram them. For example, one trireme might approach an enemy ship at an angle and sheer off most of its oars on one side, rendering it helpless; then a second attacker, stationed directly behind the first, would move in for the kill. Still another offensive tactic was to use grappling hooks or ropes to lock two ships together; the marines from one vessel then boarded the other and fought hand to hand.

These were the kinds of ships and tactics used at Lade in 494 B.C., although not all the ships got a chance to employ them. Not long after the battle began, some of the Greek contingents turned tail and ran. "As for the Samians [Greeks from Samos, an island off the Anatolian coast]," Herodotus reports,

it is said that they abandoned their place in the line, got sail on their vessels, and made for home—with the exception of eleven triremes, whose officers stayed and fought. ... The sight of the Samians under sail for home was too much for the Lesbians [from the island of Lesbos], who were next in the line. They soon followed suit, as indeed did the majority of the Greek fleet. Of those who remained at their posts and fought it out ... were the Chians [from the island of Chios], who fought a brilliant and most valiant action. (*Histories* 6.15)

Despite the heroics of the Chians, the larger Persian forces won the day at Lade.

But this first major Persian foray into the world of large sparring war fleets also marked the high point of Persian naval warfare. Four years later Darius sent a fleet across the Aegean Sea to punish two of the Greek cities, Athens and Eretria, for helping the Anatolian Greeks in their insurrection. The ships disembarked a large army at Marathon, northeast of Athens. But the Athenians proceeded to crush the invaders and capture several of the ships, after which the rest of the vessels sailed back to Anatolia. The worst Persian naval loss occurred in 480 B.C., when Darius's son, Xerxes, led perhaps a thousand or more ships to Greece. While the Persian king watched from a makeshift throne set up on a nearby hilltop, about six hundred of these ships engaged a united Greek fleet in the Salamis straits southwest of Athens. Though the Greeks had far fewer ships, they won a resounding victory. As Cornell University scholar Barry Strauss points out:

The Greeks took advantage of the unusual geography of the Salamis straits. The narrow space made it impossible for the Persians to use their superiority in [numbers and] speed. . . . Their boats collided with each other. . . . [This and other factors] turned the battle of Salamis from a hammer blow by Persia into a trap laid by Greeks. Persia hoped to crush the Greeks . . . but blundered into an ambush in which its [fleet's] very mass worked against it. Rarely have so many been hurt by so few. (*The Battle of Salamis*, p. 207)

An eyewitness account of the carnage has survived in the form of a passage from *The Persians* by the Athenian playwright Aeschylus, who actually fought in the battle. In the play, a Persian messenger returns to Mesopotamia and tells King Xerxes' mother:

A Greek ship charged first, and chopped off the whole stern of a Persian galley. Then charge followed charge on every side. At first by its huge impetus our fleet withstood them. But soon, in that narrow space, our ships were jammed in hundreds; none could help another. They rammed each other with their prows of bronze; and some were stripped of every oar. Meanwhile the enemy came round us in a ring and charged. Our vessels heeled over; the sea was hidden, carpeted with wrecks and dead men; all the shores and reefs were full of dead. Then every ship we had broke rank and rowed for life. The Greeks seized fragments of wrecks and broken oars and hacked and stabbed at our men swimming in the sea. . . . The whole sea was one din of shrieks and dying groans, till night and darkness hid the scene. (*The Persians* 406–22)

Two centuries after the Persian disaster at Salamis, which may have saved Europe from domination by a Near Eastern power, the Mesopotamian-based Seleucid monarchs also vied for power and wealth in the pivotal eastern Mediterranean region. Like the Persians, they utilized triremes and other vessels from foreign lands, especially Rhodes and other Greek islands lying off the western coast of Anatolia. In the late 190s B.C. the Seleucid king Antiochus III found himself at odds with the Romans, who had recently stunned the world by decisively defeating a large Macedonian phalanx in mainland Greece. Antiochus led an army to Greece with the intention of driving the Romans out. But instead they drove him out, and in 191 B.C. he tried to defeat them at sea near Cape Corycus on the Anatolian coast. The Roman ships were supplemented by Rhodian vessels; while Antiochus's admiral, Polyxenides, was himself a Rhodian. The Seleucid fleet ended up fleeing the scene, and the victorious Romans sank ten enemy ships and captured another thirteen. Two smaller naval encounters between the Seleucids and the Romans occurred in the following year. After the eventual decline of the Seleucid Empire, the Parthians and Sassanians who inherited the Mesopotamian plains concentrated their money and energies on developing their land forces, especially their cavalry. Neither people attempted to become a naval power.

SEE ALSO: Antiochus; Persian Empire; ships; weapons and warfare, land; Xerxes

weapons and warfare, siege

Modern scholars are unsure when the first sieges of fortified towns in Mesopotamia and surrounding regions took place. Most experts agree that the existence of fortified walls, especially brick and stone ones, around many early towns indicates that these places sometimes came under attack. All of the early Sumerian cities had brick defensive walls, for example. And much earlier, a number of towns in the Fertile Crescent were protected by formidable stone walls and towers. Among these were

Jericho, in Palestine, and Çatal Hüyük, in Anatolia. The question is: At what point did relatively brief assaults on these fortified towns and cities turn into protracted sieges utilizing specialized siege devices and tactics? At present, there is simply no way to be sure.

Assyrian and Babylonian Siege Craft What is more certain is that the Assyrians and Babylonians possessed a fairly sophisticated knowledge of siege warfare and employed it fairly frequently during their conquests of neighboring lands. It is possible that they inherited some basic ideas about siege craft from the Sumerians and earlier peoples and then added their own innovations, thereby raising it to an art. Other contemporary Near Eastern peoples, including the Hittites and the Egyptians, also conducted sieges, and it is unclear who borrowed what ideas from whom in this regard. Suffice it to say that by the mid-to-late second millennium B.C. sieges were a common feature of warfare in Mesopotamia and other parts of the Near East.

During this period and for some time to come, the Assyrians seem to have been the masters of siege warfare. This may be partly because their empire lasted a long time, and almost yearly military campaigns were conducted by most Assyrian kings. Therefore, the Assyrians had much practice in warfare and more need and opportunities to conduct sieges of enemy towns. This naturally stimulated them to devise the most effective siege techniques they could, given their level of technology and the available materials. As might be expected, town planners across the Near East responded to these advances in siege craft by developing improved, more formidable defenses. And in turn, this naturally inspired the besiegers to invent still more

ingenious methods of assault, and so on and so on.

For example, one of the earliest siege devices was undoubtedly the battering ram; it usually consisted of a large wooden, and later metal-tipped, beam carried by men or dragged by animals. The attackers used it to batter down a city's front gate or crash a hole in a section of the defensive wall. The defenders then developed countermeasures, including digging moats in front of the gate to make it more difficult for the ram to approach. They also showered arrows, rocks, and boiling liquids down onto the men and animals operating the ram. Assyrian besiegers learned to nullify these deadly rains by covering the ram and its operators with a sturdy, protective structure—later called a penthouse—made of wood, thatch, and layers of animal hides.

Meanwhile, the defenders continued to come up with their own countermeasures, including making the lower sections of their outer walls extra thick to make them stand up better to the pounding of a battering ram. This inspired the attackers to try to exploit the thinner, more vulnerable upper sections of the defensive walls. They began using scaling ladders, with which their soldiers tried to climb up and over the walls. And they had contingents of archers fire arrows at the defenders manning the tops of the walls. The defenders countered by using long poles to push the scaling ladders away from the walls. They also learned to equip the tops of the walls, or battlements, with alternating merlons (square notches) and crenels (openings), the familiar notched pattern used later in all medieval European castles; the defenders could then hide behind the merlons and shoot arrows through the crenels.

To counter the increasing strength of

the walls and their defenses, the attackers began building siege towers—tall contraptions made of wood and thatch that moved on large wooden wheels. Soldiers rode inside a tower and fired arrows into the city as they approached the walls; when the tower reached the walls, these soldiers climbed out and fought hand to hand with the defenders manning the battlements. When possible, the defenders used flaming arrows to set the towers ablaze before they reached the walls. While this life-and-death struggle ensued, still another battle between attackers and defenders was sometimes occurring far below the walls. The attackers learned to dig tunnels, later called saps, under the walls; these had two goals: either to weaken a wall enough to make it collapse or to allow the sappers to enter the city from beneath. To counter the saps, the defenders tried lighting fires that filled the tunnels with smoke, or they dug their own tunnels beneath those of the attackers, causing the upper saps to collapse.

Many of these elements of attack and defense during sieges can be seen in Assyrian relief sculptures. Particularly striking are the panels commissioned by King Sennacherib (reigned ca. 704–681 B.C.) to commemorate his siege of the Hebrew city of Lachish in Judah in 701 B.C.. (This siege is also described in the Old Testament book of 2 Chronicles.) These sculptures, found in the ruins of Nineveh by the great nineteenth-century Assyriologist Austen Henry Layard, show that the stronghold was erected atop a high mound to discourage the approach of siege devices such as battering rams and siege towers. So Sennacherib ordered a huge earthen ramp to be built in front of the stronghold. The attackers then dragged their battering ram, which was protected by a strong penthouse made of animal hides, up the ramp and

began smashing at a section of wall. Meanwhile, as the sculptures show, Assyrian soldiers climbed scaling ladders placed against the walls; they protected themselves by holding large shields made of thick layers of wicker above their heads as they moved upward. The reliefs also show that inside the town the defenders built a massive ramp of their own in an effort to bolster the portion of wall weakened by the battering ram. Despite their heroic defense, however, the city eventually fell. Sennacherib besieged another Hebrew city, Jerusalem, but failed to take it, although he later successfully laid siege to Babylon. As for Lachish, it was besieged again, using similar methods, by the Babylonians circa 588 B.C.. They also besieged and captured Jerusalem the following year.

Persian Sieges The Persians, who modeled many of their battlefield formations and tactics on those of Sennacherib and other Assyrian warrior-kings, also learned about siege tactics from the Assyrians. And some evidence for Persian sieges has survived. For example, the Greek historian Herodotus recorded how, in 494 B.C., King Darius I besieged the Greek city of Miletus in western Anatolia, which had joined in the rebellion the Anatolian Greeks had launched in 499 B.C.. Herodotus also mentions a typical outcome of successful Assyrian and Persian sieges—killing some of the losers, enslaving others, and deporting the rest back to Mesopotamia:

> [The Persians] invested Miletus by land and sea. They dug saps under the walls, brought up rams of all kinds, and, five years after the revolt [had begun] overwhelmed it. So Miletus was reduced to slavery. . . . Most of the [Milesian] men were killed by the Persians . . . the women and children were made slaves, and . . . the men in the city whose lives were spared were

sent as prisoners to Susa; Darius did them no harm, and settled them in Ampe, on the Persian Gulf, near the mouth of the Tigris. . . . In this way, Miletus was emptied of its inhabitants. (*Histories* 6.17–22)

The Height of Near Eastern Siege Warfare

Though the Assyrians, Babylonians, and Persians prosecuted many successful sieges, they did not survive long enough to witness the pinnacle of siege warfare in the Near East. During his invasion of the Persian Empire in the 330s B.C., Alexander the Great invested a number of cities that made the mistake of resisting him. Of particular note was the spectacular siege of the Phoenician city of Tyre, then controlled by Persia, in 332 B.C.

Alexander's officers and engineers owed a great deal to an earlier Greek military genius, Dionysius I, who became dictator of the Sicilian Greek city of Syracuse in 405 B.C. Dionysius and his own engineers created large mechanical crossbows. Each was attached to a wooden framework equipped with a metal winch that slowly drew back the bowstring. A barrage of wooden bolts (huge arrowlike projectiles) unleashed by these bows showered a city's battlements, allowing siege towers to get closer to the walls. Dionysius's siege towers were equipped with big wooden gangways that dropped onto the rooftops of buildings within a city. (His troops ran down the gangways and quickly took control of the buildings.)

Greek inventors also introduced torsions-powered catapults, which featured bundles of animal tendons or human hair that had been twisted tightly. When released, the pent-up energy propelled large bolts or stones up to .5 miles (.8km) or more, doing tremendous damage to stone walls and wreaking havoc in besieged towns. (The large missile shooters and catapults were the ancient equivalent of artillery.) Alexander's father, Philip II, utilized such devices in the sieges he prosecuted in northern Greece; and Alexander proceeded to employ them in his invasion of the Near East. Then, in the centuries immediately following Alexander's death, new generations of Greek inventors, engineers, and machinists produced even more lethal versions of siege artillery. The Greek Seleucids, who came to control Mesopotamia, along with their frequent enemies in Greece and Greek-ruled Egypt, used these devices. And so did the Romans, who were experts at borrowing useful ideas from other peoples and then improving on them. Under the Greeks and the Romans, the art of siege craft reached its apogee in ancient times.

SEE ALSO: Alexander III ("the Great"); Assyrian Empire; Jerusalem; Judah; Sennacherib; Tyre; weapons and warfare, land

weights and measures

Mercantile activities, including buying and selling; money exchanging; and trade, both local and foreign, as well as reckoning the sizes of land parcels and erecting large buildings, necessitated the development of standards of weights and measures in ancient Mesopotamia. These standards, which came to be used across the region and in a number of neighboring Near Eastern lands, were not invented all at once. Instead, they evolved over many centuries when and where need dictated. It appears that many were introduced, or at least modified and passed along, by the Sumerians.

Their creation of the world's first cities and large farming estates in the late fourth and early third millennia B.C. significantly increased the volume of commerce and trade in the region. This stimulated a demand for uniformity in weights and measures in order to reduce the confusion caused by using many different local systems. A similar effect occurred with the rise of empires in Mesopotamia beginning in the late third millennium B.C.; an empire's central administration imposed a uniform series of weights and measures for everyone in the realm.

By the time that the Babylonian and Assyrian empires arose, a fairly standard set of weights and measures was in general use across Mesopotamia. It was based in large degree on Sumerian models, which is evident by its frequent reliance on the Sumerian counting system, which combined a sexagesimal approach (based on the number 6) with a decimal one (based on the number 10). The Akkadian (Babylonian and Assyrian) system also employed measurements based on the approximate lengths of the human finger and forearm.

Basic Units The early basic Akkadian unit of weight was the *she* (from the Sumerian *se*), which was equivalent to 1/600 of an ounce (.05g). By the Neo-Babylonian period, dating to the mid-first millennium B.C., the *she* had been replaced by the *shiklu*, later popularly known as the shekel, equal to 180 *she*, or .3 ounces (9g). This is about the weight of a U.S. quarter. In the Akkadian system 60 shekels equaled 1 *manu*, and 60 *manu* equaled 1 *biltu*, equaling roughly 67 pounds [30kg].

Akkadian measures of length and distance were based on finger and forearm lengths. The average forearm length was later widely called a cubit, a term used frequently in the Old Testament, which was written in Mesopotamia and Palestine in the first millennium B.C. One *ubanu*, based on the Sumerian *shu-si*, or "finger,"

was equivalent to about .6 inches (1.6cm). And 1 *ammatu*, or cubit, was equal to about 15.5 inches (39cm). Large units of measure included the *kanu*, or "cane," equal to 6 *ammatu* (7 feet 10 inches [2.3m]); the *ashlu*, equal to 157 feet (48m); and the *beru*, or "league," equal to 5.25 miles (8.4km).

Because the Sumerians were the first people to employ farming on a large scale in Mesopotamia, the units they developed for measuring the areas of plots of land became universal in the region. For example, the Sumerian *sar*, or "garden," became the Akkadian *musaru*, equal to 27.5 square yards (23 sq. m). One Sumerian *iku*, or "field," became an Akkadian *iku*, equaling 100 *musaru*, or .79 acres (.32ha). And 1 Sumerian *bur* became an Akkadian *buru*, which equaled 18 *iku*, or 15 acres (6ha).

Units of volume were also important for trade, and the Sumerians and the Akkadians developed their own equivalents of modern pints, gallons, and bushels. For instance, the *sila* (the term used by both the Sumerians and the Akkadians) was equivalent to about 1.5 pints (.9l). One *massiktu*, or *pi*, equaled 60 *sila*, an amount equivalent to 11 gallons (41.6L) or 1.3 bushels. An average donkey load in ancient Mesopotamia was called an *imeru*, equal to 100 *sila*, or about 2.25 bushels.

When the Achaemenid Persians took over Mesopotamia from the Babylonians and the Medes in the sixth century B.C., Persian officials adopted a system of weights and measures similar in many ways to the traditional Sumerian-Akkadian one. Like the older version, the new one had units of length called fingers, hands, cubits, and canes, for instance. However, the actual measurements in the Persian system differed somewhat. A Persian finger (*aiwas*) was .8 inches (2cm); a hand (*dva*), equal to 5 fingers, was 4 inches (10cm); a cubit (*panka*), was 20 inches (50cm); a cane was 5 feet (1.5m); and a *parasang*, supposedly the distance a person could walk in an hour at an average pace, was 3.7 miles (6km). Some of the basic Persian units of weight were the shekel, at .3 ounces (8.3g); the *mina*, equal to 60 shekels; and the talent, equal to 3,000 shekels.

The Seleucid System Following the conquest of Persia by Alexander the Great and the wars among his successors following his death, the Greek-ruled Seleucid Empire took charge of Mesopotamia. Unfortunately, the use of weights and measures in the region now becomes somewhat uncertain because of a lack of reliable surviving evidence. It appears that Seleucus and his successors did not introduce a new system of weights and measures. Instead, they seem to have kept in place a conglomeration of older systems, each predominating in a different part of the empire. In Babylon, for example, merchants and traders probably used the Akkadian or Persian system, or perhaps both. The Seleucids also appear to have used a Greek system, specifically the Attic, which was the one used in Athens and was the most widely used system in Greece at the time. The Attic foot measured 11.6 inches (29cm); 600 of these feet equaled a stade, or *stadion*. Smaller Greek units of length included the fathom (*orgyia*), equal to 6 feet (2m); the pace (*bema*), equal to roughly 2.5 feet (.7m); and the cubit (*pekhys*), equal to about 1.5 feet (.5m). The chief Greek unit of area was the *plethron*, roughly equivalent to 10,000 square feet, in today's terms perhaps .25 acres (.1ha). A major unit of liquid measure was the amphora, roughly equivalent to a bit more than 8 modern gallons (about 39L). And one of the most common units of dry measure was the *medimnos*, probably equivalent to a bit more than 11 modern gallons (52l). The late Michael Rostovtzeff, the leading scholar of the economies of the Seleucid and other Greek kingdoms of that period, suggested that individual major cities in the Seleucid Empire may have issued their own sets of standard weights and measures with the permission and guidance of the central government. This, he says, implies

the existence in the Seleucid administration of a department of weights and measures which issued the royal standard weights [probably based on the Attic system] and controlled those issued by the magistrates [officials] of at least the most important cities of the kingdom. Unfortunately, [the matter remains somewhat vague because] there is no complete collection of the numerous weights of the Seleucid kingdom. (*Social and Economic History of the Hellenistic World*, vol. 1, p. 454)

After the decline of the Seleucid Empire, the Parthians seem to have kept the old Persian and Greek standards of weights and measures in place, although little or no evidence for Parthian weights and measures has been found. Not surprisingly, the Sassanians, who supplanted the Parthians in the region, utilized the Persian system since the Sassanians considered their realm a reborn version of Achaemenid Persia and tried to emulate the earlier Persians in numerous ways.

SEE ALSO: mathematics; money and banking; trade

women

Although the status, rights, and treatment of women varied somewhat from place to

A relief showing Assyrian women with a child among palm trees. THE ART ARCHIVE/MUSEO BARRACCO ROME/DAGLI ORTI

place and era to era in ancient Mesopotamia some general observations can be made about the majority of women in that region. First, at no time did women have political rights, such as holding public office or ruling cities or countries; the occasional exception was a queen who ruled temporarily, and with limited powers, following her husband's death. Second, in theory the social status of Mesopotamian women seems to have been roughly equivalent to that of men, especially during Sumerian times in the third millennium B.C.; however, the legal status of women was never equal to that of men. The rights and treatment of women may have been slightly better under the Sumerians because of the importance that people placed on female goddesses in their religion. Supporting this view is the fact that priestesses were common in Sumerian temples. Also, Sargon of Akkad (reigned circa 2340–2284 B.C.), though not himself a Sumerian, retained worship of these goddesses after absorbing the Sumerian cities into his empire. And he appointed his daughter to be high priestess of the moon god, Nanna, at Ur, a very prestigious position.

Women's Legal Status Nevertheless, the social and legal status of women in Mesopotamia apparently declined to some undetermined degree after the third millennium B.C. Women remained generally subservient to men. There may have been exceptions to this rule, since most of what is known about the lives of Mesopotamian women relates to upper-class urban women. Ancient writers tended to devote almost all their attention to the lives of rich, famous, and prominent folk and rarely described the lives of the poor and powerless. Information about the lower classes, making up the vast majority of ancient Mesopotamia's population, is therefore lacking. It is possible that women in poor farm households shared equally in the decision making with their husbands; this was true in many parts of ancient Europe. But it is likely that, overall, women in Mesopotamia were second-class citizens who were fairly tightly regulated by their husbands and fathers.

Certainly ancient Mesopotamian women were not legally protected to the degree that women are in most modern societies. This can be seen in some of the surviving laws of the Babylonians and the Assyrians, which either did little to protect women from physical assault or even condoned various abuses. One of the statutes in Hammurabi's famous law code reads, "If a man has struck the daughter of a free man and caused her to cast that which was in her womb [i.e., have a miscarriage], he shall pay ten shekels of silver." Thus, for causing a women to lose her baby, a man received essentially a slap on the wrist. Another of Hammurabi's laws, which follows from the one mentioned above, actually demands that an innocent woman should suffer for someone else's crime: "If that woman [who had the miscarriage] died as a result, they shall kill his [the attacker's] daughter." Another law regulating women, this one Assyrian, was discovered by the team of German archaeologists who excavated the ruins of the city of Ashur between 1903 and 1914. "Apart from the penalties for a married woman which are written on the tablet," the law reads, "a man may flog his wife, he may pull out her hair, [or] he may damage and split her ears. There is nothing wrong in this." Other surviving Assyrian laws that, to modern ears, sound overly harsh toward women include:

> If a woman, whether the wife of a man or the daughter of a man, utters vulgarity or indulges in low talk, that woman bears her own sin.

> If a woman brings her hand against a man, they shall prosecute her; 30 *manas* of lead shall she pay, [and] 20 blows shall they inflict on her.

> If the wife of a man goes out from her house and visits a man where he lives, and he has [sexual] intercourse with her, knowing that she is another man's wife, the man and also the woman they [the authorities] shall put to death.

> If a woman be dwelling in the house of [her] father, but has been given to her husband, whether she has been taken to the house of her husband or not, all debts, misdemeanors, and crimes of her husband shall she bear as if she too committed them. Likewise if she be dwelling with her hus-

band, all crimes of his shall she bear as well.

Women Workers The strict and sometimes abusive treatment described in these laws suggests that Assyrian women may have been more strictly regulated and disciplined than women in other parts of Mesopotamia; although there is no way to know how often and how literally such abuses were actually carried out. It is possible that these highly punitive laws were meant to deter unacceptable behavior and in actual practice were not always strictly enforced. Yet there is no doubt that Assyrian women were closely regulated. This can be seen in a surviving law that called for "respectable" women to wear veils when they were in public, although certain lower-class women could actually be punished for wearing veils:

> If the wives of a man or the daughters of a man go out into the street, their heads are to be veiled. The prostitute is not to be veiled. Maid-servants are not to veil themselves. Veiled harlots [prostitutes] and maid-servants shall have their garments seized and 50 blows inflicted on them and bitumen [tar] poured on their heads.

Despite their lower legal status and occasional mistreatment by men, a fair number of Mesopotamian women, perhaps most, had the right to work. Some held jobs or professions usually dominated by men. Evidence shows, for instance, that a few female scribes existed in the Old Babylonian period, during the first few centuries of the second millennium B.C.; at least ten of these were in the city of Mari on the upper Euphrates. A few women doctors, diviners, artists, and several priestesses are also mentioned in surviving sources from that period. Meanwhile, considerably larger numbers of lower-class

women worked in less-specialized jobs. A good many women labored on the land, helping their husbands with the planting, harvesting and threshing wheat, pruning vines, towing barges upriver, and doing a wide range of domestic chores.

Other women toiled in shops, especially ones that produced textiles. In Assyria, which was almost always fighting wars or putting down rebellions, it was common for a woman to run her husband's shop while he was away serving in the military. In addition, a number of women worked as maids, cooks, gardeners, and so forth in palaces or on temple estates. Still others had jobs in taverns; of these, some actually ran the establishments, others were barmaids, and still others provided entertainment by singing, dancing, and/or playing musical instruments. In general though, in keeping with the overall lower status of women, they were routinely paid only half of what men made for comparable work; and they were not paid at all for the days when they were menstruating. Also, although a woman could work in a shop or other business, she had to have her husband's or father's permission to do so.

As for their social and economic rights, ancient Mesopotamian women had far fewer than modern women do but actually more than most women in classical Greece had. Most women in Babylonia and Assyria could inherit or buy slaves and land. They could also sue in court to get the title to a parcel of land, although they could not appear in court as witnesses in legal disputes. Also, most Mesopotamian women could acquire loans and/or invest part of their dowries in an effort to make money (in the form of interest). Any profits that women made from their own investments were referred to as "hand," or "in the basket."

Persian and Greek Women in Mesopotamia

Under the Achaemenid Persians, the lives of Mesopotamian women do not seem to have changed dramatically, although there were some differences. Infant boys were notably more prized than infant girls in Persian families; so Persian mothers of boys received more praise and higher rations of food and other items than mothers of girls. Conversely, grown Persian women, at least upper-class ones (once again, more is known about them than lower-class ones), could attain high positions in business and accumulate great wealth. They could buy and sell land at will. And surviving documents show that an upper-class woman named Irdabana owned several workshops that employed both male and female laborers. The wives of two Persian kings, Darius I (reigned ca. 522–486 B.C.) and Darius II (reigned 423–405 B.C.), owned extensive estates, and surviving records describe the visits they made to these lands and the large retinues of servants that accompanied them.

It is unclear to what degree lower-class Persian women enjoyed the economic freedom accorded to their upper-class counterparts. Some ancient Greek writers, including Herodotus, claimed that average Persian women were usually secluded in their homes, as were most women in Athens and many other Greek cities in his day. However, these reports may well be misleading. It is possible that Persian women of all classes continued to enjoy the right to work and make money, as long as they had their husbands' or fathers' permission. If so, the secluded Persian women mentioned by the Greeks may have been those women whose husbands and fathers were more conservative and pre- ferred their wives and daughters to remain in the home.

More certain is the fact that the Persians condoned and practiced polygamy. According to Herodotus, most upper-class Persian men had multiple wives as well as concubines (live-in mistresses). The fact that Persian women could not have multiple husbands is a sign of women's overall social inferiority. Also, the Persians, like the Assyrians, retained the custom of obliging upper-class women to wear veils in public. However, as before, lower-class women did not have to wear veils; and the use of veils and other outer coverings by women at all social levels did not begin in Mesopotamia until medieval times, when the Muslims controlled the region.

The relative economic freedom of Mesopotamian women continued under the Greek Seleucid rulers who controlled the region in the wake of the death of Alexander the Great. Many Greek women who moved from mainland Greece to the great monarchies of the Near East happily experienced increased status and opportunities. However, as before, they and non-Greek women in the region still had no political rights and, legally speaking, remained essentially second-class citizens.

Not much is known about women in the Parthian realm that ruled Mesopotamia in the centuries following the decline of the Seleucid Empire. The third-century A.D. Roman historian Justin said that polygamy was still practiced in the region and that most women were secluded in the home; but in the absence of reliable Parthian sources, the claims of an observer from a distant enemy land must be viewed with caution.

As for Sassanian women, it appears that they enjoyed rights and treatment roughly comparable to women in the

Achaemenid Persian realm. Also, some recent research suggests that a few Sassanian women actually fought in their nation's renowned cavalry units. (This research is summarized in scholar Kaveh Farrokh's book *Sassanian Elite Cavalry*.)

SEE ALSO: clothing; Code of Hammurabi; grooming; marriage and divorce

Charles Leonard Woolley (1880–1960)

A noted British archaeologist who became one of the giants of Assyriology and Near Eastern studies and made some of the most sensational discoveries in the history of archaeology. Born in London, Woolley attended New College, Oxford, and then rapidly made a name for himself in the still-young science of archaeology. Shortly before the outbreak of World War I he engaged in major excavations at the site of the ancient Syrian city of Carchemish. There, he worked with the eccentric but brilliant British scholar, excavator, and adventurer T.E. Lawrence, who later became famous as "Lawrence of Arabia." Woolley also worked at Tell el-Amarna, in Egypt, site of the ancient city erected by the maverick pharaoh Akhenaten.

Woolley's greatest and most memorable achievements came after the end of World War I. In 1922 he headed a joint expedition of the British Museum and the University of Pennsylvania in excavations at the site of the ancient Sumerian city of Ur. During the next twelve years Woolley and his colleagues unearthed hundreds of ancient graves, including a number of tombs belonging to Sumerian royalty. The tomb of Queen Puabi and several others contained fabulous treasures, including jewelry, weapons, and other items made of gold and lapis lazuli. Woolley also investi-gated the great ziggurat at Ur and found evidence that he thought proved the reality of the great flood mentioned in the biblical book of Genesis.

Upon his triumphant return to England in 1935, Woolley, now world famous, was knighted by the queen, becoming "Sir" Charles Leonard Woolley. He went on to lead important excavations in Syria from 1937 to 1939 and from 1946 to 1949. A superlative scholar and an excellent writer, Woolley published twenty-five books, many of which have gone through numerous reprints and are still available. Among the most popular were, and remain, *The Sumerians* (1928); *Digging Up the Past* (1930); *Ur of the Chaldees* (1938); *Spadework: Adventures in Archaeology* (1953); and *Excavations at Ur* (1954).

SEE ALSO: flood legends; Ur; ziggurat

Wrath of Erra, The

An ancient Babylonian myth and epic poem that tells how Erra (or Nergal), god of the Underworld, death, and war, tried to destroy Babylon while that city's divine protector, Marduk, was away. The surviving written version of *The Wrath of Erra* (also known as *Erra and Ishum* and *The Erra Epic*) probably dates from the eighth century B.C. Beneath the surface of the story's colorful characters and events it appears to be a commentary on the ravages, and more importantly the inevitability, of war and the death and destruction it brings. The poem also reminds the reader or listener that human cities and society are transient and subject to decline or destruction at the whims of the gods. Yet even the most pitiless of divinities, including Erra, are not likely to cause the complete destruction of the world. The work concludes with a ray of hope that humanity is destined to survive the worst of catastrophes.

As the tale begins, Erra is restless and bored and laments that it has been a long time since he has been able to express his violent tendencies:

> Erra, warrior of the gods, was restless in his dwelling. His heart urged him to do battle! Says he to his weapons: "Smear yourselves with deadly venom!" To the Seven, warriors unrivaled, [he says] "Let your weapons be girded!" ... Erra's limbs are sluggish, like those of a mortal lacking sleep. He says to himself, "Shall I get up or go to sleep?"

Hoping to break out of his state of lethargy, Erra decides to destroy the city of Babylon. However, his faithful adviser, Ishum, tells him that this would not be a wise course. In response, Erra shouts:

> Keep quiet, Ishum, [and] listen to what I say as concerns the people of the inhabited world, whom you would spare. ...I am the wild bull in heaven, I am the lion on earth, I am king in the land, I am the fiercest among the gods! ... All the gods are afraid of a fight, so the black-headed folk [humans] are contemptuous! ... I will make Marduk angry, stir him from his dwelling [his main temple in Babylon], and lay waste the [Babylonian] people!

Thus, Erra disregards Ishum's advice and travels to Babylon. There, the god of the netherworld approaches the great god Marduk and accuses him of dressing in clothing unfit for a god. Unaware of Erra's ruse, Marduk becomes concerned about his appearance and decides to leave Babylon and obtain better garments. Naturally, Erra offers to watch over the city while his fellow deity is away. As soon as Marduk is gone, the god of death begins his attack.

Ishum again tries to dissuade his master from violence, but to no avail. Erra continues on his rampage, killing men, women, and children and wrecking buildings.

Eventually, however, Erra grows tired of destroying the city and departs. He meets with a group of fellow gods and justifies his actions, saying in essence that such violent acts are simply part of his nature. Then he asks the wise Ishum to explain how humanity is far from completely destroyed. The people of Babylonia will rise again, Ishum says:

> Let the people of the country, who had dwindled, become numerous again. Let short and tall alike traverse its paths. ... You shall make ... grain descend once more [on] to the land. You shall make [the] mountain deliver its yield, [the] sea its produce, [and] you shall make the ruined fields deliver produce. Let the ... ruined temples lift their heads like the rays of the sun. Let the governors of all cities make the provider for ... Babylon their lord.

Finally, the story ends with a hymn of praise for the mighty Erra, sometimes destroyer of humanity and the Earth's surface.

SEE ALSO: afterlife; Babylon; literature; Marduk; Nergal; religion

writing

The exact origins of writing are lost, probably forever, in the mists of time. Modern scholars still disagree where and when the first substantial examples of writing appeared, some favoring ancient Egypt, others ancient Mesopotamia. Those in the second group think that their argument is strengthened by the discovery in various parts of the Near East of small clay tokens dating from the eighth millennium B.C.,

A wall painting depicting Assyrian dignitaries and scribes before a king. REUNION DES MUSEES NATIONAUX/ART RESOURCE, NY

not long after the rise of settled agriculture in the region. These tokens may have been used by farmers and merchants. The theory is that they pressed the tokens into wet clay, producing marks that recorded business transactions. A certain mark stood for a sheep, another for a bushel of grain, and four of the latter marks indicated four bushels of grain. If this was indeed an early form of writing, it predates the earliest forms found in Egypt.

Over time, after the Mesopotamian plains had been settled by the peoples now called the Ubaidians and the Sumerians, a more sophisticated form of writing appeared. As near as scholars can reckon, sometime between 3500 and 3000 B.C. a complex writing system appeared in the Sumerian city of Uruk. Then it rapidly spread to neighboring towns and other sectors of the Near East. Once again, clay tablets were the basis for writing. People, mostly trained experts in reading and writing called scribes, pressed pointed sticks, reed styluses, or other objects into moist clay tablets; when the tablets dried and hardened, they became cumbersome but permanent records, the world's first ver-

sions of letters, account sheets, and books. In its most mature form, this writing system consisted mainly of small wedge-shaped marks arranged in various combinations. Modern scholars came to call it *cuneiform* after the Latin word *cuneus*, meaning wedge or nail shaped. There were between five hundred and six hundred separate cuneiform signs in all, requiring a great deal of time and effort to master.

The way these signs were used was much more ingenious and complex than the older system of pictograms and ideograms, in which a mark that looked like a sheep or stood for a sheep meant a sheep on a tablet or other surface. By the early third millennium B.C., Sumerian writing was based only in part on picture signs; it also employed the principle of homophony. In this system, the marks made by scribes stood for sounds used in speech, and the sound for a certain object or concept could be used with other such sound signs to create messages and sentences. Gwendolyn Leick, a noted scholar of ancient Mesopotamia, explains:

In Sumerian, the word "house" was a monosyllabic word. Assyriologists assume that it was pronounced like the German "e." The same sound appeared in many other contexts, such as . . . a syllable in longer words. Only the value "house" could be drawn as a picture, but this sign could be equally used for any occasion the phoneme [sound] "e" had to be written. [Over time] the meaning of signs was further enlarged. . . . The sign for "shepherd" could also stand for "to shepherd," and the combination of [the sign for] "head" with a [bowl] near the throat [meant] "to eat." (*The Babylonians*, p. 19)

About five hundred thousand cuneiform tablets using such signs have been discovered so far in Mesopotamia and other parts of the Near East. The vast majority consist of dry administrative and financial records, including bills, accounts received, inventories, volumes of grain or other foodstuffs, and measures of land parcels. Though monotonous, these reveal much about social customs and economic practices, especially among members of the upper classes, who owned the land and controlled commerce. However, some of these tablets preserve actual literature, including myths, hymns to the gods, epic tales of the adventures of human heroes, odes extolling the deeds and virtues of kings, lamentations for the fall of cities and rulers, wedding songs, and proverbs and wise sayings.

Because Sumerian cuneiform—as well as Babylonian, Hittite, and other forms of cuneiform that followed it—was so complex and difficult to learn, it was perhaps inevitable that people would eventually look for easier forms of writing. The answer to this problem proved to be alphabetic signs and scripts, in which one sign stood for a specific sound. Since there are a rather limited number of basic sounds humans can utter, such a system has far fewer signs, or letters. Two alphabetic scripts appeared in the thirteenth century B.C. or shortly thereafter in the region of Syria. One, invented by scribes in the port city of Ugarit, had about thirty letters; the other, introduced by the Phoenicians, had about twenty letters. The Greeks borrowed the Phoenician version and added a few vowel sounds, thereby creating the system that became standard in Europe and, in modified form, is still in use today. The Aramaeans also adopted an alphabetic script similar in some ways to the Phoenician one to write down their own language, Aramaic. Like the Greeks, the Aramaeans added or duplicated certain letters to stand for vowel sounds missing in the Phoenician script. Much simpler than existing cuneiform writing systems, the Aramaic version swept the Near East in the early first millennium B.C. and that language became the lingua franca, or universal tongue, of the region for centuries to come.

SEE ALSO: cuneiform; languages; literature; writing materials

writing materials

A wide variety of writing materials were used in Mesopotamia and surrounding regions over the course of ancient times. Among the earliest, and for a long time the most common, of these was the simple clay tablet. A slab of moist clay was an inexpensive, easy, and inviting medium for conveying any form of writing. It was also quite durable. The clay hardened as it dried, and it could be made even harder and longer lasting by baking it in a fire or oven. Various forms of cuneiform (wedge-shaped writing), including Sumerian, Babylonian, Hittite, and others, were committed to clay tablets from the late fourth millennium B.C. to the first century A.D. Hundreds of thousands of these tablets have survived, and some are on display in museums around the world. A typical tablet included not only a written list, message, or piece of literature but also a colophon. This consisted of a mark or marks made by the scribe as a means of identification; the colophon could include one or a combination of the following: the title of the work; a catchphrase, often consisting of the first line of the work; the scribe's name; or the page number of the tablet if it was part of a long work requiring several tablets. In the case of a personal letter, the tablet was placed in an "envelope" also made of dried clay.

Although clay tablets remained a major writing material in Mesopotamia for a long time, people did use other materials. Cylinder seals, made of clay or stone, were also fairly common. Stelae, consisting of large slabs of stone or dried clay, were also used by rulers to commemorate military victories or issue royal decrees. A cheaper, easier, and more informal medium—the ostrakon, a broken piece of pottery—was also used for scribbling simple messages or records of financial transactions of no particular literary merit or importance. Still other writing media included cliff faces (a famous example being the Behistun Rock); human-made walls; coffin lids; and even jewelry, although there was a limit to how much could be written on a piece of jewelry. Meanwhile, students and scribes in schools often used wooden boards covered in wax, which had the advantage of being reusable. They etched their writing into the wax, which hardened somewhat. Then, whenever they desired, they could add fresh wax or smooth out the old and begin writing something completely new.

Another popular writing material became common in Mesopotamia in the first millennium B.C., although it was known on a more limited basis before that. This was papyrus, a kind of paper made from a marsh plant native to Egypt. The Egyptians exported it to Greece, Italy, Palestine, and other neighboring lands throughout ancient times. The first-century A.D. Roman scholar Pliny the Elder gives this description of how it was made:

> Paper is manufactured from papyrus by splitting it [the plant's stem] with a needle into strips that are very thin but as long as possible. The quality of the papyrus is best at the center of the plant and decreases progressively toward the outsides. . . . All paper is "woven" on a board dampened with water from the Nile [to prevent the strips from drying out]; the muddy liquid acts as glue. First, an upright layer is smeared on the table—the whole length of the papyrus is used and both its ends are trimmed; then strips are laid across and complete a criss-cross pattern, which is then squeezed in presses. The sheets are dried in the sun and then joined together. (*Natural History*, 13.71–74)

Glue was used to accomplish this joining of papyrus sheets. Next, about twenty of the bound sheets were wound around a wooden dowel, making a roll usually 20 or 30 feet (6 or 9m) long. People wrote on the papyrus with a reed or a bronze pen dipped in ink manufactured from soot. Each roll, or "book," held roughly ten- to twenty thousand words of text.

When Aramaic, the alphabetic language of the Aramaeans, became widely used across the Near East in the first millennium B.C., it was often written on papyrus sheets or rolls. Assyrian scribes began using papyrus as a writing material, along with clay tablets, in the eighth century B.C.

A few centuries later the Persians, who inherited the Mesopotamian plains from the Assyrians and the Babylonians, also adopted the dual use of papyrus and clay tablets. The Greeks, who followed the Persians in the area, had been using papyrus for some time, as well as parchment made from dried and stretched animal hides. Seleucid merchants and scribes used both of these writing media as well as most of the others mentioned above.

SEE ALSO: languages; literature; scribe; writing

Xenophon
(ca. 430 B.C.–354 B.C.)

A noted Greek historian, social commentator, soldier, and adventurer who visited and wrote about Mesopotamia and its peoples in some detail in his book the *Anabasis* (or *March Up-Country*). Xenophon (ZEN-uh-phon) was born into a wealthy Athenian family shortly after the outbreak of the Peloponnesian War (431–404 B.C.), a devastating conflict in which most of the Greek city-states sided with one or the other of the two leading combatants, Athens and Sparta. His entire childhood and young adulthood took place during troubled times in which his city and fellow citizens suffered serious physical and emotional trauma as well as a major loss of prestige after the Athenians lost the war. Thus, it is not surprising that as he grew up, Xenophon became disillusioned with Athens. He was even more upset when, five years later, his friend, the eccentric philosopher Socrates, was prosecuted in court on trumped-up charges that he had corrupted the city's youth with his ideas and was then summarily executed. Xenophon was angry and bitter over what he saw as a miscarriage of justice and later vigorously defended Socrates in a treatise titled *Memorabilia* (*Memories of Socrates*).

Extremely bitter over Socrates' death and disgruntled with Athenian politics, Xenophon was also one of many Greek youths in that era who had known nothing but war. When the Peloponnesian conflict ended, thousands of young men who had been trained to fight were in need of some new outlet to channel their energies. Therefore, many became mercenaries, or soldiers for hire. This is how Xenophon joined a force of some ten thousand Greek troops who, in 401 B.C., signed on to fight for a Persian prince named Cyrus the Younger. This young aristocrat desired to usurp the throne of his older brother, Artaxerxes II, the reigning king. To this end, Cyrus gathered as many native Persian troops as he could and filled out the rest of his army with Greeks and other mercenaries. Cyrus led these forces from Sardis in western Asia Minor overland to Cunaxa, about 50 miles (80km) from Babylon in what is now Iraq.

There, Artaxerxes, who had by now learned of the rebellion, was waiting with a larger army. In the major battle that followed, Cyrus was killed and Xenophon and his fellow Greeks now found themselves stranded in a foreign land and completely surrounded by hostile forces. Artaxerxes' officers invited the Greek commander, Clearchos, to peace talks, but this was a sinister ploy, as Clearchos and most of the officers who accompanied him were slaughtered the moment they entered the Persian negotiation tent. (A few were killed later.) Outraged at such treachery, the Greek soldiers immediately chose new leaders, including Xenophon. Most agreed that there was nothing else to do but retreat and fight their way out of Persia or at least die trying. When the army was assembled, someone asked Xenophon to give

Xenophon and the Ten Thousand (a Greek force that supported Cyrus the Younger of Persia) reach the Black Sea after their long overland trek. Time Life Pictures/Mansell/Time Life Pictures/Getty Images

a speech to raise everyone's spirits. "You see," he told his comrades at the time,

> that the enemy dared not make war upon us until they had seized our leaders. . . . When they took our commanders, they thought we would be destroyed by anarchy and disorder. . . . So the enemy will find themselves mightily mistaken. For this day they will see ten thousand Clearchoses instead of one. (*Anabasis* 3.2)

With this defiant attitude, the band of Greeks set out on an incredible overland trek of more than 1,000 miles (1,609km). They weathered daunting hardships, including fending off assaults by Persian troops and fierce hill tribesmen and trudging through deep mountain snows. Eventually, most of the "Ten Thousand," as they

became known to Greeks everywhere, made it back to their homes.

However, Xenophon opted to stay in Asia a while longer, probably because he loathed the idea of returning to Athens and what he saw as a fickle, ethically challenged government. Instead, he joined a Spartan army that at the time was campaigning against Persian forces in Anatolia. Later, a Spartan king who had befriended Xenophon helped him acquire an attractive country estate near Olympia in southwestern Greece. There, Xenophon settled down and for more than two decades devoted himself to tending his lands and writing books. These included the *Anabasis*, still considered to be one of the greatest adventure stories ever penned; the *Hellenica* (*History of Greece*); the *Oeconomicus* (*Estate Manager*); the

Symposium (*After-Dinner Drinking Party*), in which his old mentor Socrates plays a key role; and some brief military treatises, among them *The Art of Horsemanship*.

Unfortunately for Xenophon, his tranquil life on his estate came to an abrupt end in 371 B.C. In that year Sparta was defeated by another major Greek city-state, Thebes; and many Spartans and Spartan sympathizers lost their lands, including Xenophon. He returned to Athens, but for reasons unknown did not stay long there. Not long after moving to nearby Corinth, he died in about 354 B.C.

In retrospect, Xenophon's personal participation in some conflicts, and nonparticipation in others, strongly affected the quality of his writing. When describing events he did not take part in, for instance in most of his *Hellenica*, he was a mediocre historian who often injected his personal moral judgments and left out important historical events. In contrast, when he witnessed battles firsthand, Xenophon was a far better reporter and produced a more reliable and moving account. The prime example is his *Anabasis*, which remains one of the most important and enlightening documents ever written about ancient Mesopotamia.

SEE ALSO: *Anabasis*; Greeks; historical accounts. And for other quotes about Mesopotamia by Xenophon, see Armenia; Battle of Cunaxa; chariots; clothing; Cyrus the Younger; Cyrus II

Xerxes
(reigned 486–465 B.C.)

An Achaemenid Persian king who succeeded his father, Darius I, and is most famous for his attempted invasion of mainland Greece in 480 B.C. Darius, who in a highly fruitful reign had extended the boundaries of the Persian Empire far beyond Iran and Mesopotamia, had three sons by his first wife. He also had four more sons by his second wife, Atossa. Of the two women, Atossa enjoyed the most influence with the king and his court. So when Darius passed away in 486 B.C., her eldest son, Xerxes (ZERK-seez), ascended the throne. An inscription on a tablet uncovered by archaeologists in the ruins of one of the Persian capitals, Persepolis, reads, "Darius also had other sons, but by the will of Ahura-Mazda [the chief Persian god] he made me [Xerxes] the greatest after himself. When Darius, my father, passed away, by the will of Ahura-Mazda I became king."

Once king, Xerxes was immediately faced with the nagging reality that he had inherited his father's vendetta against the Greeks—in particular the Athenians—for their defeat of a Persian army at Marathon, near Athens, in 490 B.C. At first the young ruler expressed little interest in pursuing his father's plans for revenge. These plans had included initiating a conquest of Europe as well as laying waste to Athens. Over time, however, some of Xerxes' advisers, who had earlier urged Darius to wage a war in Europe, began to work on him. The new king's brother-in-law, Mardonius, for example, argued that the Athenians must not go unpunished and added that Europe was a beautiful, bountiful region ripe for Persian exploitation. Eventually Xerxes relented and actually showed considerable enthusiasm for the venture. "I have found a way to win for Persia not glory only but a country as large and as rich as our own," he told his chief followers,

and at the same time to get satisfaction and revenge. . . . I will bridge the Hellespont [today the Dardanelles, the strait separating Anatolia from north-ern Greece] and march an army ... into Greece, and punish the Athenians for the outrage they committed upon my father and upon us. ... We shall so extend the empire of Persia that its boundaries will be God's own sky, so that the sun will not look down upon any land beyond the boundaries of what is ours. With your help I shall pass through Europe from end to end and make it all one country. (Quoted in Herodotus, *Histories* 7.8–9)

Egyptian Campaigns But before Xerxes' dreams of European conquest could be realized, he was forced to deal with some problems closer to home. Shortly before Darius's death, Egypt had risen in rebel-lion. His son's first priority after assuming the throne was to bring this valuable asset back into the imperial fold. By 484 B.C. Xerxes had managed to put down the Egyptian insurrection. To make it clear that he would tolerate no more such revolts, he confiscated many of the lands belonging to Egypt's local temples and imposed stricter rules and penalties on the natives. He also appointed as the Persian satrap, or governor, of Egypt someone he felt he could trust implicitly, his brother Achaemenes, named after the founder of the Achaemenid dynasty.

The trouble in Egypt had no sooner been disposed of when Xerxes faced an-other major challenge. In 483 B.C. the Persian satrap of Babylon, Zopryas, was murdered and his killer, a man named Shamasheriba, declared himself king of Babylon. Quick to respond, Xerxes sent his best general, Megabyzus, to deal with the usurper. Megabyzus easily recaptured Babylon, and per Xerxes' orders, his sol-diers tore down the city's defensive walls, demolished several of its temples, and

confiscated the estates of its wealthiest citizens.

Xerxes' handling of the two rebellions showed that he was a formidable ruler who would act swiftly against would-be rebels and transgressors. Another strength he shared with his father was his patient and thorough approach to war preparations. This became apparent in the ongoing military buildup for the invasion of Greece and Europe. Far in advance of the army's arrival, Persian engineers and laborers constructed impressive boat bridges over the Hellespont to facilitate the crossing into Europe. According to Herodotus:

> Galleys and triremes [warships] were lashed together to support the bridges—360 vessels for the one on the [Anatolian] side, and 314 for the other. They were moored slantwise ... and at right angles to the Hellespont, in order to lessen the strain on the cables. Specially heavy anchors were laid out both upstream and down-stream. ... Once the vessels were in position, the cables [made of flax] were hauled taut by wooden winches ashore. ... The next operation was to cut planks equal in length to the width of the floats, lay them edge to edge over the taut cables, and then bind them together on their upper surface. That done, brushwood was put on top and spread evenly, with a layer of soil, trodden hard, over all. Finally a paling [fence] was con-structed along each side, high enough to prevent horses and mules from see-ing over and taking fright at the water. (*Histories* 7.36–37)

Invasion of Greece It was across this makeshift but sturdy bridge that Xerxes led what turned out to be the largest single invasion force ever launched in ancient times. It consisted of roughly two hundred thousand foot soldiers and up to a thousand ships, plus tens of thousands of support personnel and camp followers. After making his way into mainland Greece, Xerxes won a technical victory at the pass of Thermopylae by killing the handful of Greeks who were defending the pass, and were led by Sparta's King Leonidas. But before they died, these few Greeks slew some twenty thousand Persians, fully a tenth of Xerxes' land forces. Though furious over these losses, the Persian monarch marched on and did manage to occupy and burn Athens. In his view, this fulfilled his father's revenge on that city. However, Xerxes' war fleet was disastrously defeated by a Greek fleet soon afterward at Salamis, southwest of Athens, as he watched in horror from a nearby hilltop. He was forced to retire to Anatolia. To make matters worse, the land army he left behind under the command of Mardonius was almost annihilated by the Greeks in the following year.

Little of a substantial nature is known about the remainder of Xerxes' reign. But a few bold highlights stand out, including the defeat of another of his armies at the hands of the Greeks circa 469 B.C. at Eurymedon in southern Anatolia; his construction of several fine public buildings, including a huge ceremonial gateway, in his capital of Persepolis; and the addition of magnificent sculpted reliefs on the massive, elegant staircases leading to the entrance of the grand audience hall in that city. Xerxes was ultimately assassinated by a group of palace conspirators and was succeeded by his eighteen-year-old son, Artaxerxes I.

SEE ALSO: Darius I; Greeks; Persepolis; Persian Empire

Yaggid-Lim
(reigned ca. 1830–1820 B.C.)

The founder of the Amorite dynasty at Mari, a prosperous trading city on the upper Euphrates River. For details, see under his more commonly used name, Iaggid-Lim.

SEE ALSO: Amorites; Iahdun-Lim; Mari

Yahdun-Lim
(reigned ca. 1820–1796 B.C.)

The son of Iaggid-Lim (or Yaggid-Lim) and the second ruler of the Amorite dynasty at Mari. For details, see under his more commonly used name, Iahdun-Lim.

SEE ALSO: Amorites; Iaggid-Lim; Mari

Zab rivers

The two main tributaries of the Tigris, one of the two major rivers (along with the Euphrates) that flow through the plains of Mesopotamia. The Zab waterways are usually referred to separately either as the Upper and Lower Zab or the Great and Little Zab. The Upper Zab rises in the mountains of southeastern Anatolia, today encompassed by Turkey, and flows for some 265 miles (426km) to its junction with the Tigris near the important city of Mosul. The Lower Zab rises in the hills of northeastern Iran and flows for 250 miles (402km) before meeting the Tigris just north of the modern town of Baiji in northern Iraq. Along with the Tigris itself, the Upper and Lower Zab and the regions along their banks were the principal focus of Assyrian civilization. The Assyrians used the rivers for transportation as well as for water for drinking, cooking, bathing, and watering crops. To facilitate the latter, they built canals that diverted water from the rivers.

SEE ALSO: Assyrian Empire; farming; Tigris and Euphrates

Zagros Mountains

A major and imposing range of mountains that borders Mesopotamia in the west and southwest and played an important part in the history of the region. The Zagros peaks make up Iraq's principal mountain chain and Iran's second-largest chain. They run for some 930 miles (1,500km) from the highlands of western Iran southeastward to a point near the Strait of Hormuz on the Persian Gulf. The highest point in the Zagros chain is the peak called Zard Kuh, rising to an impressive height of 14,917 feet (4,548m). The Zagros foothills contain numerous valleys, some of them well watered and fertile; these became the main focus of a number of ancient peoples who variously traded with, fought, or invaded the Mesopotamian plains. Among the leading peoples of the western side of the Zagros range were the Elamites, longtime rivals of the Babylonians, and the Guti, who invaded Mesopotamia in the late third millennium B.C. The eastern and northern valleys of the Zagros foothills were settled by the Medes and later by their cousins, the Persians, whose main homeland was Fars, just north of the Persian Gulf.

SEE ALSO: Elam; Guti; Medes

Zephaniah

A book of the Hebrew Old Testament that contains references to major invasions of Palestine by Mesopotamian realms as well as to the fall of one of the most formidable of them—the Assyrian Empire. The identity of the author of the book is unclear. If he was a real person, he likely traced his ancestry back to Hezekiah, a ruler of the Hebrew kingdom of Judah. On the other hand, some scholars suggest that someone else wrote the book and used the name of Zephaniah rather than his own. The period in which the book was written is also a matter of dispute. The most accepted theory is that it dates from the early seventh century B.C. Supporting this view

is the fact that it mentions Assyria's invasion of Palestine in the second half of the
preceding century. (The Assyrians destroyed the kingdom of Israel in the 720s
B.C. They also invaded Judah a few years
later but were unable to bring it down.)
The author, awed by these dire, seemingly
earth-shaking events, perhaps understand-
ably placed them in the same sort of
apocalyptic framework that appears in
Genesis when God causes the great flood
to punish humanity for its sins. According
to Zephaniah, God proclaimed:

> I will stretch out my hand against
> Judah, and against all the inhabitants
> of Jerusalem. And I will cut off from
> this place the remnant of Baal [a
> heathen idol] and the name of the
> idolatrous priests, those who have. . . .
> turned back from following the Lord.
> . . . I will search Jerusalem with lamps
> and I will punish the men . . . who
> say in their hearts, "The Lord will not
> do good, nor will he do ill."
> (Zephaniah 1.4–6, 12)

In contrast, some scholars think that the
book of Zephaniah was written later,
perhaps as late as 300 or even 200 B.C. Part
of this argument rests on the fact that the
author mentions the destruction of the
Assyrian Empire, at one point in the past
tense, which occurred more than a century
after Assyria destroyed Israel:

> And he [God] will stretch out his
> hand against the north and destroy
> Assyria. And he will make [the Assyr-
> ian capital of] Nineveh a desolation, a
> dry waste like the desert. . . . What a
> desolation she [Assyria] has become.
> . . . Everyone who passes by her hisses
> and shakes his fist. (Zephaniah
> 2.13–15)

SEE ALSO: Assyrian Empire; Bible; Judah

ziggurat

A pyramid-like structure erected in many
ancient Mesopotamian cities, usually near
a temple or as part of a temple complex,
and used for religious ceremonial purposes. The modern term is derived from
the Akkadian word *ziqqurratu*. Although
they superficially resemble Egyptian pyramids, Mesopotamian ziggurats were different in some important ways. First, whereas
Egyptian pyramids were primarily used as
tombs for kings or other noble persons,
ziggurats were seen as dwelling places of
gods and were used by Mesopotamian
priests during religious worship. Also, ziggurats were solid structures having no
internal chambers, unlike Egyptian pyramids, which were honeycombed with pas-
sageways and burial chambers. In addition, Egyptian pyramids had no stairways
on the outside and came to a point at the
top. In contrast, a ziggurat had a large
stairway, or in some cases a ramp, for
priests or kings to walk upward, and at the
top of a ziggurat was a small chapel or
temple. One way in which ziggurats were
similar to Egyptian pyramids is that both
kinds of structures were viewed as symbolic representations of the primeval, or
very ancient, mound of creation, the first
land to appear on Earth.

Typically, ziggurats were constructed
of dried mud bricks, sometimes with a
layer of more durable oven-baked bricks
on the outside. Evidence also indicates that
they were multicolored, each succeeding
level painted in a different, usually bright
color. In general, most Babylonian ziggurats were freestanding and separate from
other buildings in a temple complex. Assyrian ziggurats, by contrast, were usually
attached directly in some way to a ground-
level temple. Overall, these structures were
intended as "ladders to the gods" or

An example of a ziggurat, a pyramid-like structure used for religious ceremonial purposes in many ancient Mesopotamian cities. © ROGER WOOD/CORBIS

"stairways to heaven," so to speak, so that the priests who ascended the steps or ramp could be nearer to divine forces than ordinary people. Ziggurats also had a political dimension. In this regard, they were signs of the wealth, power, and prestige of the city-states, nations, or empires that could afford to erect them. Indeed, they were extremely expensive to build because each one took thousands of laborers many years to complete.

So far, archaeologists have found the remains of thirty-two ziggurats in and around the Mesopotamian plains. Of these, four are in southern Iran; most of the rest are in Iraq. The earliest examples were erected in the third millennium B.C., and the last appeared in the sixth century B.C. Among the best-preserved examples is the ziggurat at Choga Zanbil (or Dur-Untash), near Susa in southwestern Iran. The ziggurat at Ur in southeastern Mesopotamia, investigated in detail by the great Assyriologist Charles Leonard Woolley in the 1920s, is also fairly well preserved. In contrast, little is left of one of the greatest of all the ziggurats. This was the Etemenanki, dedicated to the god Marduk, in Babylon. Today, only a few sections of the base survive, but experts believe that in its heyday it had three large staircases leading to the upper temple, and that the temple was painted a bright indigo.

Interestingly, a number of modern architects have admired the ziggurat and copied its style in their own buildings. One of the more striking examples is the University of Tennessee's Hodges Library in Knoxville, completed in 1987; it features a series of stepped levels that resemble those of an ancient ziggurat.

SEE ALSO: building materials and methods; temples; Ur

Zimri-Lim
(reigned ca. 1775–1761 B.C.)

A noted ruler of the city-state of Mari, situated on the upper Euphrates. When Zimri-Lim was still a child, his father, Iahdun-Lim, the second Amorite ruler of the city, was murdered, possibly by one of the boy's brothers. Not long afterward, the formidable early Assyrian king Shamshi-Adad I attacked and captured Mari, forcing Zimri-Lim, then in line for Mari's throne, into exile. For several years to come, one of Shamshi-Adad's sons, Iasmah-Adad, ruled Mari. But following Shamshi-Adad's death in about 1781 B.C., Zimri-Lim returned to his native city and reclaimed the throne.

A skilled ruler and diplomat, Zimri-Lim proceeded to make valuable alliances with several Syrian city-states as well as with King Hammurabi of Babylon. This helped Mari to expand its trade and wealth. Zimri-Lim put these monies to good use, initiating building programs in Mari, including the construction of an impressive new palace. He also maintained the city's vast archive of clay tablets bearing cuneiform characters. Many of these tablets were letters exchanged by Zimri-Lim, his Assyrian predecessors at Mari, and rulers of cities across Mesopotamia and Syria. These documents discuss a wide range of subjects, ranging from serious affairs of state to relatively trivial matters such as obtaining ice to cool the king's drinks. As fate would have it, one of Zimri-Lim's correspondents in these letters, Hammurabi, turned out to be more of a nemesis than an ally. In about 1761 B.C., Hammurabi's army swept across the plains, defeated Zimri-Lim's forces, and sacked Mari.

SEE ALSO: Hammurabi; Mari; palaces

Zoroaster
(flourished sometime between 1700 and 1000 B.C.?)

A semilegendary religious prophet venerated by the ancient Persians and credited with establishing Zoroastrianism, the chief religion of the ancient Persian Empire. Zoroaster (also known as Zarathustra) was known to the Persians as Zartosht and to the ancient Greeks as Zorastres. Most modern scholars think he may have been a real person. However, they differ widely on when he lived and preached. Ancient Greek and Roman writers tended to assign Zoroaster to very early times, often as far back as 6000 B.C. The vast majority of scholars have rejected this notion, and many do not accept another common ancient claim that he lived in the seventh or sixth century B.C., not long before the founding of the Achaemenid Persian

Empire. Modern linguistic studies of early Zoroastrian writings, such as the *Gathas*, have suggested a rough date of 1700 B.C. Mary Boyce, of the University of London's School of Oriental and African Studies, the world's leading scholar of Zoroastrianism, places Zoroaster's life sometime between 1400 and 1000 B.C.

Whenever Zoroaster lived, assuming he was a real person, most of what little is known about his life comes from Zoroastrian writings, mainly the *Avesta* and the *Gathas*. It appears that he was born and raised in Iran or perhaps in Bactria (now Afghanistan), where he did much of his preaching. He had a beloved wife named Hvov and three daughters and three sons. As the story goes, at about the age of thirty Zoroaster had a vision of God, similar to the later visions experienced by Christianity's St. Paul and Islam's great prophet, Muhammad. The deity with which Zoroaster made contact was Ahura-Mazda ("the Wise Lord"), who subsequently became the main Persian god. Ahura-Mazda revealed certain truths to Zoroaster, including the existence of an ongoing battle between the forces of good and evil and the need for human beings to do good works. The prophet immediately converted his wife, children, and cousin to the new faith. But at first he had difficulty converting others; most of the residents of his hometown, for example, initially mocked him. In time, however, Zoroaster gained additional followers, and the new faith spread. Eventually it thrived in Iran, especially under the Persians. For Zoroaster's basic teachings and more about his faith, **see** Zoroastrianism.

SEE ALSO: *Avesta*; Persian Empire

Zoroastrianism

The chief religion of the ancient Achae-menid Persians and later the Sassanian Persians, a faith based on the teachings of the ancient Iranian prophet Zoroaster (or Zarathustra). There is some debate among modern scholars, however, over which Persians practiced the faith. Some experts think that only the kings, royal families, nobles, priests, and a few other upper-class individuals openly practiced it; whereas others argue that Zoroastrianism was more widespread among ordinary Persians. It is also possible that different versions of the Zoroastrian faith existed. Perhaps the king, nobles, and priests practiced an orthodox, or strict and conservative, version, while ordinary folk followed a less strict version. Until more reliable evidence comes to light, Zoroastrianism as practiced by the ancient Persians will remain somewhat mysterious.

What is certain is that during the centuries they controlled Mesopotamia and other parts of the Near East, the Achaemenid Persians did not attempt to impose the Zoroastrian faith on their subject peoples. Thus, many Persian subjects in Mesopotamia, Anatolia, Palestine, Egypt, and elsewhere continued to worship their traditional gods. A number of Persian monarchs did destroy some local temples in subject lands; but these acts were usually meant to punish a city or region for disloyalty or some other offense rather than to suppress the local religion.

Zoroastrian Gods Some of the earlier inhabitants of Iran had worshipped a number of sky gods known as *daevas*, among them Ahura-Mazda ("the Wise Lord"). It was the prophet Zoroaster, who may have lived in the mid-to-late second millennium B.C., who elevated Ahura-Mazda to the status of chief god of the faith he founded. (The Greeks identified

Zoroastrian fire altars were used by Zoroastrian priests to sacrifice animals to the god Ahura-Mazda. © ROGER WOOD/CORBIS

Ahura-Mazda with their own chief god, Zeus.)

According to legend and some basic Zoroastrian sacred writings, Ahura-Mazda revealed to Zoroaster several truths about life and the world. Among these, which became central tenets of the new faith, was that an eternal struggle between good and evil was ongoing. The combatants in this mighty contest were sometimes described as "the Truth" (*Asa*) and "the Lie" (*Drug*). In the struggle, Ahura-Mazda was the champion of truth and goodness; he was assisted by six sacred, immortal beings, the Amesha Spentas. Meanwhile, evil was propagated by a dark being or force called Ahriman. Ahriman's main followers were the old *daevas*, now designated as destructive demons.

Beliefs and Practices In the Zoroastrian

faith, human worshippers were expected to follow and support Ahura-Mazda, reject Ahriman and his lies, give aid to the poor and helpless, and revere a sacred fire that was meant never to be extinguished. In general, worshippers were supposed to have good thoughts (known to the faithful as *Humata*), say good words (*Hukhta*), and practice good deeds (*Huvarshta*). Those who followed these rules were seen as decent and upright and called *ashavans*. People who ignored or violated the rules were viewed as corrupt and were referred to as *drugvans*. The *drugvans* were supposedly condemned to spend all of eternity in a hell-like abode called the Place of Worst Existence.

As is the case in all religions, the basic beliefs of Zoroastrianism were accompanied by numerous rituals and customs. Although all the details of these practices have not survived, scholars have been able to piece together the basics of some of them. Some rituals dealt not only with sacred fire but also with the proper treatment of water. J.M. Cook, a leading expert on ancient Persia, elaborates:

> The [Zoroastrian] Persians were especially concerned with purity. Fire and water must not be defiled. It was forbidden to wash in a river, and nicety and privacy were observed in the performance of bodily functions [such as urinating and spitting]. . . . Fire being divine, burning of the dead would be pollution. Bodies were waxed before interment [burial]. . . . Sacrifices were made without fire . . . and other accompaniments that the Greeks were accustomed to. (*The Persian Empire*, p. 154)

Thus, instead of using fire burning on an altar, leading Zoroastrian priests, called Magi, sacrificed animals to Ahura-Mazda in a unique way, as described by the Greek historian Herodotus. Just before a sacrifice began, Herodotus writes,

> a man sticks a spray of leaves, usually myrtle leaves, into his headdress, takes his victim [the sacrificial animal] to some open place and invokes [calls upon] the deity. . . . The actual worshiper is not permitted to pray for any personal or private blessing, but only for the king and the general good of the community. . . . When he has cut up the animal and cooked it, he makes a little heap of the softest green-stuff he can find, preferably clover, and lays all the meat upon it. This done, a Magus [the singular of *Magi*] . . . utters an incantation [magic spell] over it. . . . Then, after a short interval, the worshiper removes the flesh and does what he pleases with it. (*Histories* 1.133)

It appears that among the other religious customs practiced by the Magi and other strict Zoroastrians was the slaying of certain kinds of animals. They viewed cattle and dogs as worthy beasts and preached good treatment of them. By contrast, they saw certain other creatures, particularly "crawling things," as evil followers of Ahriman and the Lie and advocated killing them. According to Herodotus:

> The Magi are quite different from the Egyptian priests and indeed from any other sort of person. The Egyptian priests make it an article of religion to kill no living creature except for sacrifice, but the Magi not only kill . . . with their own hands, but make a special point of doing so. [The animals they destroy include] ants [and] snakes. (*Histories* 1.142)

Historical Legacy The Zoroastrian faith did not die out long ago, as did the majority of ancient religions. Although the numbers of its adherents declined over time, today about .25 million people still follow a somewhat modernized version of the faith. Most of these people live in the Middle East, but a few reside in Europe, including roughly 4,000 in Britain.

Ancient Zoroastrianism has also had some interesting, usually subtle effects on modern Western culture. Notable was the use of the founder of the faith, under his alternate name of Zarathustra, by the important nineteenth-century German philosopher Friedrich Nietzsche (NEE-chee). In his book *Thus Spoke Zarathustra*, Nietzsche creates a somewhat fictionalized version of the prophet; in the book, the author makes Zarathustra actually reject the concepts of ultimate good and evil and acknowledge the death of God. Not long after the book was published, the great German composer Richard Strauss composed an orchestral piece based on it. And in 1967, famed film director Stanley Ku-brick used the dramatic opening section of Strauss's music in his landmark film *2001: A Space Odyssey*, which incorporates a number of Nietzsche's ideas about humanity.

This progression of certain religious and cultural ideas through the courses of many civilizations over the span of several millennia is enlightening for observers of ancient Mesopotamia and of history in general. It is an excellent illustration of how many of the ideas and customs that were native to the peoples of ancient Mesopotamia survived the ravages of time and human destruction; over time, they mutated as circumstances dictated and became intricately interwoven into the fabric of modern societies whose existence Zoroaster, Sargon, Hammurabi, Cyrus, and Alexander could never have dreamed of.

SEE ALSO: Herodotus; Magi; Persian Empire

Chronology

B.C.

ca. 10,000–9000

Agriculture begins in the Fertile Crescent, an arc-shaped region lying along the northern rim of the Mesopotamian plains.

ca. 5500

People from the Fertile Crescent begin to descend from the hills and settle in the Tigris and Euphrates river valley.

ca. 5000–3500

One of a number of scholarly estimates for the period in which the people of the Ubaidian culture live in small villages in parts of Mesopotamia.

ca. 3500–3000

The Sumerians begin to build the first Mesopotamian cities in the plain lying just northwest of the Persian Gulf; they also begin using a complex writing system that evolves into what modern scholars call cuneiform.

ca. 2300

An ambitious individual named Sargon establishes the first-known empire—the Akkadian Empire—thereby uniting northern and southern Mesopotamia for the time.

2112

Ur-Nammu, king of the city of Ur, establishes a new empire, the Third Dynasty of Ur.

2004

The Elamites, from the hills east of the Mesopotamian plains, sack Ur; the Third Dynasty of Ur falls apart.

ca. 2000

An unknown Babylonian scribe collects and writes down the epic tales of the early Mesopotamian hero Gilgamesh.

ca. 1813–1781

The reign of Shamshi-Adad, founder of Assyria's first royal dynasty and the first of that nation's rulers about whom any details are known.

1759

Babylonian king Hammurabi conquers the kingdom of Mari, located on the upper Euphrates, and soon afterward absorbs Ashur and the other Assyrian cities.

ca. 1595

Babylon is sacked by the Hittites, whose homeland lies in central Anatolia (what is now Turkey); the Hittites fail to follow up on their victory, and a group of newcomers to the region, the Kassites, establish a dynasty in Babylon.

ca. 1365–1330

The reign of Ashur-uballit I, the first major king of Assyria's second phase of expansion in Mesopotamia.

ca. 1200

Many cities in the western parts of the Near East are sacked and burned, including those of the Hittites, by waves of people from southeastern Europe; in Mesopotamia, Assyria and Babylonia largely escape the destruction.

ca. 744–727

The reign of King Tiglathpileser III, who reasserts Assyrian domination over many areas in the Near East.

ca. 722–705

The reign of Sargon II, founder of the Assyrian Sargonid dynasty, who crushes numerous rebellions and builds a new royal palace northeast of Nineveh.

ca. 668–627

The reign of Ashurbanipal, who inherits the Assyrian Empire at its height of power.

ca. 626

A Chaldean ruler, Nabopolassar, seizes Babylon and launches a war against Assyria.

ca. 615

Media's King Cyaxares attacks Assyria from the east; the following year he captures and sacks Ashur, the most sacred of Assyria's cities; Cyaxares and Nabopolassar form an anti-Assyrian alliance.

612

A combined Babylonian-Median army ravages the Assyrian heartland, destroying Nimrud and Nineveh.

ca. 605–562

The reign of the Neo-Babylonian king Nebuchadnezzar II, who oversees vast new building projects in Babylon, including temples, palaces, and the famous Hanging Gardens of Babylon.

589

Cyaxares invades the kingdom of Lydia in Anatolia.

559

A capable, ambitious Persian nobleman named Cyrus rises to the throne of Fars, a small southern Iranian vassal of the Median Empire.

539

Having conquered and absorbed Media, Cyrus captures Babylon.

525

Cyrus's son, Cambyses, invades Egypt.

ca. 522

A nobleman named Darius becomes king of the Persian Empire.

512

Darius crosses into Europe and invades Scythia, lying west of the Black Sea.

490

Two of Darius's generals land their army at Marathon, on Greece's eastern coast, where a small Athenian army defeats them.

480

Darius's son, Xerxes, invades Greece with a much larger army; the Greeks soundly defeat the Persians in a large naval battle at Salamis, near Athens.

401

Ten thousand Greek mercenaries who are backing a rebellious Persian prince find themselves stranded in the center of Mesopotamia but manage to fight their way across the plains to safety. Their story is later told by one of their number, Xenophon, in his *Anabasis*.

334

Macedonian conqueror Alexander the Great invades the Persian Empire and in a mere decade conquers it.

323

Alexander dies at Babylon, after which his leading generals, the so-called Successors, fight a series of wars for possession of his huge empire.

281

After carving out a new Near Eastern empire centered in Mesopotamia, one of the Successors, Seleucus, dies.

141

The Parthians, having risen to power in northern Iran, are in control of most of the shrunken Seleucid realm, including Mesopotamia.

A.D.

224

The Sassanians, hailing from southern Iran, overrun the Parthian Empire.

637–651

Muslim Arab armies conquer much of the Sassanian-controlled Near East, including the region of Mesopotamia.

1845–1851

British-sponsored archaeologist Austen Henry Layard excavates the Assyrian capitals of Nimrud and Nineveh, making numerous important discoveries, including magnificent carved bas-reliefs depicting the exploits of Assyria's kings.

1849

English linguist Henry C. Rawlinson makes great strides in the decipherment of the ancient Mesopotamian writing system called cuneiform.

1872

English scholar and archaeologist George Smith translates the Mesopotamian epic tale of the hero Gilgamesh, which had a profound effect on the literatures of later ancient cultures.

1902

A team of French archaeologists discovers a tablet bearing the famous law code of the Babylonian king Hammurabi.

1932

Establishment of the modern nation of Iraq, which covers much of the region of ancient Mesopotamia.

For Further Research

A Note on Primary Sources, All direct quotations in this book that are not cited in the text are taken from one of the following sixteen sources:

Jean Bottero, *Mesopotamia: Writing, Reading, and the Gods*. Chicago: University of Chicago Press, 1992.

Trevor Bryce, *The Kingdom of the Hittites*, Oxford, UK: Clarendon, 1998.

C.W. Ceram, ed., *Hands on the Past: Pioneer Archaeologists Tell Their Own Story*. New York: Knopf, 1966.

Stephanie Dalley, trans., *Myths from Mesopotamia*. New York: Oxford University Press, 1989.

The Electronic Text Corpus of Sumerian Literature, www-etcsl.orient.ox.ac.uk.

Benjamin R. Foster, *Before the Muses: An Anthology of Akkadian Literature*. 2 vols. Bethesda, MD: CDL, 1996.

A.K. Grayson, ed., *Assyrian and Babylonian Chronicles*. Locust Valley, NY: Augustine, 1975.

Internet Ancient History Sourcebook, www.fordham.edu/halsall/ancient/asbook.html.

L.W. King, trans., *The Law Code of Hammurabi*. Chicago: Encyclopaedia Britannica, 1910.

Jorgen Laessoe, *People of Ancient Assyria: Their Inscriptions and Correspondence*. Trans. F.S. Leigh-Browne. London: Routledge and Kegan Paul, 1963.

Miriam Lichtheim, ed., *Ancient Egyptian Literature: A Book of Readings*. 2 vols. Berkeley and Los Angeles: University of California Press, 1975–1976.

Livius: Articles in Ancient History, "Achaemenid Royal Inscriptions,"www .livius.org/aa-ac/achaemenians/inscriptions.html.

Daniel D. Luckenbill, ed., *Ancient Records of Assyria and Babylonia*. 2 vols. New York: Greenwood, 1968.

Leo Oppenheim, ed., *Letters from Mesopotamia: Official, Business, and Private Letters on Clay Tablets from Two Millennia*. Chicago: University of Chicago Press, 1967.

James B. Pritchard, ed., *Ancient Near Eastern Texts Relating to the Old Testament*. Princeton, NJ: Princeton University Press, 1969.

M.A. Roth, *Law Collections from Mesopotamia and Asia Minor*. Atlanta: Scholars, 1997.

Selected Translations of Ancient Sources

Arrian, *Anabasis Alexandri*, published as *The Campaigns of Alexander*. Trans. Aubrey de Sélincourt. New York: Penguin, 1971.

M.M. Austin, ed., *The Hellenistic World from Alexander to the Roman Conquest: A Selection of Ancient Sources in Translation*. Cambridge, UK: Cambridge University Press, 1981.

Bible, Revised Standard Version. New York: Thomas Nelson and Sons, 1952.

James Darmesteter and F. Max Muller, eds., *The Zend Avesta*. Whitefish, MT:

Kessinger, 2004. A collection of translations of several parts of the ancient Persian *Avesta*.

Benjamin R. Foster, ed., *From Distant Days: Myths, Tales, and Poetry of Ancient Mesopotamia*. Bethesda, MD: CDL, 1995.

Robert F. Harper, trans., *The Law Code of Hammurabi*. Chicago: University of Chicago Press, 1904.

Herodotus, *The Histories*. Trans. Aubrey de Sélincourt. New York: Penguin, 1972.

Josephus, *Antiquities of the Jews*, in *The New Complete Works of Josephus*. Trans. William Whiston. Grand Rapids, MI: Kregel, 1999.

Maureen G. Kovacs, trans., *The Epic of Gilgamesh*. Palo Alto, CA: Stanford University Press, 1990.

John Maier and John Gardner, trans., *The Epic of Gilgamesh*. New York: Vintage, 1981.

Plutarch, *Life of Alexander*, *Life of Artaxerxes*, and other biographies of ancient figures (parts of his larger work, *Parallel Lives*), in *Plutarch: The Age of Alexander*. Trans. Ian Scott-Kilvert. New York: Penguin, 1973; and in *Plutarch's Lives of the Noble Grecians and Romans*. Trans. John Dryden. New York: Random House, 1932.

Leroy Waterman, ed., *Royal Correspondence of the Assyrian Empire*. 4 vols. Ann Arbor: University of Michigan Press, 1930–1936.

Xenophon, *Anabasis*. Trans. W.H.D. Rouse. New York: New American Library, 1959.

———, *Cyropaedia*. Trans. Walter Miller. 2 vols. New York: Macmillan, 1914.

———, *Hellenica*, published as *A History of My Times*. Trans. Rex Warner. New York: Penguin, 1979.

Selected Modern Sources

Alexander the Great, the Greeks, and the Seleucid Empire

Paul Cartledge, *Alexander the Great: A New Life*. New York: Overlook, 2004.

J.F.C. Fuller, *The Generalship of Alexander the Great*. Cambridge, MA: Da Capo, 2004.

Peter Green, *Alexander of Macedon, 356–323 B.C.: A Historical Biography*. Berkeley and Los Angeles: University of California Press, 1992.

———, *Alexander to Actium: The Historical Evolution of the Hellenistic Age*. Berkeley and Los Angeles: University of California Press, 1990.

———, *The Greco-Persian Wars*. Berkeley and Los Angeles: University of California Press, 1998.

John Lazenby, *The Defense of Greece*. Bloomington, IL: David Brown, 1993.

Nick Sekunda and John Warry, *Alexander the Great: His Armies and Campaigns, 334–323 B.C.* London: Osprey, 1998.

Susan Sherwin-White and Amelie Kuhrt, *Hellenism in the East: The Interaction of Greek and Non-Greek Civilizations from Syria to Central Asia After Alexander*. London: Duckworth, 1987.

———, *From Samarkhand to Sardis: A New Approach to the Seleucid Empire*. London: Duckworth, 1993.

Philip de Souza, *The Greek and Persian*

Wars, 499–386 B.C. London: Osprey, 2003.

The Archaeological Rediscovery of Mesopotamia

Charles Burney, *From Village to Empire: An Introduction to Near Eastern Archaeology.* Oxford, UK: Phaidon, 1977.

C.W. Ceram, *Gods, Graves, and Scholars: The Story of Archaeology.* Trans. E.B. Garside and Sophie Wilkins. New York: Random House, 1986.

Austen Henry Layard, *Nineveh and Its Remains.* 2 vols. London: John Murray, 1867.

———, *A Popular Account of Discoveries at Nineveh.* New York: J.C. Derby, 1854.

Seton Lloyd, *The Archaeology of Mesopotamia.* London: Thames and Hudson, 1985.

———, *Foundations in the Dust: A Story of Mesopotamian Exploration.* New York: Thames and Hudson, 1981.

———, *The Ruined Cities of Iraq.* Chicago: Ares, 1980.

E.M. Meyers, ed., *The Oxford Encyclopedia of Archaeology in the Near East.* 5 vols. New York: Oxford University Press, 1997.

George Smith, *Assyrian Discoveries.* New York: Scribner, 1875.

Charles Leonard Woolley, *Digging Up the Past.* Baltimore: Penguin, 1937.

———, *Ur Excavations.* 8 vols. London: British Museum, 1934–1982.

Gordon D. Young, *Mari in Retrospect: Fifty Years of Mari and Mari Studies.* Winona Lake, IN: Eisenbrauns, 1992.

Art, Architecture, and Sculpture

L. Sprague de Camp, *The Ancient Engineers.* New York: Ballantine, 1995.

Peter Clayton and Martin Price, eds., *The Seven Wonders of the Ancient World.* New York: Barnes & Noble, 1993.

Dominique Collon, *First Impressions: Cylinder Seals in the Ancient Near East.* London: British Museum, 1995.

Henri Frankfort, *Art and Architecture of the Ancient Orient.* New York: Penguin, 1971.

Gwendolyn Leick, *A Dictionary of Near Eastern Architecture.* New York: Routledge, 1988.

André Parrot, *The Arts of Assyria.* New York: Golden, 1961.

———, *Sumer: The Dawn of Art.* New York: Golden, 1961.

Julian Reade, *Assyrian Sculpture.* London: British Museum, 1998.

John M. Russell, *Sennacherib's Palace Without Rival at Nineveh.* Chicago: University of Chicago Press, 1992.

The Assyrians and the Babylonians

L. Delaporte, *Mesopotamia: The Babylonian and Assyrian Civilization.* Trans. V. Gordon Childe. New York: Barnes & Noble, 1970.

Mark Healy and Angus McBride, *The Ancient Assyrians.* Oxford, UK: Osprey, 1991.

A. Kirk Grayson, *Assyrian Rulers of the Third and Second Millennia B.C.* Toronto: University of Toronto Press, 1987.

Mogans T. Larsen, *The Old Assyrian City-State and Its Colonies.* Copenhagen: Akademisk Forlag, 1976.

Gwendolyn Leick, *The Babylonians*. London: Routledge, 2003.

Joan Oates, *Babylon*. London: Thames and Hudson, 1986.

A.T. Olmstead, *History of Assyria*. Chicago: University of Chicago Press, 1968.

H.W.F. Saggs, *Babylonians*. Berkeley and Los Angeles: University of California Press, 2000.

————, *The Greatness That Was Babylon*. New York: New American Library, 1963.

————, *The Might That Was Assyria*. London: Sidgwick and Jackson, 1984.

Donald J. Wiseman, *Nebuchadnezzar and Babylon*. Oxford, UK: Oxford University Press, 1995.

Crafts, Commerce, Trade, and Travel

Lionel Casson, *The Ancient Mariners*. Princeton, NJ: Princeton University Press, 1991.

————, *Ships and Seafaring in Ancient Times*, London: British Museum, 1994.

————, *Travel in the Ancient World*. Baltimore: Johns Hopkins University Press, 1994.

Jan G. Dercksen, *Trade and Finance in Ancient Mesopotamia*. Leiden: Netherlands Historical-Archaeological Institute, 1999.

J.D. Hawkins, ed., *Trade in the Ancient Near East*. London: British School of Archaeology in Iraq, 1977.

Peter R.S. Moorey, *Ancient Mesopotamian Materials and Industry*. Oxford, UK: Clarendon, 1994.

————, *Materials and Manufacture in Ancient Mesopotamia*. Oxford, UK: B.A.R., 1985.

A. Leo Oppenheim et al., *Glass and Glassmaking in Ancient Mesopotamia*. Corning, NY: Corning Museum of Glass, 1970.

General Works on History and Culture

Norman B. Hunt, *Historical Atlas of Ancient Mesopotamia*. New York: Facts On File, 2004.

Samuel N. Kramer, *Cradle of Civilization*. New York: Time-Life, 1978.

Gwendolyn Leick, *Historical Dictionary of Mesopotamia*. Lanham, MD: Scarecrow, 2003.

————, *Mesopotamia: The Invention of the City*. London: Penguin, 2001.

————, *Who's Who in the Ancient Near East*. London: Routledge, 1999.

R.J. Matthews, *The Early Prehistory of Mesopotamia, 500,000 to 4,500 B.C.* Turnhout, Belgium: Brepolis, 1999.

Fergus Millar, *The Roman Near East, 31 B.C.–A.D. 337*. Cambridge, MA: Harvard University Press, 1993.

A. Leo Oppenheim, *Ancient Mesopotamia: Portrait of a Dead Civilization*. Chicago: University of Chicago Press, 1977.

Susan Pollock, *Ancient Mesopotamia*. New York: Cambridge University Press, 1999.

Julian Reade, *Mesopotamia*. Cambridge, MA: Harvard University Press, 1991.

Michael Roaf, *Cultural Atlas of Mesopotamia and the Ancient Near East*. New York: Facts On File, 1990.

Georges Roux, *Ancient Iraq*. New York: Penguin, 1992.

H.W.F. Saggs, *Civilization Before Greece and Rome*. New Haven, CT: Yale University Press, 1991.

J.M. Sasson, ed., *Civilizations of the Near East.* 4 vols. New York: Scribner's, 1995.

Wolfram von Soden, *The Ancient Orient: An Introduction to the Study of the Ancient Near East.* Trans. Donald G. Schley. Grand Rapids, MI: William B. Eerdmans, 1994.

Gods and Religion

Jeremy A. Black and Anthony R. Green, *Gods, Demons, and Symbols of Ancient Mesopotamia.* London: British Museum, 1992.

Jean Bottero, *Religion in Ancient Mesopotamia.* Trans. Teresa L. Fagan. Chicago: University of Chicago Press, 2001.

Thorkild Jacobsen, *The Treasures of Darkness: A History of Mesopotamian Religion.* New Haven, CT: Yale University Press, 1976.

Rustom Masani, *Zoroastrianism: Religion of the Good Life.* New York: Macmillan, 1968.

Kazko Watanabe, ed., *Priests and Officials in the Ancient Near East.* Heidelberg, Germany: C. Winter, 1999.

The Hittites, Hebrews, and Other Near Eastern Peoples

Maria E. Aubert, *The Phoenicians and the West.* Trans. Mary Turton. New York: Columbia University Press, 1993.

Trevor Bryce, *Life and Society in the Hittite World.* Oxford, UK: Oxford University Press, 2002.

Michael D. Coogan, ed., *The Oxford History of the Biblical World.* New York: Oxford University Press, 1998.

John Curtis, ed., *Later Mesopotamia and Iran: Tribes and Empires, 1600–539* B.C. London: British Museum, 1995.

Yisrael Eph'al, *The Ancient Arabs: Nomads on the Borders of the Fertile Crescent.* Leiden, Netherlands: Brill, 1982.

Roberta L. Harris, *The World of the Bible.* London: Thames and Hudson, 1995.

Walther Hinz, *The Lost World of Elam: Recreation of a Vanished Civilization.* London: Sidgwick and Jackson, 1972.

Donald B. Redford, *Egypt, Canaan, and Israel in Ancient Times.* Princeton, NJ: Princeton University Press, 1992.

Mathew W.A. Waters, *A Survey of Neo-Elamite History.* Helsinki, Finland: Neo-Assyrian Text Corpus Project, 2000.

Gernot Wilhelm, *The Hurrians.* Warminster, UK: Aris and Phillips, 1989.

Laws and Justice

G.R. Driver and John C. Miles, *The Assyrian Laws.* 2 vols. Oxford, UK: Clarendon, 1935.

———, *The Babylonian Laws.* 2 vols. Oxford, UK: Clarendon, 1968.

Martha Roth, *Law Collections from Mesopotamia and Asia Minor.* Atlanta: Scholars, 1995.

Literature, Myths, and Flood Legends

J.A. Black, *Reading Sumerian Poetry.* Ithaca, NY: Cornell University Press, 1998.

S.G.F. Brandon, *Creation Legends of the Ancient Near East.* London: Hodder and Stoughton, 1963.

Samuel N. Kramer, *From the Tablets of Sumer.* Indian Hills, CO: Falcon Wings, 1956.

———, *Sumerian Mythology.* New York: Harper and Row, 1972.

Wilfred G. Lambert, *Babylonian Wisdom Literature*. Oxford, UK: Clarendon, 1960.

Wilfred G. Lambert and Allan R. Millard, *Atrahasis: The Babylonian Story of the Flood*. Oxford, UK: Clarendon, 1969.

Gwendolyn Leick, *A Dictionary of Near Eastern Mythology*. London: Routledge, 1998.

Henrietta McCall, *Mesopotamian Myths*. Austin: University of Texas Press, 1990.

Piotr Michalowski, *Letters from Early Mesopotamia*. Atlanta: Scholars, 1990.

Olof Pedersen, *Archives and Libraries in the Ancient Near East*. Bethesda, MD: CDL, 1998.

William Ryan and Walter Pitman, *Noah's Flood: The New Scientific Discoveries About the Event That Changed History*. New York: Simon & Schuster, 1998.

Nathan Wasserman, *Style and Form in Old Babylonian Literary Texts*. Leiden, Netherlands: Brill, 2002.

The Persians, Parthians, and Sassanians

Alessandro Bausani, *The Persians: From the Earliest Days to the Twentieth Century*. Trans. J.B. Donne. London: Elek, 1971.

M.A.R. Colledge, *The Parthians*. London: Thames and Hudson, 1967.

J.M. Cook, *The Persian Empire*. London: Dent, 1983.

John Curtis, *Ancient Persia*. Cambridge, MA: Harvard University Press, 1990.

Kaveh Farrokh, *Sassanian Elite Cavalry*. London: Osprey, 2005.

Ilya Gershevitch, ed., *The Cambridge History of Iran*, Vol. 2. *The Median and Achaemenian Periods*. Cambridge, UK: Cambridge University Press, 1985.

A.T. Olmstead, *History of the Persian Empire*. Chicago: University of Chicago Press, 1948.

Josef Wiesehofer, *Ancient Persia from 550 B.C. to 650 A.D.* London: Tauris, 1996.

Society and Everyday Life

Zainab Bahrani, *Women of Babylon: Gender and Representation in Mesopotamia*. London: Routledge, 2001.

H.S. Baker, *Furniture in the Ancient World*. London: Connoisseur, 1966.

Stephen Bertman, *Handbook to Life in Ancient Mesopotamia*. New York: Facts On File, 2003.

Jean Bottero, *Everyday Life in Ancient Mesopotamia*. Baltimore: Johns Hopkins University Press, 2001.

Georges Contenau, *Everyday Life in Babylon and Assyria*. London: Edward Arnold, 1964.

L. Hartman and A. Leo Oppenheim, *On Beer and Brewing Techniques in Ancient Mesopotamia*. Baltimore: American Oriental Society, 1950.

Karen R. Nemet-Nejat, *Daily Life in Ancient Mesopotamia*. Peabody, MA: Hendrickson, 1998.

Michael B. Poliakoff, *Combat Sports in the Ancient World*. New Haven, CT: Yale University Press, 1987.

Nicholas Postgate and J.N. Postgate, *Early Mesopotamia: Society and Economy at the Dawn of History*. New York: Routledge, 1994.

Daniel C. Snell, *Life in the Ancient Near East, 3100–332 B.C.* New Haven, CT: Yale University Press, 1997.

Klaas R. Veenhof, ed., *Houses and Households in Ancient Mesopotamia*. Istanbul: Netherlands Historical-Archaeological Institute of Istanbul, 1996.

The Sumerians

Harriet E.W. Crawford, *Sumer and the Sumerians*. Cambridge, UK: Cambridge University Press, 2004.

Thorkild Jacobsen, *The Sumerian King List*. Chicago: University of Chicago Press, 1939.

Tom B. Jones, ed., *The Sumerian Problem*. New York: John Wiley, 1969.

Samuel N. Kramer, *History Begins at Sumer*. Philadelphia: University of Pennsylvania Press, 1981.

———, *The Sumerians: Their History, Culture, and Character*. Chicago: University of Chicago Press, 1971.

Charles Leonard Woolley, *The Sumerians*. New York: Norton, 1965.

Weapons and Warfare

Arthur Cotterell, *Chariot: The Astounding Rise and Fall of the World's First War Machine*. New York: Overlook, 2005.

Robert Drews, *The End of the Bronze Age: Changes in Warfare and the Catastrophe ca. 1200 B.C.* Princeton, NJ: Princeton University Press, 1995.

Richard A. Gabriel and Karen S. Metz, *From Sumer to Rome: The Military Capabilities of Ancient Armies*. New York: Greenwood, 1991.

John Hackett, ed., *Warfare in the Ancient World*. New York: Facts On File, 1989.

Adreinne Mayor, *Greek Fire, Poison Arrows, and Scorpion Bombs: Biological and Chemical Warfare in the Ancient World*. New York: Overlook Duckworth, 2003.

Yigael Yadin, *The Art of Warfare in Biblical Lands in the Light of Archaeological Study*. 2 vols. New York: McGraw-Hill, 1963.

Web Sites

The International History Project, "Persia." (http://ragz-international.com/persians.htm). A brief but informative overview of Persian history, with numerous links to related topics.

Livius: Articles in Ancient History, "The Sassanids," (www.livius.org/sao-sd/sassanids/sassanids.htm). An excellent overview of the major rulers and events of the Sassanian Empire. Available through links, the Livius history series also has fine articles on Assyria, Darius I, Persepolis, the Seleucid Empire, ziggurats, and many other topics relating to the civilizations of ancient Mesopotamia.

Ms. Croft-Crossland's Standard World History, "Babylonians." (http://home.cfl.rr.com/crossland/AncientCivilizations/Middle_East_Civilizations/Babylonians/babylonians.html). Though brief, this synopsis of ancient Babylonia is well written and includes some striking photos of surviving artifacts. Available through links, Croft-Crossland's series also has informational articles on the Sumerians, Assyrians, Hittites, Hebrews, and other important ancient Near Eastern peoples.

Index

Ancient Mesopotamia

About the Author

Historian and award-winning writer Don Nardo has published many books about the ancient world, including *Life in Ancient Athens*; *The Etruscans*; *Life of a Roman Gladiator*; *Religion in Ancient Egypt*; literary companions to the works of Homer, Sophocles, and Euripides; histories of the Assyrian and Persian empires; and Greenhaven Press's encyclopedias of ancient Greece, ancient Rome, and Greek and Roman mythology. He lives with his wife, Christine, in Massachusetts.

About the Consulting Editor

Robert B. Kebric is senior professor of ancient history at the University of Louisville in Kentucky. He is the author of four books (including the critically acclaimed *Greek People*) and numerous articles and essays, and has been a consultant for Time-Life Books and other presses and international news agencies.